STAIRS TO
FIRST FLOOR

IVREI CHAIM'S HOUSE

W.C.

SUKKAH

AIRS TO
FLOOR

STAIRS TO
LADIES GALLERY

R' YITZCHAK TOIVYA'S
MIKVEH

RABBI
ARYEH LEIBISH'S
HOUSE

CORRIDOR

HAIM'S
MENT

DIVREI CHAIM'S
BEIS MIDRASH

RABBI
ARYEH LEIBISH'S
KVITTEL AND *TISCH*
ROOM

CORRIDOR

HAIM'S
TISCH ROOM

DIVREI CHAIM'S
SEAT

ENTRANCE

ENTRANCE

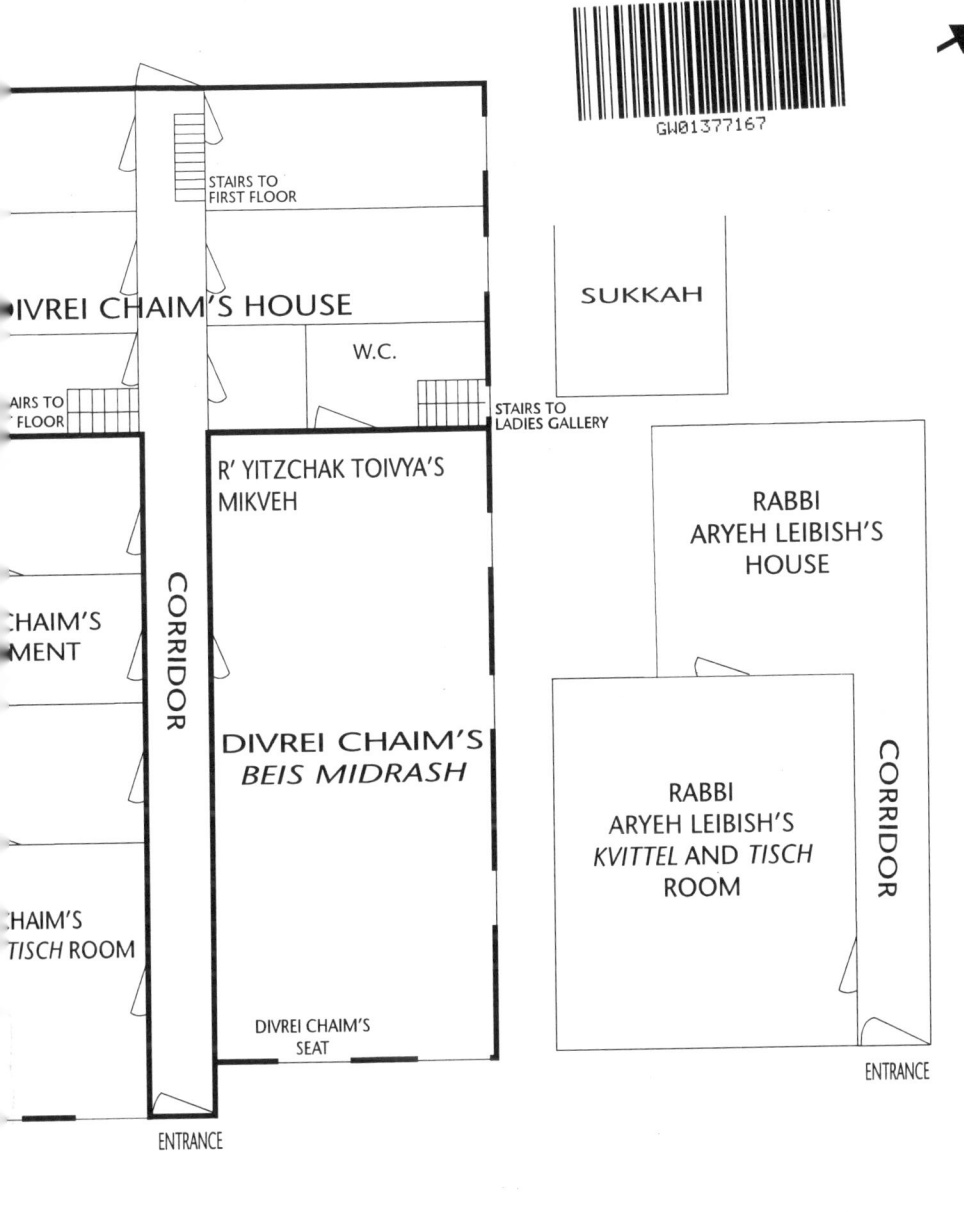

KAZIMIERZA ROAD

LEHRER
Y

THE VANISHED CITY OF TSANZ

DAVIDSON

THE VANISHED CITY OF TSANZ

Shlomo Zalman Lehrer
and Leizer Strassman

Mishnas Rishonim
TARGUM/FELDHEIM

First published 1997
Copyright © 1997 by S.Z. Lehrer and L. Strassman
ISBN 1-56871-130-1

First Yiddish edition published September, 1994
Second Yiddish edition published May, 1997
First Hebrew edition in preparation

All rights reserved

No part of this publication may be translated, reproduced, stored in a retrieval system, or transmitted in any form or by any means, electronic, mechanical, photocopying, recording, or otherwise, without prior permission in writing from both the copyright holder and the publisher.

Published by:
Targum Press, Inc.
22700 W. Eleven Mile Rd.
Southfield, MI 48034

in conjuction with:
Mishnas Rishonim

Distributed by:
Feldheim Publishers
200 Airport Executive Park
Nanuet, NY 10954

Distributed in Israel by:
Targum Press Ltd.
POB 43170
Jerusalem 91430

Printed in Israel

מזכרת נצח לעילוי נשמת

ר' מרדכי ב"ר יהודה אליעזר הלוי שטראסמאן

נפטר בשי"ט בערב שבת
כ"ז טבת תשנ"ו

ת.נ.צ.ב.ה.

ב"ה
אנטווערפען, תש
JACOB JACOBSSTRAAT, 22

משרד הרבנות
על יד
הקהלה החרדית
מחזיקי הדת

ב' לחודש אשר ישועות בו מקיפות תשנ"ד

ידיד נפשי ואהוב לבי מוהר"ר ר' **שלמה זלמן לעהרער** שליט"א העלה על גבי הכתב תולדות העיר צאנז וגדוליה, למותר הוא להציג את ידידי החביב אשר הרבה שנים הוא מתעסק בעירנו בתורה ובגמילות חסדים ורוב היום הוא מקדיש להרבצת תורה ברבים.

ידידי הנ"ל הוא ראש הגבאים של "צדקת רבי מאיר בעל הנס, כולל חיבת ירושלים". משרת הגבאות שלו איננה לשררה אלא ממש כעבדות, הוא עוסק בכל הדברים הגדולים והקטנים הנצרכים לטובת הכולל בבחינת "האי צייד כי משכח רברבא שקיל ומשכח זוטרא שקיל".

הנני מעיד שכל דבריו בספר זה הם אמתיים ועל שכמותו אמרו חז"ל "אילו יהבו ליה כל חללא דעלמא לא הוי משני בדיבורא".

ספר זה ודאי יהיה לתועלת למען ידעו דורות הבאים את קורות יהדות פולין וחכמיה וגדוליה בכלל ועיר צאנז בפרט, מתחילת ישובה ובפרט מתקופת מרן בעל הדברי חיים זי"ע עד חורבנה עם חיסול הגעטא ע"י הנאצים ימ"ש בשנת תש"ב. ויהי רצון שנזכה בקרוב לביאת משיח צדקינו במהרה בימינו אמן.

חיים קרייזווירטה
אב"ד דפ"ק אנטווערפען

Rabbi ELCHONON HALPERN
189, GOLDERS GREEN ROAD,
LONDON, N.W.11.
Phone: 01-455 6298

אלחנן בהר״ר דוד ז״ל היילפרין
מראדומישלא-קאשוי
רב ור״מ בלונדון נ.וו.
חבר הרבנות דהתאחדות קהלות החרדים

ד׳ פ׳ צו, לסדר הוא העולה על מוקדה על המזבח כל הלילה עד הבוקר, י״א ניסן,
נשיא לבני אשר, תשנ״ד לפ״ק פה גאלדרסגרין יצ״ו

מע״כ יד״נ וידיד נפש כל חי, המופלא ומופלג בתוי״ר ובחסידות, באמונת ה׳ טהורה
העומדת לעד, מוה״ר **שלמה זלמן לעהרער** שליט״א אב״י בעוב״י ק״ק אנטווערפען יצ״ו.

אחדשה״ט, קבלתי מכתב-תעודת הגר״ח קרייזווירטא, גאב״ד מחזיקה״ד דעירכם
שליט״א, המעיד על מדת אמיתת מעכה״ר, ואמיתת הדברים שבפעלו הנעלה על העיר
צאו״ז המהוללה, דיירי׳ מגזע גאון הגאונים הנודע ביהודה זלל״ה, ואח״כ נתוסף ונעלה
הקודש ע״י אא״ז גאון ישראל וקדושו הדברי חיים זי״ע וצאצאיו גאוני וצדיקי הדורות עד
מלחמת השואה ועד בכלל, הי״ד וזי״ע.

מה אומר ומה אדבר, הנני רק כיהודה ועוד לקרא, כי דבר גדול עשה בעמיו, להנציח
מאורעות העיר הנ״ל החריבה בעוה״ר, וביותר הצליח להנציח גבורי העיר, הקהל הקדוש
בכלל, ובפרט חכמי׳ וצדיקי׳ ובין האמרות טהורות יש ללמוד לקח, הנהגות גדולי וצדיקי
הדור, שביקרוה, בכדי להכיר תכונתה, ועיניהם והוקירו רום ערכה, חכמי׳ וצדיקי׳, גם אם
לפעמים השקפותיהם שונות, ואלו ואלו לש״ש מתכוונים, חבל על דאבדין ולא משתכחין,
ועל כולם יתברך וישתבח ויתפאר, שזכות אבותיו של מעכה״ר, ומעשיו הכבירים לצדקת
רמבעהנ״ס כולל גליציא, עמדו לו למגן, לגלגל זכות גדולה על ידו, למען ידעו דורותינו
אחרינו, קורות יהדות גליציא, [חלק חשוב ממדינת פולניא]. ויה״ר שיקויים בנו מ״ש שמחנו
כמות עינותנו, ונזכה לחזות בעינינו בשוב ה׳ שיבת ציון יגל יעקב ישמח ישראל.

ידידו עוז דושה״ט מברכו בכל הטוב, חג הפסח כשר ושמח

הק׳ אלחנן בהרר״ד היילפרין, מראדומישלא קאשוי.

רגילני לרמז בשם העיר הלזו, משכן כבוד אא״ז הדברי חיים זי״ע, שכידוע בשער בת
רבים, אמרת בנו הצדיק משינאווא זלל״ה, שלהיות אביו ז״ל גדול בשלושה עמודי העולם,
תורה, עבודה, וגמ״ח, אין כי עפר משלו, ואושר בזה תיאורו במצבת ציונו "יחוד בדורו",
הרי מלת צאני״ז, מרמזת על כל אלה, אות צ׳ ע״יש כח הצדקה שלו שהפליא כל יודעיו,
אות נ׳ ע״יש כח התורה, חמשים שערי בינה אות ז׳ ע״יש כח העבודה כמו״ש שבע ביום
הללתיך, ואות א׳ שביניהם, ע״יש הקב״ה אלופו של עולם, שאליו ית״ש יחד כל עבודתו
עבודת הקודש. [כידוע דברי המהר״ל מפראג ז״ל, אותיות גולי״ה וגאולי״ה שוות, ואות
א׳ המרמזת על הקב״ה אלופו של עולם, מבדלת ביניהם, כי גאולי״ה, בלא אמונת א׳ עולם
גולי״ה תחשב והבן].

צאנז, די הייליגע פארשווינדענע שטאט

משה הלברשטאם
מו"ץ העדה החרדית
ראש ישיבת "דברי חיים" טשאקאווע
מח"ס שו"ת "דברי משה"
פעיה"ק ירושלים תובב"א
רח' יואל 8 טל' 370514

בס"ד

שמחתי באומרים לי וכן בראותי תכריך כתבים לידידי יקירי מאד נעלה ורב חביבי ה"ה הרה"ח המפואר התורני ירא ושלם, ורודף צדקה וחסד, מוה"ר ר' **שלמה זלמן לעהרער** שליט"א, מעי"ת אנטווערפען, וראש הגבאים ממש של צדקתנו צדקת רבי מאיר בעל הנס לעדת גאליציא, אשר העלה על הכתב קורות העיר צאנז מקום הולדתו בו וימי נעורו. משכן כבוד אא"ז הגה"ק מרן בעל דברי חיים זי"ע ועכ"י ובניו וצאצאיו אחריו ממשיכי דרכו הגה"ק זצוקלל"ה הי"ד.

ידידי הרה"ח הנ"ל הנו מהיחידים, יחידי סגולה, שנשארו לפליטה מעיר צאנז, שעדיין זוכר את העיר בתפארתה בימי קדם, על רבבות תושביה היהודיים, תלמידי חכמיה ופשוטי עם, אנשי החסד, וכן הנהנים מיגיע כפם בתום ויושר, שקידשו שם שמים בחייהם על אדני התורה והחסידות, ובמותם ובעלותם על המוקד ה' על קידוש שמו יתברך, ואין כל בריה יכולה לעמוד במחיצתם כמאמר חז"ל, הי"ד.

שוחרי תורה וחסידות בכלל, ומוקירי בית צאנז בפרט, בודאי יכירו טובה למחבר הדגול שליט"א שהשקיע מאונו והונו דמים תרתי משמע, במשך שנים רבות, להעלות זכרונותיו על הכתב למען יעמדו לימים רבים, ולמען ידעו דור אחרון את אשר עשה לך עמלק, עד יקום ד' וינקום דם עבדיו השפוך, וימחה שמו של עמלק, ותרוממנה קרנות מדיק, וזכר צדיקים וחסידים לברכה ברו"ג, אמן.

Contents

PREFACE 9
FOREWORD 11

PART I

Introduction 17

CHAPTER 1
The Early History of the Town 21

CHAPTER 2
Blood Libels 28

CHAPTER 3
Galicia under Austria 31

CHAPTER 4
The Early Rabbanim 39

CHAPTER 5
The Divrei Chaim 43

CHAPTER 6
The Yartzeit of the Tsanzer Rav 75

CHAPTER 7
The Kreiser Rav 81

CHAPTER 8
  Rabbi Aryeh Leibish Halberstam 90
CHAPTER 9
  Rabbi Mordechai Zev Halberstam 112
CHAPTER 10
  Saintly Personalities 118
CHAPTER 11
  Jewish Life in Tsanz 148
CHAPTER 12
  Charity and Good Deeds 181
CHAPTER 13
  Minhagim of Tsanz 205
CHAPTER 14
  The Buxbaum Family 226

PART II

INTRODUCTION 243

Chapter 1
  The Outbreak of War 247
CHAPTER 2
  The Ghetto and the First Labor Camp 279
CHAPTER 3
  The Last Year in the Tsanzer Ghetto 286
CHAPTER 4
  The Final Days 306
CHAPTER 5
  Kiddush Hashem and Heroism 323
CHAPTER 6
  My Own Experiences 334

CHAPTER 7
Auschwitz 350

Chapter 8
Szwientochlovitz 362

CHAPTER 9
From Buno to Liberation 378

CHAPTER 10
In Belgium 391

PREFACE

More than fifty years have passed since the total destruction of my birthplace, Tsanz. With the approach of the month of Elul in 5699 (1939), before the outbreak of war, people felt that difficult times loomed ahead. Yet even in their wildest imaginations, none foresaw the devastating tragedy that was about to overtake the Jews. When Hitler and his murderous thugs declared war, we had some taste of the terrible days that lay ahead: on the very first day that they marched into the town of Przemyzl they murdered six hundred Jews, among them many Jews of Tsanz.

After the war, very few people wrote about their harrowing experiences. They were simply too busy trying to rebuild their cruelly shattered lives. In addition, many who had lived through the ghettos and extermination camps were ill and not physically capable of writing. Others were still suffering from shock and could not bring themselves to set down all they'd been through. I myself belonged to the class of the physically ill.

It is only thanks to the encouragement of my son-in-law Reb Yehudah Eliezer Strassman that this book came into being. I tried to persuade him that I was not a writer and there was so much to write that I would not know where to start, but he persistently urged me not to give up the idea. He told me it was incumbent upon future generations to know to what degree of depravity a so-called intelligent, cultivated nation could stoop in their efforts to exterminate the Jewish people. The Germans may not have received their just revenge, and

The Vanished City of Tsanz

many Nazi murderers are still on the loose, but it is the duty of the survivors to record all that we have suffered, as the *pasuk* says, "Remember what Amalek did to you."

In response to my son-in-law's prodding, I began jotting down short stories which I remembered from bygone years on scraps of paper. My son-in-law did extensive research on the history and customs of Tsanz. In this way, with our combined efforts, we put together this book over a ten-year period.

After everything was collected and we had some idea of the book's general contents, we realized how much was still missing. I then added more descriptions and anecdotes, until we were satisfied with the final result.

I would like to give acknowledgments to my son Reb Hershel Lehrer and my grandsons Reb Leibel Strassman and Gershon Tiefenbrunner.

Since this book is a remembrance to the Tsanz of old, I originally wrote it in Yiddish, the language in which Tsanzer Jews used to converse and write. I did my best to remember all that I had seen in my childhood and record it as accurately as possible. I also tried to write down my personal experiences in the nightmarish death camps in their correct, chronological order, right up to the liberation. I hope that because of this book my children and grandchildren and all future generations will know and remember the devastating tragedy which struck the Jewish nation. They should know of the destruction of the six million precious Jewish souls, *hy"d*, who were brutally murdered. The *pasuk* says, "Remember what Amalek did to you"; we hope that the second half of the verse will also be fulfilled: "Obliterate the memory of Amalek; do not forget."

Shlomo Zalman HaLevi Lehrer (Buxbaum) of Tsanz
Adar I 5754

FOREWORD

With boundless gratitude to Hashem, we are happy to finally publish *The Vanished City of Tsanz*, a book of many years' work. I am greatly indebted to my daughter-in-law Tsirelle for undertaking the great task of translating this book into English. Her work has been of great value.

Some ten or twelve years ago I asked my father-in-law to record whatever he remembered of life in Tsanz. I told him there were very few people who remembered the life of prewar days, and it would be a shame for that era to be completely erased. At that time, I intended this narrative to be written for the family only. However, Rabbi Moshe Halberstam, *rosh yeshivah* of Divrei Chaim Yeshivah and *dayan* for the Eidah Chareidis, who somehow found out about the research I was doing on Tsanz, encouraged me to publish my father-in-law's work. My father-in-law is head of the *gabbaim* of the *tzedakah* Rabbi Meir Ba'al HaNess Kollel Chibas Yerushalayim L'Adas Galicia and is therefore in steady contact with Rabbi Moshe. Rabbi Moshe said, "Whatever your father-in-law writes is reliable, and who else remembers the Tsanz of old as well as he?"

When I approached Rav Moshe Halberstam, *shlita*, and asked him if I may translate and publish this book into English, he said to me, "Please don't call it a book. This is not a book but a *sefer*." Then he added, "Yes, you may translate the *sefer*, since

The Vanished City of Tsanz

today the overwhelming majority of Orthodox Jewry are English-speaking, so that the English-speaking public will also have the opportunity to know what the Tsanz of old used to look like."

I did extensive research on the history of Tsanz. A source of information was the stories I heard on many occasions from the Pshevorsker Rebbe of Antwerp, Grand Rabbi Yaakov Leiser, *shlita*. When I came across any new information, I carefully reviewed it with my father-in-law to ensure that everything written be as accurate as possible.

We originally named the book *Tsanz, die heiliger fershvinderner shtodt*, "Tsanz: the holy, vanished town." "Tsanz," because only a small part of the book involves my father-in-law's actual experiences, the larger portion being about his hometown, Tsanz; "the holy, vanished town," because there is very little left of the area itself. The Germans had stored their weapons in a castle situated directly behind the saintly Divrei Chaim's house. Shortly before the war's end, partisans blew up the castle. The castle collapsed and with it the entire Jewish Street. The Talmud Torah, the mikveh, the *batei midrash*, and the home and *beis midrash* of the Divrei Chaim — everything was blown to bits. Today the entire area is covered with grass. The sole remaining building, which is still standing, was the shul, which has stood for over 220 years. It is said that the Divrei Chaim used to daven there sometimes. Today, the entire area is covered with grass.

The Chassidic Jews in Tsanz did not allow themselves to be photographed. There are therefore very few pictures of prewar times. Most of the photos we have today were taken by the Nazis during the war. In addition, when the Jews were in the ghetto, they were forced to hand in a photo of themselves to the *Judenrat*.

When we chose the cover picture, we did not know whether it was a photo of the Divrei Chaim's youngest son, Rabbi Yeshayele Tzechover, or the Stropkover Rebbe, Rabbi Avraham Shalom, *zt"l*. Rabbi Elchanan Halpern, *shlita*, of London clarified the matter for us and told us that the picture is of the Stropkover Rebbe and his *gabbai*, Reb Chaim Yaakov Leiser. The *bachur* at the forefront is Reb Moshe

FOREWORD

Englander from Krenitz (now living in New York). The photo was taken in Krenitz. The present Stropkover Rebbe, Rabbi Avraham Shalom, *shlita*, told me that Reb Moshe Englander had told him that his great-grandfather, the Stropkover Rebbe, was very particular not to have his photograph taken. This picture, however, was taken with his permission. He said at the time that he wanted the photo to be circulated so that future generations would know what a genuine Rebbe used to looked like.

Speaking of Reb Moshe Englander, I would like to thank him for the information he offered about the Englander family. I would also like to thank another family member, who chooses not to be mentioned by name, for checking the accuracy of all that I have written about the Englander family and for adding a few points.

Great thanks are due to Rabbi Dombey and the staff at Targum Press.

I would like to acknowledge the following for providing us with invaluable information: Rabbi Moshe Halberstam; the Tsanzer survivors Reb Chaim Weiss of Tsanz (now living in Jerusalem), Reb Nechemia Shengut, Mr. Leibish Blumenfeld, Mr. Gertner of Petach Tikvah, Mr. Wolf Knobbel, Mr. Moshe David Lauer, Mr. Toivya Katz, Mr. Moshe Keller, and Mr. Avraham Hollander; Mr. Yechezkel Blumenfrucht of Cracow (Antwerp); and last but by no means least, Professor Jonathan Webber of Oxford, who is an expert on the history of Jewish Galicia and has given us many hours of his precious time.

After we published the Yiddish version of this book, Rabbi Eziel Herbst of Tsanz (London) told us a few interesting stories that his grandfather Reb Shloime Herbst personally remembered from his youth about the Divrei Chaim and his son the Kreiser Rav, which we have included in the second Yiddish edition and in this English edition as well. We are very grateful to him for giving us all the information and also for his comments and corrections to the first edition.

Yehudah Eliezer HaLevi Strassman

I
THE TSANZ THAT WAS

INTRODUCTION

Deep in the Carpathian Mountains, where the Kamienica River flows into the Dunajec River, is my birthplace, New Tsanz. There my family lived for many generations. My grandfather's grandfather Rabbi Nassan was a *dayan* in Tsanz when the holy Divrei Chaim was the *Rav*. He was called Reb Nassan Dayan. His father, Rabbi Yitzchak Ravreveter, was *rosh beis din* when Rabbi Baruch Landau was *Rav* in Tsanz, before the Divrei Chaim even came to the town.

I lived in Tsanz from the day I was born until the Jewish community's final extermination at the hands of the Nazis in Elul 5702 (1942).

The Vanished City of Tsanz

Sadly, after the war very little was left of the town in general and my family in particular. Among the few survivors of the town were some who undertook the effort to publish a memorial book, which was very well written. However, they omitted one aspect, the most important one — the religious life. Reading their book, one could be led to believe that the town of Tsanz consisted mainly of nonreligious Jews, with only a handful of religious Jews among them. The book elaborates on the town's irreligious organizations, expending hundreds of

Kasimir's castle

pages in describing them. I was not even aware of the existence of these organizations until I read this book. In reality, these irreligious organizations, if they did indeed exist, were very small and insignificant, because Tsanz was one of the most Orthodox and Chassidic-oriented towns in prewar Galicia.

To illustrate my point: the *beis midrash* where I davened had five to six hundred congregants. Every single one of them wore a *shtreimel*. And this was just one of many Chassidic *batei midrash*! Tsanz had a population of thirty-five thousand, twelve thousand of whom were Jewish. The overwhelming majority were Chassidically inclined.

INTRODUCTION

I have therefore taken the time and effort to write about my birthplace, Tsanz, so that my children, grandchildren, and all descendants of Tsanz will appreciate what wonderful fathers and grandfathers they had. May they never forget what a beautiful heritage they possess and what Tsanz actually represented.

CHAPTER 1

THE EARLY HISTORY OF THE TOWN

The Establishment of Sanz

The town of Sanz was established in the year 5052 (1292). At that time it belonged to the bishop of the city of Cracow located a hundred kilometers away. Originally, the town was named "Kamienica," after an old village nearby whose name was derived from the Kamienica River.

Twenty years later, ownership of the town was passed to a "horse rider" (knight) whose name was Sandamer. From that time on, the

Sanz in earlier times

town was officially named *Nowy Sacz*, "New Sanz," and the small village nearby, *Stary Sacz*, "Old Sanz." The majority of the town's population at that time were German colonists, and until the year 5261 (1501) the official town records were written in German. When the Germans became assimilated with the Poles, the town registers began keeping their records in Polish.

Officially the Jews were permitted to reside in Sanz only from the year 5433 (1673), but it is known that twenty years prior to that a shul with a *Rav* was already established there.

The Jews were granted residency in Sanz, despite vehement protests from the town priests, due to the bloody years of 5408–5409 (1648–1649), the years of the Cossack uprising.

The Gezeiros Tach V'Tat: The Cossack Uprising

In the year 5395 (1635) and 5396 there had been uprisings of the Cossacks in the town of Preyeslov, in the Ukraine. The Cossacks, who were natives of the area, were skilled and warlike horsemen. They had been long-oppressed by the Polish overlords and literally starved for bread. Finally, they resolved to throw off the yoke of their masters and organized a revolution. Since many of the barons fled their wrath, the Cossacks released all their pent-up anger and frustration on the help-

THE EARLY HISTORY OF THE TOWN

less Jews. The Cossacks were filled with suppressed hatred for the Jews, who were forced by the Polish barons to be their tax collectors, moneylenders, estate administrators, and tavern keepers — all representing the hated Polish oppressor.

It took three months for the Polish army to suppress the revolt. With that it seemed that the matter was resolved. However, this was far from true. In the year 5408 the Cossacks and their peasant allies of the Ukraine and Middle Russia appointed Bogdan Chmielnicki to be their leader. He was then in his early fifties, a devout Orthodox Greek who loathed Roman Catholics and despised Jews. As a young man he had served as a cavalryman in the forces of the Poles and Cossacks against the Turks. He had attempted numerous unsuccessful business ventures and was bitterly disappointed that he had not attained any significant rank within the Polish army, despite being a courageous warrior. He was willing and unafraid to risk all in order to vindicate his religion, talents, and ambition.

In Nissan 5407, a major disagreement erupted between him and the town squire of Czehryn. The squire ordered his soldiers to smash Chmielnicki's house down and take his wife captive. After this incident, the embittered Chmielnicki left his town, deserted the Poles, and joined the Cossack Zaporozhian group. This rabble consisted mainly of escaped criminals, highwaymen, and dispossessed serfs. They were, however, all skilled soldiers equipped with intrepid ingenuity; above all, they had nothing to lose.

Bogdan Chmielnicki possessed all the qualities of leadership, and with his cunning mind, personality, and military acumen he welded these people into a fighting force. When he emerged with the battle cry "Freedom from the Polish Roman Catholics!" almost the entire Ukraine joined his campaign. The Tartars, too, gave Chmielnicki their full support.

In Nissan 5408, Chmielnicki marched across the Dnieper westward into Poland. Successes in the battles of Zheltye Vody and Korsun won him widespread support from the peasant masses who now saw him as their potential savior and leader. By Cheshvan 5409 he had already advanced to Lemberg, Galicia. The Poles, realizing that they

The Vanished City of Tsanz

were dealing with a mighty power, sought to appease the army. They granted the Cossacks autonomy for a state and gave Chmielnicki the title "baron" in return for his commitment to pay at least lip service to Polish sovereignty.

The war left a trail of violence and enmity between the ethnic groups of Poland and the Ukraine. Polish nobles were held for ransom and tortured to death even after the ransoms were delivered. Numerous quarrels between the Cossacks and Tartars left death and destruction amidst those former allies.

During the stormiest fighting, the Cossacks never forgot their venomous hatred against the Jews and vented their long-suppressed rage on them at every opportunity. Throughout the war it was the Jews who suffered more than any other citizens. The *sefer Yovan Metzulah*, which describes the events of those years, records that in the years 5408–5413, the Cossacks wiped out three hundred flourishing Jewish communities. Some of the victims were skinned alive, their flesh thrown to the dogs. Others had their hands and feet severed before being thrown under a horse's hooves to be trampled to death. Not always were these pain-racked victims thrown to the horses; some had deep wounds cut into them and then were thrown on the streets to wallow in the dirt until they slowly died from the excruciating suffering. Others were simply buried alive. The Cossacks would snatch infants out of their mothers' laps and cut them open, cleaning out their innards as one does with fish. Children were pierced with spears, their bodies roasted on open fires and brought to their mothers to be eaten.

The Tartars were not to be outdone in cruelty. However, they had shrewd business minds and reckoned that there was money to be made in their brutal deeds. They knew well that the Jews would pay a hefty price for the redemption of captives, so they captured Jews and sold them to Turkish slave dealers, who sold them to Jews in Italy. Thirty thousand Jews were saved from death in this manner.

The Cossacks had announced that any Jew who would convert would be saved. Out of hundreds of thousands of Jews very few took up the offer. After the battle of Tulchin, at which the treacherous Polish sold out their Jewish allies to the common Cossack enemy, 150 Jews

THE EARLY HISTORY OF THE TOWN

died with the Shema on their lips. Not one embraced Christianity. This poor showing so enraged the Cossacks that they slaughtered many of the previous few converts.

Officially, peace had been made. However, it lasted only for half a year, until Pesach 5409. By then, the partnership between the Cossacks and the Tartars was beginning to disintegrate as the Tartars had already derived all the benefit they could from the alliance. In addition, the Poles bribed them with gold and other valuables, which persuaded them to go over to the Polish side. With the Tartars as allies, the Poles were ready to renew their battle against the Cossacks and Ukrainians.

With both the Poles and the Tartars against him, Chmielnicki was not as powerful as he had been, and in Av 5409 he had no choice but to sign a peace treaty with the Poles.

In the winter of 5410, the Va'ad Arba Aratzos (which was established in 5293 [1533] and remained in existence until 5524 [1764]) designated 20 Sivan to be a *ta'anis tzibbur* (public fast) as a remembrance of the catastrophic tragedy which had befallen European Jewry. They chose this particular day because on 20 Sivan 5408, the river in the town Nemirov grew red with the blood of the hundreds of Jews who were brutally slaughtered there.

Despite the peace treaty, the years of death and destruction weren't over. In 5411 the Cossacks once again renewed their battle against the Poles. A year later, the Tartars struck an alliance with the Cossacks a second time, and the bloody war flared up again. Not long afterwards, a cholera epidemic broke out. In Sanz, where Chmielnicki and his bloodthirsty gang did not enter to wreak murder and destruction (they only advanced till Lemberg), the disease claimed thousands of victims.

The End of Chmielnicki

In 5414, Chmielnicki turned to the Russian czar for help. He agreed to place his Cossacks under Russian rule in return for partial autonomy for his Cossack state. However, Chmielnicki was an unreliable ally: when Russia invaded Poland later that same year, Chmielnicki started maneuvering for an alliance with Sweden, who then controlled large areas of Poland. By joining with the Swedes, Chmielnicki hoped to achieve complete independence for his Cossack state and at the same time deal mortal blows to both his Polish enemy and his Russian friends. The negotiations with Sweden lasted a long time and only ended with Chmielnicki's death in 5417. After his demise, the Poles and the Russians made peace. The Cossack autonomy was completely curtailed by Russia, so that in the end the Cossack revolution, after having caused hundreds of thousands of deaths, had achieved none of its goals. A great heroic statue of one of mankind's worst sadistic murderers — Bogdan Chmielnicki — stands until this day in Kiev: one man's killer is another's hero.

In those days, the aftermath of war was liable to result in even more deaths than the war itself. This was because very little was sown during wartime, and even that which had been planted was trampled or robbed by the invading army. This resulted in years of severe famine. In addition, thousands of dead bodies lay sprawled on the streets, spreading infection and illness for many weeks until they were finally buried. Many tens of thousands of soldiers lay wounded in their dirty, dilapidated barracks without medical care, spreading contagious diseases and epidemics to which countless victims fell prey. In Sanz alone the population dropped dramatically, from five thousand souls to thirteen hundred. Many houses were left empty and deserted, and consequently, in the year 5433 (1673), the Jews were permitted to populate the town in order to bring life back into the city.

Early Shuls

The exact date of when a minyan was first formed in Sanz is unknown. By the year 5417 (1657) a wooden shul existed, but its origin is lost to history.

The old ledgers lying in the Sanzer town hall record that a Jew by the name of Avraham lived in Sanz in the year 5229 (1469). Eventually he moved to Cracow. In the year 5253 (1493) we find another Jew in Sanz, also by the name of Avraham. Nothing more is known until the

THE EARLY HISTORY OF THE TOWN

year 5360 (1600), when we hear of a few Jews living on the royal grounds. Despite the prohibition on Jewish residence in Sanz we know that in 5413 (1653) there was a minyan and that the town had a *Rav*. Finally, in the year 5433 (1673), the Jews were permitted to live in the town, as we have mentioned.

In 5455 (1695) the wooden shul became too crowded for the steadily growing Jewish population. The Jewish community forwarded a request to the town's magistrate for a plot of land on which to build a new brick shul. The magistrate was ready to grant his permission, but the local priests went to great lengths in their determination not to let the plan materialize. Their efforts succeeded, and the Jews were forced to continue praying in the small, wooden shul until the year 5529 (1769). That year, a raging fire broke out in Sanz, razing half the town to the ground. Among the buildings burned down was the old wooden shul. Three hundred Jewish families were financially ruined because of the fire. But that did not deter the church from asking the Jews to pay for all the damages, claiming that the fire started in the house of a Jew named Judka.

Gradually, the town of Sanz recovered from the devastating damage caused by the fire and became reestablished.

CHAPTER 2

BLOOD LIBELS

The Blood Libel of 5511 (1751)

The years between 5457 (1697) and 5523 (1763) marked a bleak and tragic period in the history of Polish Jewry. Almost every year another blood libel was fabricated against them. In 5511 a Polish youth in Sanz was found murdered. (Some say he had mysteriously vanished.) Immediately, rumors began circulating among the gentiles, claiming that the boy occasionally stole cholent from the baker and the Jews had decided to dispose of him once and for all. At the same time, a certain Mr. Deptovitch was found dead from unnatural causes.

At that time there lived in Sanz a man by the name of Reb Yaakov the son of Reb Abbish who owned a tavern. One night a non-Jewish student slept in his tavern. He left the next morning on a visit and was never heard from again. That same day Reb Yaakov was honored by a visit of four distinguished Jewish guests. Two of them were from the town of Tarnow, one was the Shendishover Rav from Cracow, and the fourth was a son-in-law of a Hungarian *Rav*.

Since Reb Yaakov was one of the prominent members of the Sanzer Jewish *kehillah*, a priest by the name of Viton pointed an accusing finger at him and said that Reb Yaakov had a hand in the murders of the young thief and Mr. Deptovitch, and that he had personally killed the student who'd stayed in his inn. Viton said that there was evidence to his claim: blood splattered on the walls of Reb Yaakov's storehouse. Reb Yaakov tried to explain that the blood was from a chunk of slaughtered cow which he had hung in his storehouse, a common practice in those days, but his pleas fell on deaf ears.

The gentiles unanimously concluded that the visit of four Jews, including a *Rav* and a *Rav*'s son-in-law, was clear evidence that they had come to consult with Reb Yaakov on how to "squeeze Christian blood" for the purpose of baking matzos for Pesach.

Reb Yaakov was also accused of practicing sorcery in order to murder his victims from afar. In those times the Poles were extremely primitive and superstitious. They used to organize processions where they burnt old, innocent hags at the stake for the supposed crime of practicing witchcraft. Amongst this sort of backward peasantry, a tale such as was told about Reb Yaakov was enthusiastically accepted.

Reb Yaakov was tried in court for his "crime." When he steadfastly refused to confess to committing something he did not do, the judge ordered him to be tortured. He was placed on a rod and stretched out three times until his joints cracked. Still, the courageous Reb Yaakov was adamant. Though suffering immense torture, he refused to throw the guilt on any other Jew.

His ordeal wasn't over. The torturers took Reb Yaakov and burnt his body. Yet Reb Yaakov did not give in, and while his body was being scorched he proudly declared, "Even if you were to burn me to ashes, I will not confess to something of which I know nothing."

It is not known how the story concluded. But one thing is clear: even if Reb Yaakov emerged alive from this horrifying ordeal, he must have remained a cripple for life.

The Blood Libel of 5521 (1761)

Barely ten years had elapsed since the blood libel against Reb Yaakov ben Reb Abbish, when a new libel was fabricated, this time involving a whole family.

In Pasadov, a village close to Sanz, lived an innkeeper by the name of Yosef Markovitch, with his wife and daughter, his son-in-law, Mr. Ohrnovitch, and another girl, a relative of Reb Yosef. The innkeeper was nicknamed Reb Yosef Bobover (probably because he came from

The Vanished City of Tsanz

Bobov, a city close to Sanz).

One day, a three-year-old boy disappeared from the village. He vanished not long before Pesach — a perfect excuse for the gentiles to put the blame on the Jews for using the child's blood for matzah. For some unknown reason, they accused Reb Yosef of having committed the murder. All five members of his family were thrust into the Sanzer prison and subjected to merciless torture in an attempt to force them into confessing.

The young girl was the first to submit to their cruelty. She admitted to everything they accused her of and even agreed to convert in order to save her life.

Reb Yosef, however, refused to confess. The judge ordained that his refusal to admit his guilt stemmed from the Jewish people's tremendous willpower and amazing stubbornness. To prove his guilt, the judge summoned the three women to give evidence to Reb Yosef's crime. His wife and daughter-in-law had already undergone unbearable suffering. They had refused to give false evidence or to convert to Christianity despite all, until they were told that the men were dead. When they heard this, they surrendered completely and agreed to testify that they had seen Reb Yosef murder the child. They reasoned that since he was dead it couldn't do any harm to say that they saw him kill the child. Immediately after their confession, they were killed.

Reb Yosef was tortured horribly, his skin flayed and his body drawn and quartered. His son-in-law, Mr. Ohrnovitch, was told that if he converted to Christianity he would be beheaded, but if he refused he would get the same death as that of his father-in-law. Mr. Ohrnovitch staunchly stuck to his claim of innocence until the very end, but when he witnessed the ghoulish scene of his father-in-law Reb Yosef's terrible death he agreed to convert rather than undergo the same macabre ordeal.

After this tragic event had occurred, no body of a gentile child was ever discovered.

CHAPTER 3

GALICIA UNDER AUSTRIA

Galicia Becomes Part of Austria

A year after the fire in 5529 (1769), the entire area which today we call Galicia was invaded by the Austrian empress Maria Theresa's troops. Sanz was surrounded by a wall until it was conquered by Austria. In 5553 (1793) a large part of the wall was removed; in 5564 (1804) the remainder was taken away, except for a small portion which remained until the Second World War.

When Austria took over, the fashion of building brick houses began, although the majority of the houses were still made of wood. The new Austrian regime permitted the Jews to build a new shul despite the fierce opposition of the Catholic church. This shul still stands to this very day.

As in the majority of shuls in Galicia, a few steps led down to the entrance of the new shul. The place where the *ba'al tefillah* stood was level with the rest of the floor, unlike many other shuls of that day, where the *ba'al tefillah* descended a centimeter or two. The women's section was built above a room adjoining the shul at the back called the *polish* and not above the shul itself. Most of the shuls in Galicia were built with this layout.

The shul was not completed until 5536 (1776), because the church constantly tried to impede its progress. Though the shul is still in existence today, it is used now only as a museum and not as a place

The Vanished City of Tsanz

of prayer. However, the fact that it exists at all is indeed miraculous, for the Germans attempted to destroy everything in connection with Judaism right down to the tombstones of the cemetery before deporting the Jews of Sanz to the gas chambers of Belzec.

Apart from the main shul, another shul, Beis Nassan, also survived the Nazi destruction of Sanz. It stands today on Jagiellonska Street, in a courtyard leading to the road. Someone who resides on the second floor keeps the key. The Nazis did not notice this shul because the exterior appears to be a small extension of a house. In addition, the shul stood directly in front of their headquarters, and it did not occur to the Nazis that a shul could exist right in front of their noses.

The Sanzer shul

Schools

In the year 5542 (1782), Austria divided Galicia into eighteen districts. New Sanz and its surrounding area became a district of its own. Every small community belonged to one of four larger communities called *Vojavodas*. Sanz belonged to the community of Cracow.

In an attempt to Germanize Galician Jewry, Emperor Joseph II permitted the Jews to enroll in the state schools. However, his efforts did not meet with much success. When Galicia was under Polish sovereignty, the Va'ad Arba Aratzos wielded a powerful influence over all the Jews, acting as an independent regime headed by *rabbanim* and *parnasim* which had the final say in all Jewish matters. Consequently, the entire Jewish population remained strictly religious. Though the Va'ad no longer existed in Joseph's time, its influence was still felt.

When the emperor perceived that permission for Jews to attend gentile state schools did not achieve anything substantial, he founded German Jewish schools. This, too, did not see much success. The determined emperor did not give up and tried yet another tactic. He sent for a German Jew by the name of Hertz Homburg to head the German Jewish schools in the hope that he would succeed in modernizing the Galician Jews.

The Galician Jews were filled with apprehension when they heard of Homburg's imminent arrival. Hertz Homburg was known to be a close friend of Moses Mendelsohn, the founder of the Reform movement, who was infamous for his translation of the *Chumash* into German. This work was shunned by the majority of leading *gedolim* and was placed under a ban.

The friendship of Hertz Homburg and Moses Mendelsohn went so deep that Mendelsohn entrusted Homburg with the education of his own children. It is interesting to note that all of Mendelsohn's sons, and likewise the four sons of Homburg, eventually converted to Christianity. It is no wonder then that the Jews of Galicia knew well what the name Hertz Homburg implied and dreaded his arrival.

Hertz Homburg came to Galicia in the year 5548 (1787) and settled in the city of Lemberg. Knowing the purpose of his visit, not a single Jew in Lemberg was willing to rent him an apartment. Having no choice, Homburg was forced to take an apartment in the gentile district. He wasted no time but set to work immediately. He found no willing assistants among the Galician Jews, but, undaunted, he imported Jewish teachers from Germany. The financial burden of supporting the school and its teachers was imposed upon the local Jewish communities.

In 5558 (1798), a German Jewish school was established in Sanz. Not a single Jewish child stepped over its threshold because, of all the towns in Galicia, it was in Sanz especially that the Jews were most particular not to let their children speak any language other than Yiddish.

In 5548 (1787), Emperor Joseph decreed that in the duration of one year all the Jews in Galicia were obliged to choose a German surname for themselves. This law applied only to the Jews; the gentiles were permitted to keep their Polish surnames. The German surnames which the Jews chose are the names which we still carry to this very day.

When Emperor Joseph died, the Jews appealed to the new emperor, Leopold, to free them from the burden of having to support the German Jewish schools and their staff. In the meantime Hertz Homburg did not stand on the sidelines. He requested that Emperor Leopold forbid the Jews from wearing beards and sidelocks and abolish Jewish *chadarim*, which, he claimed, hindered the development of culture among the Galician Jews.

A fierce controversy broke out among the Galician Jews and the German supporters of Hertz Homburg. The quarrel lasted many years, until 5562 (1802), when Homburg fled Galicia in humiliation.

In the year 5566, Emperor Franz issued a decree that all German Jewish schools must be closed down. As a devout Catholic, Emperor Franz feared that these schools would introduce free thinking in his empire, which he considered worse than having ultra-Orthodox Jews in his kingdom. For this reason, too, he did not prohibit the wearing of beard and sidelocks. In addition, Emperor Franz struck a pact with the Pope in which he delegated everything involved in the field of education into the hands of his Catholic priests. The Jews were permitted to study in Catholic institutions, but the schools reeked of anti-Semitism. The Jewish children were made to sit on specially designated benches in order not to "infest" the Christian children with their presence. In Sanz the Jews shunned the priests' gracious kindness in allowing the children to attend their schools.

The Sanzer shul

The beginning of 5560 (1800) saw a new influx into Sanz, the immigration of a few hundred families from Germany. Austria granted them homes, gardens, and land for free. They frequented a church near the Jewish Street (or, as it was called in Yiddish, *"der Yiddisher Gass"*), which the Jews dubbed "the Shwabisha church," since the immigrants came from Shwaben, Germany.

Interestingly, the Jews and Germans got along reasonably well. This was because of the similarity between the German and Yiddish language and because the Germans constituted a minority. Nobody would have believed that 150 years later their great-grandchildren would claim to be *Volksdeutsche* (of German descent) and join Hitler Youth Clubs, where they would be taught how to exterminate the Jewish nation. After the war these Germans fled to Germany for fear of retribution. When I was in Sanz in 5753 (1993) I saw their deserted church and school still standing empty.

Austrian Decrees against the Jews

Empress Maria Theresa despised Jews and imposed many heavy taxes on them, including the wedding tax, an enormous amount of money. Emperor Joseph increased the tax even more and added a new decree: a head tax. Only Jews were obligated to pay this tax, and those who could not afford it were declared *"bettel* Jews" (beggar Jews) and driven from the land.

Emperor Joseph also enforced a kosher-meat tax. This raised the cost of meat to such an extent that only the very wealthy could afford it.

Even harsher was the candle tax enforced by Emperor Franz, a nephew of Emperor Joseph. In reality, the idea was formulated in the times of Leopold, but he was emperor for only two years and did not have the chance to implement the law. Sadly, the whole idea of a candle tax was introduced by a Jew. The story goes as follows:

We have already mentioned Hertz Homburg as the one who fought a bitter struggle with the Galician Jews in an attempt to establish German Jewish schools. He constantly sought ways to become rich at the expense of his Jewish opponents. He once consulted a certain Solomon Kowler from Lemberg, and they decided on the idea of a candle tax.

The first step of their plan was to inquire of the Austrian government if a candle tax was against the policies of Austrian law, which allowed freedom of religion. When they were answered in the negative, they suggested this law. The government immediately agreed.

The decree was as follows: The eldest of every Jewish family was obligated to pay half a "twenty" (a currency in those days) for two of the candles lit in honor of Shabbos. A *Rav* had to pay for five candles. A *gabbai* of a *beis midrash* had to pay for four candles. A community rabbi had to pay for seven candles. A *Rav* was not permitted to let a Jewish couple get married until the father of the bride or groom presented a declaration that he had paid five gulden, the tax for the *chuppah* candles. If two families lived in one room, both families had to pay a whole twenty, since each family benefited from the light which emanated from the other's candles. Even the poorest widow and a new couple directly after their wedding were forced to pay this tax.

Every week, one had to pay the tax for the forthcoming week. It was forbidden to pay for more than one week at a time. If by Shabbos one had not paid, he was fined a penalty of one gulden — the equivalent of three twenties. If by the next Shabbos he still had not paid the half a twenty plus the penalty, his clothing and bedding were confiscated.

Jewish officials were given the task of collecting the tax. They were called *"lecht pachters."* Every year an auction took place for the "privilege" of becoming a *lecht pachter*. The person who contributed the greatest amount of money was chosen. In those days, the Jews lived in abject poverty, and it was heartbreaking to hear the bitter wailing that prevailed in poor homes every Friday. It was only the hardhearted and brutal people who fought for the privilege of becoming a *lecht pachter*.

In order to ensure that no one would light candles for which he did not pay tax, the government forced the eighteen community rabbis to assemble in Lemberg and jointly draw up a warning of excommunication to anyone who would violate the law. The government argued *dina d'malchusa dina*, "the law of the government is law according to Judaism." Lemberg had no *Rav* at that time, only two Jewish courts of justice.

Solomon Kowler managed to manipulate the government to force the two greatest rabbis of the time — the well-known *gaon* Rabbi Tzvi Hirsh Meisels, *av beis din* of Zolkowa, and the *gaon* Rabbi Yosef Asher Ehrenberg, *av beis din* of Premishlan — to announce in shul that if anyone violated the law a shofar would be blown (as is the custom with excommunications), and the person would be put into *cheirem*.

Solomon Kowler was given the right to implement the collection of the tax in every town. Hertz Homburg received 2 percent of all the money collected. There was nothing the Jews could do to counteract this severe tax. However, the entire nation turned against Homburg and molested him mercilessly, until he had to flee Galicia in disgrace and humiliation, as we have written earlier.

The *Rav* of Pshevorsk, Rabbi Yaakov Leiser, *shlita*, related the following incident in connection with this tax:

There was a certain man who used to visit the Divrei Chaim, and every time he undertook the journey, he lost some money. Once the Gorlitzer Rav, the son of the Divrei Chaim, asked this person, "Why do you persist on coming here? Don't you see that you are suffering financial losses as a result?"

The Gorlitzer Rav mentioned the man's name to his father, the Divrei Chaim. The Divrei Chaim remarked, "How long was it that he was a *lecht pachter?*"

The Pshevorsker Rav explained that in his previous *gilgul* the man had been a *lecht pachter*, and by constantly losing money he was amending his former misdeeds.

There were other taxes, too. Among them was a tax for a minyan with a *sefer Torah* and a tax for a minyan without a *sefer Torah*. There was a shul tax, a cemetery tax, and an endless array of others.

The Austrian government also issued a decree that all the Jews must belong to a community and that those who lived in the surrounding villages were obligated to daven in town at least during the High Holy Days. Officially this was for the Jews' benefit, so that they would be able to observe their religious rites more fully. In reality it was for the government's own interest — to enable them to keep strict control over where the Jews lived and thereby make the collection of the various taxes easier.

CHAPTER 4

THE EARLY RABBANIM

We know of only four *rabbanim* who presided in Sanz during the period discussed in the previous chapters. The first *Rav* we know of was Rabbi Moshe Yerucham. The second *Rav*, who took on his position in the year 5467 (1707), was called Rabbi Moshe. The only thing we know about him is that he had a son by the name of Chaim. Another *Rav* was Rabbi Tzvi Hirsh the son of Rabbi Yosef, who became *Rav* in Sanz in the year 5524 (1764). We know no other details about these *rabbanim*.

Rabbi Baruch Landau

In the year 5533 (1773), Rabbi Baruch, the son of Rabbi Moshe David Landau, became the official *Rav* of Sanz. He was a close relative of the chief rabbi of Prague, Rabbi Yechezkel Landau, known as the Noda BiYehudah.

In 5590 (1830) the Divrei Chaim was taken on as a *moreh tzedek dayan*, as is recorded in his *kesav rabbanus*. But after an incident occurred from which Rabbi Baruch Landau perceived the great saintliness of the Divrei Chaim, Rabbi Baruch stepped down from his position in his old age and handed over the rabbanus to the Divrei Chaim.

The Vanished City of Tsanz

The story goes as follows: A controversy concerning a large amount of money once erupted between two prominent merchants. The merchants came to the Divrei Chaim, who settled the dispute satisfactorily. However, the *pesak* greatly enraged Rabbi Baruch Landau. He drew up a letter in which he outlined the argument and the Divrei Chaim's *pesak* in a manner which would put the verdict of the Divrei Chaim in a poor light. He sent a letter to the *gaon* Rabbi Yaakov Lisser, author of *Chavos Da'as*, who was then acting as *Rav* in Strij. At the end of the letter, he added the following note: "A certain man whom I do not care to mention by name, who does not bear a single ordination as *Rav*, has dared to judge and pass judgment without permission from any court of law or accepted *dayan*... It is obvious that his judgment is invalid as he is not worthy of acting thus..."

When the Lisser Rav received the letter, he agreed fully with Rabbi Baruch and was very annoyed that a person not well versed in halachah dared to pass judgment not in accordance with the law. In his response to Rabbi Baruch, he included the words: "It is forbidden for [the man concerned] to judge in laws pertaining to permitted and forbidden [property] and money matters."

When the response reached Sanz, opponents of the Divrei Chaim gleefully pounced on the sharp condemnation. They argued that the eldest and most respected of *poskim* in those times had forbidden the Divrei Chaim to judge. The revelation caused a tremendous uproar, and the Chassidim of the Divrei Chaim felt belittled and degraded in the face of his opponents and the rest of the general population.

When the Divrei Chaim heard of this, he wrote a sharp reply to the Lisser Rav. He explained the full details of the case and the reasons for his *pesak*, clearly pointing out that it was in full accordance with Jewish law. When signing his name at the end, he added, "son-in-law of the *gaon* Rabbi Baruch Frankel, *av beis din* of Leipnik."

Upon reading the letter, the Lisser Rav immediately understood that he was dealing with a great man whose *pesak* had been halachically correct. He realized that the previous description of the case had been misleading.

THE EARLY RABBANIM

The Lisser Rav responded to the Divrei Chaim's letter with warmth and geniality. He addressed him with great respect and showered him with honorary titles befitting an elderly and esteemed person. In his letter he fully justified the Divrei Chaim's judgment.

The Lisser Rav summed up his letter with the following words: "Many years ago, when the Leipniker Rav was still alive, I once mentioned to him that there were no *rabbanim* in the new generation who could take the place of the elderly *poskim* in judging difficult cases. The Leipniker Rav consoled me, saying that his son-in-law Rabbi Chaim was suitable to take over the leading *poskim*. In addition, he even believed he could become the next *gadol* of the generation."

When the letter arrived in Sanz, everybody unanimously admitted that the Divrei Chaim was right. The *Rav*, Rabbi Baruch Landau, read the letter and declared that only the son-in-law of the Leipniker Rav was worthy of being *Rav* in the town. He stepped down from his position and handed over the leadership of the town to the Divrei Chaim. Rabbi Baruch remained *Rav* of the Sanzer *kreis* (district).

Rabbi Baruch Landau passed away in the year 5608 (1848). A dome was built above his grave. Nine years later, in 5617, Rabbi Aharon Halberstam, the Divrei Chaim's son, took over his position as *Rav* of the Sanzer *kreis* (thus his title, Kreiser Rav). Rabbi Elimelech Elazar Ehrenberg, author of *Arzei Levanon*, writes that before the Kreiser Rav became *Rav*, his brother Rabbi Meir Nassan acted as the Kreiser Rav.

(There are contradicting opinions as to whether Rabbi Baruch Landau indeed voluntarily handed over his position to the Divrei Chaim. There are those who believe that Rabbi Baruch passed away as early as 5590 and that the Divrei Chaim came to Sanz to act as *Rav* in his stead. However, it is likely that this is based on guesses only.)

The First Rabbinical Dynasty

The Divrei Chaim was not the first Rebbe in Sanz. In the period prior to that of the Divrei Chaim, Rabbi Asher Zalke, the son of Rabbi Tzvi, acted as Rebbe. He had been one of the students of the Chozeh of Lublin. In the *kesav rabbanus* of the Divrei Chaim, Rabbi Zalke is listed as one of the Sanzer *dayanim*. His grave was set apart in the Sanzer cemetery and had a dome built over it.

Rabbi Chaim Sanzer

Rabbi Chaim Sanzer, a world-renowned *Rav* who belonged to the famous *chachmei klaus* (a group of the greatest *gedolim* of that time who learned all day in the *beis midrash*) of Brod, originated from Sanz. He was born in the year 5480 (1720) to Rabbi Menachem Nachum of Sanz. His mother was a daughter of Rabbi Shmuel Shmelke Horowitz, the *av beis din* of Shendishov and later the *Rav* of Tarnow for forty years. Rabbi Shmelke was also the grandfather of the two saintly brothers, the Hafla'ah and the Rebbe Reb Shmelke of Nicholsburg.

Rabbi Chaim Sanzer was a fiery *misnagid* and considered the path of Chassidus, founded by the Ba'al Shem Tov, a new and strange one. Nevertheless, it is said that the Ba'al Shem Tov said of Rabbi Chaim Sanzer that he had both the appearance and the soul of the *tanna* Rabbi Yochanan ben Zakkai.

It was told in Sanz that Rabbi Chaim Sanzer had many similarities to the Sanzer Rav, the holy Divrei Chaim. Both prayed with intense fervor, and both were extremely learned in the open and hidden mysteries of the Torah. Rabbi Chaim Sanzer authored many *sefarim*, of which only a part was actually published.

Rabbi Chaim Sanzer was also known for his many deeds of kindness and charity. He was always concerned that the poor people of the town would not be destitute. He was also very zealous, and if he ever saw a defilement of Jewish law, he would not hesitate to outrightly voice his disapproval. Rabbi Chaim Sanzer passed away in Brod on 6 Shevat 5543 (1783).

CHAPTER 5

THE DIVREI CHAIM

Sanz Becomes Tsanz

Tsanzer Chassidim did not spell "Sanz" with a *samech*; rather, they wrote "Tsanz," with a *tzaddi*. The reason behind it is as follows: An inhabitant of Sanz once paid a visit to Reb Meirel Premishlaner. As he handed Reb Meirel a *kvittel*, the *tzaddik* saw the name Sanz written on the piece of paper. The aged rabbi remarked, " 'Sanz' is not spelled with a *samech* but with a *tzaddi*, because Tsanz is the residence of the *gadol hador*." Reb Meirel was, of course, referring to the Divrei Chaim. Since then, Tsanzer Chassidim spell the town Sanz with a *tzaddi*. (The fact is, though, that before this incident, in the year 5493 [1733], two of the leaders of the Tsanzer community signed a document, "Menachem Nachum from Tsanz" and "Meir Katz from Tsanz," spelling "Tsanz" with a *tzaddi*. However, most people from Tsanz wrote Sanz with a *samech*.)

His Early Years

There is a difference of opinion as to the exact birth date of the Divrei Chaim, Rabbi Chaim Halberstam. He was born in Tarnegrod, according to one source in the year 5553 (1793) and according to another in the year 5557 (1797). The Tzieshinover Rebbe of Brooklyn, Rabbi Shalom Yechezkel Rubin-Halberstam, who was a student of my father, wrote that he had browsed through the official state records

The Vanished City of Tsanz

of Tarnegrod and clearly saw that the Tsanzer Rav's birth was registered in the year 5557. Those who believe that he was born in 5553 claim that the official town records are not at all reliable, since many people used to register births a few years later, in order to evade forced army conscription. In general, the Polish state records from this time are not as organized and reliable as the records of other European countries, and it is therefore more than likely that the date registered is indeed incorrect.

Reb Chaim's father, Reb Aryeh Leibish, was a *dayan* in the town Przemyzl during the last few years of his life. On his father's side, Reb Chaim was a descendant of Rabbi Tzvi Hirsh, the *Rav* of Halberstadt. Reb Chaim changed his family name from "Halberstadt" to "Halberstam" since he maintained that many towns were named after foreign deities. He would never refer to a town by a name, apart from the town of Duklah, since Duklah is mentioned in the Torah (Bereishis 10:27). The Divrei Chaim was also a descendant of the Maharshal. On his mother's side, he was a descendant of the Chacham Tzvi.

As a child, the Divrei Chaim was a weak lad who limped on one foot. It was said that the assistant teacher in *cheder* beat him, leaving him with a permanent limp. My father once told me that the assistant used to drag the Divrei Chaim to *cheder* every morning. One day, the little boy asked the assistant, "Why do I have to be dragged to *cheder* every day, while my father is graciously asked if he wants to go someplace?" He received no satisfactory response to his query, but the next morning, when the assistant came to take him to *cheder*, he said to him, "Chaim, please come to *cheder*." Little Chaim pertly answered, "I would love to go, but I would like to follow in the footsteps of my father. He does not go everywhere he is asked to go, and I wish to act likewise."

Even as a young child, the Divrei Chaim was known as an *ilui*. My father told me the following story which he heard about the Divrei Chaim:

When the Divrei Chaim was a little boy of nine or ten years old, someone asked him, "Why is it that when one person says to another, '*Shalom aleichem*,' the other answers back, '*Aleichem shalom*'?"

THE DIVREI CHAIM

The Divrei Chaim answered, "The Gemara says when somebody wants to bring an *olah* or a *chatas* he should say '*olah LaShem*' or '*chatas LaShem*' and not '*LaShem olah*' or '*LaShem chatas*.' The reason is that if he said '*LaShem*' first and died before he could say '*olah*' or '*chatas*,' he would have said Hashem's name in vain. The same is true of '*shalom aleichem*.' Shalom is a name of G-d. The person who begins the greeting may say '*shalom aleichem*,' because it says that whoever greets his friend first will be blessed with long life. For him there is no danger that he will die before he can say the word '*aleichem*.' But there is always the possibility that the one who answers might die, so he has to say '*aleichem shalom*.'"

The Divrei Chaim was attracted to Chassidus from a very young age. His first rebbe was Reb Yossele HaLevi of Tarnegrod, a brother of the Chozeh of Lublin. As a young boy, the Divrei Chaim begged his father to take him along on a visit to the Chozeh. His father was a strong *misnagid*, yet he relented before his son's earnest pleas and traveled with him to the Chozeh. The visit left such a profound impression on the child that he regularly visited the Chozeh, right up to his mentor's death in the year 5575 (1814).

It appears that the Divrei Chaim's mother did have some Chassidic inclination. The story goes that when she was pregnant with the Divrei Chaim she went to the Chozeh with a *kvittel*. The Chozeh told her that she would give birth to a son who would light up the world with his wisdom. Indeed, the Divrei Chaim proved his words correct.

The Divrei Chaim got married at the age of seventeen to the daughter of Rabbi Baruch Frankel-Teumim, *av beis din* of Leipnik, author of *Baruch Ta'am*. At the tender age of eighteen he was accepted as *Rav* in Rudnik, a town close to Ropshitz. From there he would travel to the Ropshitzer Rav, Reb Naftali, who was one of the well-known Chassidim of the Chozeh. The Divrei Chaim always considered himself a Chassid and disciple of the Ropshitzer Rav. Many of the popular *niggunim* commonly sung in Tsanz originally stemmed from Ropshitz. When the Ropshitzer Rav, of saintly memory, passed away in the year 5587 (1826), the Divrei Chaim left Rudnik.

The Divrei Chaim Becomes Rav

The Divrei Chaim customarily delivered a *pilpul* on Shavuos day. One Shavuos, after the Divrei Chaim had concluded his *pilpul*, he announced, "Yossel Ropper has paid attention and has understood every word."

This mysterious statement left the Chassidim perplexed, as Yossel Ropper had passed away years before. Soon enough, the Divrei Chaim shed light on his mysterious declaration. He recounted what happened to him when he came to Tsanz the very first time to be accepted as *Rav*. He had barely dismounted from the wagon when all the learned scholars of the town surrounded him, eager to launch into a deep Torah discourse with him. Amidst the confusion, a simple young man by the name of Yossel Ropper suddenly made his appearance and quietly informed the *Rav* that he had something of urgent importance to discuss with him. He led the *Rav* out of the circle of admirers into a private room. There he offered the *Rav* some food and drink and with warmth and concern respectfully said to him, "The *Rav* is probably tired and hungry from his travels. Please refresh yourself and then rest a little."

"Yossel Ropper revitalized my waning energy after my tiring journey," concluded the Divrei Chaim. "Therefore, even though he was an ignoramus in this world, in the World to Come he understands every word of my complex discourse." It seems that, in the merit of having assisted the Divrei Chaim, Yossel Ropper was granted the privilege of becoming familiar with the wonderful treasure of Torah learning.

In the first year of the Divrei Chaim's stay in Tsanz, he and his family resided at the home of the community leader, Reb Yidel HaKohen Hollander, at Reb Yidel's expense. The story goes that Reb Yidel Hollander once wanted to test whether the new *Rav* bore any favoritism toward anyone. He considered himself the perfect candidate, since he was a close friend of the *Rav*, having arranged for the *Rav* to obtain his position in Tsanz and opened up his home to him and his family, providing him with all his needs.

THE DIVREI CHAIM

Thus, Reb Yidel conspired with a friend of his. The plan was that the friend would approach the Divrei Chaim with a complaint against Reb Yidel. The friend followed Reb Yidel's exact instructions and consulted with the *Rav*, complaining that Reb Yidel owed him a large amount of money which he refused to repay. He demanded that the *Rav* summon Reb Yidel to a *din Torah*.

The *Rav* promptly called his messenger and bade him to draw up an official summons to Reb Yidel Hollander to appear before the *Rav* for a *din Torah*.

Reb Yidel received the expected summons and brazenly answered, "I, being the head of the community and a wealthy merchant, do not have time in my busy schedule to accommodate a petty *din Torah*."

The messenger dutifully reported Reb Yidel's words to the Divrei Chaim. Undeterred by the bold reply, the Divrei Chaim sent the messenger back to Reb Yidel with a sharp command that he must appear before him. Once again, Reb Yidel responded to the messenger, "I am hard-pressed with all my business affairs. Right now I simply do not have the time, but when I find some free moments I will make the effort to present myself. Meanwhile, please tell the *Rav* that I do not want to be bothered with this affair any longer."

When the Divrei Chaim heard this audacious response, he ordered the messenger to return immediately to Reb Yidel and strongly warn him that should he not appear immediately before the *beis din* an injunction would be issued against him.

As soon as Reb Yidel heard of the extreme step which the *Rav* was ready to carry out, he rushed to the Divrei Chaim's home and admitted that it had all been a ploy. "It is now clear to me without any doubt that the *Rav* is unquestionably worthy of acting as *Rav* of Tsanz," he warmly declared.

After that incident Reb Yidel showered the *Rav* with all he could possibly require and bought him a magnificent apartment where he resided for many years, until the Neugroschl family, Tsanzer Chassidim from Vienna, built him a large house and *beis midrash*.

The Vanished City of Tsanz

Rabbi Eziel Herbst from Tsanz (now living in London) told that before Reb Yidel bought the Divrei Chaim his magnificent apartment he lived in the home of Rabbi Eziel's great-great-grandfather, Reb Shloime Herbst, for over three years. In 5636 (1876), not long after the Divrei Chaim's death, his son the Shinover Rav came to live for one year in Tsanz. He went to Reb Shloime's apartment and said that he would like a bed placed in the exact spot where his father, the Divrei Chaim, used to learn. As soon as the bed was placed there, the Shinover Rav lay down and fell asleep. He slept for so long that his Chassidim thought he would miss *minchah*, so they started banging on the door till he woke up. When the Shinover Rav awoke he said, "One can tell that somebody has learned *Torah liShmah* here. It's a long time since I have felt so good when I slept."

Eighteen years after the Divrei Chaim was appointed *Rav* of Tsanz, in 5608, a bill was introduced in the Austrian government that gave equal rights to all its citizens, including Jews. This wrought a remarkable improvement in the Jews' general social and economic situation.

As soon as the new law was enforced, the Jews' response was to finally move out of the stifling ghetto quarters to other parts of town. This step met with resentment by the ever-present anti-Semites all over the land. They strongly protested to the young emperor, Franz Joseph, claiming that he was breaching the traditional Polish laws by allowing the Jews to infest the Polish settlements with their unwanted presence. However, Franz Joseph showed admirable strength of character and refused to be swayed by their stories. He steadfastly maintained that he would stick to what he had originally planned: to give unlimited living rights and trading opportunities to the Jews. In Tsanz the wicked anti-Semites did not give up their evil plans, and they persistently fought against the Jews until they finally capitulated in 5627 (1867), when they perceived that Franz Joseph was adamant in his decision.

Life before the Telegraph

In the year 5523 (1863) the first telephone-telegraph office was established in Tsanz. Up until then all the towns in Galicia were

THE DIVREI CHAIM

completely secluded, cut off from any means of communication. The following story gives us a bit of a picture of what this meant.

In the town of Duklah there lived a *shamash* by the name of Reb Tzadok HaKohen Steiner. Once, when he locked up the shul for the night, he unwittingly locked in his twelve-year-old son, Yaakov. Yaakov had been playing outside, and when he had grown weary of his frolics he had gone inside, lain down on one of the benches, and fallen fast asleep. His father, assuming Yaakov was still happily playing in the courtyard, locked the door and went home.

When Yaakov awoke, everything was dark and eerie. The bewildered boy tried to exit via the door, but it was firmly locked and bolted. His alarm growing, the boy attempted to escape through one of the windows, but they were one and a half meters high, and there was no way such a young boy could reach it. Terrified, the boy cowered under one of the benches in the corner of the shul.

When Reb Tzadok arrived home unaccompanied by his son, his wife asked him, "Where is Yaakov?"

Reb Tzadok looked around him in alarm and said, "I have no idea! The last time I saw him he was playing in the shul courtyard."

Their concern growing with each passing minute, the couple began searching for him in all possible places. After hours of worried searching and still no trace of their son, Reb Tzadok suggested to his panic-stricken wife, "Perhaps the boy is locked up in the shul?"

This seemed the only possible place left, and so, accompanied by a concerned neighbor, they went in the direction of the shul. Reb Tzadok held a lantern in his hand and with trembling fingers opened the door. He stepped inside, but the feeble light of the lantern did not illuminate the frightened boy cowering under the bench. After a quick look around, a disappointed Reb Tzadok turned to his wife and neighbor and said, "No. The boy is not here."

Meanwhile, Yaakov, who had spent the past few hours in the lonely, dark shul in heart-stopping fear, had heard the key turning in the lock. His terror reaching a hysterical pitch, he had been overcome with relief to hear his father's voice. When he heard his father say he was not there, he cried out in frustration, "I *am* here!" Thus Yaakov

The Vanished City of Tsanz

was rescued. However, the sheer fright of the past few hours proved to be too much for the poor boy. After uttering those words, he was struck dumb and could speak no more.

Reb Tzadok agonized over his son's handicap. In desperation, he took him to the Dukler Rav, Reb Avigdor, a brother of the Divrei Chaim. Reb Avigdor wrote a letter to his brother the Divrei Chaim explaining the situation.

Duklah is approximately sixty kilometers from Tsanz, but in those days the roads were rough and unpaved. The messenger had to journey first through Zmigrod, after that through Gorlitz, then Gribow; finally, three weeks later, he reached Tsanz. The Divrei Chaim answered the letter, saying that "within a short time I will journey to Duklah." It took four weeks for this message to reach its destination.

Another four passed, and in the eleventh week of the boy's sudden illness, the Divrei Chaim finally arrived at Duklah. The stricken lad was brought before him.

The Divrei Chaim opened an *alef-beis* book and asked the boy to recite the letters. His request was met with stony silence. The Divrei Chaim then gave the boy a tap on his right shoulder with his pipe. Still no response. The Divrei Chaim gave the boy a tap on his left shoulder with his pipe. This met with the same result. The Divrei Chaim gave the boy a tap between his shoulder blades, and, miracle upon miracles, the boy began to recite the *alef-beis* as commanded!

The Pshevorsker Rav, *shlita*, said that this was the first story that he ever heard from his Rebbe, the Koloshitzer Rav. He heard it in Duklah in the year 5686 (1926). The Pshevorsker Rav, *shlita*, himself remembered the boy, grown up, as Reb Yaakov the *shamash*. Reb Yaakov had taken over his father's position after his death. He remembered him as an old man of over seventy years who had a slow, slurred speech. The elderly people of the town said they remembered that the Divrei Chaim had said at the time, "The lad was lucky that he was not yet of bar mitzvah age, because if he would have been, the souls that come into the shul at night would have called him up to the *sefer Torah*, and the boy would have died of sheer terror."

THE DIVREI CHAIM

This amazing story must have occurred before 5623 (1863), because after that time Reb Avigdor could have sent a telegram relaying his message to his brother, and it would have been unnecessary for the boy to have suffered for eleven long weeks until he could be cured of his ailment.

The Shalom Zachor

In Tsanz there was a custom to serve *arbis* (chickpeas) and small cakes in the shape of a heart at every *shalom zachor*. These cakes were called "*zachor kichelech*." My father explained to me that the custom of serving cakes was because the occasion was called a "*se'udas shalom zachor*," and in order for a *se'udah* to be called thus, *mezonos* must be served.

The Divrei Chaim unfailingly attended every *shalom zachor* that took place in town. After he had finished his *tisch* Friday night, he would be escorted by a multitude of Chassidim to the home of the *ba'al simchah*. He would take a bite of the delicacies being served, and after blessing the parents of the newborn and all the other relatives in the home, he would depart.

One Friday night a man named Reb Yaakov Engelhart, who was known as "Yaakov the son of *hakodesh* (the martyr) Reb Moshe Maliss," celebrated a *shalom zachor*. He lived in the part of the town called the Piekela, a suburb which was quite a distance from the Divrei Chaim's home. It was a cold, winter Shabbos. The Divrei Chaim had finished his *tisch* very late, so it was after midnight when he set out on the long walk to the home of Reb Yaakov.

Reb Yaakov and his family had long given up hope of receiving any more guests, and they had all gone to bed. They were awakened by the escorts of the Divrei Chaim, who tapped on the windowpanes. Feeling both honored and embarrassed they hastily got ready to welcome their highly esteemed visitor. The Divrei Chaim tasted a few of the *arbis*, drank a "*l'chaim*," and blessed the father, mother, and child. As Reb Yaakov escorted the Rebbe to the door, he wondered aloud, "If I would not have seen it with my own eyes, I would never have believed that the old Rebbe would come all this way merely to taste a few *arbis*!"

It was said that Reb Yaakov Engelhart had received a blessing of long life from the Divrei Chaim. Indeed, he was the eldest person in Tsanz, and at the grand old age of one hundred years, he himself would trudge to the well with two buckets on his shoulders and carry them back home filled to the brim completely unassisted! Immediately after the Divrei Chaim passed away, Reb Yaakov purchased a plot of land near his burial place. He lived another sixty years after that, and after his death at the age of 107, he was indeed buried in the spot of his choosing.

This Reb Yaakov, as we mentioned earlier, was called "Yaakov the son of *hakodesh* Reb Moshe Maliss." His father was called thus because of the following:

A large group once traveled from Tsanz to a wedding in Sighet, Marmarosh. On the way they were attacked by a vicious band of gypsies who robbed them down to their last farthing. Still not satisfied, the bloodthirsty gang wanted to murder the entire group. Displaying amazing courage and self-sacrifice, Reb Moshe Maliss stepped forward and offered that the gang satisfy their blood lust on him and let the others free. The gypsies agreed and murdered the martyr Reb Moshe, allowing the rest to continue on to the wedding unharmed.

Market Day

The market days in Tsanz used to take place on Tuesdays and Saturdays. This posed great difficulties for the Jewish dealers who used to actively participate. The Divrei Chaim intervened on their behalf to the city council to change the market day from Saturday to Friday. His efforts bore fruit, and the change was brought into effect. This proved to be of great benefit for all the Jews who had stalls in the marketplace.

The Chassidim inquired of their *Rav*, "Why did you ask the day to be changed to Friday? Would it not be more convenient if the market day took place on Thursday, allowing time on Friday for Shabbos preparations?"

THE DIVREI CHAIM

The marketplace in Oswiecim in 5665 (1905), later to aquire terrible repute under its German name, Auschwitz

Market day in Strij, Galicia, 5665 (1905)

The Vanished City of Tsanz

The Divrei Chaim replied, "When the Jews hastily dismantle their stalls and pack away their merchandise two hours before Shabbos arrives and rush to complete their Shabbos preparations and ritual bath in time for candle lighting, a tremendous impact is wrought in Heaven at their great dedication and self-sacrifice in honor of the Shabbos. It is worth the Friday rush and pressure for the influence it wreaks in Heaven!"

The Tsanzer Rav's Charity and Good Deeds

The marketplace of Tsanz with the town hall in the middle

A distinguished German *rabbiner* from Berlin once passed through Tsanz and stepped in to see the Divrei Chaim. In the midst of their conversation he remarked, "Your method of charity distribution is unsatisfactory. Money is given out to all who are willing to accept it, whether the receiver is in need of it or not. Back home in Germany, we take great care to ensure that the beggar is indeed in need of the donation. If not, the money is not granted."

The Divrei Chaim replied, "The difference between you and me is as follows: You do not give money to a hundred paupers for fear that one of them may not be worthy of the donation. I, on the other hand, give charity to a hundred paupers in the belief that perhaps one of them indeed needs the money..."

A Shabbos in Tilitsh

In the era of the Divrei Chaim, it wasn't as common as it is today for people to spend their summer vacations in holiday resorts. Instead, the Rebbes used to travel to the countryside, where they lodged at the homes of local Jews. Almost all the outlying villages were populated by a number of Jews who made a living by journeying into town to sell eggs, poultry, milk, and butter.

Tilitsh, a small village, was located a few kilometers away from Tsanz. Reb Berel Tilitsher, a Tsanzer Chassid, invited the Tsanzer Rav to visit him in the countryside for a few weeks so that he could benefit from the fresh air. Much to his delight, the Tsanzer Rav accepted his invitation.

Needless to say, many Chassidim joined the Tsanzer Rav in Tilitsh over Shabbos. Chassidim often visited their Rebbe when he was away from home, because then it was easier to be granted an audience and be given a *berachah* for all their personal needs.

On Shabbos morning, many Chassidim thronged to the village lake to immerse themselves. When the village squire, a man named Krashinski, and his son saw this, they were furious with the Chassidim for "polluting" the water. They enticed the peasants to grab sticks, axes, and pieces of iron and drive the Chassidim from the lake.

Reb Berel Tilitsher ran toward Krashinski and his son and begged them to allow the Chassidim to immerse in peace. He assured them that the Chassidim would not contaminate the water and promised each peasant who was present a sack of flour in return for leaving the Chassidim alone. The peasants accepted the offer, and the following day they turned up in masses to demand "fees" for their services. Reb Berel Tilitsher handed each of them a sack of flour.

The saintly Divrei Chaim heard all the commotion and, turning to his host, Reb Berel, asked him, "What is all the noise and tumult about?" Reb Berel Tilitsher related the entire story and told the Divrei Chaim all that had occurred when the Chassidim wanted to immerse themselves.

The Divrei Chaim casually responded, "They are mentally deranged people!" That day both troublemakers, Squire Krashinski and his son, indeed became mentally ill and had to be sent to a lunatic asylum.

The Vanished City of Tsanz

The Undrawn Picture

It was Pesach in the year 5702 (1942). The World War was raging. The Jewish Police were carrying out one of their dreaded *oblaves*, when they would seize people and herd them onto trucks to be deported to the notorious death camp Puskow. I just happened to be on the streets at that time, and in great panic I fled into the cellar of Baruch Fendler's herring store.

The Gorlitzer Rav's son, about whom it was said looked exactly like the Divrei Chaim

There I sat, huddled together with a few other Jews the entire night, until we heard the commotion outside subsiding and knew that the *aktion* was over. As we sat there, we came across a mound of old paper, yellowed with age, which recorded court trials. In those days, when paper was expensive and valuable, the court used to sell their records fifty years after their use to merchants to wrap their merchandise in.

Our nerves taut with apprehension, we whiled away the tension-filled hours reading through the court dealings which had taken place so many years ago. We came across one particularly interesting case. It dealt with a certain Lemberg newspaper that sued the saintly Tsanzer *tzaddik*, the Divrei Chaim himself. What happened was that the newspaper, hearing of this "wonder *rabbiner*," wanted to feature an article about him. They sent a professional artist to Tsanz to sketch the countenance of this "wonder rabbi."

The artist arrived at Tsanz and rented an apartment right across the street from the Divrei Chaim's home so that when the rabbi would walk to the *beis midrash* or mikveh, he would be able to sketch his appearance. However, halfway through his project, the artist became paralyzed and was unable to continue.

The newspaper editors took the Divrei Chaim to court, claiming that he had cursed the artist and caused his handicap as a punishment for attempting to draw a picture of him. They demanded compensation for the artist.

It so happened that the Divrei Chaim was ill at the time and was unable to personally attend the trial. The accusation was written up and sent to him at home, with a demand for his response. The *Rav* sent his *gabbai*, Reb Refael Tzimmetbaum, known as "the tall Refael," to stand in court in his stead. He ordered him to say the following words in his defense:

"From the moment I was able to think for myself, I firmly resolved never to harm a single person, be it Jew or gentile." The court accepted his words, and the Divrei Chaim was acquitted.

(In Tsanz it was known that no picture of the Divrei Chaim exists. The Banier Rav of Antwerp, Rabbi Yissachar Ber Dachner, of saintly memory, once said that the picture of the Divrei Chaim which is accepted in the world today is in reality a picture of one of his grandchildren, Rabbi Elisha Halberstam, a son of the Gorlitzer Rav. Elderly Chassidim who remembered the saintly Divrei Chaim remarked that he looked exactly like his grandfather. This picture was drawn in order to give an idea of what the Divrei Chaim looked like.)

"Buy the Whole Estate"

Chaim Schenker of Chrzsanow had an opportunity to rent an *arenda* (a guest house) in Oswiecim (Auschwitz). He had some doubts about the location, because the Jews of that town were considered progressive, so he traveled to Tsanz to ask the Divrei Chaim what he should do.

The Divrei Chaim told Chaim that it was his duty to relocate to Oswiecim, because as a result other Chassidic Jews would also move there, and thus his move would have an influence on the whole town.

The Vanished City of Tsanz

Chaim moved to Oswiecim and rented the *arenda* from Count Roosocki.

In those days the entire economy in that district was based on raising crops, whose prices were low because the surrounding countries placed a high import tax on all grain. Therefore the population was impoverished. The first year was very difficult for Chaim Schenker because there was a drought and the peasants stopped coming to town. Business dropped sharply, and Chaim was afraid he would not be able to pay his rent. He decided to travel to Tsanz and ask the Divrei Chaim whether he should move back to Chrzsanow.

When Chaim Schenker entered the room of the Divrei Chaim, before he could even open his mouth, the Divrei Chaim said to him, "Listen, Chaim, if you don't have enough money to pay the rent, you should buy the whole estate."

The management of the Oswiecim, Zasole, Brzezinka (Birkenau), and Babice estates was in the hands of a Polish administrator who lived in a splendid villa. He was a drunkard and reduced the count's property, embezzled his funds, and treated the workers on the estate brutally. He could do so easily because the count rarely visited Oswiecim, since he had large estates in Stanislawow and Lublin and lived in his Lemberg palace for most of the year.

Once Count Roosocki paid a surprise visit to the estate, where he felt animosity toward him on the part of the workers. Investigating the cause, he uncovered many complaints against the administrator. The count then took the records of the estates and studied them. To his horror he found that his administrator was not only wicked, but he was a thief as well. The count sent for the administrator, but the latter had already made good his escape.

Count Roosocki was forced to remain and take care of the neglected estate. He despaired of his task and decided to sell the estate, but the administrator had already sold the crops before the harvest, and all the count's efforts to dispose of the property were in vain.

The Austrian government was at that time planning the Vienna-Cracow-Lemberg railway line, which would pass through Oswiecim. Count Roosocki submitted a plan in which the railway line would pass

THE DIVREI CHAIM

through his estate. He then applied for a loan from a mortgage bank for agriculture. In view of his application for the railway to go through his land the bank upped the value of his land and approved a sizable low-interest loan on a long-term payment plan.

However, later the town council of Oswiecim protested against the construction of a railway through the town. The farmers joined the protest because they were afraid that sparks from the locomotives would set their fields afire. These protests were sent to Vienna. The count feared that the cancellation of the government's plan to build the railway and the high appraisal of his property would involve him in legal difficulties if he were to try to reduce the appraisal. He therefore decided to sell the estate at any price. He then remembered Chaim Schenker, whom he had encountered when signing a contract for the lease of the *arenda*.

The count sent for Chaim and said to him, "I want to sell you all my estates in Oswiecim, Zasole, Brzezinka, and Babice. You won't have to pay the purchase price in cash. You can take over the mortgage registered against the estates in the Land Registry office. These are to be paid on convenient terms over a period of ten years." The count went into detail about the purchase-price arrangement, but Chaim was paying scant attention. His mind was on the words that the Divrei Chaim had said to him only a few days earlier: "Listen, Chaim, if you don't have enough money to pay the rent, you should buy the whole estate."

Straight after the sale, luck was with Chaim wherever he turned. The Austrian government set aside the petitions of the town council and farmers of Oswiecim. Thanks to the high appraisal of Count Roosocki, the price paid by the Austrian government to the railway to pass through Chaim Schenker's estate covered the mortgage in its entirety. Not long after that the British government greatly reduced the import duty on grain. Because of that, other countries also reduced their import duty, and the price of grain soared. Chaim Schenker became the richest man in the whole district.

(I heard this story from the Pshevorsker Rebbe. Later, in the archives of the charity Rabbi Meir Ba'al HaNess Kollel Chibas

The Vanished City of Tsanz

Yerushalayim, I discovered a more detailed account written by a great-grandson of Chaim Schenker.)

The Tsanzer Rav's Avodas Hashem

The following is from the recorded memories of an elderly gentleman who was fortunate enough to have seen the holy Tsanzer Rav, Rabbi Chaim Halberstam, in his final years. The story portrays to some extent the tremendous *avodas Hashem* which the Divrei Chaim displayed, nullifying his own will completely for the Will of his Creator. This is what this man related:

> My father was a fiery Chassid of the Tsanzer *tzaddik*, Rabbi Chaim Halberstam. Our Shabbos table was replete with stories about his saintliness. My father's words had a remarkable impact on my young, impressionable mind. I was made to understand again and again that the Tsanzer *tzaddik* had a soul holier and loftier than other mortals. I yearned with every fiber of my being just to catch a glimpse of the holy man, who was quite elderly.
>
> One seder night my father informed me of incredibly wonderful news. Immediately after Pesach he would take me along with him to Tsanz to consult with the *tzaddik* about which yeshivah I should attend. That was in the year 5632 (1872). I was ten years old at the time.
>
> I was so overcome with joy that the entire *yom tov* I could not close an eyelid. My childish mind tried to conjure up images of the saintly *tzaddik* I had heard so much about. He must surely resemble an angel!
>
> There were few train routes on the trip we were about to undertake, but only on a short stretch of the journey were we afforded that luxury — from Dembitz to Tarnow. The rest of the way we hitched wagons from one *shtetl* to the next.
>
> On the way from Tarnow to Tsanz we were caught in a torrential downpour. Our only means of protection was a massive, empty liquor barrel.

THE DIVREI CHAIM

More dead than alive, we finally arrived at our destination. My joy at arrival was so intense that I soon forgot all the suffering I had been forced to endure in order to get there.

We arrived on a Thursday. At our lodgings we were told the sad news that the Tsanzer Rav had returned a mere half-hour before from the cemetery, where he had seen his daughter, Reb Leizerke's wife, buried. The news hit my father like a thunderbolt. As for me, my bitter disappointment surpassed even his.

"We will certainly not be allowed entrance until after the *shivah*," my father said with a heavy sigh. "I cannot afford to wait that long. We have no choice but to return home tonight without even having seen the saintly *tzaddik*."

However, my father was known in Tsanz and was therefore granted special permission to daven with the *Rav*'s minyan in the large room which adjoined his private chamber. The *Rav*'s door was slightly ajar, and I peeked into his room in order to finally catch a glimpse of the *tzaddik* I had heard so much about. Suddenly a side door opened, and a small, elderly man limped into the room with amazing sprightliness. He headed toward the water, washed his hands, and pranced about the room, reciting the blessing *asher yatzar* in a loud voice, with intense devotion.

I stood motionless, transfixed at the scene unfolding before my eyes. I could not believe that I had actually merited to see the *Rav* in real life! That first impression I have of the *Rav* remains engraved in my memory, the image of an angel of G-d.

The Tsanzer *tzaddik* was wont to move about a lot while praying and to utter exclamations out loud as a result of his intense fervor. Even when sitting with his Chassidim or conversing with a group of people, he would suddenly get up and begin dancing around the room, repeating aloud again and again, "There does not exist a vacant space where Hashem is not found!" This unexpected outburst would throw a trembling and fear on all who witnessed it.

He would also often sing the well-known song composed by the Kalever Rebbe, which concluded with the above-mentioned words. This song unfailingly strengthened belief in G-d, both in the one who sang it and in all who heard him, that G-d's presence fills the entire world. It is pointless to probe into the mystery of His ways, for the more one tries to satisfy one's questions, the more perplexed one becomes. The only solution, therefore, is to unquestioningly accept His oneness and complete Divinity. The approximate translation of the song is as follows:

"The blasphemers challenge,
'Where is G-d?'
Oy vey, what do we tell them?
There does not exist a vacant space where Hashem is not found.
There does not exist a vacant space where Hashem is not found.
The drunkards ask,
'What does G-d do?'
Oy vey, what do we tell them?
Oy vey, what do we tell them?
Les machshavah tefisah bai klal — It is beyond human comprehension to grasp the ways and existence of the supreme G-d."

As the Rebbe would finish singing this moving melody, he would emit a deep, soul-stirring cry — *"Les machshavah tefisah bai klal."*

That Thursday night, when we were fulfilling the mitzvah of *sefiras ha'omer*, the Rebbe danced with such intense fervor and enthusiasm that the great impression it ingrained on me then remains until today. And all this was a mere three or four hours after his daughter's funeral. A person who could so completely obliterate his own feelings and emotions for the sake of G-d, a person who could reach this ultimate degree of the requirement "Serve Hashem with joy," cannot be an ordinary mortal but must have reached the level of an angel of G-d!

THE DIVREI CHAIM

The Shabbos of the *shivah* week, the Rebbe *feered tisch* as usual. Many people in white *bekishes* (other Rebbes) were present at the *tisch*, among them the *tzaddikim* Rabbi Hershele Lisker, the Radomsker Rebbe (author of *Chesed L'Avraham*), who was a renowned *ba'al tefillah* and *sheliach tzibbur* at *shacharis*; the Ilinover Rebbe, Reb Chananyele, who was *sheliach tzibbur* for *mussaf*, and Reb Aharon Cracower.

I vividly recall the Rebbe's words at the *tisch*: "A person must constantly be on guard like a soldier in the army. He is fighting a permanent battle with his *yetzer hara*, and the only way he can triumph over his enemy is by serving Hashem with joy. A truly faithful soldier does not desert the battlefield, even if he is heavily wounded, as long as he has the slightest bit of energy left in him. The heavy burden of daily problems should not sidetrack a person in his *avodas Hashem*, for this is the purpose of his creation."

Indeed, it was in this very field that the Tsanzer Rebbe was not only an eloquent speaker but the epitome of what he preached.

Those who heard him sing the moving melody *"An'im Zemiros,"* which discusses the yearning of the soul to come closer to G-d, those who saw his indescribable enthusiasm and loftiness at the words "As I speak of Your glory my heart yearns for Your love," which he sang with a beautiful and soothing tune, clasping both ends of his *bekishe* in his hands, must undoubtedly admit that they had witnessed a truly faithful soldier in the army of Hashem!

The Bar Mitzvah Bachur

Reb Shmuel Herbst became bar mitzvah in 5636 (1876), the year of the Divrei Chaim's passing. In compliance with the Tsanzer custom, Reb Shmuel went to the Divrei Chaim on the day of his bar mitzvah to have the *Rav* put on his tefillin for the very first time. When the Divrei Chaim took the tefillin he noticed that the *kesher* of the

The Vanished City of Tsanz

tefillin shel rosh was made according to *nosach Sefard*. (Before the war I had never heard of the *kesher* that the Klausenberger Chassidim call the "Tsanzer *kesher*." I have been told, though, that they say that the Tsanzer Rav used this *kesher*, and the Klausenberger Rav's grandfather, the Gorlitzer Rav, was the only one who took to using it.) He immediately ordered the *shel rosh* to be carried back to the *sofer* to be changed to *nosach Ashkenaz*, saying that this was the custom in Tsanz. While the arrangements were being made, he asked the nervous bar mitzvah *bachur* to say his *pshetl*.

When the tefillin were brought back from the *sofer*, the Divrei Chaim turned to the boy and said, "You should know that while we don tefillin Hashem does so, too. At that time we are in direct contact with Hashem. Therefore you should not utter any words other than prayer while you are wearing the tefillin, not even in Lashon HaKodesh."

The Divrei Chaim began the solemn ceremony of putting the tefillin on the boy. Together they recited the prayers *"V'Eirastich"* and *"Kadeish Li Kol Bechor."* Then the *Rav* said, "I want to hear you recite the morning blessings."

Young Shmuel began with *"Adon Olam"* and continued with *"Yigdal."* The Divrei Chaim then said to the boy, "Why are you saying '*Yigdal*'?"

Shmuel motioned with his hand that the *Rav* had warned him not to speak when wearing tefillin. The Divrei Chaim said, "You are right. But if you have something important to say, you may raise the *tefillin shel rosh* with your right hand and speak."

Shmuel did as he was bidden and then explained to the Divrei Chaim that he used to daven with his grandfather Reb Shloime in the town shul, where they davened *nosach Ashkenaz* and said *"Yigdal."* (The shul was the only minyan in the whole of Tsanz which davened *nosach Ashkenaz*.)

The Divrei Chaim closed his eyes in deep devotion for a few minutes, while the young boy stood respectfully with the *tefillin shel rosh* in his right hand. Suddenly the Divrei Chaim opened his eyes and announced, "If you have davened *nosach Ashkenaz* until now, you

THE DIVREI CHAIM

should continue with *nosach Ashkenaz*. But if you daven in my *beis midrash* and are asked to daven in front of the *amud*, you should begin with '*Hodu*' and not with '*Mizmor Shir*' *(nosach Sefard)*."

The Gorlitzer Rav, Rabbi Baruchel, happened to be in Tsanz at the time. He approached his father and said, "Tatte, don't you rule differently in your responsa?"

"If I have ordered him to daven *nosach Ashkenaz*, I know what I am doing. Please do not ask me about it again," retorted the Divrei Chaim.

After davening, the Gorlitzer Rav walked up to Shmuel and, holding him playfully by the ear, said to him, "I tremble when I speak to my father, yet you recited a *pilpul* to him and conversed with him as if you were his friend!"

Reb Shmuel was a miracle child, born through the Divrei Chaim's blessing. The story is as follows:

Reb Shmuel's father, Reb Henoch, was the son-in-law of Reb Nuta Greenberg, who lived in Tarnow. Reb Nuta was a Ropshitzer Chassid whom the Divrei Chaim knew from the days when he used to travel to the Ropshitzer Rav, Reb Naftali. After his marriage, Reb Henoch was supported by his father-in-law.

Reb Henoch managed to get a concession to buy cigarettes directly from the government, who had the sole monopoly on all tobacco sales. One Shabbos, a delegation from the army arrived at his home and demanded that he give them the key to his warehouse so they could take cigarettes. According to the agreement that Reb Henoch had with the government, the army had the right to demand the key. Though permitted according to halachah, nevertheless Reb Henoch refused to give them the key on Shabbos.

Fearing the consequences of his brazenness, he deserted his entire business and fled to Tsanz to his father. His father-in-law was furious and followed him to Tsanz to complain to the Tsanzer Rav about his son-in-law's foolhardiness, because in those days obtaining a grant to sell cigarettes was a difficult and lengthy procedure.

As soon as Reb Nuta entered the Divrei Chaim's room, the *Rav* said to him, "*Shalom aleichem!* What do you say about your son-in-law? I mean to say, I want to know if I am a good teacher. Have I educated him well?"

After hearing these words, Reb Nuta had to swallow all his criticism. But after dinner Reb Nuta blurted out, "Rebbe! Is this the right way? A young man has a decent business, and he drops everything when according to halachah this wasn't even called for?"

The Divrei Chaim appeased him. "I don't know what all this concern is about. You are afraid he won't have any income? I promise you he will have a *parnasah*. Lend him five hundred gulden, and I will persuade his father to lend him five hundred gulden. I give you my word that he will repay you."

The Divrei Chaim ordered Reb Henoch to purchase alcohol. At that time it seemed a foolish thing to do, because there was plenty of alcohol on the market.

Reb Henoch, who was childless, remained in Tsanz with his father, and the alcohol was stored away. Meanwhile, it became impossible to obtain alcohol due to problems of transport because of bad weather. The price of alcohol doubled. Still, the Divrei Chaim did not let Reb Henoch sell. When the price rocketed sky-high the Divrei Chaim said, "Now you may sell." Reb Henoch repaid his father and father-in-law and managed a thriving alcohol business.

Some people who noticed Reb Henoch's success in business began to envy him. One person said to him, "Henoch, you have been privileged to be in the *Rav*'s attendance many times, but you will never have children." This was two years after his marriage.

The incident was reported to the Divrei Chaim. That night, when Reb Henoch visited the *Rav*, the *Rav* put his arm on his shoulder and paced up and down the room. Then he stopped and said to the bewildered Reb Henoch, "You are despondent because of what that fellow said to you? I promise that you will have a son."

Rabbi Yossele Neustater, known as the *"Gitter Yid,"* happened to be in Tsanz at the time. The *Gitter Yid* never accepted *kvittelech* while he was in Tsanz. One evening after supper, the Divrei Chaim said to him, "I know you have a *minhag* not accept *kvittelech* while you are here, but I ask you to accept a *kvittel* from this young man. I promised him a son, and I want you to help me." Soon after, Reb Henoch had a son, Reb Shmuel, who remained his one and only child.

The German Chassid

A Tsanzer Chassid was forced to move to Bad Neuheim, Germany, for financial reasons. Since there was no Chassidic *beis midrash* there, the Chassid began to appear regularly at the main shul. He was given a seat next to an affluent German young man, a moneylender by occupation. The German made few attempts to converse with his *"Ost Jude"* (Eastern European Jew) neighbor, and the two men had very little to do with each other.

One day, during davening, the Tsanzer Chassid noticed that his wealthy German neighbor was not his usual self. His straight-backed carriage had stooped a little, and his face looked pale and drawn. Concerned, the Tsanzer Chassid asked his neighbor if anything was the matter, but the German merely shrugged off his queries, saying that everything was all right. His Galicianer neighbor noticed, though, that the German's appearance became more and more haggard with each passing day. He pressed him once again to tell him what the problem was. Finally, the German said, "Do you really want to know?"

"Yes," answered his neighbor. The German young man then invited him to his office.

In his office, the German released all barriers and began sobbing bitterly. "My business," he explained through his tears, "is that people

A Galician Jew, mid-nineteenth century

The Vanished City of Tsanz

who marry off their children pay installments of money to me over a number of years, receiving a lump sum at the required time. In the meantime, I invest their money in other businesses, with a *heter iska*. Recently a number of these businesses have declared themselves bankrupt. I have absolutely no way of repaying all those who have entrusted me with their money. It seems to me that the only way to get myself out of this is to commit suicide!"

The Galician Chassid drew back in shock when he heard these words. "How can a Jew speak like that?" he exclaimed. "Take your own life? A Jew who believes in the Creator?"

"But what can I do?" cried the anguished German.

"Personally I can do nothing to help your situation," replied the Chassid, "but I have a Rebbe in Galicia, a great *tzaddik*, the Tsanzer Rav, who will surely be ready to assist you."

"Will he be able to lend me money?" inquired the German dolefully.

"I do not know what he will do, but I am confident that if you write him a letter explaining your situation he will surely help you," the Chassid assured him.

The German wasted no time and wrote a letter to the Tsanzer Rebbe, describing his miserable situation. A short while later, he received a thick envelope from Tsanz. The Rebbe wrote to him as follows: "A person may not despair even in the most critical situation. He must have faith in the Creator. I am sending you a sum of money as a loan, with which you should continue to do business. With G-d's help you will succeed and be able to repay the loan."

Indeed, the German young man invested the money, and his business flourished. A few years passed thus, with his business growing successfully.

One night the German young man dreamed that an old man appeared to him and declared, "You owe me money."

In the morning, he rushed to the Galician Chassid and told him of his dream. When he described the countenance of the old man, the Chassid cried out, "*Gevalt!* That is the Tsanzer *tzaddik!* But since he is no longer alive, I don't know how you can repay him."

THE DIVREI CHAIM

As time went on, the German's business continued to flourish, and he moved to Frankfurt to further expand his activities. One night the Tsanzer *tzaddik* again appeared to him in a dream and said, "My son Shalom Elazar is about to marry off a child. However, he lacks the necessary funds. I request of you to repay him the loan which you owe me."

The German awoke very early and caught the first train to Bad Neuheim. He rushed to his friend the Tsanzer Chassid, told him of his dream, and asked him where he could find Rabbi Shalom Elazar, the *tzaddik*'s son. "I know he lives in Hungary," said the Chassid, "but I am not sure where. Go to Budapest, and there you will certainly find out."

The German hastened to Budapest, where he was told that Rabbi Shalom Elazar lived in Ratzferd. Arriving in Ratzferd, the German went to his home and asked the Rebbe, "Are you *Herr Rabbiner* Halberstam?"

"I am," said the *Rav*.

"Then I have something of the utmost importance to tell you," said the German. Rabbi Shalom Elazar led him to a private room.

"I hear that the Rebbe is about to marry off a child," began the German. "I would like you to draw up an exact account of how much the wedding will cost you."

Rabbi Shalom Elazar summoned his son Reb Zishele and asked him to draw up an account of all the expenses. The German told him to give generous approximations. When Reb Zishele had finished his accounting the German was astonished to see that the grand total amounted to the exact amount which the Tsanzer Rav had lent him!

The German then related the entire story and concluded, "I am now repaying the debt which I owed your father." In addition to the repayment, he handed him a generous amount of money as a wedding present.

(This story was related to me by Mr. Yehudah Maharam Stern of Antwerp. He heard it from HaRav Unger, *shlita*, of Bnei Brak, who heard it firsthand from Reb Zishele.)

The Vanished City of Tsanz

The Train Line

Somebody once came to the Divrei Chaim with the news that a new railroad was being built which would run through the town. The Divrei Chaim responded that as long as he was alive no such venture would materialize. So it was. The first train line leading into Tsanz was built in 5636, right after the saintly *tzaddik* had passed away.

The reason for the delay was an interesting one. What happened was that the Austrian government offered a tidy sum as compensation to all the farmers whose fields would be transversed by the train line. Consequently, many farmers were interested in having their fields cut by the track. They approached the architect responsible for designing the plan and bribed him to have their fields cut by the line. The architect willingly obliged, and so it came to be that the train would travel a full twenty minutes in a zig-zag fashion without covering any distance at all! I still remember traveling that way before the war.

When word of this reached Vienna, the guilty architect was brought to trial. However, the architect never reached the dock. He committed suicide before the trial was to take place.

The Beis Din Goes to Prison

It happened in the year 5636 (1876). In Tsanz there lived a salt dealer by the name of Yossel Amaizen, known as Yossel Zeltzer, due to his trade. Yossel Zeltzer was a respectable person and quite a learned man, but also extremely strong-willed and stubborn. If he decided on something, nobody would dare contradict him or try to get him to change his mind.

Once, the *beis din* sent him a summons to appear before a *din Torah* against a certain Kalman Pearlstein. Yossel Zeltzer refused to comply with the order. "If Kalman Pearlstein has a complaint to make, let him present it before a secular court of law," he said to the *beis din* messenger.

At this point it is necessary to note that in Tsanz they were very particular never to bring their cases before a gentile court. The highest

THE DIVREI CHAIM

court of justice, whose verdict was unanimously accepted, was the *beis din*. A person who brought his complaint against another person to a gentile court was shunned and disgraced by the whole town. Should it happen that a person refused to accept the ruling of the *beis din*, he had one other alternative: to bring his case to the supreme judge, the Divrei Chaim himself. Everybody without exception trembled at the words of the Divrei Chaim. Nobody dared to disobey a summons to the *beis din*. Yet here, without any reason, a certain Yossel Zeltzer, an ordinary, respectable businessman, who even had a seat by the eastern wall of the *beis midrash*, actually dared to refuse to appear before the *beis din*. Such brazen audacity had never been heard of before in Tsanz!

The *beis din* received Yossel Zeltzer's reply with great anger and indignation. They immediately issued another, stronger summons. However, Yossel was unmoved and stuck to his former decision. "If Kalman Pearlstein demands something of me, let him bring me to court. I will not go to a *din Torah!*"

In ordinary circumstances, the Tsanzer *beis din* consisted of three members: Reb Berish Pearlstein, the *rosh beis din*; Reb Ellish; and my great-grandfather, Reb Moshe. However, Reb Berish Pearlstein was Kalman Pearlstein's uncle and therefore, according to Jewish law, could not act as judge. Therefore the *Rav*'s son himself, who was then acting as a substitute for the *dayan*, the Kreiser Rav, Reb Aharele, was one of the signers of the summons. As a result, the *beis din* was even more enraged to receive Yossel Zeltzer's response. To actually violate the *Rav*'s son's word — what unheard-of chutzpah!

The *beis din* sent the messenger a third time with a warning that should he once again refuse to appear for a *din Torah*, he would be placed in *cheirem*.

Yossel Zeltzer was unmoved and coolly sent back the bold reply, "Tell the *beis din* that if they put me in *cheirem* I will put them into prison!"

This was the final straw. News of Yossel's audacious reply spread like wildfire through the city of Tsanz. The whole town was enraged beyond words. To show such disrespect to the most distinguished members of the community was unforgivable.

I was never able to find out whether the *beis din* actually carried out their threat of an official *cheirem*, which entails lighting candles and blowing shofar. Some people told me that the *cheirem* was carried out quietly. Others claim that the *beis din* never actually carried out their threat. Whatever the case, what is certain is that the second day after Yossel had responded with his shocking statement, the people came to shul to see scrawled over the wall in bold, black letters, "Yossel Zeltzer, *yemach shemo*, is in *cheirem*." It was then that bitter, unrestrained fighting broke out in Tsanz.

As already mentioned, Yossel Zeltzer was terribly stubborn. He was a man of means, and he went to all extremes, using his wealth and influence to carry out his threat: "If you put me in *cheirem*, I will put you into prison."

Yossel filed an official complaint against the *beis din*. His strongest complaint was against Reb Aharele, the Kreiser Rav, the Tsanzer Rebbe's son.

Reb Aharele was very beloved by the Tsanzer Chassidim, being a person of great humility and unassuming piety. Like his namesake, Aharon HaKohen, he loved peace and would pursue peace. Owing to these attributes, he was not as strict as his brother Reb Baruchel Rudniker, who later became the Gorlitzer Rav. Yossel Zeltzer knew this well and therefore chose Reb Aharele as his victim in order to carry out his triumph to the last detail.

Yossel was unperturbed by the fierce reaction of his fellow townspeople, and he continued to go to shul every morning as if nothing had happened. Everybody was infuriated by his indifference, and many fiery quarrels broke out between the people and Yossel Zeltzer and his children. The situation reached a point where Yossel was forced to turn to the police for protection. Even this did not deter the people who continued to molest him and his children.

Zeltzer wanted to sue the *beis din*, but he found nobody willing to testify against them. Fiercely determined to see things through to the bitter end, he brought in secular judges to personally witness how the town youngsters were relentlessly embittering his life. The mid-

THE DIVREI CHAIM

dle-aged, sensible men of the town begged the youngsters not to be so rash and overzealous in their deeds. They pleaded with them to refrain from attacking Zeltzer in the presence of the judges, to no avail. The youngsters unceasingly tormented Zeltzer. *Talleisim* and towels were mercilessly thrown in his direction. One towel actually landed on one of the judges himself, inflaming the situation even further.

The day of the court case arrived. Sadness and apprehension prevailed in the town. The whole town assembled in groups to recite tehillim and plead on behalf of their beloved *Rav* and his *dayanim*. A grave and tense atmosphere reigned among the entire Jewish community as they nervously awaited the outcome of the trial.

Remarkably strange was the attitude of Reb Aharele's father, Rabbi Chaim Halberstam, the Divrei Chaim himself. There was hardly any mention of the turbulent events in his home. Elderly Chassidim remember that on the day the trial proceedings were to begin, Reb Aharele's wife, the Kreiser *rebbetzin*, entered the room of her saintly father-in-law and implored him with tears in her eyes to pray on behalf of her husband. Upon hearing the heart-rending pleas of the *rebbetzin*, the *Rav* got up and in great agitation called out, "One may not! One may not! '*Kol mai d'avid Rachmana l'tav avid* — Whatever Hashem does is for the best.' " She argued that it would be a *chillul haShem* if her husband were imprisoned. When the Divrei Chaim heard that, he cried out, "A *chillul haShem!* A *chillul haShem* is when one forgets Hashem for one moment!"

The Mitteler Belzer Rav, Rabbi Yehoshuale, was in Tsanz at the time for the engagement of his granddaughter to the Divrei Chaim's youngest son, Rabbi Yeshayale.

The Divrei Chaim's children were quick to realize that there was no way they could get the Divrei Chaim to appeal to the authorities on the Kreiser Rav's behalf. In desperation, they approached the Belzer Rav and begged him to try to persuade the Divrei Chaim to do something about the situation. They knew that the Divrei Chaim's words would carry enormous weight in the opinion of the judges.

When the Belzer Rav, Rabbi Yehoshuale, parted with the Divrei Chaim, he asked him to request of the authorities not to imprison the

The Vanished City of Tsanz

Kreiser Rav and his two *dayanim*. When the Divrei Chaim heard the request of the Belzer Rav he fell into a deep meditation. When he came out of his reverie, he related to the people surrounding him the following tale:

The Maharam of Rottenberg (Rabbi Meir ben Rabbi Baruch, one of the famous *ba'alei haTosafos*) was arrested while attempting to escape from Germany into France. His captors demanded an exorbitant sum for his release. The wealthy people in town were prepared to procure the price, but when the Maharam discovered the amount of money required he immediately sent a strong message to those involved, warning them that on no account should they give the astronomical sum. He claimed that were his captors' greed satisfied on this account, there would be no end to their malicious schemes in order to elicit greater sums of money.

"The saintly Maharam of Rottenberg," concluded the Divrei Chaim, "succeeded, despite his captivity, in establishing a small yeshivah of select students in his fortress. Right there in his prison he managed to serve Hashem with all his heart and soul."

A restless quietude settled in the room when the *Rav* ended his speech. All who were assembled now knew with a dreaded certainty that nothing in the world could be done to assist Reb Aharele and his *dayanim* in their plight. They would have to face their sentence of six weeks' imprisonment.

The three distinguished Torah scholars sat in prison for six interminably long weeks. In the duration of that time, another tragedy befell the Tsanzer community: the holy Divrei Chaim passed away on 25 Nissan 5636 (1876). The Kreiser Rav, Reb Aharele, was permitted to leave the prison walls for his father's funeral. He was taken under heavy police escort and led back immediately after it was over.

After this episode, Yossel Zeltzer's children strayed completely off the Jewish path. As for Yossel himself, he suffered complete financial ruin and was shunned by the religious community for the rest of his life until his death.

CHAPTER 6

THE YARTZEIT OF THE TSANZER RAV

The twenty-fifth of Nissan is the yartzeit of the great and saintly *gaon*, Rabbi Chaim Halberstam of Tsanz, author of *Divrei Chaim*. On that day, approximately fifty thousand Jews would come to Tsanz, to the *tzion* (grave) of the Tsanzer *tzaddik*. By the thousands they flocked from far and near, not only from Poland but also from Germany, Austria, Czechoslovakia, Hungary, Rumania, and even from as far as Amsterdam, Antwerp, Vienna, Berlin, and Leipzig.

This day was hallowed and respected not only by the Tsanzer Rav's Chassidim but by the entire general population. Weighty business transactions, *shidduchim*, employment agreements — everything came to a halt and remained suspended until the following day.

The day on which the *tzaddik* passed away was called *"Yoma D'Hilula,"* meaning "a day of great joy," surpassing even the joy of a wedding. Those who were worthy of witnessing the supreme happiness and closeness to Hashem which reigned on that day testified that it was indeed worthy of that name.

The Ohel

The *ohel* (a little house built over the grave) of the Tsanzer *tzaddik* was larger than most. Opposite the door of the shelter, near the eastern

The Vanished City of Tsanz

wall, the *Rav* himself was laid to rest. To his right lay his son Rabbi Aharon, known as the Kreiser Rav, and to his left lay his son Reb Meir Nassan. Years later, the Rebbes of Shinov, Reb Moishele and his son Reb Leibish Mordechai, were also buried there. Each of the five graves was surrounded by a tall, iron fence. The dimensions of the shelter were approximately eight meters long, six meters wide, and four meters high.

With time, the *ohel* was extended. At the edge of the shelter lay the Divrei Chaim's son-in-law Reb Yitzchak Tuvia Rubin, Reb Naftali Tzvi, and Reb Leibele, the Glisker Rav, who lived on the Piekela in Tsanz. On the other side lay Rabbi Aryeh Leibish Halberstam, who also acted in place of his father, Rabbi Aharon, as Tsanzer Rav, and his brother Rabbi Shalom, known as the Piekeler Rav.

In all, there were ten graves in the shelter of the Divrei Chaim. The Tsanzer Rav Rabbi Aryeh Leibish Halberstam was the last to be laid to rest there. Before his demise a mutual agreement was struck between the children of the Divrei Chaim — the *admorim* Rabbi Shalom Elazar of Ratzferd and Rabbi Yitzchak Yeshayah of Tzechov, who lived in Cracow, and Rebbetzin Nechumele of Tsanz and Gitshe the Gliner Rebbetzin — with the approval of the Tsanzer Rav, Rabbi Aryeh Leibish Halberstam, that apart from Rabbi Aryeh Leibish no more bodies would be buried in the shelter.

The shelter was painted a glossy white and had three windows. A *ner tamid* burned steadily on the grave of the Divrei Chaim. The grave was surrounded by many candles and oil lights, which visitors to the *tzion* would light when they came to pour out their troubles.

In the summer months especially there were many visitors to Tsanz. The town happened to be located close to many holiday resorts such as Krenitz, Shavnitz, Kroshtzinka, Glemboka, Piwnitzna, and Muszyna. As a result, many people would come to Tsanz to pray at the *tzion* of the Divrei Chaim on their way home from vacation.

There was a group of *"kvittel* writers" and people selling candles at the *ohel*. Beadles of local *batei midrash* would offer to recite "*Keil Malei Rachamim*" for people who came to commemorate their relatives' yartzeits. On all the graves in the *ohel* there stood large charity

THE YARTZEIT OF THE TSANZER RAV

An old picture of the Divrei Chaim's ohel

boxes in the name of Rabbi Meir Ba'al HaNess. This charity was greatly revered by all the Tsanzer *rabbanim* and has remained respected by their Chassidim to this very day.

The twenty-fifth of Nissan, the yartzeit of the Divrei Chaim, falls three days after Pesach. The day was commonly known in Tsanz as "the third day of Pesach." Already on Chol HaMo'ed the first of the "summer birds" were seen in Tsanz — those who would visit their relatives in Tsanz over Pesach, well in advance of the great day, the *Yoma D'Hilula*. Directly after Pesach, the real excitement began. Entire families would stream in from the small villages surrounding Tsanz. A strict warning was proclaimed by the Tsanzer Rav's grandchildren that no women approach the *ohel* on the day of the yartzeit, in order to prevent mingling of men and women. On the day after the yartzeit, however, women would come from far and wide to visit the *ohel*.

The huge attendance from all over Galicia necessitated extra trains to Tsanz from many Galician towns. Thousands of Chassidim gath-

The Vanished City of Tsanz

ered together from Germany, Austria, Czechoslovakia, and Hungary. Some came on special trains running for that purpose and others, by bus. A joyous atmosphere prevailed.

The joy and excitement was especially prevalent on Kazimierza Street, better known as *"der Yiddisher Gass."* Most of the *batei midrash* were located on that street, as well as the *beis midrash* and home of the Divrei Chaim himself. *Der Yiddisher Gass* and all the other roads leading to the cemetery were lined with countless street vendors selling all sorts of wares. A great number of them sold religious articles, and cries of "Tefillin, mezuzos, *talleisim, kemei 'os, segulos,* candles, pamphlets! Come and buy!" filled the air. Business flourished as thousands of visitors thronged around the stalls and money and goods changed hands. The Hungarians were especially profitable customers since they had an age-old custom to buy all their religious requisites in Tsanz.

The stalls were also filled to overflowing with a wide range of goods. From raw fabrics to ready-made clothing and shoes — everything was available. The population in Tsanz were able to draw a livelihood for a few months just from the business they did that day! The restaurants and hotels were filled to capacity, and the owners enjoyed a thriving business.

The majority of the Jewish population were concentrated in the city center so that most of the shops in the marketplace were owned by Jewish proprietors. The tradesmen, too — the tailors, shoemakers, locksmiths, electricians, watchmakers, printers, artists, doctors, and coachmen — were mostly Jews.

Inside the *ohel*

THE YARTZEIT OF THE TSANZER RAV

In front of the *ohel*, 5751 (1991)

The *ohel* after the war

The coachman Reb Shabsai Phiaker was known as a devoutly religious person. He would always vie for the privilege of driving the great Rebbes to the *tzion* of the Divrei Chaim. The Bobover Rav, Rabbi Ben Tzion Halberstam, would not travel with any other coachman to the cemetery.

At the Tzion

Already a considerable distance from the cemetery, the streets were packed with swarms of people heading in the same direction. Not everybody succeeded in reaching the shelter on that day. Only those who pushed their way among the thousands of people were privileged to actually reach the *tzion*. It was no mean feat. One had to elbow one's way and jostle among throngs of other people who had the same intention.

The Vanished City of Tsanz

The great joy of the day was complemented by the many *simchah*s which took place. Hundreds of plates were broken, marking the traditional custom at a *tena'im* (engagement). In those days people were reluctant to travel due to the difficulty in journeying. The roads were either stony, winding dirt paths or in dire need of repair. Train connections were poor, and costs were heavy. Therefore if two families from different locations were interested in matching their children, they would postpone the meeting until the day of the yartzeit in Tsanz, when they intended to travel in any case. Another reason for the many engagements was that Chassidim did not pronounce an engagement official until they had received their Rebbe's blessing. Since communication in those days was time-consuming and difficult, the parties involved would wait until this great day when they would be sure of personally meeting their Rebbes in Tsanz.

The *ohel*

CHAPTER 7

THE KREISER RAV

With the passing of the Divrei Chaim on the twenty-fifth of Nissan, his son Reb Aharon, the Kreiser Rav, took on the position of *Rav* in Tsanz. By rights the position belonged to the Divrei Chaim's eldest son, the Shinover Rav, but he publicly renounced the privilege in favor of his brother. Reb Aharon acted as *Rav* in Tsanz for almost thirty years, until his death in 5666 (1906).

It is interesting to note that after the Divrei Chaim, no one called himself the "Tsanzer Rav." Reb Aharon was called the Kreiser Rav because he refused to be called by his father's title. He said that after his father, the Divrei Chaim, there could be no other Tsanzer Rav. His son Rabbi Aryeh Leibish, who was *Rav* in Tsanz after his father, and the Kreiser Rav's grandson Rabbi Mordechai Zev, who served as *Rav* after his father, both called themselves "Gribover Rav" for that reason.

The Official Crowning

This is the tale of how the Shinover Rav renounced his position as Tsanzer Rav in favor of his brother:

Following the Divrei Chaim's death, the Shinover Rav moved to Tsanz to accept the mantle of *rabbanus*. A controversy ensued: some people felt that the Shinover Rav, being the eldest, ought to become

Rav, while others believed that the Kreiser Rav deserved to take over the leadership, since his father had appointed him Kreiser Rav in his lifetime.

One Shabbos morning before davening, the Kreiser Rav, accompanied by many Chassidim, Reb Shmuel Herbst among them, went to visit the Shinover Rav. When the Shinover Rav saw his esteemed visitor, he ran toward him and said, "Ah, my brother. My brother is here." He offered the Kreiser Rav a seat and requested coffee to be brought in for him.

"What is the reason for your visit?" asked the Shinover Rav.

"I came to discuss a piece of *Zohar*," answered the Kreiser Rav, "but I would like nobody but Reb Shmuel Herbst to be present."

The Shinover Rav ordered Reb Shmuel to take the *Zohar* off the shelf and place it on the table. He then asked Reb Shmuel to leave the room. The Kreiser Rav showed the Shinover Rav at which point he had encountered a difficulty, and the Shinover Rav enlightened him with an explanation. When they had finished, they arose, and the Shinover Rav accompanied his brother out to the street.

That evening, at *se'udah shelishis*, the Shinover Rav gave a speech in which he officially declared that he was handing over the mantle of *rabbanus* to his brother, the Kreiser Rav.

The Robbery

In the year 5650 (1890) a devastating fire broke out, which razed most of the houses in town to the ground. The population barely had time to recuperate from this blow when, four years later, once again disaster struck: in 5654 another fire destroyed half the town. Yet again the people had to set about picking up the pieces of their shattered lives and rebuilding their ruined homes from scratch. This time, bitter experience had taught them to use bricks and not wood as their building material. They had built their homes with wood after the fires of the years 5529 (1769) and 5650, with catastrophic results.

The people had not yet recovered from the shattering blows of the two consecutive fires when a new tragedy struck in the year 5658. This

THE KREISER RAV

sorrowful turn of events was dubbed "The Robbery." It came as a result of the poor system of inheritance which was prevalent at that time. Galicia was divided into sections of land, each owned by an individual farmer. When he died, his portion was equally divided among his children. If a farmer had ten children, who each had ten children of their own, his grandchild would end up receiving only a hundredth of his grandfather's original portion. This resulted in extreme poverty. It came to a point that the farmers literally did not have bread with which to feed their starving families.

An evil priest, Stanislaw Stayalowski, saw this as the perfect opportunity for exploiting his unquenchable lust for power. He incited the vulnerable farmers against the Jews, claiming that the Jews were at fault for all their misfortunes. The result was inevitable: the starving farmers did not need much convincing and immediately let loose upon the hapless Jews like a pack of wild animals. Their pillage began in the town Wieliczka but quickly spread throughout the entire Galicia.

In Tsanz, even the so-called decent gentiles aided the plunderers in their acts of robbery and theft. The police were unsympathetic and did not make any effort to stop the looting; their efforts extended only so far as to keep the hooligans from actual murder.

The Jews sent a delegation to Vienna, begging the government to put a stop to the senseless pillage. The president of Austria, Gratz Tuhn, cordially accepted the delegation and promised to do all he could to assist them. Indeed, on that very day he sent his army to take strict measures to prevent further acts of crime and to punish those who had robbed and stolen. Very soon hordes of military police were seen enforcing order throughout Galicia, and in a short time the rioting was completely dispelled.

Several weeks after peace had been restored, the Kreiser Rav, Reb Aharon, gave a speech. He declared that the recent tragedies had come as a Divine punishment for laxity in religious duties, as people had joined the many political groups that had just begun to sprout — the Socialists, Zionists, Communists. He strongly warned everyone to pull themselves together and be more stringent in all aspects of Jewish law. The Kreiser Rav based his statement on the startling fact that from the

The Vanished City of Tsanz

year 5529 (1769) until 5650 (1890), there had never been such a severe fire in Tsanz. In addition, from 5529, when Galicia came under Austrian rule, until 5650 there had never been a single pogrom or libel in Galicia.

Generally, the government did not oppress the Jews physically. The only burden which they forced upon the Jews was extremely heavy taxes. This ended in 5608 (1848) when Emperor Franz Joseph came to power. He acted favorably toward the Jews and removed the taxes which had unjustly been imposed on them.

To understand why the Galician Jews still speak of Emperor Franz Joseph with great respect and affection, one must first understand how liberal Emperor Franz Joseph was to the Jews. To do this I would like to present a brief overview of the economic situation under Emperor Franz Joseph from 5608 until 5674 (1914).

The Monopolies

From the year 5608 and onwards, the Austrian government did not extract heavy taxes from its citizens. There was only one official tax, the *ainkunft* tax (income tax). The authorities were very lax in enforcing even this, so that very few people bothered to pay it. The government chiefly collected its dues through a system of monopolies, notably on tobacco and liquor.

The entire tobacco industry, as well as all tobacco plantations, belonged to the government, which was the sole manufacturer of all types of tobacco, cigarettes, cigars, and snuff. The companies which sold its products were called "*farlags*." The *farlags* also sold currency and postal stamps.

The government granted special permission to private businessmen to open such *farlags*. Each important city had its main *farlag*, which sent details of all its income to the secretary of finance. The smaller *farlags* sent their details to the main *farlag* in the vicinity. The government determined the retail price. The *farlags* received a certain percentage of the revenue.

Similarly, the government was the sole producer of liquor. Here, too, they gave special grants to private people to be alcohol wholesalers. These wholesale companies were called *propenatzias*. The shops which bought the alcohol to sell to the consumers were called *shenken*.

In order to open a *shenk*, one needed a government grant. The amount of grants issued in one town by the government was proportionate to the number of people who lived in the town.

The *farlags* and *shenken* of all the towns and villages belonged to Jewish proprietors. The salt monopoly was also chiefly in Jewish hands. The businesses were obligated to be open on Shabbos, so the Jews used a special *heter* to allow gentiles to run their shops on that day.

In general, the economic and social situation of the Jews in those days was relatively good. Jews were granted official positions in a variety of civil services: judges, tax collectors, members of the council and the postal service, and train-station managers.

This idyllic situation only lasted until 5660 (1910). The change for the worse was not enacted by the government in Vienna but by the Poles themselves.

At that time, Emperor Franz Joseph was ill and did not have the strength to fight the constant battle on behalf of the Jews. Certain political parties took advantage of this and aimed to pry the monopoly trades out of Jewish hands. They opened large companies in the big cities, with affiliated branches in the small villages. The main wholesalers did not suffer from this, because the companies continued to purchase their stock from them. However, it was a tremendous blow to the smaller Jewish traders.

The New Political Parties

It was in that era that many political groups, such as those of the Socialists, Zionists, and Communists, were organized. Sadly, the groups attracted many religious youths, causing them to stray off the Orthodox path. Only one devoted party member with an eloquent tongue was needed to ensnare countless young men. The many ideal-

The Vanished City of Tsanz

istic youngsters with happy dreams of freedom and justice were easy prey for the speaker's promise of a glorious future.

Fortunately, in Tsanz the situation was under control. However, the Kreiser Rav took every precaution, and he held many lectures in which he warned the youngsters of the dangers of these groups. In fact, a renowned recruiter to Zionism, M. D. Berel, who was especially sent to Tsanz by the Zionist organization to spread Zionism in Tsanz, wrote in his article in *Sefer Sanz* that when he arrived at Tsanz in the year 5660 he was met by an impenetrable wall. To illustrate the extent of Orthodoxy in the town, he pointed out that there were only two or three men who did not wear a *shtreimel* in the whole of Tsanz on Shabbos. Secular books and newspapers were shunned by the community and were not even read for "medical purposes." When he hung up a Magen David as a tribute to Zionism, the Chassidim accused him of profaning all that it symbolized. They tore off the Magen David embroidered on the *paroches* and all the other Magen Davids sewn on their tallis and tefillin pouches. One of Mr. Berel's devoted followers, enraged by this slight to his leader's dignity, stealthily entered the *beis midrash* in the darkness of night and carved a Magen David in the Kreiser Rav's *shtender* with a knife. The next morning, when the Kreiser Rav noticed the vandalism, he ordered that the *shtender* be removed from the *beis midrash*.

Yehudah Knebbel, a secularist who also wrote an article in *Sefer Sanz*, gave an idea of the situation in Tsanz. He wrote, with bitterness and anger, that the majority of the community were Chassidim and that the important communal decisions were laid down by them. He complained further that all his and his party's efforts to usurp the Chassidim's communal power proved to be of no avail. Indeed, Tsanz remained one of Europe's most religious communities until the war.

Unfortunately, most of the communities were not so strong, and many youngsters succumbed to the pressure. Soon the situation was totally out of control; many religious communities were thrown into a deep depression. Before the Tzieshinover Rav, author of *Divrei Simchah*, passed away, his nephew, the Koloshitzer Rav, Rabbi Chuna Halberstam, approached his deathbed and cried out in despair, "Uncle,

THE KREISER RAV

what will become of this world?"

"Be comforted. It is said that before the coming of Mashiach the *neshamos* which do not need much amendment will be sent down on this world," answered the saintly Tzieshinover Rav, promising that times would get better.

Honestly Earned Money

Once, on an *erev Yom Kippur*, long after *minchah*, the Kreiser Rav was still sitting at his table surrounded by many Chassidim, taking *kvittelech*. Rabbi Eziel Herbst told us that his grandfather, Reb Shloime, happened to come into the room just then. The thought flitted through his mind: *Erev Yom Kippur, so late in the afternoon, and the Rav still takes kvittelech with money*. The Kreiser Rav, reading his thoughts, turned toward Reb Shloime and said, "Reb Shloime, you should know that one is allowed to take honestly earned money right up to the *zeman*."

Of Yartzeits and Tachanun

The Banier Rav, Rabbi Yissachar Ber Dachner of Antwerp, once related a conversation which took place between the Gorlitzer Rav, Rabbi Baruch Halberstam; Rabbi Shloimele Halberstam, the first Bobover Rav; and the Kreiser Rav, Rabbi Aharon Halberstam. They noted how convenient it was that the Divrei Chaim had passed away on a day when Tachanun isn't said, so there was no question as to whether or not to omit Tachanun.

In the midst of the conversation, one of the three *tzaddikim* declared, "We can do this, too." His declaration was confirmed by the other two. Indeed, all three *tzaddikim* passed away on Rosh Chodesh, when Tachanun is omitted — the Gorlitzer Rav on Rosh Chodesh Adar, the Bobover Rav on Rosh Chodesh Tamuz, and the Kreiser Rav on Rosh Chodesh Av.

(As an added note, the Divrei Chaim was of the opinion that Tachanun should be recited on a Rebbe's yartzeit. He gave the reason

The Vanished City of Tsanz

for his opinion: Should someone have begun saying Tachanun and pronounced Hashem's Name and others would not say it, this person would have said the Name in vain.)

As mentioned above, the yartzeit of Reb Aharon falls on Rosh Chodesh Menachem Av. The Pshevorsker Rebbe, *shlita*, recounts that when Reb Aharon was born, his father, the Divrei Chaim, asked his Rebbe, Reb Naftali, the Ropshitzer Rav, what to name his son. The Ropshitzer Rav told him to give the name Aharon, a name that had not been used in the family before.

The Tsanzer Rav wrote a letter to his father-in-law, the Baruch Ta'am, the Liepniker Rav, telling him that he had named his son Aharon. The Baruch Ta'am sent him a sharp reply: "Are you from a family of converts that you gave him a name picked at random from the Torah?" However, seventy years later, the Ropshitzer Rav's foresight became clear, for Reb Aharon passed away on Rosh Chodesh Av, the yartzeit of Aharon HaKohen, the only yartzeit mentioned in the Torah.

Tsanzer Chassidim further relate that prior to his passing Reb Aharon, the Kreiser Rav, went to immerse himself in the mikveh. The Banier Rav, Rabbi Yissachar Dachner of Antwerp, recalls that as the *Rav* emerged from the mikveh, his attendant touched him. The *Rav* descended into the mikveh to immerse himself again. After that he bade farewell to his sister Nechumele who lived close to his home, in the Divrei Chaim's house. Not a single *sefer* written by the Kreiser Rav exists today because he single-handedly burned all his writings on the day before his passing.

Rabbi Eziel Herbst told us that Rosh Chodesh Av, the day the Kreiser Rav was *niftar*, was on Friday. When he returned from immersing himself in the mikveh and bidding farewell to his sister, Reb Shloime Herbst entered the room. When the Kreiser Rav saw him he said, "Shloime, it's good that you are here. I have not yet put on Rabbeinu Tam's tefillin. Please help me put them on." After he removed his tefillin, he was *mekabel Shabbos*. He made Kiddush when it was still afternoon even though in Tsanz they were particular never to accept Shabbos before the *zeman*. When he was finished, he lay down on his bed and passed away peacefully.

THE KREISER RAV

It was later noticed that at the moment of his death his *Chumash* was opened to the parashah which recounts Aharon's demise, *parashas Mas'ei*, on the page which bears the *pasuk* "Aharon HaKohen ascended Mount Har according to the words of Hashem, and he died there."

The Banier Rav related that on the day of the Kreiser Rav's wedding, his bride-to-be locked herself in a room and refused to be led to the *chuppah*. When asked why she did not want to be wed, she replied that the wives of her future father-in-law and brothers-in-law all died young, and she was afraid she would share the same fate.

Her fear was reported to the Divrei Chaim, and he answered, "I promise that she will outlive him." The Kreiser Rav was close to eighty years old when he passed away; his *rebbetzin*, Chana Elka, lived another seven years after his death. Her grave is on the right-hand side of the door at the entrance of the *ohel*.

The Kreiser Rebbetzin's grave

CHAPTER 8

RABBI ARYEH LEIBISH HALBERSTAM

His Appointment as Rav

The Kreiser Rav, Rabbi Aharon Halberstam, did not mention in his will which of his two sons, Reb Aryeh Leibish or Reb Shalom, was to replace him as *Rav* of Tsanz. His third son, Reb Shmelke, did not live in Tsanz and in any case was a merchant.

Those who were close to the Kreiser Rav surmised that Rabbi Aharon did not leave the instruction in his will on purpose, because his younger son, Rabbi Aryeh Leibish, was more suitable for the position than his elder brother, Rabbi Shalom. It must be understood, though, that Rabbi Shalom, too, was a great and pious man.

The problem was resolved in a highly unusual and unexpected manner. There was a custom in Tsanz to honor the *Rav* of the town by making him *sandak* at every bris. While the debate as to who should be *Rav* was going on, a son was born to the Menner family. The family faced a difficult dilemma: who should be honored? The *gabbai* of the Tsanzer Rav's *beis midrash* was reluctant to get involved in any quarrels. He therefore advised the baby's father to invite both brothers and have them brought in the same carriage to the *beis midrash* where the bris was due to take place. Let the problem take its own course!

RABBI ARYEH LEIBISH HALBERSTAM

When the two brothers arrived at the *beis midrash*, the baby's father opened both doors to enable the brothers to enter together. The *gabbai* announced at the appropriate time, "The Tsanzer Rav is hereby honored to be *sandak*."

A suspenseful silence hung in the *beis midrash*. The assembled waited with bated breaths. Who would volunteer? The brothers looked at each other in confusion. Who did the *gabbai* mean? The silence was broken by the voice of Rabbi Shalom.

"Aryeh Leibish, Tsanzer Rav, take the child," he called out.

At that moment, the outcome was clear to one and all. Rabbi Shalom had gracefully handed over the mantle of the Tsanzer *rabbanus* to his younger brother, Rabbi Aryeh Leibish.

The baby's father had acted with foresight and wisdom. The result was indeed finalized at that bris; Rabbi Aryeh Leibish took over from his father, who had taken over from his father, the Divrei Chaim, as *Rav* of Tsanz.

The Tsanzer Rav, Rabbi Aryeh Leibish, carrying his *sefer Torah*, welcoming the Polish president, together with his brother, the Piekeler Rav, Rabbi Shalom; the *rosh hakahal*, Ailish Klapholz; Gershon Herzberg; and Chaim Berliner, in November 1929

The Vanished City of Tsanz

Rabbi Aryeh Leibish Halberstam was a great and holy man, one of the worthiest grandchildren of the saintly Divrei Chaim. This is not the place to describe his greatness and piety at length. I will therefore try to relay the essence of his personality in a few brief paragraphs.

A Love for Children

Rabbi Aryeh Leibish had a special love reserved for young children. He used to daven in the great *beis midrash*, known as the Gribover *beis midrash*, which accommodated more than five hundred members. When he entered the large, impressive building and noticed a young child davening in a distant corner, he would walk over to the child and gently prod, "Daven a little louder, my child, so that I can answer amen." After davening, he would frequently call in the children and offer them a fruit, asking them to make a loud blessing so that he could answer amen.

Another Bris Incident

Rabbi Aryeh Leibish had a Chassid who lived in Cracow. The Chassid was childless, and he used to beg the rabbi at every opportunity to bless him with a child.

Finally the Rebbe acquiesced and gave his blessing, on condition that he, Rabbi Aryeh Leibish, would be honored as *sandak*. Sure enough the blessing materialized, and the Chassid asked the *Rav* to be *sandak* at the bris.

The *Rav* journeyed to Cracow especially for the occasion. The child was brought into the *beis midrash*, and the *Rav* took him into his arms. To everyone's surprise, the *Rav* took one look at him and announced, "The child is yellow. I cannot be *sandak* at his bris." So saying, he set about on the long, tedious journey back to Tsanz without even having presided at the bris. The Chassid, though, had done as the *Rav* had asked; he had honored him to be *sandak*.

Avoiding the Draft

In Poland, when a boy turned twenty-one he was summoned to a committee of three doctors. He was given an overall health check, and if the results met the required criteria, he was drafted into the army. Many of the religious youth who were summoned to the examination turned to Rabbi Aryeh Leibish in deep distress, begging him for a blessing to be saved from such a calamity. Apart from the hardships a drafted boy would be forced to endure, he had the added problem of not being able to get married until the years of service were over.

The Tsanzer Rav, Rabbi Aryeh Leibish, advised the youths to assist in whatever way possible with the entire procedure of baking matzah — from the initial grinding of the wheat to the kneading and rolling out of the dough, right up to its final stage of preparation. Rabbi Aryeh Leibish promised the so-called *shtellers* (those who were eligible for draft) that if they would sweat because of their efforts in baking matzah they would be relieved of having to sweat in the army.

The boys were justified in their fear and dread of being conscripted, since Jewish soldiers were especially subject to great suffering. The army did not provide them with kosher food or cooking facilities. In addition, they suffered terribly from the jeering and scoffing of their anti-Semitic officers.

In our home there was a large mill with two great wheels designed to grind the flour for matzah. Two youths used to laboriously turn the wheel, producing fine, powdery flour. I vividly recall watching the boys take turns working the mill when the *shemurah* flour for the pre-Pesach matzah was ground. The *Rav* was present at the time, and as they worked, each boy mentioned his and his mother's name, as is the custom when handing a *kvittel* to a Rebbe.

Only a Scare

A father and his son once came to Tsanz from a distant town. The purpose of their journey was to plead for a blessing from Rabbi Aryeh Leibish that the son be exempt from army duty. The son was a tall,

The Vanished City of Tsanz

broad-shouldered young man of good health. Unfortunately, the *Rav* had locked himself in his rooms on the very day of their visit with a strong warning that no one and nothing should disturb him.

The distraught pair tried to plead with Rabbi Aryeh Leibish's children to make an exception in their case. The *Rav*'s children refused because they were afraid to disturb their father in the face of his stern warnings. However, they took pity on them and agreed to send in a *kvittel* with the *shamash*, Reb Yechiel Gottlieb, who was still a *bachur* at the time.

Reb Yechiel, who provided the *Rav* with all his needs, was the only one permitted to enter his room. Reb Yechiel took the *kvittel*, walked into the *Rav*'s private room, and placed the *kvittel* on the table before him. The *Rav* carefully read it and remarked, "*Nu*, he will make a good soldier!"

Meanwhile, the father and son were nervously waiting outside the door. When they heard what the *Rav* had said, they were brokenhearted. Was this why they had undertaken the arduous journey? Disappointed and filled with despair, they made their way back home.

The ominous moment when the young man was to be presented before the military committee approached. In desperation, the father and son decided to approach the *Rav* and try their luck once again. They traveled all the way to Tsanz and met with an exact rerun of their previous visit. The *Rav* had locked himself in his rooms on the day of their visit with a strong warning that no one disturb him. The *Rav*'s children refused to go into their father's room but as before sent in the *shamash*.

There was one slight deviation from the previous time: when Reb Yechiel entered the room and told the *Rav* that the father and the son were here again and the boy was waiting outside in great trepidation, Rabbi Aryeh Leibish answered, "Go and tell him he should not be afraid, for no harm will befall him, and he will soon be freed from army service."

Reb Yechiel delivered the message to the relieved pair outside and then went into the room adjoining the *Rav*'s private chamber. Rabbi Aryeh Leibish rose from his seat and followed him into the room. "Yechiel," he declared, "that person is afraid, but you should not be afraid? One must be afraid, because with fear one is absolved of true tragedies!"

The outcome of the boy's appointment with the army committee was as the *Rav* had predicted. He was dismissed from army service for no valid reason even though he was a picture of health.

When Reb Yechiel Gottlieb related this story, he commented that in the horrifying war years there were many times when he saw no hope for his salvation. His life would hang on a thread, and he would be overcome with terror. However, Hashem's boundless kindness saved him time and time again from certain death. Reb Yechiel always concluded this story with the words, "All this I attribute to the advice of the *Rav*: one must be afraid, for with fear one is released from tragedy."

Chanukah Lights

The Tsanzer Rav, Rabbi Aryeh Leibish, lit Chanukah lights relatively late, at 8:30 P.M. A large crowd gathered at his house to take part in the beautiful and uplifting experience. The *Rav* chose people with melodious voices to lead in singing *"Ma'oz Tzur."* After the soul-stirring harmonic choir was over the *Rav* quietly whispered to himself the *pesukim* of *"Yosheiv B'Seiser."* Then he would sing *"Mizmor Shir," "LaMenatzei'ach BiNeginos," "Rannenu Tzaddikim,"* and a few *pesukim* of chapter 119 of Tehillim. He would then gaze pensively at the flickering candles for half an hour. The first night of Chanukah, year after year, he would seat himself at his table and recount the following:

> The Tsanzer *zeida* (the Divrei Chaim) used to tell stories at the lighting of the Chanukah candles. The first story related by my grandfather is of an elderly lady who was blessed with a large family of grandchildren and great-grandchildren. The family lived in great poverty.
>
> One day she assembled the entire family and said to them, "How long can we tolerate living in such destitution? We must

think of a way to rid ourselves of this terrible poverty. Yet how can we begin if we do not even own one possession on which to build our plans?"

At this, one of her grandchildren piped up, "*Bubbeshe*, we do have something in the house. We have a chicken egg."

"Wonderful!" exclaimed the elderly woman. "I have a plan. We will establish a livelihood with this egg. We will take it to my neighbor who has a hen and ask her to allow the hen to sit on the egg. The egg will hatch a little chick. The chick will grow up and will eventually lay eggs of its own. We will give these eggs to other chickens to hatch until we will own a large coop with many chickens. We will then sell the chickens in exchange for a calf. We will raise the calf until it matures into a cow which will give milk and bear more calves. We will sell the calves and with the money build a house of our own..."

The children listened with increasing delight to their *bubby*'s plan. Suddenly, one of the children accidentally gave the table a little shake, and the egg fell on the floor and smashed. The children stared in horror as they saw all their glorious hopes and dreams trickling away into a white and yellow puddle. The old lady groaned in despair. "Oh, dear, now nothing will become of my brilliant plan."

The moral of the story is applicable to each of us. As soon as a person reaches the age when he is able to reason, he starts building glorious plans for his future. He plans to climb and climb until he reaches the pinnacle of the ladder of success. Suddenly the egg smashes. The man dies with none of his dreams and ambitions fulfilled.

The second story he would tell went as follows:

There once lived a man who had a very weak memory. His memory was so poor that he used to wake up in the morning and forget where he had put his clothing the night before! The frustrated man came up with a brilliant solution for his pressing problem. He would carefully note down where he had placed each item of clothing. The next day he would only have to glance at the paper next to his bed, and he would be able to get dressed without delay. So it was. That evening, the man took a pencil and paper and conscientiously wrote down where he had put his clothing: "Trousers are on the chair, shirt is on the trousers, vest is on the shirt, shoes are under the bed, and I am in the bed."

In the morning the man woke up rejoicing. Today he would not spend time in confusion and worry. He could get dressed immediately. He looked at his paper and happily followed the instructions written down. Indeed, everything was exactly in the marked place, except for one object. He looked in puzzlement at the words "I am in the bed." He raised the bed covers and thoroughly searched all over the bed. His search proved fruitless: he was not there! Greatly disappointed in his well-thought-out plan, he cried out, "Where am I?"

The moral of the story is that a person spends all his life planning for his physical needs. Sadly, he is so busy with his worldly affairs that he neglects his spiritual needs, until he realizes where his folly has led him and cries out, "Where am I?" But by then it is too late...

When the *Rav* had finished retelling the two tales, he would read out loud a piece about Chanukah from the *sefer Divrei Chaim*. He would do this every night of Chanukah, but few people understood it because it was based on Kabbalah.

A Complete Recovery

Mr. Shmuel Korngut of Antwerp told me the following story:

It was around the year 5685 (1925). I was a child of four years and fell deathly ill with *scralatin* (scarlet fever, a children's disease). The illness caused two large sores to spread over my throat. The sores soon became infected with pus, until it reached a point when the secretion was choking me and it became difficult for me to breathe. The doctors warned my parents that there was no option other than to operate on the affected area.

My father was a devoted Chassid of Rabbi Aryeh Leibish, and he resolved to travel to Tsanz to consult with the *Rav*. He traveled from Tarnow, where we lived, and arrived at the *Rav*'s home late at night. He found the *Rav* deeply immersed in his learning. When my father "gave *shalom*" to the *Rav*, the *Rav* asked him if he was earning a living and how his business was doing. My father replied, "I have come for a blessing for the recovery of my son Shmuel ben Ruchamah."

The *Rav* did not reply but continued his studies. A short time elapsed, and the *Rav* once again inquired, "How is your business doing?"

My father once again replied that the purpose of his present visit was to elicit a blessing for his son's recovery. This happened a few times, with the *Rav* always resuming his studies in between.

The *Rav* then asked him if he had gone to pray at the *tzion* of the holy Divrei Chaim, and he inquired as to what the doctors had advised. My father told him of the doctors' urgent desire to operate. The *Rav* replied that an operation was indeed necessary, but they shouldn't operate on the throat; instead the upper part of the child's arms should be cut open.

My father did not question the *Rav*'s statement. He went to the *tzion* of the Divrei Chaim, as the *Rav* had told him to do, and then traveled back home to Tarnow.

Upon his arrival, he told the doctors the rabbi's advice. The doctors adamantly refused to go along with this seemingly absurd suggestion, but my father insisted that they follow the *Rav*'s orders.

While my father was away, my illness had reached a critical peak, and I stopped breathing completely. Frantically, my mother sealed her lips around mine and did mouth-to-mouth resuscitation. In the process, the pus lining the right side of my throat was shoved into my right arm, and the pus lining the left side was shoved into my left arm. When the doctors did the surgery according to the *Rav*'s orders, they discovered the infection in both of my upper arms. They removed the pus, and I was soon on my way to a quick recovery. I still have the surgical scars on my arms. To this day, I am particular to give *tikkun* in shul on 21 Adar, the yartzeit of the *Rav*.

Opposing the Rav

In Hungary there were two Jewish communities: the Orthodox community, which served the religious Jews, and the Neologen community for the less religious. In Galicia, separate communities for the religious and nonreligious had never been established. Consequently, the Orthodox leaders of the community had to fight a constant battle to gain the upper hand in all religious matters. Whether the issue concerned ritual slaughter, mikveh, *eiruv*, or modesty, it was always a struggle to ensure that the decision made was in accordance with Torah-true values.

I would like to relate a story which I myself witnessed. The incident took place at the home of the Tsanzer Rav, Rabbi Aryeh Leibish Halberstam.

In autumn of 5691 (1930) elections took place in the Tsanzer community, an event that occurred once every five years. The elections were officially recognized by the government, as was the position of *Rav*. The nonreligious parties campaigned strongly against the *Rav*'s followers. In the way of politics, they promised a rosy future for the population if they would be elected, a future in which all religious services such as ritual slaughter, mikveh, and burials would be drastically reduced in price and practically given away for nothing. How they would finance everything they conveniently forgot to mention.

One of the *Rav*'s greatest opponents, Mr. Y. B., was a very rich man and actually *shomer Shabbos* himself. He resented the fact that the committee was in the hands of the ultra-Orthodox, and he did

The Vanished City of Tsanz

everything in his power to assist the nonreligious in the elections. Though the majority of the Jewish population were Chassidic, the danger of losing was still very real, for a number of reasons. The first was the terrible poverty which existed at that time. It was feared that the glorious picture of prosperity which the nonreligious painted would influence the general population to vote in their favor. The nonreligious parties were well aware of this weak point, and they targeted their propaganda at the simple, uninformed Jews. Another problem was that the religious parties themselves were divided into various groups — Tsanz, Shinov, and Bobov. Needless to say, this greatly diminished their combined power.

Mr. Y. B. was a very wealthy man who lived in an impressive mansion and owned a large flour business. The Tsanzer Rav, Rabbi Aryeh Leibish, summoned him to his home and said to him: "You should know that even if you win the elections, you cannot force me to step down from my position as *Rav*. The reason I am fighting to have the community in my hands is solely for the benefit of the religious Jews. I want to be able to supply them with all their religious needs such as ritual slaughterers, G-d-fearing *dayanim*, and *mikva'os*. I therefore request of you: give up your campaign against us, for it will bring you no good."

Mr. Y. B. shrugged his shoulders and ignored the *Rav*'s warning. He continued distributing propaganda and other harmful literature against the rabbi's party. Strangely enough, at around that time, in the days of Selichos of 5691, Mr. Y. B. suddenly fell ill. His situation steadily deteriorated with each passing day until the doctors gave up all hope. In desperation, Mr. Y. B. sent his wife and children to the *Rav* to beg forgiveness and implore him to save his life.

In Galicia there was a custom that if a person was dangerously ill, the *gabbai* would open the door of the *aron kodesh* and allow the invalid's female relatives to approach in order to cry and pray on his behalf. This was called *"ainreisen."*

On Shemini Atzeres of 5691, while the *Rav* was distributing wine to his followers, the distraught wife and daughters of Mr. Y. B. entered the room. With tears in their eyes, they begged the *Rav* to forgive and

RABBI ARYEH LEIBISH HALBERSTAM

The *kehillah* headquarters, opposite the Beis Nassan shul, in 5753 (1993)

pray for their husband and father. The *Rav* replied, "I warned him to pull back from the propaganda against the Chassidic community."

The women beseeched the *Rav* to forgive Y. B. The *Rav* placed his arms on the table and rested his head on his arms for a few minutes. At last he lifted his head and said, "the Tsanzer *Zeida* (the Divrei Chaim) said that if one wants to have a great request fulfilled '*darf men oisreisen a zshobra*' ('one needs to tear out a rib,' — to make a great sacrifice). If they want me to forgive him, they should promise now, before we got to shul, to donate five hundred dollars to marry off a poor orphan."

Mr. Y. B.'s wife and daughters began bargaining, claiming that the amount demanded was far too exorbitant (before the war five hundred dollars was a huge fortune). At this, the *Rav* got up and said, "If that is the case, we will now go to the *hakafos*." Immediately after *yom tov*, Mr. Y. B. passed away.

This incident caused great unrest among the Jews. It was clear to all the fate of one who opposed the *mara d'asra*. One does not stand up against *gedolim!*

That year, the Chassidic party won the elections with an overwhelming majority.

The Only One Released

In the year 5692 (1932) my eldest brother, Moshe, was learning in Cracow, in Yeshivas Keser HaTorah D'Radomsk. Being of draft age, he was summoned to a military committee to ascertain whether he was fit to be sent to the army. The law in Poland was that a boy weighing less than fifty kilos was exempt from army service. With this in mind many boys starved themselves in order to obtain an exemption and thereby avoid the harsh conditions they were subjected to among the anti-Semitic Polish soldiers.

The boys would afflict themselves to extreme degrees. They stayed up nights in the *beis midrash*, trudged on foot from one town to the next, and ate and drank only the minimal amount in order to appear haggard and underweight.

It happened once that twenty youths, my brother among them, arranged to walk from Cracow to Wieliczka, a journey of approximately twenty kilometers, in the middle of the night. On the way they came across a large, hefty *valtz rod*, a heavy wheel which was harnessed to two horses and dragged on the stony paths in order to press the stones into the ground — a steamroller without steam. Desperate to lose weight, the boys tied themselves to the *valtz rod* and attempted to lug it a few kilometers.

Luck was not with them. They were spotted by the Poles in one of the villages they traversed. The Poles immediately alerted the police, reporting that the Jews had stolen a *valtz rod* and were dragging it away under the cover of night. The police arrived at the "scene of the crime" and took down the names of all the youths. They ordered the boys to replace the *valtz rod*.

The police were quick to guess the purpose behind the boys' actions, and they spitefully handed in the list of names to the military committee, informing them of their attempt to evade military service.

The day of the fateful decision arrived. The boys were summoned to the committee according to alphabetical order. When one of the listed boys entered the room he was immediately conscripted without even having been examined by one of the doctors. This was their penalty for having tried to afflict themselves in order to appear underweight.

My brother, Moshe Lehrer-Buxbaum, was not one of the first names to appear in the official records, and so he was not immediately called in. Before long, he grasped what was happening to the listed boys. Terrified of sharing their fate, he telephoned my father in a panic.

The fact that he managed to contact my father in Tsanz was in itself no mean feat. In the street where we lived there were only one or two telephones. If a person without a telephone wanted to place a call to somebody in a different town he would have to go to the post office and book a conversation for a certain time a few hours later. My brother scheduled a telephone conversation in the Cracow post office for 11 P.M. At the appointed time my brother poured out his tale of woe, begging my father to go to the Tsanzer Rav, Rabbi Aryeh Leibish Halberstam, with a *kvittel* that he should be spared military service.

Immediately after the phone call, at around midnight, my father went to the Tsanzer Rav. I was privileged to be taken along.

At the *Rav*'s home we met another gentleman who had come for the same purpose. He was a wealthy wheat merchant, a Tsanzer Chassid by the name of Shimon Weg. His son Aharon was a tall, robust lad, a picture of health and vitality.

Reb Shimon handed the *Rav* a *pidyon* of five zlotys. The *Rav* put the entire amount into the great, square-shaped, tin *pushka* of Rabbi Meir Ba'al HaNess, which was ever present on his desk. Reb Shimon then handed him another *pidyon* of five zlotys. The *Rav* did the same.

This occurred a few times. Rabbi Shimon handed the *Rav* a sum of money, and the *Rav* put it directly into the *pushka*, saying that "Rabbi Meir can accomplish more than I." After Rabbi Shimon had given the ninth donation, he asked the *Rav* to keep something for himself. The *Rav* consented and kept the tenth and final *pidyon* of five zlotys.

The *Rav* blessed Reb Shimon and said, "Rabbi Meir will see to it that Aharon does not become a soldier." Indeed, Aharon was released despite his healthy appearance.

The Vanished City of Tsanz

It was my father's turn to consult with the *Rav*. As he handed him the *kvittel*, my father related to the *Rav* all that had happened to Moshe, that he was in very grave danger of being conscripted.

My father handed the *Rav* a *pidyon* of five zlotys. The *Rav* put the entire amount in the *pushka* of Rabbi Meir Ba'al HaNess and said, "If one needs a salvation, one must turn to Rabbi Meir Ba'al HaNess. Rabbi Meir will see to it that Moshe does not become a soldier."

Amazingly enough, Moshe was the only one of the twenty boys who had no defect and yet was exempted from army service.

In Tsanz there was a boy called Toivya Klieger. He had lost a lot of weight by afflicting himself. Yet this alone was not enough; one also needed "connections" with the doctors. Of the three practicing doctors, Toivya succeeded in bribing only the two deputy doctors.

When Toivya appeared before the medical committee the two deputy doctors determined that he was not fit to serve in the army. The chief doctor seemed to agree, but he insisted on seeing Toivya fully dressed before finalizing his exemption.

Toivya got dressed and once again entered the room. The chief doctor confronted him with a startling question, "Are these clothing yours, or are they stolen?"

Totally confused, Toivya answered that they were his own. "The shirt, too?" probed the doctor. Toivya answered in the affirmative. At this, the doctor stuck his fist in the collar of his shirt and showed the other doctors that the size of the shirt was much larger than the size of the boy's neck. Triumphantly he declared, "This proves that the boy starved himself in order to evade military duty. For this alone he deserves to be conscripted. Have him sent to Katowitz, to the cavalry."

Not Suitable to Be a Soldier

HaRav Yissachar Shlomo Halberstam, *shlita*, *Rav* of Beis Midrash D'Chassidei Koloshitz in Bnei Brak, related to me an event which had occurred to his father, Rabbi Baruch, a son of Rabbi Elisha of Gorlitz.

Rabbi Baruch was one of the youths who afflicted himself in an attempt to lose weight and thereby avoid military duty. He came to the *Rav*, Rabbi Aryeh Leibish, with a *kvittel*. The *Rav* said to him in surprise, "Why do you come to me? Your father himself is a Rebbe." Rabbi Baruch replied that since the committee to which he had to present himself was located in Tsanz, he decided to give his *kvittel* to the *Rav* of that place.

The *Rav* took the *kvittel* and put the entire donation into the *pushka* of Rabbi Meir Ba'al HaNess. (The *Rav* never used the *kvittel* money for his private use; he lived on the salary he received as *Rav* of the town.) He then took Rabbi Baruch's arm and rolled up his sleeve. He looked at his arm and said, "You are not suitable to be a soldier in the army."

The blessing came true. When he was examined by the doctors, they looked at his arm and said the exact same words: "You are not suitable to be a soldier in the army." Rabbi Baruch was released.

The Missing Shtreimel

It was *parashas Shekalim*, in the year 5692 (1932). A large crowd of Chassidim had traveled to Tsanz to spend Shabbos with the *Rav*, Rabbi Aryeh Leibish. In Tsanz everyone donned his *shtreimel* on Shabbos morning from after Kedushah until after *leining*. That Shabbos after Kedushah a great tumult was heard from a corner of the *beis midrash*. Word spread quickly: the son-in-law of the very wealthy Reb Nassan Pshevorsky had mislaid his *shtreimel*, known to be the most expensive one in the *beis midrash* and perhaps in the entire Tsanz, purchased for the extravagant sum of three hundred dollars.

Amidst all the to-do the *Rav* became aware of the cause of the commotion. He summoned the two *gabbaim* of the *beis midrash*, Reb Nesanel Lauer and Reb Elisha Gertner, and told them to announce that not a single congregant could leave the *beis midrash* until they had been searched. The two *gabbaim* stood at the door and inspected each person who left.

It was to no avail. The culprit was not found, and the mystery of the missing *shtreimel* remained unsolved. Later in the day, when the *Rav* was

The Vanished City of Tsanz

Moshe David Kornhauser

Mendel and Moshe, sons of Reb Zalman Yidel, the last Shinover Rav

at home at his *tisch* together with his guests (all visiting Chassidim ate together with the *Rav*), the *Rav* gazed intently around the table and asked, "Is the young man from Neumark present at the *tisch?*"

The *Rav* was answered in the negative. He summoned two *bachurim*, Nassan Shanzer and Mendel Saphir, and ordered them to go to the lodging of the young man and collect the *shtreimel*.

Barely fifteen minutes had elapsed before the two youths appeared, triumphantly bearing the missing *shtreimel*. Needless to say, the guilty thief was never seen again in Tsanz. The Tsanzer Rav's Chassidim claimed that this was an open miracle; the non-Chassidic Jews attributed the discovery to the *Rav*'s keen wit, that he had merely observed that the young man from Neumark was the only Chassid absent from his *tisch* and therefore surmised that he was the guilty one!

The Stopnitzer Rebbetzin

An elderly *rebbetzin* lived in the same apartment building as Rabbi Aryeh Leibish. She was a relatively wealthy woman, since her children regularly sent her money from America, but she had a reputation of being very stingy.

On Purim in the year 5694 (1934) this *rebbetzin* demanded that a *yeshivah bachur* come to her home to read the megillah. There were a hundred poor *bachurim* in Tsanz, and, knowing full well that the *rebbetzin* could afford to pay for the service requested, not a single *bachur* volunteered to read the megillah for her free of charge. However, the *rebbetzin* insisted that it was her right to have a *yeshivah bachur* read for her without payment.

Finally, one *bachur* by the name of Baruch from the town of Suche consented to read the megillah for her at no charge. The other *bachurim* were surprised at him; why should he do this for her? Baruch, however, reassured them that he knew what he was doing.

So it was. Baruch appeared at her home at the designated time and obligingly began reading from the megillah. When he reached the words "on that night the king's sleep was disturbed," he stopped and calmly rolled up the megillah. The *rebbetzin* began protesting. "*Nu?*" In reply the *bachur* held up two fingers, implying that he would only read further if she paid him two zlotys. The *rebbetzin* badgered him again. "*Nu?*" But the *bachur* continued to hold up his two fingers. Reluctant to speak during the reading of the megillah, the *rebbetzin*, having no choice, opened her purse and gave two zlotys to the poor *bachur*.

As soon as he finished his job the *bachur* fled from her home. The *rebbetzin* indignantly marched to the *Rav*'s apartment to complain about the brazen cheek of the *bachurim* of his yeshivah. The *Rav* listened to her words of outrage and smiled. "I never knew I had such clever *bachurim* in my yeshivah," he remarked.

A True Tzaddik

On 25 Nissan, the yartzeit of the saintly Divrei Chaim, the many great rabbis who came to Tsanz for the occasion would all visit the Tsanzer Rav, Rabbi Aryeh Leibish. The *Rav* was occupied the entire day entertaining his numerous esteemed guests.

Each guest was honored by the *gabbai* with a tray of fruit, cakes, and drinks. Being a devout Chassid of Rabbi Aryeh Leibish, I would spend the day of the yartzeit at his home. I was interested in listening to the many stimulating conversations and discourses of Rabbi Aryeh Leibish and his guests. In addition, I was interested in the remaining food, which was given to us children after each visit. (A piece of cake or apple was a

The Vanished City of Tsanz

delectable treat for a child who lived in those poverty-stricken times.)

Among the Tzanzer Rav's regular visitors on the day of the yartzeit were Rabbi Shalom Eliezer; Rabbi Yeshayele from Tzechov; the Stropkover Rav; the Stitshiner Rav; the Tzieshinover Rav; and the Munkatcher Rav, author of *Minchas Elazar*. The latter made it his first priority to visit the *Rav* as soon as he arrived at Tsanz. He had developed a very close rapport with the *Rav* and once concluded a lengthy conversation with him with the following words: "Tsanzer Rav, you are the greatest *tzaddik* of the generation. Why don't you make an effort to hasten the final redemption?"

Rabbi Aryeh Leibish had replied, "Munkatcher Rav, you know very well what my grandfather the saintly Divrei Chaim once said: 'When I was young I wanted to correct the world. As I grew older I thought, *If only I could be worthy of correcting the misdeeds of the people of my town*. I became a little older and thought, *If only I could be worthy of correcting the misdeeds of my own family*. Now I say, *If only I can be worthy of correcting my own misdeeds*.' "

It is common knowledge that the Lubliner *rosh yeshivah*, Rabbi Shimele Zshelichover, once told his acquaintances that he was traveling to meet a true *tzaddik*. He did not specify whom he was referring to. It turned out that it was Rabbi Aryeh Leibish. Rabbi Shimele once wrote to his pupil, Rabbi Chaim Kreiswirth, currently *Rav* in Antwerp, that on *parashas Terumah-Tetzavah* he was to travel to Tsanz, to the elderly *tzaddik, shlita*.

Rabbi Aryeh Leibish subsisted solely on his rabbinical salary. The money he received with the *kvittelech* went straight into the large Rabbi Meir Ba'al HaNess *pushka*, which was a permanent fixture on his desk. A Chassid once gave the *Rav* a donation with his *kvittel*. Observing that the *Rav* put the money straight into the *pushka*, he gave the *Rav* a second *pidyon* and asked him to keep it. The *Rav* seemed to agree, but as soon as the Chassid left, he was seen putting that sum directly into the *pushka*.

A Chassid once traveled to Tsanz to consult with Rabbi Aryeh Leibish about a prospective match for his sister, who lived in a distant town. The Chassid asked for the *Rav*'s opinion, but the *Rav* failed to reply. The Chassid traveled home no wiser than when he had come.

A short time later he came again, hoping to elicit some response. As soon as he arrived in Tsanz he entered the *Rav*'s *beis midrash* and stood at the far end of the room, where he began davening. In the middle of davening the *Rav* sensed the Chassid's presence. He turned from his place and walked to the Chassid, who was standing at the far end of the *beis midrash*, at the western wall. He whispered into his ear that the match was not suitable for his family, and they should not go along with the proceedings. A while later it was indeed revealed that the family of the suggested match had a great blemish on its reputation.

Guidance from Rabbi Aryeh Leibish

Rabbi Aryeh Leibish had five sons. The eldest was Rabbi Mordechai Zev, who became *Rav* after him. The next was Rabbi Moishele, followed by Rabbi Shemayah, Rabbi Efraim, and Rabbi Hersh. All of them were distinguished *talmidei chachamim*. Rabbi Hersh was a fur merchant and had a reputation for being extremely honest in all his dealings. He was so trusted that when the non-Jewish fur dealers of the villages had a dispute among themselves, they would bring their complaints to Rabbi Hersh and unquestioningly accept his ruling.

Rabbi Hersh was of a nervous disposition, and he was wont to daven quickly. Rabbi Aryeh Leibish once noticed this and called him aside. "You, as the son of the Tsanzer Rav, should daven slower and with a little more *kavanah*," he rebuked him. He went on to show him how the week's *sidrah*, *parashas Chayei Sarah*, taught one how to daven.

The Torah tells us that when Eliezer entered Lavan's home, "they put food before him and he said, 'I will not eat until I have told you what I have to say,' and he [Lavan] said, 'Speak,' and he [Eliezer] said, 'I am the servant of Avraham.'" The *pasuk* can be explained as follows: Lavan gave Eliezer food, but Eliezer declined to eat until he had davened. Lavan thereupon replied, "Speak," i.e., daven quickly and be over with it, upon which Eliezer answered, "I am the servant of Avraham," i.e., being the servant of Avraham my davening must be different from that of an ordinary servant. "Similarly," the Tsanzer Rav pointed out to his son, "your davening must be different from the davening of an ordinary person."

Once, someone in the *beis midrash* said Kaddish D'Rabbanan before *"Hodu."* When he finished the Kaddish another person who had just entered the *beis midrash* began saying Kaddish, too. The latter, being a mourner, was obligated to say Kaddish, and since he had arrived when the first mourner was in the middle of saying Kaddish, he let him finish and then began himself. Rabbi Aryeh Leibish called him and said he had not done the right thing; Kaddish is said after a *niftar*, and he had said Kaddish after a person who was still alive...

21 Adar: A Day of Good Omen

On 21 Adar 5686 (1926), on the yartzeit of Rabbeinu HaKadosh Rabbi Elimelech of Lizensk, the Fristiker Rav, Rabbi Menachem Mendel Halberstam, passed away. When Rabbi Aryeh Leibish was told of his passing he remarked, "A clever person; he chose a good day." Nine years later, in the year 5695 (1935), Rabbi Aryeh Leibish passed away on Sunday, 21 Adar I.

The grave of Rabbi Aryeh Leibish Halberstam, Tsanzer Rav until 5695 (1935)

RABBI ARYEH LEIBISH HALBERSTAM

I would like to note that elsewhere I have seen written that the death of Rabbi Aryeh Leibish is recorded to have occurred in 1932. I personally testify that this is an error, for I myself was assisted by him in donning my tefillin on the day of my bar mitzvah a week after Shavuos in the year 5694 (1934). I was the last person whom Rabbi Aryeh Leibish assisted in donning tefillin, because shortly after my bar mitzvah he was struck with his final illness.

CHAPTER 9
RABBI MORDECHAI ZEV HALBERSTAM

After the death of the Tsanzer Rav, Rabbi Aryeh Leibish Halberstam, his eldest son, Rabbi Mordechai Zev, took over the rabbinical post of Tsanzer Rav. Rabbi Mordechai Zev had already begun serving as *Rav* in the town of Gribow during his father's lifetime in 5665 (1905). One of his main priorities upon inheriting his father's position was to concern himself with the running of Yeshivas Bnei Torah, which had been founded by his father. My father served as *rosh yeshivah* there.

Rabbi Mordechai Zev was acclaimed by the *gedolim* of the generation as a *poseik* in halachah. One of the *gedolim* in whose esteem he was greatly held was the famous Tarnapoler Rav, Rabbi Menachem Munish Babad, author of *Chavatzeles HaSharon*, one of the greatest *gedolim* in prewar Galicia.

My father, Rabbi Nosson Mordche, received his rabbinical ordination from the Tarnapoler Rav at the same time as the Tsanzer Rav, in 5688 (1928). My father told me that he had read the ordination which the Tarnapoler Rav had written in regard to the Tsanzer Rav, Rabbi Mordechai Zev. Among other descriptions he had written, "He is well versed in *Shas* and the *poskim* of the *rishonim* and *acharonim*.

RABBI MORDECHAI ZEV HALBERSTAM

He has a sharp mind and vast knowledge. He is G-d-fearing and worthy of succeeding his ancestors in the rabbinical leadership of the town Tsanz."

Rabbi Mordechai Zev was a firm leader who did not buckle even under severe pressure. In the summer of the year 5699 (1939), just before the outbreak of World War II, the *Rav* was staying in the health resort Piwniczna. I, being rather pale and weak, was allowed to accompany the *Rav* during his stay in the spa, which lay between Tsanz and the more famous resort of Krenitz.

Once, the *Rav* summoned the local butcher, wanting to clarify a matter of kashrus. (Piwniczna was under the jurisdiction of Tsanz.) The butcher refused to come and brazenly quoted a *Rashi* which implied an insolent response to the *Rav*'s request.

The *Rav* warned that he would do better by coming immediately, but the butcher refused. The *Rav* thereupon issued a proclamation that his meat was as good as *treif*. At this the butcher hastily came to the *Rav* to apologize and retract his impudent response, but he was told that for the next fourteen days the *Rav* refused to hear an apology. The penalty thus remained in place for the next two weeks, after which the *Rav* removed the ban.

Being in such close proximity to the *Rav* in Piwniczna afforded me a wonderful opportunity to perceive his greatness. His *hasmadah* in learning was truly amazing. He would stay awake entire nights learning. At 6 A.M. he would have his daily mineral bath, to which I was privileged to accompany him.

One morning, on the way to the bathhouse, an anti-Semitic lout of about twelve years flung a stone at the *Rav*'s shoulder and yelled, "You stinking rabbi! Hitler will be after all of you." This was a typical example of Polish anti-Semitism. The *Rav* turned to me and said, "Let us hurry, because if not, he will throw another stone at us." Alone with the *Rav* it would have been suicidal to do anything to the boorish youth, for with one shout, all the *goyim* of the village would have been after us.

When war broke out and the Nazis began rounding up the Jews, it soon became obvious that their first victims were the rabbis and spiritual leaders. The Tsanzer Rav and his *rebbetzin* secretly fled to Tarnow as soon as they recognized the danger. In Tarnow they were protected and sheltered by the *Rav*'s devoted Chassidim.

During their stay in Tarnow Rabbi Mordechai Zev's *rebbetzin* fell ill. The *Rav* did not have the means with which to pay for the required treatment. His Chassidim in Tsanz offered to provide him with the necessary sum, and so, in 5701 (1941), the *Rav* once again undertook the dangerous journey. Disguised as a farmer, complete with horse and wagon, he succeeded in reaching Tsanz undiscovered. The Tsanzer Chassidim collected the required sum, and the *Rav* traveled back to Tarnow.

In 5703 (1942), when I was transferred from the camp in Muszyna to the Tarnow ghetto, I was told by the few remaining Jews of the ghetto (who were deported to Auschwitz together with me a short time later) what had happened to Rabbi Mordechai Zev. He had been in hiding in Tarnow when the Nazis organized a major manhunt and rounded up ten thousand Jews, his *rebbetzin* among them. Rabbi Mordechai Zev emerged from his hiding place donned in his tallis and tefillin and announced himself with the words, "I want to go *al kiddush haShem*, together with all the other Jews."

The victims were herded onto trucks and driven to a forest approximately seven kilometers from Tarnow, to a place called Zbylitowska-Gora. There they were all shot into a mass grave. Fifty years later I visited Zbylitowska-Gora and saw the tombstones erected there with the inscription "Here is the grave of ten thousand Jews of the Tarnow ghetto. This, too, is the grave of eight hundred Jewish children who were brutally murdered by the Nazis in Tamuz 5702." According to the information that I gathered in the Tarnow ghetto, the Tsanzer Rav, Rabbi Mordechai Zev, and his *rebbetzin* are among the *kedoshim* buried there.

Rav of Old Tsanz

If you read the first chapter of this book, you will remember that there are two towns called Tsanz. New Tsanz is the subject of this book. Old Tsanz is about seven kilometers from New Tsanz. The Old-Tsanzer Rav, Rabbi Avigdor Tzvi, the son of Rabbi Yechiel

RABBI MORDECHAI ZEV HALBERSTAM

Nassan Halberstam, was born in 5644 (1884). Rabbi Avigdor Tzvi married his cousin, becoming the son-in-law of his great-uncle Rabbi Aryeh Leibish, *Rav* of Tsanz. His grandfather Rabbi Moshe, the father of Rabbi Yechiel Nassan, was a son-in-law of the Kreiser Rav. Rabbi Moshe, who was a son of the Gorlitzer Rav, would joke that he was the most unfortunate of all the Tsanzer grandchildren. The Divrei Chaim had a policy not to give money to his children or grandchildren. When one of his children married off a child of his own, he would ask the Divrei Chaim for money for the sake of the future grandchild — who was not yet a grandchild of the Divrei Chaim. Rabbi Moshe complained that his father and father-in-law were both children of the Divrei Chaim, and he therefore could not receive money from his grandfather! In fact, however, the Divrei Chaim gave him his writings, which were later to become his famous *sefer*, *Divrei Chaim*, to be organized and published. So through that he was no worse off financially than any of the other descendants of the Divrei Chaim.

Rabbi Avigdor was appointed Old-Tsanzer Rav in 5665 (1905), when he was only twenty years old. However, his residence remained in the Piekela district of Tsanz, and twice a week he traveled to Old Tsanz to carry out his rabbinical duties. He was a great *poseik* in halachah and an expert in

The grave of the last Tsanzer Rav, Rabbi Mordechai Zev Halberstam, among the ten thousand *kedoshim* buried in Zbylitowska-Gora on 26 Sivan 5702 (1942)

The Vanished City of Tsanz

judging the most complicated court cases. He always shunned honor.

After his father's death in 5694 (1933) he was appointed Bardiaver Rav in place of his father. With the outbreak of the second World War he came back to his birthplace, Tsanz, since he felt that in times of trouble his place was with his fellow citizens. He took up residence in his former home on the Piekela. The Piekela was thought to be a safer place, since the laborers lived in that ghetto.

We have mentioned before that when the war broke out, the Tsanzer Rav, Rabbi Mordechai Zev, moved to Tarnow because the first victims the Nazis took were the rabbis and spiritual leaders. Being that Rabbi Avigdor, the Old-Tsanzer Rav, was a son-in-law of the former Tsanzer Rav, Rabbi Aryeh Leibish, and a brother-in-law of the present *Rav*, Rabbi Mordechai Zev, and being very much revered by the Tsanzer population, he was considered *Rav* of the town after Rabbi Mordechai Zev moved to Tarnow. Since it was the custom in Tsanz that the *Rav* act as *sandak* at every bris, the Old-Tsanzer Bardiaver Rav was offered the honor of *sandak* at all the *brisos* during the war.

The Old-Tsanzer Rav acted as *sandak* for the very last Jewish

Rabbi Avigdor Tzvi Halberstam, the Bardiaver and Old-Tsanzer Rav

baby who was born in the Tsanzer ghetto before its final liquidation. When he entered the *beis midrash*, the congregation gazed at him strangely, since the S.S. had just shorn off his long, black, impressive bushy beard. All that remained was his large mustache. The Old-Tsanzer Rav said sadly, bitterness choking his voice, *"Vos kikt ets mich oon? Ich bin es* — Why are you all staring at me? It's me!" With tears in his eyes he pronounced the name of the child: Moshe Uri. The child was named Moshe after his father and Uri after his grandfather Uri Greenberg, who had both been murdered just a short time earlier by the Nazi beasts.

The Old-Tsanzer Rav perished in Belzec together with all the other Tsanzer *Yidden* on 16–17 Elul 5702 (1942).

CHAPTER 10

SAINTLY PERSONALITIES

Rabbi Chuna Hersh Rubin of Sakmar

Of the many personalities of prewar Tsanz who were exemplary in their good deeds and *avodas Hashem*, Rabbi Chuna Hersh Rubin stands out clearly in my memory.

Rabbi Chuna Hersh was a son of Rabbi Naftali Rubin, the *Rav* of Vizhnitza, Galicia, a son-in-law of the Divrei Yechezkel, the Shinover Rav. In Tsanz he was known as the Sakmarer Rebbe, since his previous dwelling place had been the town of Sakmar. Having been childless for many years, he had come to live in Tsanz, hoping that a "change of place brings change of luck."

(In Tsanz, the town of Satmar was called "Sakmar" since Satmar is the name of an *avodah zarah*. The Sakmarer Rebbe, Rabbi Yoel Teitelbaum, also referred to the town as Sakmar. Another reason for calling the town so was because the Divrei Chaim never referred to any town by its proper name, apart from the town of Duklah, which is mentioned in the Torah.)

Rabbi Chuna Hersh prayed with intense devotion and the utmost concentration. His love of G-d and his fellow men was truly incredible. When he made a blessing, he dwelled on every word, and one could see that he meant it with every fiber of his being. Many Chassidim who strove for perfection in *avodas Hashem* came to his *beis midrash* just to observe him. He frequently acted as *ba'al tefillah*, and when he did he shed heartfelt tears. Yet at the same time he was a man who was always happy and content.

Witnessing Rabbi Chuna Hersh lighting Chanukah lights was unforgettable. Many Chassidim would come and watch as he lovingly prepared the wicks and poured the olive oil in the menorah. As he recited the blessings with burning enthusiasm and an intense love of G-d, a feeling of tremendous awe befell the gathered crowd. I remember until this day the sweet experience of observing Rabbi Chuna Hersh in his holy *avodas Hashem*.

Every night of Chanukah Rabbi Chuna Hersh would arrange a *milchig* meal for the assembled congregation in which he personally ensured that the poor people were well taken care of. The meal consisted of bread, cheese, and potato *gritz* (soup). Rabbi Chuna Hersh would lecture on *divrei Torah* from the *sefer Zera Kadosh*, which was written by his grandfather Rabbi Naftali of Ropshitz. The assembly then sang "*Ma'oz Tzur*," "*Shir HaMa'alos*," and *pesukim* from "*Ashrei Temimei Derech*," chapter 119 of Tehillim..

Rabbi Chuna Hersh had four staunch supporters: Reb Avraham David Schiff, Mendel Wagshal, and the brothers Itzikel and Yosef Roth. The other congregants of his *beis midrash* were poor people whom Reb Chuna Hersh himself would help, ensuring that they had sustenance and the means to marry off their children.

Rabbi Chuna Hersh showed amazing self-sacrifice when it came to helping others. In the winter of 5693 (1933) Reb Itzikel Roth, who owned a shop of shoemaking equipment, owed his wholesaler in Bochnia approximately one thousand zlotys. The deadline by which the debt had to be settled was on a Friday. When Friday arrived, Rabbi Itzikel still did not have the money. That night the wholesaler had him thrown into jail.

A prison in Poland at that time was a horrifying place. Years after this story took place, I myself had an opportunity to experience firsthand what Polish prison life was all about. At the outbreak of the war, in Elul 5699 (1939), the Tsanzer Jews tried to flee, imagining that they could elude the Nazis' long claws. At the time of our flight the Polish prison wardens opened their prison doors and allowed the

The Vanished City of Tsanz

convicts to go free. They were a shocking sight. Their complexions were waxen and yellow, and they were partially blind from sitting in the prison cells in total darkness for so long. They were ill from lying on cold stone floors for many years. They had been literally left to rot for their prison terms. They stumbled down the street in the daylight, their hands groping for the walls, trying to get their bearings. This gives us some idea of the appalling conditions to which Reb Itzikel Roth was subject on that Shabbos.

Knowing it was Shabbos and there was nothing anyone could do, the people agreed that Rabbi Chuna Hersh should not be told what had happened to his Chassid Reb Itzikel, lest Rabbi Chuna Hersh's Shabbos be disturbed. They warned everybody not to reveal that Reb Itzikel had been imprisoned and told his son David to explain away Itzikel's absence with the excuse of a common cold.

Every Friday night Rabbi Chuna Hersh would observe all his congregants, concerning himself with the welfare of each. After davening the congregants would file past Rabbi Chuna Hersh and wish him "good Shabbos." When it was Reb Itzikel's son David's turn, Rabbi Chuna Hersh inquired, "Where is your father? I did not see him here today."

"He has a cold," replied David.

The people imagined that with this the subject was closed. However, later, at his *tisch*, as Rabbi Chuna Hersh was eating his soup he announced, "I insist on knowing what is the matter with Reb Itzikel." (Reb Itzikel never missed Rabbi Chuna Hersh's *tisch*.) Nobody volunteered any information.

Rabbi Chuna Hersh summoned David Roth and said to him, "Please tell me the truth. What is the matter with your father?" David conceded defeat and told him what had transpired, adding that it was decided to conceal the truth from the *Rav* so that he would not be disturbed on Shabbos.

Rabbi Chuna Hersh arose in agitation and said, "What? We will eat *lokshen mit yoich* (noodles and soup) on Shabbos while a fellow Jew languishes in prison? Impossible! Tomorrow morning in my *beis midrash* we will not say the *berachos* until Reb Itzikel is released and can daven with our minyan. If this doesn't appeal to anybody here, he can daven elsewhere!"

The assembled tried to persuade Rabbi Chuna Hersh that on Shabbos there was nothing to be done, but Rabbi Chuna Hersh was adamant: when someone is in prison one could not sit with folded arms, even on Shabbos. He ordered a gentile to be summoned before him and for somebody to find out the address of the Bochnian wholesaler's representative in Tsanz. They succeeded in reaching the representative at his address, but he claimed that he was unable to do anything without the explicit permission of his boss in Bochnia. Undaunted, Rabbi Chuna Hersh took the gentile with him to the post office to contact his employer in Bochnia by phone. The bargaining went on for the better part of the night until the wholesaler finally agreed to allow them to give his representative in Tsanz merchandise to the value of a thousand zlotys. Rabbi Chuna Hersh himself collected the merchandise. The entire procedure lasted until Shabbos midday.

Rabbi Chuna Hersh succeeded in his mission. That Shabbos, *berachos* commenced at 1 P.M. in Rabbi Chuna Hersh's *beis midrash*, with Reb Itzikel Roth davening at that minyan, as the *Rav* had prophesied. After davening the congregation broke out in joyous dancing and singing in celebration of the great mitzvah of redemption of captives which had been accomplished that Shabbos.

A later incident earned Rabbi Chuna Hersh another devout Chassid. On 25 Nissan 5698 (1938) the Koloshitzer Rav, Rabbi Chuna Halberstam, and Rabbi Itzikel of Pshevorsk, who later lived in Antwerp, arrived in Tsanz for the yartzeit of the Divrei Chaim. The Rebbes decided to use the opportunity to collect money for a needy orphan bride from a respected family. They went through the marketplace, being careful in their choices of whom to collect money from for this important purpose. Rabbi Chuna Hersh accompanied the distinguished visitors.

A certain Mr. Sigmund Reicher sold dishes and porcelain in one of the shops in the marketplace. The rabbis did not visit his shop since he had such a tiny mezuzah on the door that it was barely discernible and because he sported a small, trimmed beard. However, Sigmund

Reicher badly wanted them to allow him to donate money since his wife was very ill and he needed the merit. After he had explained the situation to the distinguished Rebbes, Rabbi Chuna Hersh asked him, "Does your wife cover her hair?"

"No," he replied.

Rabbi Chuna Hersh said to him, "If you take upon yourself three things — that you do not trim your beard, that your wife cover her hair, and that you nail a kosher mezuzah on your door — we will accept your donation. In this merit your wife will quickly recover."

Reicher agreed and miraculously his wife recovered. After that, Sigmund Reicher became one of Rabbi Chuna Hersh's greatest Chassidim and supporters.

More Great Deeds

Reb Yechiel Tepper and his family lived on the street known as *"der Yiddisher Gass."* The Tepper family struggled hard to earn a living. They would go out into the woods and pick raspberries, then press raspberry juice on their own little press. It was backbreaking work. Obviously, they could only do business in the summer season when the raspberries were ripe. In addition, their workroom was in a dark, windowless room with no door to the street. Entry to the room was via their house only.

Suddenly Reb Yechiel Tepper passed away, and his widow and orphans were left bereft of any means of sustenance. When Rabbi Chuna Hersh became aware of their bitter plight he went straight to their home to see what could be done for them. "We carry the responsibility for this family," he said.

Rabbi Chuna Hersh looked around the dark, dank workroom and fell upon a plan. He would convert the room into a grocery store.

His first step was to approach the landlord of the apartment building, Reb Yaakov Shia Ehrlich, a distinguished personality, and ask him permission to knock an opening in the wall so that there would be access from the street. Reb Yaakov Shia agreed to this reasonable request.

SAINTLY PERSONALITIES

After the building project had been carried out, Rabbi Chuna Hersh provided the widow with groceries with which to stock her store. He approached Reb Mendel Wagshal (one of the four supporters mentioned above), who also owned a grocery store where one of the Tepper sons was employed.

"Until now the *bachur* worked in your shop; now let him work for his mother and for the orphans. As for you, Mendel, you will deliver the merchandise to the store, and I will guarantee payment," said Rabbi Chuna Hersh.

Needless to say, Reb Mendel obeyed Rabbi Chuna Hersh. Thanks to Rabbi Chuna Hersh's effort, the widow and children earned a respectable livelihood.

Once, an elderly gentleman from Bekovsk came into Rabbi Chuna Hersh's *beis midrash* and began unpacking his wares: *talleisim, tzitzis, sefarim*. Rabbi Chuna Hersh noticed how the old man dragged about his parcel of wares with great difficulty, with his last ounce of strength. He took pity on the old, broken man and said to him, "How much do you earn a week from traveling with this package of goods?"

"Five zlotys," answered the old man.

Rabbi Chuna Hersh's home, with his *beis midrash* on the first floor

"If so," responded the *Rav*, "remain in my *beis midrash*. I will supply your weekly income of five zlotys, and my *rebbetzin* will provide you with all your other needs."

The man from Bekovsk lived in Rabbi Chuna Hersh's *beis midrash* in Tsanz from that day until the outbreak of war in Elul 5699.

One day a boy from Czechoslovakia by the name of Meir appeared at the home of Rabbi Chuna Hersh. The boy had fled his home fearing a reprisal from the army for evading military duty. Rabbi Chuna Hersh took him in and had the boy learn an occupation as a plumber. He paid for his apprenticeship and eventually married him off, providing him with a furnished apartment and all other household requirements. The young, bewildered lad grew up into a confident man with a respectable occupation. His wife bore him several children, and together they built a beautiful Jewish family.

I remember when, on Purim 5695 (1935), after reading the megillah, Rabbi Chuna Hersh brought in a tray loaded with a delicacy called *noont*, a treat consisting of crushed nuts coated with honey. He distributed a portion to all his congregants, many of whom were paupers for whom this was a one-time luxury. When the *rebbetzin* protested that there would be no remaining *noont* for her *mishlo'ach manos*, the *Rav* replied, "Do not worry. You will receive *mishlo'ach manos* and will thus have things to send to others, but if we don't provide for the poor, who will?"

It was Rabbi Chuna Hersh's specialty to care for widows and orphans and for other unfortunate, broken souls. His home was always open to every indigent.

In wartime he fled to Vizhnitza where he perished *al kiddush haShem* with all the Vizhnitzer Jews in 5702 (1942).

The Koloshitzer Rav

The Koloshitzer Rav, Rabbi Chuna Halberstam, visited Tsanz several times a year. He was hosted by Reb Abbish'l Kleinberger, who lived in the center of the marketplace. Reb Abbish'l, a Koloshitzer Chassid, owned a tavern and a hotel, but he did not accept payment

SAINTLY PERSONALITIES

from anybody who could not afford it and never from any Rebbe.

It was said that when the Koloshitzer Rav's mother gave him a packed lunch for *cheder*, he would distribute the food to his classmates and leave nothing for himself. This characteristic of his remained until his dying day: he would give everything he owned to other unfortunates, leaving nothing for himself.

The Koloshitzer Rav was an exceptional *oveid Hashem*. He was remarkably pious and G-d-fearing, even in comparison to other *gedolim* of the prewar generation. It was a pleasure to listen to his heartwarming prayers and to hear him learning. He was always happy and ready with a good word and a warm smile. The following story illustrates the great love he had for other people.

Many poor people would approach the Koloshitzer Rav for a donation. Once, a tall, robust, healthy-looking man put a small yarmulke on his head and came to the Koloshitzer Rav to ask for money. The *Rav* did not have any money on his person, so he turned to his Chassidim and asked if anybody could lend him some. The Pshevorsker Rav, *shlita*, and, *l'havdil bein chaim l'chaim*, Reb Shmelke Goldklang, who were there, offered him half a zloty. The Koloshitzer Rav took the money and handed it to the beggar. However, the worthy fellow considered the proffered amount too little and refused to accept it. He indignantly turned to leave the room. Seeing this, the Koloshitzer Rav ran to the door and begged the man to accept the money since he simply did not have any more to offer. The fellow graciously agreed to his request.

This incident greatly vexed Rabbi Chuna's *gabbai*, Reb Mendel. The beggar was a young, healthy man, he protested, who only put on a yarmulke so that he could beg for money. Let him go and work to earn a living, he declared.

The Koloshitzer Rav replied that this was not so. Before a person is born, it is decreed in Heaven whether he will be strong or weak, rich or poor. "If it is indeed as you say," said the *Rav*, "it would only be necessary to announce whether he will be strong or weak, because if he is strong he can work and is automatically rich. Rich and strong are individual qualities independent of each other. If it is decreed in

Heaven that he be strong and poor, he is given lead in his feet (he is very lazy), and he can therefore do nothing to earn money."

The Strange Dream

When he was on a visit to Antwerp as guest of honor at the annual dinner of Rabbi Meir Ba'al HaNess Kollel Chibas Yerushalayim, Rabbi Shmelke Pinter of London told me another interesting story about the Koloshitzer Rav.

Rabbi Shmelke had a brother, Avraham, who was twenty-five years older than he. Reb Avraham's father-in-law, the Bochnier Rav, Rabbi Asher Meir Halberstam, was a grandson of Rabbi David Keshanover, a son of the Divrei Chaim.

Avraham told his brother Reb Shmelke that on Shabbos *parashas BeHa'alosecha*, in 5695 (1935), the Koloshitzer Rav was visiting Krosno. The Bekovsker Rav, Reb Shmelke's father, wrote to his son Avraham and told him to travel to Krosno to spend Shabbos with the Koloshitzer Rav. Though not a Koloshitzer Chassid, Avraham went out of respect for his father's wishes.

Rabbi Chuna Halberstam, the Koloshitzer Rav

Shabbos afternoon, after the *tisch*, Avraham took a nap. He dreamed he saw the Divrei Chaim standing with a jug in his hand and a towel on his shoulder. Turning around to face the assembled people, he asked, "Who knows the *shiur* of *netilas yadayim?*"

Somebody replied, "The greater *shiur*" (as *paskened* by the Noda BiYehudah).

The Divrei Chaim replied, "Eh, the smaller *shiur*." At that point, Avraham woke up and hurried off to daven *minchah*.

earn a living, he declared.

The Koloshitzer Rav replied that this was not so. Before a person is born, it is decreed in Heaven whether he will be strong or weak, rich or poor. "If it is indeed as you say," said the *Rav*, "it would only be necessary to announce whether he will be strong or weak, because if he is strong he can work and is automatically rich. Rich and strong are individual qualities independent of each other. If it is decreed in Heaven that he be strong and poor, he is given lead in his feet (he is very lazy), and he can therefore do nothing to earn money."

The Strange Dream

When he was on a visit to Antwerp as guest of honor at the annual dinner of Rabbi Meir Ba'al HaNess Kollel Chibas Yerushalayim, Rabbi Shmelke Pinter of London told me another interesting story about the Koloshitzer Rav.

Rabbi Shmelke had a brother, Avraham, who was twenty-five years older than he. Reb Avraham's father-in-law, the Bochnier Rav, Rabbi Asher Meir Halberstam, was a grandson of Rabbi David Keshanover, a son of the Divrei Chaim.

Avraham told his brother Reb Shmelke that on Shabbos *parashas BeHa'alosecha*, in 5695 (1935), the Koloshitzer Rav was visiting Krosno. The Bekovsker Rav, Reb Shmelke's father, wrote to his son Avraham and told him to travel to Krosno to spend Shabbos with the Koloshitzer Rav. Though not a Koloshitzer Chassid, Avraham went out of respect for his father's wishes.

Shabbos afternoon, after the *tisch*, Avraham took a nap. He dreamed he saw the Divrei Chaim standing with a jug in his hand and a towel on his shoulder. Turning around to face the assembled people, he asked, "Who knows the *shiur* of *netilas yadayim*?"

Somebody replied, "The greater *shiur*" (as *paskened* by the Noda BiYehudah).

The Divrei Chaim replied, "Eh, the smaller *shiur*." At that point, Avraham woke up and hurried off to daven *minchah*.

The Vanished City of Tsanz

At *se'udah shelishis*, Avraham noticed the Koloshitzer Rav standing with a jug in his hand and a towel over his shoulder, exactly as he had seen the Tsanzer Rav in his dream. The Koloshitzer Rav turned to face the assembled and asked, "Who knows the *shiur* of *netilas yadayim?*"

"The greater shiur," answered Avraham.

He intentionally gave that response, eagerly waiting to see what the Koloshitzer Rav's reply would be. As he had expected, the Koloshitzer Rav replied, "Eh, the smaller *shiur*," exactly as the Tsanzer Rav had said in his dream.

The Pshevorsker Rebbe, *shlita*, has another interesting story about that Shabbos in Krosno. A man was given an *aliyah*. The *gabbai* asked the person for whom he wanted to make a *"Mi SheBeirach."*

"For all the Koloshitzer Chassidim," answered the man.

When the Koloshitzer Rav heard these words, he went white and said, "This is party politics. One is forbidden to go in the ways of the heathens."

The Stropkover Rav

The Stropkover Rav, Rabbi Avraham Shalom Halberstam, was a son of the holy *Rav* of Shinov. The Divrei Yechezkel went every year to Tsanz for the yartzeit of his grandfather, the holy Divrei Chaim and stayed with the hospitable Reb Yeshayah Mandel.

If the Stropkover Rav gave somebody a *berachah* he was guaranteed that it would come to fruition. Every year, his host gave the Stropkover Rav a *kvittel* in which he asked for children. The Stropkover Rav would shower him with blessings of every type, except that of children.

The Stropkover Rav limped on one foot. Rabbi Halpern of London told me that he himself witnessed the following:

The Stropkover Rav learned very diligently many hours of the day. He learned very quickly, so much so that people could be forgiven for thinking that he did not learn very deeply.

SAINTLY PERSONALITIES

Once the people sitting in his *shiur* smelled singed meat. To their horror they saw that the top of the Rebbe's cigar had dropped onto his boot and burnt a hole right through, singeing his foot. The Stropkover Rav was concentrating so hard on what he was learning, he didn't even feel it.

The year 5689 (1929) brought a worldwide economic crisis. In such a time the first thing a person does is to stop buying luxury articles, so one of the first places to feel the pinch was Antwerp, where most of the Jews dealt in diamonds. When the Stropkover Rav heard about the crisis in Antwerp, he asked if there were any wealthy people left in the town. When he was informed that there were still a few rich men, he traveled to Antwerp and collected a large amount of money. He then asked the charity *gabbaim* to send him all the people who had been left impoverished and gave these people the money he'd collected. After that he left for home.

The Stropkover Rav got an eye infection that seriously affected his eyesight, so much so that he was nearly blind. He decided to travel to Vienna to a renowned eye specialist.

The specialist looked into the Stropkover Rav's eye and said that there was nothing he could do to save his sight. When the Stropkover Rav heard this he got up and walked out. He then asked for a telephone book and told his *gabbai* to open the book under "eye doctor," count till the eighteenth doctor, and make an appointment.

The doctor chosen examined the *Rav*'s eyes and found nothing seriously wrong. The Rebbe needed only to smear an ointment on his eye, and it would get better. When he was told what the famed specialist had said, he looked again into the Rebbe's eyes and repeated that there was nothing seriously wrong. But just to be sure, he added, ask a third doctor. The Rebbe did so, and the third doctor said the same as the second. The Stropkover Rav went home cured.

Once an elderly woman, the daughter of the *dayan* of Komarner, came to the Stropkover Rav and cried that she had never found a *shidduch*. The Stropkover Rav, who was then a widower of about sixty-five years, said to her that if in a short time she still hadn't found her intended he would take her as a wife. She agreed if he'd promise her a son. The Stropkover Rav did so, and she soon became the Stropkover Rebbetzin.

Ten years after his wedding, his wife still hadn't borne a son. She reminded her husband of his promise. The Stropkover Rav asked her to forgive him his promise. When she said that she still wanted a son, he said, *"Nar blaibt nar und mekach blaibt mekach"* (a fool remains a fool, and a sale remains a sale). A year later her son, Yosef Yom Tov, was born.

The Stropkover Rav was *niftar* on the first day of Shavuos, at the age of eighty-five. His wife and son, Yosef Yom Tov, perished in the war in 5702 (1942).

The Labover Rav

The Labover Rav, Rabbi Shmuel Aharon Miller, was a frequent visitor to Tsanz. He was born in 5625 (1865) to Rabbi Naftali, a *poseik* in Gorlitz.

The village of Labowa was situated between Tsanz and Krenitz. The Jews there lived in extreme poverty and were unable to support their *Rav*. Not only did he have to provide himself with sustenance, but he also provided for his congregation and assisted them in marrying off their children.

The Labover Rav was a great *talmid chacham*. It was considered a rare privilege to receive the authority to *pasken she'eilos* from him. He founded a yeshivah where he himself learned with the *bachurim*. He was also actively involved with the organization

Rabbi Shmuel Aharon Miller, the Labover Rav

Shemiras Shabbos, which aimed to ensure the preservation of Shabbos in Krenitz.

On his regular visits to Tsanz, he was usually hosted by his distinguished relative Reb Shabsai Miller (whose son Akiva Miller lives today in Monsey, New York). Sometimes he would stay at our home. On one occasion when he was staying with us, he asked my mother at breakfast on Sunday morning whether she had any remaining challos from Shabbos. My mother asked him why he insisted on eating only the challah from Shabbos. He replied that he did not eat bread bought from the Jewish bakery, since the bakers who worked there overnight did not wash their hands for *negel vasser* at daybreak. (My father, too, did not eat bread bought from a baker, for the same reason.)

A Tsanzer *bachur*, who was a great *talmid chacham* but unfortunately not very G-d-fearing, once came to the Labover Rav to receive rabbinical ordination.

"Did you study *Orach Chaim, Hilchos Shabbos?*" inquired the *Rav* of the lad.

"Yes," was the response.

"How do you cut your nails?" probed the *Rav*. "In the order of the fingers or not?"

"In the order," replied the boy.

"But it is written in *Orach Chaim* 241 and 261, 'When one cuts his nails one should not do it in order, but should begin with the fourth finger of the left hand and with the forefinger of the right hand.' "

The *bachur* quickly excused himself. "The Magen Avraham says the Arizal was not particular about this."

"The Ari HaKadosh could afford to be lax with this custom, but you have no right to, since the Magen Avraham himself concludes that 'one should be stringent,' " responded the *Rav* sharply.

As a result of this interchange, the *bachur* was refused rabbinical ordination.

At the outbreak of war, the Labover Rav moved to Tsanz together with his son, the *tzaddik* Rabbi Yoelish. In the Tsanzer ghetto Rabbi Yoelish was caught by the S.S. and held hostage. He was imprisoned in the Tarnow gaol, where he was tortured to death.

His father perished in the Belzec extermination camp together with all the Tsanzer Jews on 16–17 Elul 5702 (1942).

Rabbi Shimele Zshelichover

Rabbi Shimele came to live in Tsanz in 5677 (1917) at the age of forty. By that time, he had already reviewed the entire *Shas* fourteen times! He stayed there for a while, acting as a *melamed*, until his acceptance of the position of *rosh yeshivah* at the Warsaw Mesivta.

Rabbi Shimele Zshelichover was born in 5637 (1877), a year after the Divrei Chaim's passing. He was a Koznitzer Chassid who frequently recounted stories about his Rebbe. I still remember one story:

A contagious childhood epidemic had broken out in his hometown of Zshelichov. The Koznitzer Rebbe quoted from the *Zohar* in *parashas Pinchas* that ten *talmidei chachamim* should go to all four corners of the stricken town and recite the parashah of *ketores*. His instructions were carried out, and the epidemic subsided.

When Rabbi Shimele left Tsanz to travel to Warsaw, many *talmidei chachamim* accompanied him to the train station. At the station, his talmidim asked him to "give them *tikkun*." (It was customary to "give *tikkun*" — that is, a *berachah* that some spiritual lack be repaired — to one who had passed away and to people setting out on a journey.) Rabbi Shimele replied that he would offer them an option: either they would tell him the reason for giving *tikkun* and he would then give it to them, or he would tell them the reason for *tikkun* instead of giving it.

His *talmidim* did not know the reason, so he said, "I will tell you the reason as explained by Rabbi Shimon of Jaroslaw."

He explained as follows: It is hard to understand why it is permitted for a person to leave his town to seek *parnasah* in another place, for Hashem provides sustenance to all his creations from the biggest to the smallest. If a person is destined to have no *parnasah*, of what good will it be to him to fight Hashem's will? The *Chovos HaLevavos* writes in *Sha'ar HaBitachon*, "A *tzaddik* once went to a distant place to seek *parnasah* for his family. A priest of idol worshippers came toward him, and the *tzaddik* said to him, 'How blinded you

SAINTLY PERSONALITIES

are and how little wisdom lies in your idol worship.' "

"What is your religion and whom do you serve?" asked the idol worshipper.

"I believe in the Creator Who can do everything and gives sustenance to His creations from the greatest down to the tiniest," answered the *tzaddik*.

"Where are you heading?" inquired the priest.

"I am going to seek *parnasah* in another town," replied the *tzaddik*.

"Your actions contradict your words," scoffed the idol worshipper.

"How so?" queried the *tzaddik*.

"If you would sincerely believe that the Creator gives sustenance from the greatest to the smallest of his creations, you would believe that He could provide you with sustenance in your own town just as He could provide you in another town, and you would not bother to undertake such a long journey in search of livelihood."

Rabbi Shimele Zshelichover

Shimon Wechter, Rabbi Shimele's *talmid*, and Yaakov Aharon dem Rav's, Rabbi Aryeh Leibish's grandson

The Vanished City of Tsanz

After hearing these words, the *tzaddik* went straight home and never left his town again.

"If so," continued Rabbi Shimon of Jaroslaw, "it would seem that a person should always fulfill the verse 'Worthy is he who stays in his home.' But if a person is forced to leave his town in search of *parnasah* or for another reason, it surely means that the person needs to amend something in the other town. Hashem therefore arranges that the person ends up where he is needed. For this reason, it is customary to ask of a person who enters or leaves a town to give *tikkun*, since the purpose of his coming or going is to amend something."

"I have given you the reason for *tikkun*, and I am therefore absolved of my duty to give *tikkun*," concluded Reb Shimele.

Rabbi Shimele stayed in Warsaw for a few terms only (six months to a term), since Rabbi Meir Shapiro, the founder of Yeshivas Chachmei Lublin, offered him the position of *mashgiach* and *rosh yeshivah* in his yeshivah. After leaving Lublin, Reb Shimele settled in Cracow where he remained until the extermination of the Cracow ghetto in 1943. He was killed *al kiddush haShem* with all the other Cracow Jews.

Until war disrupted the routine of daily life, Reb Shimele would travel from Cracow to Tsanz every year for a visit of two weeks on *parashiyos Terumah* and *Tetzaveh*. Prior to his departure from Cracow, he'd inform his close acquaintances that he was journeying to meet a true *tzaddik*.

The Tsanzer Rav, Rabbi Aryeh Leibish, would accord Rabbi Shimele great honor, enjoying intimate discussions with him behind closed doors for hours at a time. After Rabbi Aryeh Leibish's death, his son Rabbi Mordechai Zev followed his father's lead, also treating Rabbi Shimele with great respect. He always saw to it that Rabbi Shimele departed Tsanz with a royal farewell and a sizable amount of money. Rabbi Shimele's *talmidim*, too, provided their beloved *Rav* with a large sum.

Rabbi Shimele would expound on *Chumash* with *Rashi* on Friday night in the Tsanzer Rav's *beis midrash*. He was especially apt at explaining clearly and lucidly the chapter of the building of the Mishkan according to *PaRDeS* (*peshat, remez, derush, sod*). Hundreds

SAINTLY PERSONALITIES

Moshe Eliezer Bochner, Reb Abbele Sucha's son, and on his right, Hersh dem Rav's, Rabbi Aryeh Leibish's son

of people attended his *shiur*, including the greatest *talmidei chachamim* in town and all his former students. Rabbi Shimele himself did not attend the *Rav's tisch*, yet he never commenced his *shiur* until the *tisch* was over.

On a visit to London on 28 Adar II 5757 (1997) I davened in the Beth Midrash Tiferes Amram. The *Rav* there, Rabbi Jungreis, learned *Mishnah Berurah* after davening. He said that it mentions that one should say Pesukei D'Zimrah, as if one is counting money. The Pri Megadim says that this means a half-hour. This reminded me of a visit by Reb Shimele sixty years ago when he davened in the Tsanzer Rav's *beis midrash*. He davened Pesukei D'Zimrah slowly, word by word, with a beautiful tune. All of us boys stood around and watched him. It took him a half-hour to daven Pesukei D'Zimrah and he did it every single day.

On Lag Ba'Omer, all the Tsanzer children and *yeshivah bachurim* went on an outing. They took along cake and eggs for lunch, and of course the all-important bows and arrows, symbolic of the rainbow which was never seen during the lifetime of Rabbi Shimon bar Yochai.

When Reb Shimele was a *melamed* in Tsanz, before being appointed *rosh yeshivah* of the Warsaw yeshivah, his *talmidim* told him about this Tsanzer custom. He replied that he, too, had a custom on Lag Ba'Omer, the yartzeit of Rabbi Shimon Bar Yochai: to learn the sayings of that *tanna* by heart. He proposed to his *talmidim* that they sit at their tables with a Mishnah open before them while he sat in his place and recited by heart all the places in the whole of *Shas* where Rabbi Shimon's name was mentioned. Some of his students agreed to the plan and stayed with him. The day grew dark, but Rabbi Shimele was still there, quoting Rabbi Shimon bar Yochai from *Shas*...

The Great and Saintly Reb Abbele Sucha

One of the well-known personalities of prewar Western Galicia was the pious Reb Abbele Bochner, known as Reb Abbele Sucha. I had the opportunity of becoming acquainted with Reb Abbele on his annual visit to Tsanz on the yartzeit of the Divrei Chaim.

Reb Abbele limped and dragged his right foot. According to his son Reb Moshe Eliezer Bochner, who lived in Tsanz, this happened when Reb Abbele was visiting Cracow. He went to the mikveh at dawn, and, finding the gate surrounding the mikveh locked, he tried to jump over it. He fell and broke his right leg. The doctor who came to inspect the injury strongly advised that the leg be put in plaster of paris or he would remain a cripple for life.

Reb Abbele inquired of the doctor whether he would be able to go to the mikveh with his foot in a cast. The doctor replied in the negative. Reb Abbele said, "Then I will not allow my foot to be put into a cast. Hashem will heal it without plaster of paris." As a result, he had a permanent limp in his right leg.

It was an awesome experience to watch Reb Abbele pray. He stood at prayer literally as a servant would stand to the attention of his master. He recited Pesukei D'Zimrah word for word, with the utmost concentration. At Shema he fell on the floor under the table out of sheer trembling. There he would remain with his head between his legs for a quarter of an hour, until he had finished reciting Shema.

SAINTLY PERSONALITIES

Then he would jump up and continue to daven.

Being of low stature, when he passed a mezuzah he would enthusiastically jump up and kiss it with both hands. And he never slept on a mattress or used a pillow. Such was the behavior of the past generation's pious men.

Reb Abbele's son, Reb Moshe Eliezer Bochner, was a son-in-law of Reb Shalom Reb Baruchel's, who was an excellent *melamed*. A pupil of his once moved the clock five minutes ahead of time so that he could go home five minutes earlier. When Reb Shalom Reb Boruchel's found out later that he had finished giving lessons five minutes earlier, he cried out "*Gevalt!* My whole life I have been careful not to take a even a groschen from anybody, and now you go and make me in my old age a real thief. You will all have to learn five minutes longer today, so that I can pay back the lost five minutes to your fathers."

Reb Moishele Rubin

Among the many personalities who lived in Tsanz, one must not omit mention of Rabbi Moishele Rubin. He was a son of Rabbi Yitzchak Toivia and Rebbetzin Nechumele, a daughter of the Divrei Chaim. Rabbi Moishele Rubin lived with his mother in the apartment of his grandfather the Divrei Chaim. Reb Moishele was a respected personality, especially renowned for his goodheartedness. He was one of the rare citizens of Tsanz who had mastered the Polish language. He therefore had the distinguished position of metrical leader, the person officially responsible for registering the births of Jews in Tsanz. At one point, he was a serious candidate for the *rabbanus* in Tarnow. He also authored a *sefer*.

In the Tsanzer district, there were approximately 150 Jewish soldiers drafted in the army. Occasionally, the military officials would allow its Jewish soldiers to spend *yom tov* in Tsanz. It was a joy and an honor for a family to have a Jewish soldier as its guest. On Pesach night in particular, the men would vie for the privilege of inviting a Jewish soldier for the seder.

The Vanished City of Tsanz

In 5698 (1938), the chief general of the Tsanzer district refused the Jewish soldiers permission to partake of the seder at private families. Instead, he ordered a communal seder for the 150 soldiers to take place in the presence of himself and his officers. He was curious to see what exactly this much-spoken-of seder entailed.

Reb Moishele Rubin together with the Bobover Rav

This arrangement gave rise to a major problem: if gentiles were present at the seder, what would happen with the wine? How could one make Kiddush and drink the four cups on wine which the gentiles might touch? As a result, all the usual do-gooders in town were reluctant to volunteer to lead the seder.

Reb Moishele himself volunteered to solve the problem. He maintained that it was a *chillul haShem* to refuse the chief general's request, and it could very well be that the general would in his anger forbid the soldiers to leave their barracks on Pesach.

So it was that Reb Moishele led a festive seder for the soldiers in the orphanage of Mashler. He wisely avoided the problem of the wine

SAINTLY PERSONALITIES

by ordering the wine bottles and tumblers to be decorated with opaque red and white paper. Officially, the paper served to symbolize the red and white flag of Poland. This gesture left the chief general and his companions suitably impressed by the laudable patriotism of its Jews, who proudly displayed the Polish flag even at their seder.

After the seder was finished Reb Moishele asked the general if he had enjoyed it. "Yes, very much indeed," replied the officer. Reb Moishele asked him if he had any questions.

The general said, "I have a question that has been bothering me for a long time. When a Pole opens a grocery shop or any other business, another Pole will never open a shop selling the same article, in the same street, opposite his fellow. But when a Jew owns a shop, another Jew is very likely to open a shop selling the same products in that very street, heartlessly robbing him of his regular customers."

"A minister once asked a great *Rav* the very same question that you asked in even stronger terms," replied Reb Moishele. "I will answer you with the same reply that the *Rav* gave that minister.

"It was in the time of the Russian czar Nikolai. The Russian minister of education, Plevai, arranged a conference in Petersburg with all the great *rabbanim* of the time. The purpose of the meeting was to discuss the problems involving the Jews. The spokesmen for the *rabbanim* were the *ge'onim* Rabbi Yitzchak Elchanan Spector, Rabbi Chaim Brisker, and Rabbi Elya Chaim Meisels of Lodz.

"The minister of education, notorious for his anti-Semitism, began by deprecating the Jews with a variety of demeaning and unflattering comments. He pointed out that among all the nationalities to be found in Russia — Russians, Poles, Gruziner, Lithuanians, and Ukrainians — one would never find a gentile who would be ready to tear the last piece of bread from his colleague's mouth, as the Jews were wont to do. The gentile tailors, shoemakers, and ironmongers lived peacefully side by side, whereas the Jews thrived on fierce competition and would be ready to drown each other for the sake of a few coins! One Jew would open a shop, and soon ten other Jews would be selling the very same products. They were ready to tear each other to pieces for a couple of groschen. What a corrupt nation!

The Vanished City of Tsanz

"When Minister Plevai finished his hate-filled tirade, the Lodzer Rav, Rabbi Elya Meisels, spoke up.

" 'Esteemed Minister,' he began, 'I would like to pose a question. Have you ever wondered why animals do not devour one of its own species — a lion would not consume a lion, and a wolf would not kill a wolf — yet it is a common occurrence for fish to swallow each other alive?'

" 'Tell me why,' replied the minister, his curiosity aroused.

" 'It is because all other living creatures have the big, wide world at their disposal,' explained the *Rav*. 'The woods, the trees, the mountains, are free for them to romp in and search for food. They see an endless expanse of opportunity to satisfy their needs. The fish, however, are trapped in the sea. They cannot, and may not, leave their prison to reach dry land because they know it spells their death. Out of sheer hunger, they swallow each other alive, the stronger fish prevailing over the weaker.

" 'It is the same with us Jews. You gentiles are open to the opportunities which the whole of Russia has to offer. However, we Jews are enclosed in ghettos imposed by your government. We may not reside or trade on any other streets. What do you expect us to do?'

"The same applies to us," continued Rabbi Moishele Rubin. "In 5696 (1936), ritual slaughter was condemned, and a law was passed which officially boycotted the Jewish butcher shops. Large butcher shops were opened near the local Poles. In 5697 the government decreed that all businesses must display their name on a plaque outside their offices. This was so that the Jewish businesses could be easily recognized and avoided. Polish louts stand outside the Jewish shops, discouraging customers from patronizing the stores. *Nu*, what should the Jews do? They have no choice but to compete with the Jew next door."

This reply greatly appealed to the general's sense of justice. He was also well satisfied with the entertainment that had been provided for him and benignly allowed the soldiers to daven and share their meals in Tsanz the following morning and the next seder night and day. The Tsanzer Jews, too, were very grateful to Rabbi Moishele for his genius in solving this tricky problem.

SAINTLY PERSONALITIES

With the outbreak of war, Rabbi Moishele fled to Lemberg with his family. When the Russians invaded Lemberg, they offered all Jewish residents the option of adopting Russian citizenship. Rabbi Moishele chose not to accept it and was sent to Siberia along with others like him. It turned out that most of the Jews who opted for this alternative saved their lives, for more than half of those who were sent to Siberia survived the war, whereas those who remained in Lemberg were killed by the Nazis when Germany invaded East Galicia.

The last Tsanzer *rosh hakahal* Reb Shalom Yonah Tenzer's son, Reb Shlomo, who was exiled together with Rabbi Moishele Rubin, writes about Rabbi Moishele in his autobiography:

> I would like to put down on paper a scene in my memory which I will never forget. For it is something unforgettable, and it gives us something of an idea of how Polish-Jewish prisoners were treated by the Russians in Siberia.
>
> On the first day of Rosh HaShanah, I saw Rabbi Moishele Rubin, a direct grandchild of the saintly Divrei Chaim, walk past my window. He was wearing a torn silk *chalat* which was tied at the waist with a piece of string instead of a *gartel*. A giant ax was flung over his shoulder. Bitter tears streamed over his fine, handsome features and ran down his impressive white beard. At his side walked his *rebbetzin*, and from her eyes, too, flowed an incessant stream of tears.
>
> Can one ever forget such a sight?
>
> I was lying in my bed at the time, ill and very weak. When I saw the saintly Rabbi Moishele and his pious wife pass my window thus, I began weeping uncontrollably, and my fever became dangerously high.
>
> I was later told what had happened afterwards in the forest. The work brigades were usually dispersed throughout the dense forest, but on this day the workers defied officers' orders and gathered in one location. Together they davened while sawing wood. Rabbi Moishele was the *ba'al tefillah*. When he cried out the word "*hamelech*," all the people in unison cried out the word

"hamelech" after him. The Russians did not know what had hit them! Everybody davened as much as they remembered by heart. Rabbi Moishele recited the Shemoneh Esreh from memory, and they all said it after him with broken hearts and voices choking with emotion. The Russian guards, themselves prisoners, sympathized with their fellow exiles and tried to work with them as quickly as possible in order to complete the quota and be able to return to their barracks. The second day of Rosh HaShanah, the Russians remained behind, and only the Jews were sent to work. However, they did not do much work and returned home after a while.

In Elul 5702 (1942), many Polish Jews were released, among them Rabbi Moishele Rubin. Rabbi Moishele and the other Polish Jews settled in Dziambul, the largest and oldest town in Kazakhstan. There, Rabbi Moishele learned with the children the entire day. He did not take money; he lived on the parcels he received from the Hatzalah every month.

A few months before the war ended, Rabbi Moishele fell ill with typhus. He succumbed to the disease and passed away. Thousands of people attended his funeral, because he was beloved by Polish and Russian Jews alike. He was buried in the new cemetery in Dziambul.

The Lubliner Rav's Visit to Tsanz

In the year 5692 (1932), the *Rav* of Lublin and founder of Yeshivas Chachmei Lublin, Rabbi Meir Shapiro, came on a visit to Tsanz. He was given a royal welcome by the *Rav*, Rabbi Aryeh Leibish, and treated with fitting respect. Despite their differing opinions on many diverse affairs, the *Rav* ordered the *rosh hakahal*, Reb Shalom Yonah Tenzer, and his own Chassidim to greet the Lubliner Rav with great honor and to provide him with money for his yeshivah. The *rosh hakahal* faithfully fulfilled the *Rav*'s request on both counts.

The Lubliner Rav delivered a speech in shul to a packed audience. People stood on the windowsills in an attempt to catch his words. He

SAINTLY PERSONALITIES

gave a discourse on the subject of *chinnuch* of children. He based his speech on the *pesukim* of *parashas Bo*, where Moshe says to Pharaoh, "With our young and our old we will go, with our sons and daughters...to celebrate a festival for G-d." Pharaoh replies, "May G-d be with you as I send you and your children." Moshe did not mention the small children, but Pharaoh did, for he knew Moshe would not leave the children behind for fear that Pharaoh would convert them. Therefore Moshe said to Pharaoh "to celebrate a festival for G-d," implying that for a festival one needs the children, for without the children, it is no festival. "With our young and our old we will go" — the young must emulate and be educated by their elders.

Rabbi Meir Shapiro then went on to lament the plague of controversy. It bodes only evil, he declared, bringing proof from Yaakov Avinu. The *pasuk* in *parashas VaYeitzei* tells us, "And he took from the stones of the place and put them at his head." Rashi comments that the stones quarreled about who should lie under the *tzaddik*'s head. Hashem caused a miracle to happen, and they became one large stone. The question then arises: if Hashem had made a miracle with the stones, why did he not turn it into a cushion at the same time so that Yaakov Avinu could lie comfortably? "This teaches us," continued the Lubliner Rav, "that the result of a quarrel could only be a large stone, but certainly not a cushion."

When the Tsanzer Rav accompanied the Lubliner Rav to the door, the latter remarked, "Chazal tell us, 'A man should not depart from his friend without mentioning a halachah to him.' The first halachah in *Shulchan Aruch* is, 'Be strong as a lion to do the will of G-d.' I therefore bless you that you should be healthy and strong." This blessing was particularly suitable, for the Tsanzer Rav was named Aryeh, and he was very weak at the time.

After that the Lubliner Rav went to visit the *rebbetzin* Nechumele, the daughter of the saintly Divrei Chaim, who lived in her father's house.

As he entered the apartment he noticed the *zecher l'churban* opposite the door. He inquired of the *rebbetzin* whether this *zecher* had existed in the times of the Divrei Chaim. The *rebbetzin* answered in the affirmative, adding that the Divrei Chaim had knocked out the

The Vanished City of Tsanz

plaster to reveal the bricks underneath with his own hands. She went on to disclose the tale behind the deed.

The *tzaddik* Rabbi Hillel Kolomayer used to travel from place to place giving *mussar*. Once, during a stay in Tsanz, he paid a visit to the Divrei Chaim. The Tsanzer Rav said to him, "You may give me a bit of *mussar*, too."

Rabbi Hillel replied, "Rebbe, I have something to ask you. Where is the *zecher l'churban* which every Jew must have in his home?"

"You are right," replied the Divrei Chaim, and without delay he took a ladder and a hammer and set about knocking out a *zecher l'churban*.

The Lubliner Rav showed great interest in the story and commented, "It is a momentous occasion for me to be in the home of your holy father, the Tsanzer Rav, and to see with my own eyes that he positioned the *zecher l'churban* opposite the door, because there is a dispute in Gemara about this. The Gemara tells us that if a person paints his home, he should leave a part uncovered, as a remembrance of the Beis HaMikdash. Rabbi Chisda says that it must be opposite the door. The question is whether he meant above the door or facing the door. I am now convinced that he meant facing it. This is logical, for this way everybody who enters the house can see the *zecher l'churban*.

"We have a proof from *Bava Basra*," continued the Lubliner Rav. "The Gemara tells us that if a person discovers a palace which a *ger* had left as an inheritance (he had no children or relatives to inherit it), the *din* is that everybody who makes a *chazakah* in his property is *koneh* (acquires) it. Even a person who plasters a piece of wall in the house acquires it. How much must he plaster to acquire the house? Rabbi Yosef answers that one *amah* is enough. Rabbi Chisda adds that it must be opposite the door. The Rashbam says that it must be opposite the door because then it can be seen better.

"Since the Rashbam says that it must be opposite the door because it can be seen better, the same *din* applies to the *zecher l'churban*. But even so I still had my doubts. Now that I see what your father did I am happy to know that what I thought is right."

SAINTLY PERSONALITIES

The *rebbetzin* Nechumele related another story about Rabbi Hillel Kolomayer and her father, the Tsanzer Rav. Rabbi Hillel once resolved to travel to a small town infamous for its lowly inhabitants to deliver *mussar* there.

A night before his scheduled departure, Rabbi Hillel had a dream in which a person with a radiant countenance appeared before him and warned him not to visit the town, for its inhabitants had plotted to murder him if he would try to give them *mussar*.

The next morning Rabbi Hillel, who did not know the Tsanzer Rav at the time, told his friends of the dream, describing in detail the person who had spoken to him. His friends told him that, according to his description, the person who had come to him was without a doubt the saintly Tsanzer Rav. Rabbi Hillel decided there and then to travel immediately to the Tsanzer Rav.

As soon as he arrived in Tsanz he went in to see the Divrei Chaim. An awesome trembling gripped him when he saw, to his astonishment, that the person standing before him was the very person who had visited him in his dream and saved him from death!

(Part of this story was related to me in a letter from the Tzieshinover Rav of Brooklyn, Rabbi Shalom Yechezkel Shraga Rubin-Halberstam, a student of my father in Tsanz and a grandson of Rebbetzin Nechumele.)

Everything Needs Mazal

There is another interesting story about the visit of the Lubliner Rav, Rabbi Meir Shapiro, which I find appropriate to mention here.

There were six *melamdim* in the Tsanzer Talmud Torah. Two of them served the higher classes: Rabbi Hershel (known as "Tall Hershel") and Rabbi Shimon Yachtzel. Rabbi Shimon was a G-d-fearing person and an excellent *melamed*. Rabbi Hershel, on the other hand, was not very skilled in the field, although he was a great *talmid chacham* and very pious. It came to a point that the *menahel* of the Talmud Torah, Reb Shmuel Yaakov HaKohen Holtzer, was looking for an excuse to dismiss Tall Hershel from his position.

The Vanished City of Tsanz

When the Lubliner Rav visited Tsanz, he was invited by Reb Shmuel Yaakov Holtzer to tour the Talmud Torah and test the *talmidim*. The Lubliner Rav toured the classrooms with a distinguished crowd of escorts. I was in *cheder* at the time. Since we were learning *masseches Kiddushin*, Rabbi Meir Shapiro asked an exceptionally bright student by the name of Yechezkel Frankel, "Tell me, why did Reish Lakish shout here?" referring to a certain *gemara*.

We had not reached that part of the Gemara yet, and the boy did not understand the *Rav*'s question. Bewildered, he answered innocently that nobody had shouted. Of course, we boys found the incident highly amusing and broke out into laughter. Rabbi Shimon Yachtzel then explained to the Lubliner Rav that we had not yet reached that page in the *massechta*. However, the *Rav* was hard pressed for time, and he did not ask anymore questions in our class.

Rabbi Shalom Yonah Tenzer, the last *rosh hakahal*

The next classroom he visited was Tall Hershel's class. The Lubliner Rav asked, "Who can comment on the *sugyah* of '*Kovsah*'?" Tall Hershel pointed to his star pupil, Moshe Yehoshua Tzimmer of Keshanov, who had come to Tsanz to learn. He had a sharp mind and happened to know the *sugyah* of "*Kovsah*" extremely well. The boy gave an excellent discourse on the *sugyah* with which the *Rav* was well satisfied. He left it at that and did not test any other boys. Thus it turned out that Tall Hershel's pupils, who were on a relatively low standard, appeared to excel in their studies over the other students.

After this incident, the *menahel* of the Talmud Torah did not dare voice any further complaints against Tall Hershel. This was a true illustration of what our Sages tell us: "Everything depends on *mazal*, even a *sefer Torah* in the *heichal.*"

The Visit of the Gerrer Rebbe

In Menachem Av 5699 (1939), a month before the outbreak of the war, the Gerrer Rebbe, Rabbi Avraham Mordechai Alter, the Imrei Emes, made a stop in Tsanz on his way to Shtavnitz.

As the Rebbe stepped off the train, his traveling companions immediately set about seeking a car to take him to town. This was no mean feat, since there were very few automobiles available at that time. The Gerrer Rebbe requested that a hired wagon take him into town.

The Rebbe got onto the coach and asked the driver to lead him to the *Yiddishe Gass*. As they traveled through the cobbled roads, he ordered the driver to stop at the house where the Divrei Chaim used to live. The Imrei Emes remained seated in the coach and just looked at the Divrei Chaim's house in silence for a few minutes. Then he ordered the driver to ride back to the station, where his car was waiting. (The Gerrer Rebbe, Rabbi Pinchas Menachem Alter, *zt"l*, reminded me of this story when I visited him on 12 Elul 5748 [1988]. He had been with his father, the Imrei Emes, at the time.)

During his visit to Shtavnitz, the Gerrer Rebbe went for a walk with a crowd of his Chassidim. On the way they encountered a gentile driving a wagon loaded with hay. The sight of such a large crowd of Chassidim with beards and *payos* enraged the gentile, and he drove his horses directly into the crowd. However, the Gerrer Chassidim did not let themselves be treated this way. They jumped onto the wagon as one and gave the deserving malefactor a good beating.

Seeing that his deed had not turned out as intended, the hapless gentile began shouting, "Police!" When the police arrived, their initial reaction was to file a report against the Chassidim. However, a member of parliament, Reb Leibel Mintzberg, happened to be one of the crowd. He approached the police chief and introduced himself as a member of the Polish parliament. He politely explained what had

The Vanished City of Tsanz

actually occurred and demanded that justice be dealt. In actual fact, nothing ever became of it because war broke out a month after the incident.

When the Gerrer Rebbe was in Shtavnitz, he stayed in the same hotel as the last Tsanzer *rosh hakahal*, Reb Shalom Yonah Tenzer. The Rebbe showered him with honor. On Friday night he had Reb Shalom Yonah daven in front of the *amud*.

On Shabbos morning, only ten men were permitted to daven indoors with the Rebbe. Everyone else prayed in the garden. The Gerrer Rebbe ordered that Reb Shalom Yonah Tenzer join his minyan. Later, at the *tisch*, the Gerrer Rebbe said, "See what merit the town of the holy Divrei Chaim has to have such a Chassidic Jew as *rosh hakahal*." (It was rare for a Chassidic Jew to be *rosh hakahal* because he had to speak Polish fluently to be able to communicate with the government and town council.)

CHAPTER 11
JEWISH LIFE IN TSANZ

Der Yiddisher Gass

The center of Jewish life revolved around *der Yiddisher Gass*, "the Jewish Street." It was known in Polish as Kazimierza Street, named after Emperor Kasimir the Great. A spiritual atmosphere, such as one experiences in the streets of Jerusalem, reigned there.

The first house on *der Yiddisher Gass* was occupied by the current Tsanzer Rav. In my time, Rabbi Aryeh Leibish Halberstam lived there. After his passing, his son Rabbi Mordechai Zev Halberstam inherited the house together with his father's position.

The second house on the Jewish Street had belonged to the Divrei Chaim. It was later occupied by his daughter, the pious and wise Rebbetzin Nechumele, and her husband, Rabbi Yitzchak Toivia Rubin. Rabbi Yitzchak Toivia had his *beis midrash* there. It was known as "Rabbi Yitzchak Toivia's *beis midrash*" or "the Bobover *beis midrash*," since the Bobover Chassidim davened there before acquiring their own two Bobover *shtieblach*. It was in that *beis midrash* that the Divrei Chaim himself used to daven.

The next building housed the Gribover *beis midrash*, where the Tsanzer *rabbanim* — the Kreiser Rav, Rabbi Aharon; Rabbi Aryeh Leibish; and Rabbi Mordechai Zev — davened. It was a very large *beis midrash*, boasting some five to six hundred congregants. This impressive building had been donated by the Neugroschl family of Vienna.

The Vanished City of Tsanz

Once, the Divrei Chaim undertook to collect a large amount of money in order to marry off an orphan, the daughter of a *talmid chacham*. When the Neugroschl family offered to donate the entire amount, the Divrei Chaim was overjoyed, and he blessed them with riches and prosperity for all future generations. Indeed, his blessing materialized, and they became very wealthy. They always remained steadfast supporters of the Tsanzer *rabbanim* and their children. (This

Kazimierza Street, also known as *"der Yiddishe Gass"*

story was related to me by Reb Chaim Falik's Kernkraut, who used to write the *kvittel*s the people gave to the Kreiser Rav, Rabbi Aharon.)

The Batei Midrash

The *Rav*'s *beis midrash* did not have pillars to support the large women's section, as was the norm; instead it was supported by strong steel girders. These girders were sent by train from the Neugroschl family in Vienna especially for the *beis midrash*. When the train arrived with the steel girders, the entire town went to the station to witness the unloading of this fascinating material.

JEWISH LIFE IN TSANZ

I still remember when electric lights were installed in the Gribover *beis midrash*. The year was 5690 (1930). The walls of the *beis midrash* were so thick that it took a considerable amount of time until a hole was bored through them to install the electric wires. Although electricity had been introduced in Tsanz in the winter of 5671 (1911), the same year that the sewage system was put in place, it was only the very wealthy who could afford it. Electricity only became available to the general public twenty years later.

Most homes, including mine, were illuminated by paraffin lamps. These gave off a relatively strong light, since the people could afford only weak electric bulbs. In the whole of the large Gribover *beis midrash* there were only ten electric light bulbs. When people with poor eyesight or the elderly wanted to learn they would put a candle on the table next to their *sefer*, just as they did before electricity was brought into the *beis midrash*. Paraffin lamps were never used in a *beis midrash* because of the bad smell; it was either candles or electricity.

On Shabbos the *batei midrash* were beautifully illuminated by big chandeliers called *"hengel leichters."* Together with the electric light bulbs they gave off a bright light and a *Shabbosdiger ta'am*. In the large Gribover *beis midrash* there were ten such chandeliers, each one

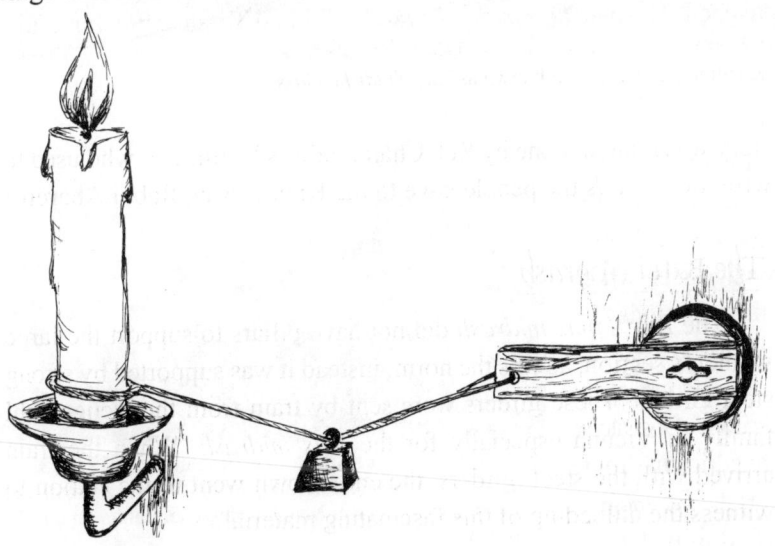

A Tsanzer Shabbos clock

The Vanished City of Tsanz

holding fifteen candles.

It is interesting how the Shabbos clock in the *beis midrash* operated. A piece of wood was placed on a switch. A string was tied to one side of the wood. In the middle of the string hung a weight, and a ring was attached at the other end. This ring was put onto a candle that stood nearby. When the candle burnt down till where the ring was placed, the wax melted and the ring fell down. This caused the weight to drop, pulling down the wood, which made the switch turn, extinguishing the electric lamp.

Another sort of Shabbos clock featured a piece of string tied to the winder of an alarm clock. A nail which formed a circuit with the wire of the lamp was tied to the other end. When the winder slowly turned, the nail was pulled up and thus contact was lost and the light extinguished.

Most *batei midrash* in Tsanz were built on a corner so that the entrance to the men's and women's sections were on different streets.

The Shinover *beis midrash* was also situated on the *Yiddisher Gass*. It boasted a large number of congregants. Nearby were two Bobover *shtieblach* in which a few hundred Chassidim davened. Next was the Chassidic *beis midrash* in which the Piekeler Rav, Rabbi Shalom, a son of the Kreiser Rav and a brother of the Tsanzer Rav Rabbi Aryeh Leibish, davened. The next *beis midrash* was the Talmud Torah. After that came the *beis midrash* Chevrah Shomrim, then the *beis midrash* Chevrah Tehillim and the town's official synagogue, which still exists today.

There were ten *batei midrash* in the *Yiddisher Gass* alone. In addition, there was the *beis midrash* of Rabbi Chuna

In the Beis Nassan shul on Lag Ba'Omer 5753 (1993). From right to left: Leibel Strassman, Jacob Miller, Zalman Lehrer, Leser Strassman, Mayer Mandel, Herschel Lehrer, and Rabbi N. Kornwasser

JEWISH LIFE IN TSANZ

Hersh Rubin of Sakmar; the building of the Reb Benzion'lech; the Yad Charutzim, a minyan for the laborers; Beis Nassan, which still exists today; and Chevrah Shloimelech. More *batei midrash* existed on the Piekela and in other places in town.

It is incomprehensible to me to this very day that, at a time when the general population lived in dire poverty and were cramped in tiny living quarters, they managed to build large, magnificent *batei midrash* and shuls. This illustrates the great *mesirus nefesh* our parents had for a mitzvah.

The Jewish Hospital

In the year 5668 (1908), a longed-for dream was finally realized: after many years of effort and struggle, a Jewish hospital was opened. Situated on Kraszewskiego Street, the hospital was a true salvation for Jewish invalids, who would otherwise have been placed in a gentile hospital, where a large cross was prominently hung opposite each bed.

The hospital was made up of two stories, with four large, airy wards. Each ward had eight beds. In addition, there were several consulting rooms for doctors, a small operating theater, a laboratory, and a kitchen. Adjoining the hospital was a smaller building with twelve beds for patients suffering from contagious diseases. The hospital had a large, scenic garden dotted with benches for those patients whose conditions permitted them to stroll in the fresh air.

The Jewish hospital was active until the outbreak of World War I in 5674 (1914). At that point, the community leaders were forced to close it down due to financial difficulties. The building became neglected and was in dire need of repair and maintenance. The final blow came when the waters of the Kamienica River rose and flooded the town. It tore down entire houses and uprooted trees. The hospital, too, suffered vast damage when the waters tore away parts of its sturdy walls of cement and iron. The waters entered through a window and seeped into the foundation, so that the very structure was in danger of collapsing.

Thus stood the sad remains of the building for many long years, until 5696 (1936), when Reb Shalom Yonah Tenzer was elected *rosh hakahal*. Reb Shalom Yonah, when campaigning before the elections, promised that the hospital would be rebuilt if he would win the seat. He indeed kept his promise.

The money for rebuilding was not taken from the communal treasury; a separate fund was set apart for this purpose. The town's wealthy philanthropists donated tidy sums for this cause as well. The two brothers Leibele and Berel Kinderman, who were building contractors, greatly assisted in rebuilding the hospital. They also undertook the rebuilding of the northern wall of the town's official shul, which still stands today. The refurbishing took two years and was completed just before the outbreak of World War II. The hospital proved to be of vital service in the war.

The small building nearby which had served as the ward for contagious diseases was turned into a *hachnasas orchim* home by Reb Avraham David Shiff. Reb Avraham David would tour the *batei midrash* at night and invite all the poor people who did not have anywhere to go to his *hachnasas orchim* home. There they received something to eat and drink. He personally helped them wash themselves before going to sleep. This was indeed a remarkable kindness, for many paupers bore an offensive odor from months of travel from not having washed their lice-infested bodies. Reb Avraham David and his good-hearted family washed, cleaned, and changed the bedding of the *hachnasas orchim* home every day.

Rosh HaKahal

According to an age-old Austrian law, the Austrian government was in total control of the lives of its Jewish citizens. The Jews were given the right to create a committee in the capital city of every province. The committee was named *"der Judishen Kultus Gemeinde"* (the Jewish Culture Committee). The committee consisted of twelve men and a president, the *rosh hakahal*, who was also the official spokesman and representative of the Jews of that town and its surrounding regions.

JEWISH LIFE IN TSANZ

The committee and its *rosh hakahal* was elected every four years by all the members of the Jewish community who held voting rights. Its duties included voting and supplying an income for a *Rav*, *dayanim*, and *shochetim*; providing for a shul, mikveh, cemetery, and other religious needs; maintaining a Talmud Torah and yeshivah; and supporting the poor and needy, especially before Pesach. The committee also usually supported a Jewish hospital, an old-age home, and an orphanage.

In order to cover its expenditures, the committee was entitled to levy a tax on all the animals and fowl which were slaughtered and on all the income of the cemetery. The committee also had a right to tax all the Jews, each according to what he could afford. The committee's budget had to be approved by the town officials.

After the first World War, Poland became independent. Up until then it had comprised several territories which were under the governorship of three kingdoms: Austria, Russia, and Germany. Each of these regimes established their own laws concerning the Jews. Generally speaking, the Polish government adopted the Austrian *Kultus Gemeinde* law, with minor alterations.

According to Polish law, the committee was divided into two bodies: the advisory board and the acting council. The advisory board established the budget and appointed employees in accordance with the acting council's recommendation. The acting council took charge of administrative duties. The chairman of the acting council was the *rosh hakahal*.

The *Rav* was a permanent member of the acting council. The committee did not have the right to

Galician wayside encounter, 5655 (1895)

accept an application from a *dayan* or *shochet* without the *Rav*'s prior approval.

Every Jew, even those who had not paid the community tax, had a right to vote for committee members. The one exception was those who were employed or supported by the committee, for they were obviously biased. The elections needed the approval of the ministry as well as the committee.

The position of *rosh hakahal* was recognized by Polish government officials. It was usually occupied by a doctor or lawyer, because he had to be well versed in the Polish language in order to be able to communicate with the officials.

Moshe Efraim Gottlieb, a Tsanzer chazzan

In Tsanz, Dr. Steinmetz was the second-to-last *rosh hakahal*. His deputy was Reb Ellish Klapholtz. Although Dr. Steinmetz was the official *rosh hakahal*, it was Reb Ellish who was generally accepted as having the position. Dr. Steinmetz knew that he owed his having been elected to the Chassidic Jews, and he therefore willingly obliged with whatever the *Rav* and his committee requested.

At the last elections of the committee, in the year 5696 (1936), Reb Shalom Yonah Tenzer campaigned for the position. He was one of the wealthiest Jews in Tsanz. In addition, he was a *talmid chacham* and well versed in the Polish language, thus capable of communicating with the Polish officials. Reb Shalom Yonah was elected for the position of *rosh hakahal*. This was a historic event, because it had been many years since the *rosh hakahal* sported a beard and *payos*. He was among the very few Chassidic *roshei hakahal* in Galicia.

Unfortunately, Reb Shalom Yonah Tenzer was the last *rosh hakahal* in Tsanz. On Monday, *erev Sukkos* 5699 (1939), he summoned the committee members to a meeting and announced his resignation, since the position exposed him to great danger. With that he adjourned the last meeting of the Tsanzer committee.

Reb Shalom Yonah moved away from Tsanz, to Lemberg. There he perished with all the other Lemberg Jews.

The Mikveh

The mikveh was situated at the bottom of a hill at the end of the *Yiddisher Gass*. It was at the foot of the castle's fortress, close to the Dunajec River. The Divrei Chaim himself *kashered* the mikveh and used it regularly all his life. His children, grandchildren, and all the Chassidim used that mikveh as well. Today the place is a field overgrown with grass and weeds. There is no sign of the mikveh which was once there. It has been wiped out, together with the other houses and *batei midrash* of the glorious dynasty of Tsanz which once was.

The mikveh boasted a sauna which operated on *erev Shabbos* and *yom tov*. The sauna had steps going up; the higher one ascended, the more intense the steam became. The steam was created by a huge oven in the cellar which heated the stones adjoining the sauna room. A gentile poured boiling hot water on the stones to generate the steam.

It was impossible to heat the mikveh entirely since the mikveh was connected to a spring. The water from the spring entered the mikveh via a large hole. When hot water was poured into the mikveh it immediately escaped through the hole. The mikveh was heated by a huge tank above the pool. Attached to the tank was a long pipe which was suspended above the water. Hot water was poured into the pool every hour, but this served to keep the water warm for a short time only. One could see that the mikveh was in direct contact with the spring because when it had rained and the water had risen, the waters of the mikveh rose, too.

During the *yamim tovim*, when more than two thousand people used the mikveh, the mikveh waters were as thick as broth by the second day of *yom tov*! This did not deter the Chassidim from using it before davening. When the second day of *yom tov* was on Friday, however, the Chassidim did not go to the mikveh Friday afternoon in honor of Shabbos.

The mikveh was divided into two, the second half being set aside for women's use. The entrance to the women's mikveh was on a different street. On Friday the women's mikveh was used by the men as the "better class" section.

There was another mikveh in town, known as the "Schreibers baths." The Chassidim did not use this since it was not under the jurisdiction of the *Rav*, and it did not use springwater.

A third mikveh, on the Piekela, was under the jurisdiction of the *Rav* and was used by Chassidim who lived on the Piekela and in other areas far from the Divrei Chaim's mikveh.

Shabbos

Before the war, the city of Tsanz had a population of thirty-five thousand, a third of which were Jewish. The majority of Jews were Chassidim, who were mainly concentrated in the center of town. Most of the upper-class streets, including the street bordering the marketplace, were inhabited by Jews. Friday night, an hour before candle lighting, the sound of hundreds of shop shutters being slammed shut resounded through the streets. The atmosphere of the coming of Shabbos permeated every corner. Hundreds of Jews were seen making their way to the *mikva'os*. Jews of all ages, *tzitzis* flying behind them, went scurrying through the streets carrying covered pots containing steaming cholent and kugel to the bakers who would keep the food warm in their tremendous ovens.

In Tsanz there was a Chevrah Shemiras Shabbos whose duty it was to ensure that all the shops were closed on time. *Minchah* was davened half an hour after candle-lighting time. No earlier *minyanim* were arranged, even on the late summer nights.

Most towns and villages in Galicia had an *eiruv*, and Tsanz was no exception. The *kehillah* had appointed a *mashgiach*, Reb Mendel Peterfreund, to ensure that the *eiruv* was still intact. On Shabbos afternoon Reb Mendel inspected the *eiruv* again. If it was broken, the *mashgiach* went to the *gabbaim* of all the *batei midrash* in town. Each *gabbai* announced in his *beis midrash* that the *eiruv* was broken and that it was forbidden to carry until further notice.

I once asked my father why he did not carry on Shabbos. Did he feel the *eiruv* was not kosher? He answered that there was no question that the *eiruv* was kosher according to all opinions. The reason why he and others did not carry was because one might transgress Shabbos by accident if the *eiruv* broke on Shabbos. This could happen in Poland, where the *goyim* would purposefully tear down the *eiruv*.

The *batei midrash* and Chassidic *shtieblach* were filled to overflowing on Shabbos and *yom tov*. It was sheer pleasure to hear the beautiful melodies coming from the Gribover, Bobover, and Shinover *batei midrash*. They had especially stirring tunes for *"Lecha Dodi"* and *"Keil Adon."* Every few weeks they would replenish their repertoire of tunes.

The town synagogue boasted an excellent cantor, Reb Moshe Efraim Gottlieb. He was also a very pious Jew. The davening there was lively and resonant, accompanied by clapping of the hands at opportune moments.

On Friday night an unbraided challah, called a *koilish*, was served; on Shabbos morning a braided challah was eaten. My father told me that the reason was because one had to honor the daytime meal more, and the braided challah was nicer.

In every household, *zemiros* were sung after each course, whereas at the *tisch* of the Rebbes the *zemiros* were sung only after the meat was served. The Shinover Rav, author of *Divrei Yechezkel*, once asked his son-in-law Rabbi Naftali Rubin, Vizhnitzer Rav in Galicia, "Why don't you sing between courses?" The Vizhnitzer Rav later remarked that he understood from those words that he would not become Rebbe. It was indeed so; he never acted as Rebbe, but his son, the above-mentioned Rabbi Chuna Hersh, did.

The Pshevorsker Rebbe, *shlita*, recalls that when the Fristiker Rebbetzin, the *tzaddeikes* Feige Baila Halberstam, a daughter of the Shinover Rav, was on a visit in the village of Yashlitzk, she advised the women to say the following short *tefillah* on Shabbos and *yom tov* morning: *"Ribbono shel olam*, give me, forgive me, and do not take

The Vanished City of Tsanz

from me." After this, she counseled, they should make Kiddush on a mug of coffee.

On the long winter Friday nights, the *bachurim* would meet in the *batei midrash* and learn together. The older *bachurim* would test their younger counterparts and learn Chassidic *sefarim* on the *sidrah* with them. This would be followed by the singing of Shabbos *zemiros*. In the summer, when the windows were open, the beautiful, moving melodies coming from the Tsanz, Bobov, and Shinova *batei midrash* blended together. It was sheer bliss to walk through the streets and hear the resulting effect.

The men used to go to the *rebbishe tischen,* and when they were over they met in the *batei midrash*. Some of them would learn *Chumash* with *Rashi* and *Or HaChaim HaKadosh*. Others would attend *shiurim* such as my father's on *Chumash* with *Alshich*.

Almost all the *batei midrash* commenced davening on Shabbos morning between nine and nine-thirty. There was one exception, however: a small minyan known as the *"hashkamah minyan* of Rabbi Nuta Shlomo Shlussel." They davened at the break of dawn. Generally speaking, the *batei midrash* finished davening between twelve and one midday. The honor of taking out and putting back the *sefer Torah* was given only

The fish street

to a *gabbai* of a charity institute. During *minchah* on Shabbos, those who were given an *aliyah* were not called by name. The *gabbai* would approach the person and request him to go up to the *sefer Torah*. The *Rav* was always given *hagba'ah* at *minchah* on Shabbos.

After *minchah*, everybody would go home to wash for *se'udah shelishis*. After *minchah* no one would greet another with *"gut Shabbos"* anymore. After eating at home, the people would make their way back to the *beis midrash* before *bentching*. They would take along a piece of challah, which they would eat in the *beis midrash* and then *bentch. se'udah shelishis* was always eaten in the dark. The *zeman* for *motza'ei Shabbos* was kept according to the ruling of Rabbeinu Tam. After *ma'ariv*, the *Rav* made Havdalah in the *beis midrash*. Every week he would honor another person with leading the singing of *"HaMavdil."*

Shamashim

In every *beis midrash*, where people learned all day, one would have a snack at the *kremel*. This was a sort of mini-snack bar which

The Dzikover Rav, the Imrei No'am's *gabbai*, together with Tsanzer Jews in Vienna

The Vanished City of Tsanz

was run by the *shamash* of the *beis midrash*. Every *shamash* had the right to open a *kremel* and keep the profits. There were *kremelech* in Bobov, Shinova, Sakmar, Reb Chuna Hersh's *beis midrash*, and in the large Gribover *beis midrash*, where the Tsanzer Rav used to daven.

The *shamash* of the Gribover *beis midrash* was Zelig Landau. He sold tea and *yablonik*, a drink made from dried pears boiled in water. To make the tea he used a big tea urn called a samovar. This was heated with wood coals. From time to time, the whole *beis midrash* was full of smoke until the wood coals would ignite.

He also used to sell strawberry ice cream. Since Zelig didn't have a machine to make the ice cream, he had to use the services of his daughter Taube. She would sit for hours hidden away in a corner of the corridor of the Gribover *beis midrash*, turning the wooden handle of the mixer, which was a sort of bowl within a bowl. The outer bowl was packed with ice, and the inner bowl was full of mashed strawberries. Ever so often her father would come to see how she was getting on. One portion of the ice cream cost ten groshen, but not everyone was able to afford such a luxury, even for so low a price.

The *shamash* also sold small pies. These were filled with large, cooked raisins and a little cinnamon, which the *shamash*'s wife used to cook. She would use the water in which she cooked the raisins for the dough, so that one could make the *berachah borei minei mezonos* on the pies.

In 5698 (1938) Mr. Hershel Stein came from America on a visit to his hometown Tsanz. When Hershel was in the Gribover *beis midrash*, Zelig Shamash invited him to try his ice cream. While Hershel was in the middle of eating the ice cream Zelig asked him, "What do you think of my merchandise?"

Hershel answered, "Wonderful! In the whole of America there does not exist such good ice cream." He paid more than he was asked. Zelig was very satisfied and proud that ice cream was a novelty even in America.

Hershel Stein returned to Tsanz a year later. When he missed the last train out of Tsanz, even his American passport did not help him. Until 1941 he was kept in a special house in the ghetto with a large sign on the front door on which was written, "American citizen." Before Pesach they told him that he would be taken to the camp in Salzburg, Austria, where all the Americans were being kept till after

Vizhnitza, Galicia, 5660 (1900)

the war. They even allowed him to take matzos with him.

An S.S. man, Lapitski, was meant to accompany him there. The day after he left the ghetto the S.S. murderers sent a telegram stating the Mr. Stein had died of a heart attack.

Reb Lemil Shamash

Reb Lemil served as *shamash* in Tsanz until his passing in the year 5694 (1934). Every Friday night before candle lighting, he would go to the main shul and the *batei midrash* on the Jewish Street and knock three times with a wooden hammer to remind everybody that Shabbos was approaching.

Reb Lemil Shamash also awakened the townspeople on the first day of Selichos, *erev Rosh HaShanah*, and the day before *erev Yom Kippur*. At 3 A.M. he would call out in a sweet, singsong chant, "*Yiddelech, Yiddelech*, arise for Selichos. Get up for *avodas haBorei*." His soft voice pierced the stillness of the night, waking everyone in a pleasant manner.

The Vanished City of Tsanz

Collecting Money

It was customary for the yeshivos to send out their *bachurim* and young boys to collect money in the *batei midrash* during Selichos and davening. Many of the men were none too happy about this, for it disturbed their prayers, yet the custom was maintained, since it had been introduced by the Divrei Chaim.

When I was a young boy, even before my bar mitzvah, I was already sent to collect money for *tzedakah* during Selichos. I asked my father, Rabbi Nosson Mordche, "Why am I sent to collect at such a young age? I am not even bar mitzvah yet, and, owing to my size, I am more often than not merely brushed aside so that I do not disturb the Selichos. I end up with very little money, so why am I sent at all?"

"You are not only sent to procure money," replied my father. "The purpose of sending you is so that when, G-d willing, you grow up and Hashem will help you to be able to give, you will think back and empathize with the feelings of the poor person who must stretch out his hand in request for a donation."

Elul and Tishrei

With the conclusion of the month of Av, the atmosphere of the time designated for *teshuvah* could already be sensed. The awe and trepidation for the Day of Judgment was clearly visible on the drawn faces of the townspeople during the month of Elul.

Yom Kippur Katan was only said on *erev Rosh Chodesh Elul*. A recently published *sefer* stated that Yom Kippur Katan was said in Tsanz on *erev Rosh Chodesh Nissan*. This is an error; nobody in Tsanz but Bobover Chassidim said Yom Kippur Katan then.

Beginning on Rosh Chodesh Elul, eighteen chapters of Tehillim were said every day. However, *"L'David Hashem Ori"* was not said in Tsanz. On the first day of Selichos, *erev Rosh HaShanah*, and the day before *erev Yom Kippur*, the people awoke at 3 A.M. The entire Tehillim was then recited. This took two hours, until 5 A.M., when Selichos commenced.

JEWISH LIFE IN TSANZ

On Rosh HaShanah, the entire town turned out to wish the *Rav* a good year. The poor said *shehecheyanu* on red melon, since this was the cheapest fruit. Wealthier people would buy grapes or pineapple.

Davening commenced at 7:30 A.M. on Rosh HaShanah. *Shacharis* and *leining* were finished by twelve, after which there was an hour break. During this time the *Rav*, as official *Rav* of the town, would blow shofar in the main shul. After the break, *mussaf* began. It ended at about 5 P.M. The *se'udah* was hurriedly eaten, and then we went back to the *beis midrash* in time for *minchah* and Tashlich. It was a wondrous sight to see thousands of Jews making their way to the two rivers which flowed in Tsanz.

On the day before *erev Yom Kippur*, all the *korbanos* were read from a *sefer Torah*. After this reading, the Shinover Chassidim would go to Tashlich.

On *erev Yom Kippur* there was a great hustle and commotion in the Jewish Street. There were many things to be seen to. First came *kapparos shloggen*. The *shochetim* would spend the night making their rounds of the *rabbanim* and other distinguished people to slaughter their chickens so that they would be able to fulfill the mitzvah of *kisui hadam*. At dawn, the *shochetim* slaughtered the *kapparos* of the remaining townspeople in the courtyard of the Tsanzer Rav. Hundreds of Jews came with their own *kapparos* so that they, too, could fulfill the mitzvah of *kisui hadam*.

Then there was the clamor for the mikveh. Hundreds of Jews, young and old, crowded the small mikveh area. The custom was to immerse three times on *erev Yom Kippur*: in the morning, before *minchah*, and after the *se'udah hamafsekes*, before Kol Nidrei.

Sounds of well-wishing could be heard from all directions: *"Ir zolt eich oisbeten a git gebentcht yar mit a gemar chasimah tovah."* In Tsanz, *erev Yom Kippur* was the only time when people would shake hands. (When a stranger came from another town, they would also extend their hands.)

Finally, there was the rush for Kol Nidrei. Thousands of Jews, men, women, and children, streamed toward the *beis midrash* in time for the *tefillah*. The *batei midrash* were filled to capacity.

The Vanished City of Tsanz

First, Tefillas Zakkah was recited. Then the people would beg forgiveness from each other for any sins they might have committed and wish each other that their *tefillos* would be accepted. After that, Kol Nidrei began.

As mentioned above, Rabbi Moshe Efraim Gottlieb, the cantor of the town shul, was a G-d-fearing person as well as an excellent chazzan. He learned his profession in Odessa under the auspices of religious *chazzanim*. The townspeople flocked to the shul during the breaks between *shacharis* and *mussaf* of Rosh HaShanah and Yom Kippur to hear him daven *Malchiyos, Zichronos*, and *Shofros*. People were especially eager to hear him daven *"U'Nesaneh Tokef"* and *"K'Vakaras Ro'eh Edro,"* whose tunes he composed himself. His melodies were interwoven with piety and fear of G-d.

After Yom Kippur everybody wished each other, *"Ir zolt hobben alles gits oisgebeten."* The next morning, and up until Hoshana Rabbah, everybody wished each other *"a git kvittel."* Before breaking their fast, they blessed the new moon. Immediately after eating something, the townspeople set to work constructing their sukkos. The Poles knew that *motza'ei Yom Kippur* was the time to drive through the Jewish Street with wagons piled high with *sechach*.

The buying and selling of *esrogim* began. The windows on the Jewish Street were splashed with huge notices displaying large signs: *"Esrogim, lulavim,* and *hadasim* can be purchased here at very reasonable prices."

All the children of the Talmud Torah and *chadarim* were occupied with creating decorations for the sukkah. The *yeshivah bachurim* especially worked long and hard to construct master creations for the *rebbishe* sukkos of Tsanz, Bobov, and Shinov. Their efforts were richly rewarded, for under the beautiful, impressive *ushpizin* and other decorations which they had crafted, their names were proudly displayed. There was fierce competition among the Chassidim, each determined that their Rebbe should have the most beautiful sukkah in Tsanz. People would visit the *rebbishe* sukkos to determine which was the most tastefully decorated.

The custom was to wash for *se'udas yom tov* every day of the holiday, even on Chol HaMo'ed. Those who bore the name of the day's *ushpizin* placed wine before the *rabbanim* in honor of the *ushpizin*. The last two days traditionally belonged to two *shochetim*: Rabbi Yosef Herbst and Rabbi David Appel. They would give farfel and kishke in honor of their *ushpizin*. During *minchah* of *yom tov* it was customary to "make a *rekidah*" (dance) when the second half of "*Aleinu*" was said ("*V'al kein nekaveh...*"). The custom to make a *rekidah* was also followed on Shabbos Chol HaMo'ed, during "*Bo'i b'shalom...*" of "*Lecha Dodi.*"

The Tsanzer Rav used to hold a *tisch* on Shemini Atzeres. First *minchah* was davened, then bottles of wine were placed on the table. The names of all the wine *shtellers* — people who had donated the bottles of wine — were announced. The *Rav* then distributed the wine to all the people assembled. Afterwards they broke out into enthusiastic dancing and singing. In this manner, they escorted the *Rav* into the shul to where they danced *hakafos*. In shul, *ma'ariv* was davened (except for the *Rav* and his Chassidim, who davened *ma'ariv* in his *beis midrash* a little later), then they danced *hakafos*. There were fifty *sifrei Torah* in the shul, which were distributed among the congregation. The entire Chassidic assembly danced with great fervor and joy.

The *hakafos* proceeded according to the Tsanzer *nosach*. Before the dancing commenced, the people encircled the *bimah* with the *sifrei Torah*. The *sifrei Torah* were then set aside on a table, and the dancing began. Nobody but the *Rav* held a *sefer Torah* in his arms during all the *hakafos*.

After the *hakafos* the reading from the Torah took place — not from *V'Zos HaBerachah* but from the parashah of Yaakov and Eisav. Then the assembly led the *Rav*, amidst singing and rejoicing, to his own *beis midrash*. There the *Rav* davened *ma'ariv* and began dancing the seven *hakafos* again. By now it was 11 P.M.

The *Rav* would dance at the southern side of the *beis midrash* with a small *sefer Torah* in his arms. He alone danced in motion whilst the boys and youths encircled him, watching him dance. At the same time they sang and clapped their hands. Only the married men danced around the *bimah*. Each *hakafah* had its own special tune, which was sung only at the *hakafos*. During the year, too, only the *Rav* sang the special *rebbishe* tunes. After each *hakafah*, a person with a musical voice was selected to sing one of the tunes designated for *hakafos*.

The *hakafos* lasted until 2 A.M. Afterwards, the *Rav* was escorted home, where he washed for the *yom tov* meal. The *Rav* never held his *tischen* in the *beis midrash*, but in his own home, which was the custom of most Galician Rebbes.

On Simchas Torah eve the *Rav* would throw apples to the people. They would catch these apples and keep them as a *segulah* for many good things.

Shovevim

All the *batei midrash* of Chassidei Tsanz, Bobov, and Shinova were filled to capacity on Thursday nights in the weeks of *Shovevim*. The sound of Torah learning resounded throughout the night, the sweet voices of youth blending with the deeper voices of the adults. Even the workers who had to stand the next day in the marketplace with their bundles of wares so that they could earn some money for Shabbos learned the entire night. One person would learn *Chok L'Yisrael*, another would learn Gemara, and a third would say Tehillim. The younger *bachurim* reviewed the Gemara they had learned during the week. The older *bachurim* learned in pairs. This would continue until *parashas Mishpatim*, except in a leap year, when it went on for two more weeks until *parashas Tetzaveh*.

Deep in the night, the Tsanzer Rav Rabbi Aryeh Leibish, and later, his son Rabbi Mordechai Zev, would come into the *beis midrash* and stroll past the tables where the men were learning. Thus he infused the *bachurim* with renewed enthusiasm to continue learning.

At 2 A.M. the young *bachurim* went to the baker, Reb David Leib, a goodhearted fellow. He would donate freshly baked *beigelach* to the deserving young boys who had stayed up learning.

Shavuos

The *ba'al tefillah* sang *"Ahavas Olam"* at *ma'ariv*. Though the men had been up all night saying *Tikkun Leil Shavuos*, *shacharis* was at 9:30 A.M. as usual. At daybreak they would go to the mikveh, then go home to sleep until *shacharis*. After *mussaf*, Kiddush was recited, and cheesecake and cheese *kreplach* were served. After half an hour elapsed, we washed for a *se'udas yom tov* of fish and meat. When *yom tov* fell out on Shabbos, those who lived near a *beis midrash* separated their meal into two parts by davening *minchah*, so the second part of the meal would be considered *se'udah shelishis*.

A Hachnasas Sefer Torah

The sheer joy which accompanied a *hachnasas sefer Torah* is difficult to portray. The entire town, men, women, and children, turned out to take part in the *simchah*. Two candles in silver or copper candlesticks burned at every window on the streets through which the *sefer Torah* was carried. When the *sefer Torah* arrived at the *Yiddisher Gass*, it was met by men dancing with the other *sifrei Torah* in their hands and by children carrying burning torches. All the *hachnasas sifrei Torah* took place at night, to show honor for the Torah, since the sight was much more magnificent in the darkness.

There was one exception to this rule. In 5691 (1931), a *sefer Torah* was given on Shavuos day, before the Torah reading. The *sefer Torah*, written by the pious Reb Binyamin Flaster, was tiny, a mere thirty centimeters long. It was presented by Reb Efraim Halberstam, a son of the Tsanzer Rav Rabbi Aryeh Leibish to his father's *beis midrash* in memory of his only daughter, Chana Elka, who passed away on 2 Iyar 5689 (1929) at the age of eighteen. Reb Efraim especially ordered the *sefer Torah* to be made so small so that his father, Rabbi Aryeh Leibish, being weak in his old age, would be able to dance the *hakafos* with it. The *sefer Torah* was called "the *Rav*'s *sefer Torah*."

The *sefer Torah* miraculously survived the war and is now in the Divrei Chaim *beis midrash* in Jerusalem, owned by the Tchakover

Rebbe, Rabbi Naftali Halberstam, *shlita*. (Others say that this is actually an older *sefer Torah*, dating back to the days of the Divrei Chaim himself.)

(As a side note, Mr. Yechezkel Blumenfrucht, who lived in Antwerp and experienced the horrors of the concentration camps together with me, told me that he had been among the last Jews to be deported from Cracow and had tried to save the Rema's *sefer Torah*. They had taken the *sefer Torah* to a person named Glanzer, whose son lives today in Kiryas Yoel, Monroe. He possessed a Czechoslovakian passport, and they assumed that this would protect him from deportation. When they realized that if you were a Jew it made no difference to the murderers what nationality you were, they handed the *sefer Torah* to a priest for safekeeping. Reb Yechezkel maintains that the *sefer Torah* must still be concealed somewhere today.)

A Rebbishe Chasunah

In Tsanz, a *rebbishe simchah* was everybody's *simchah*. A typical example was when Nechumele, the Divrei Chaim's daughter, married off her grandchild, the daughter of her son-in-law Rabbi Moshe Nesanel. The entire town turned out to participate in this momentous occasion. Everybody shared the joy of the celebrating families.

When an *aufruf* of a *rebbishe* child took place, the Jewish musicians would band together that *motza'ei Shabbos* and strike up the tune of *"HaMavdil,"* while the *bachurim* sang along.

If the *chasan* was from another town a large crowd would assemble at the train station to meet him and his parents. A few young men on horses dressed up as Cossacks in full uniform and formed a band, complete with trumpets and drums, in true military style.

As soon as the *chasan* alighted the train, the crowd broke out in joyful dancing and singing. After exiting the train station, the *chasan* and his parents mounted waiting coaches and drove into town, accompanied by all who had come out to meet them. The "Cossacks" on the horses rode before them, then the musicians, then the *chasan* and his family, and finally the entire crowd. Thus they entered the town and

JEWISH LIFE IN TSANZ

Welcoming a *chasan* for a *rebbishe* wedding

were escorted to their lodging place in true splendor!

At last the great day of the wedding arrived. The enthusiastic dancing and singing lasted throughout the night and into the next morning. The latest tunes resounded in the Jewish Street, particularly the song *"Kol Rinah,"* for which a new tune was composed for every *rebbishe* wedding in Tsanz.

Two *badchanim*, Reb Yosef Yidel Tsunger from Tsanz and the Chassidic *talmid chacham* Reb Toivyele from Tarnow, dressed up and sang humorous ditties. First they would announce the *rebbishe* wedding presents and the family wedding presents, all in perfect rhyme. Then they would portray the scene of an ever happy poor man and a downcast wealthy man. Reb Toivyele alone would then present himself as a half German Jew, half Chassid. The mere sight of him on the table dressed up as a modern Jew and a Chassidic Jew in one was enough to amuse and delight the audience.

The following are some of the things he said which I remember:

When the Heavenly court appointed positions to each angel, three angels got the positions of Torah, *avodah*, and *gemilus chasadim*. The angels asked, "What are we supposed to do?"

The Heavenly court answered, "The Torah angel should see to it that the *batei midrash* are full day and night with people learning. The *avodah* angel should see to it that everybody davens and does mitzvos."

The angel of *gemilus chasadim* then asked, "What should my job be?"

The Heavenly court answered, "You should see to it that people give one another snuff to smell."

"The first two angels are given such important jobs, and me you give snuff to sniff?"

They answered him, "Sometimes your job stands much higher than their job. Their job is not even worth a sniff of snuff if the learning is not honest."

He also said:

On Rosh HaShanah three miracles happened — one for Hashem, one for the Satan, and one for the Jews.

The miracle for Hashem was that Avraham did not slaughter Yitzchak. In all our *tefillos* we remind Hashem about *akeidas Yitzchak*. If Avraham would have slaughtered Yitzchak, then Hashem would never be able to repay the *Yidden*.

The miracle for the Satan is that we have to blow shofar from the small side to the wide side, so he can still make his escape through the wide side. If we would have to blow the shofar from the wide side to the small side, the Satan would get stuck in the middle, and he would suffocate.

The miracle for the Jews is that we have to say chapter 47 of Tehillim seven times. If we would have to say chapter 119 seven times, two days Rosh HaShanah would not be enough.

Thus the wedding stretched until the early hours of the following morning.

The family of the *chasan* would form its own minyan at the *chasan*'s home. "*Magen Avos*" was recited, in spite of the fact that the *Shulchan Aruch* says that one should not say it in a place where there isn't a regular minyan. (The Arizal rules that one should say "*Magen Avos*.") Before davening on Shabbos morning, a large crowd would come to the *chasan*'s home and escort him to shul, to the accompaniment of a special tune.

The Divrei Chaim initiated the custom that weddings should take place Friday afternoon an hour before candle lighting, so that the wedding expenses would be minimized. Most of the *chuppah*s took place outside the shul, never in the shul itself, for in Tsanz the women did not enter the shul building. Some *chuppah*s took place in private homes.

On Friday night the townspeople visited the *chasan* and *kallah*. One person would bring a kugel, another a cake, a third a drink. They would sing and make merry so that it was indiscernible whether this was a *simchah* of a poor person or a wealthy one. The highlight of the *simchah* was on *motza'ei Shabbos*, for then the *machatanim* were well rested. At the large *melaveh malkah*, the guests were served the standard menu in those times: potatoes and borsht. The *badchanim* entertained the guests with amusing stories and rhymes until deep into the night. If the *machatanim* were from another town, they would journey home after Shabbos. The *chasan* wore his *shtreimel* and *bekishe* for the seven days of *sheva berachos*, even though there were no *sheva berachos se'udos* except on Shabbos. Only Rebbes and wealthy people celebrated a *sheva berachos se'udah* every night.

Brisos

The *shalom zachar* on Friday night was in the room where the new mother was lying. The room was partitioned by a makeshift wall called a Spanish *ventel*.

All the *brisos* took place in the Tsanzer Rav's *beis midrash*. The Tsanzer Rav would be honored as *sandak* for every bris in town. Until the day of the bris, ten boys would stop at the new mother's home every day on their way home from *cheder* and say Shema at the cradle of the newborn. One needed special permission from the assistant principal to go. The boys vied for the privilege of being chosen, since the visit was invariably rewarded with a sweet. The competition was particularly fierce on the seventh day, the night before the bris, called the *"vach nacht."* On that night, every boy would be given a small, plaited challah in addition to his sweet.

On the *vacht nacht*, the father would stay awake until after midnight. The next day, the bris *se'udah* took place, also in the room of the new mother. There may not have been much food at the *se'udah*, but there certainly was rejoicing in abundance. The songs *"Odeh," "Baruch Elokeinu,"* and *"Yom L'Yabashah"* were sung.

The Town Shochetim

In the years 5690–5699 (1930–1939), there were four *shochetim* in town: Rabbi Pinchas Birnbaum, his son-in-law Rabbi Meilich Altman, Rabbi David Appel, and Rabbi Yosef Herbst, who was known as the Briggeler *shochet*. His son, Reb Chaim Herbst, also received authority to slaughter in Tsanz. He practiced as *shochet* for only two weeks before he fled to Russia after hearing rumors of war breaking out. There he stayed for the duration of the war. He lives today in America, where he is one of the distinguished Bobover Chassidim in Boro Park.

The Divrei Chaim encouraged the *kehillah* to give generous wages to the *shochetim* so that they need not be dependent on, or in fear of, the butcher's whims. The *shochetim* were the first to receive *sherayim* at the Rebbe's *tisch*. The *Rav* would regularly remind the *shochetim* to go to sleep on time so that they would be well rested and refreshed when doing their work.

The responsibility for *shechitah* and collecting its profits were sold by the community to the highest bidder, on a lease of three years. It was sold at a public auction, and the one who succeeded in obtaining it was fortunate indeed.

In Tsanz the *shochetim* made a point of always inviting guests, in order to counteract the trait of cruelty inherent in their profession. Every needy or indigent person was sent to one of the *shochetim* where he was assured a full, nourishing meal. The mentally ill, whom people were afraid to take into their home for a Shabbos meal, were sent to the *shochetim*, who never turned them away.

When a *shochet* celebrated a family *simchah*, he provided food for all the townspeople in full bounty. Guests were not limited to Shabbos and *yom tov* only; throughout the week the door of the *shochet's* home was open to all who were hungry.

Once, at a Friday night *sheva berachos* that Rabbi Yosef was celebrating for his child, a large pot of farfel and kishke was placed on the table. Unfortunately, Rabbi Yosef's well-meaning daughters — and there were quite a few — had each added salt to the farfel, being unaware that so had the others. The result was a pot of food which was indisputably inedible. The food remained uneaten.

The guests stood up for the dancing. After they had finished, they noticed that the pot of food had been emptied clean. The culprit was quite noticeable, for the fat was dripping from the corners of his *bekishe*. The man, a gravedigger, was terribly poor, with a large family to feed. He had stuffed his pockets with the food, hoping to use it to feed his family for the following week. This is but another illustration of the extreme poverty which existed in Tsanz.

Tsanz Chazzanim

No description of Tsanz is complete if it fails to include the excellent *ba'alei tefillah* and the beautiful tunes which the town boasted.

The davening on Shabbos and *yom tov* was accompanied by many tunes. Many of the *niggunim* which are sung throughout the Jewish world today originate from Tsanz. There are Chassidim who have laid claim to these tunes as being theirs; sadly, there is no one left of the previous generation to challenge the truth of these claims. Even the tune which I have heard entitled "The Rebbe Rabbi Elimelech's Dance" is in reality a Tsanzer *niggun*. Few seem to realize that many of the moving tunes which are sung by Jews throughout the world are Tsanzer *niggunim*.

In a description of Tsanzer *ba'alei tefillah* and tunes, Reb Abbish Meir Bransdorfer, who lived in the times of the saintly Divrei Chaim, deserves first mention.

The Vanished City of Tsanz

The Divrei Chaim once motioned to his usual *ba'al tefillah* to go to the *amud*. However, for whatever reason, the *ba'al tefillah* demurred. The Divrei Chaim said to him, "You think I have no one to send to the *amud*? I have Abbish Meir." Having said that, he sent Reb Abbish Meir to lead the davening. Reb Abbish Meir was not a *ba'al tefillah*, nor did he have a good voice. Yet he was a Tsanzer Chassid, and if the Rebbe told him to go to the *amud*, he went! As soon as he approached the *amud*, miraculously he found he had a lovely, musical voice. After that, he became the regular *ba'al tefillah* for the Divrei Chaim until the *Rav*'s passing.

Reb Abbish Meir davened at the *amud* every *Shabbos mevarchin hachodesh*. He also acted as *ba'al tefillah* on all the other special Shabbosos and *yamim tovim*, without accepting payment. His income was what he received as the *Rav*'s *kvittel* writer and treasurer of his household. After midnight, the *Rav* would dictate to him answers to questions which he had received from all over the world.

Reb Abbish Meir sang at every *tisch* before the *Rav*'s discourse on the parashah. He would sing "*Deror Yikra*" and "*Shabbos HaYom*" at *se'udah shelishis*. When Rabbi Abbish introduced a new tune, he could judge by the *Rav*'s reaction whether it appealed to him or not. If the *Rav* did not join in with enthusiasm, he knew not to sing that particular tune anymore.

There were other men with good voices who also composed *niggunim* for the Divrei Chaim, but Reb Abbish Meir was considered the best by far. He composed hundreds of *niggunim*, among them the well-known "*Azei BaShelishi*" from the Shavuos *yotzros* and many other tunes which are sung in the Chassidic world today.

It was said that Reb Abbish Meir could compose a tune while standing at the *amud* or during the singing of *zemiros*. More often, Reb Abbish Meir would go to the window when he had an inspiration for a tune and softly hum to himself while tapping on the window in rhythm. When he was satisfied, he summoned Reb Hershke Klezmer, who had a knack for catching on to a tune and could also read and write musical notes. Reb Hershke would listen carefully to the melody and then write down the notes.

JEWISH LIFE IN TSANZ

After Reb Hershke had written down the notes, Reb Abbish Meir once again sang his tune while Reb Hershke played along on his violin. They would do this several times in the presence of other singers until all had caught on.

Reb Hershke Klezmer himself also composed tunes. His consisted mainly of dance tunes, while Reb Abbish Meir's were usually waltzes, marches, and slow tunes, called *"wollechen"* in Yiddish.

With the passing of the Divrei Chaim, Reb Abbish Meir was left without means of support. He established an inn in the marketplace and was very successful. However, after a while, the town's council withdrew their permission for him to continue with his flourishing business. Once again left without livelihood, Reb Abbish Meir took on the position of chazzan in Cracow, in the Chassidic *beis midrash* Chadashim. He remained there until his death in 5684 (1924).

Hersh Leib Bakon was another popular chazzan in Tsanz. His hometown was Kolbosov, where he was born in 5635 (1875). When his parents realized that their young son was blessed with a good voice, they sent him to learn *chazzanus* in Tarnow with Reb Abbish Meir's brother, Reb Elya Bransdorfer.

Hersh Leib got married in the year 5655 (1895). His father-in-law being from Tsanz, he went to live there. Ten years later he was offered the position of chazzan in Keshanov. He, too, composed hundreds of tunes which are still in use today. He passed away in 5688 (1928).

Among the well-known *chazzanim* of Tsanz in the prewar years was Reb Chaim David Blum. Reb Chaim David, too, composed many tunes which are popular to this very day. I recall with nostalgia Reb Chaim David's davening on Shabbos morning in Rabbi Aryeh

Hersh Leib Bakon

The Vanished City of Tsanz

Leibish's *beis midrash*. He transported the congregants to a different planet with his fervent prayers and soul-stirring melodies. When he left the *amud*, he would be sweating from exertion. Every year he would travel to Kashow, Czechoslovakia, for the *yamim nora'im*, since there were many Tsanzer Chassidim there who derived great joy from hearing the Tsanzer *nosach*. He would take along two young boys with musical voices to assist him — my older brother Hersh and Mendel Tzimmer. When the two boys returned to Tsanz, they were the envy of all the other boys in town because they had been privileged to have traveled abroad and they had enjoyed the unheard of luxury of eating grapes whenever they pleased. Grapes were a very expensive delicacy, usually purchased only for someone who was very ill.

From Tsanz, Reb Chaim David Blum went to live in Keshanov, where he was offered a position as chazzan. There he stayed until he was murdered in the extermination of the entire town. (His son, Reb Moshe, and his daughter live in New York today, where they have established Torah-observant families.)

Chaim David Blum

The chazzan Rabbi Abbish'l Melitzer was a son of Rabbi Elimelech Horowitz of Cracow, the Melitzer Rav. Rabbi Abbish'l had a very regal countenance. Even gentiles would stop on the streets when they saw him and ask wonderingly, "Who is that person with the impressive bearing?" He was a *ba'al tefillah* and singer for the Tsanzer Rav in the Gribover *beis midrash* after Reb Chaim David left for Keshanov. The majority of his tunes were those which his father, the Melitzer Rav, had composed. Many of his tunes are sung in the Chassidic world today, among them the popular melodies "*Yedid Nefesh*" and "*Rannenu Tzaddikim*."

JEWISH LIFE IN TSANZ

(The Melitzer Rav, Rabbi Elimelech Horowitz, lived in the Radomishel ghetto during the war. When the Nazis received the order to make the ghetto *Judenrein* they did not have the means with which to deport the Jews to Belzec for extermination because the town did not have a train station. The solution was simple: the Nazis forced the Jews to dig a mass grave in the cemetery and murdered them there.

When the Jews were being driven to the cemetery, the Melitzer Rav perceived what fate had in store for them. He turned to his murderers and begged them to give him a piece of bread and to let him wash for *hamotzi* before finishing him off. The murderers agreed to his request. The

From right to left: Yaakov Hersh Mustbaum, Stengel, Nechemiah Berliner, Mendel Torum, Zalman Shein, Naftali Epstein, Leiser Unger, Mendel Rosenblum, Yosef Berliner, Alter Katz, Yoske Torum, David Drenger

Melitzer Rav washed right there before the gaping grave and ate his final meal together with his Chassidim. He gave them a Torah discourse and then enthusiastically broke out into a new tune which he had composed on the spot, *"Nishmas Kol Chai."* He and his Chassidim began dancing and singing in the face of their tormentors and the open grave. Soon after, the Nazis began their shooting spree, and one after the other, the bullets silenced the dancing Jews forever. Thus perished the

Jews of the town Radomishel and its district, together with the Melitzer Rav.)

The Bobover *shtieblach* in Tsanz also had excellent singers and *ba'alei tefillah*, among them Rabbi Shlomo Herbst, whose son Rabbi Eziel Herbst is one of the distinguished Bobover Chassidim in London today, and Aharon Itcha Wolf, a relative of mine.

The Shinover *beis midrash*, too, boasted, a good *ba'al tefillah* — Reb Itzikel Englander, one of the respected Shinover Chassidim in Tsanz. When he davened *mussaf* on the *yamim nora'im*, the congregants would get carried away by his heartfelt, tearful *tefillos*.

Other popular *ba'alei tefillah* were Reb Chaim Akiva Klagsbald and his son Reb Moshe Klagsbald. Reb Moshe used to travel to Kashow to daven before the *amud* after Reb Chaim David Blum had gone to live in Keshanov. He eventually settled in Bendin where he was offered a position as chazzan.

Reb Shaul Braunfeld was another *ba'al tefillah* in the Shinover *beis midrash*. He davened in the Chevrah Shomrim on the *yamim nora'im*. I was one of his assistants there. He could also compose tunes and was familiar with the use of musical notes.

In the *beis midrash* of Rabbi Chuna Hersh Rubin, known as the Sakmarer Rebbe, one of the *ba'alei tefillah* was Reb Yosef Leiser. He was a close relative to the Pshevorsker Rebbe, *shlita*, of Antwerp.

The world-renowned chazzan Shlomo Mandel was also born in Tsanz, on Yom Kippur 5670 (1910). He acted as chazzan in Johannesburg where he was very beloved by the population.

The Chevrah Nichum Aveilim

In Tsanz, there was a *chevrah nichum aveilim*. When my father sat *shivah*, I noticed that every day another neighbor would bring in food. Apart from arranging this, they also placed a large, unlocked *pushka* in the mourner's home. I asked my father why they left the *pushka* open. He replied that since the mourner was forbidden to work, he might have difficulty supporting his family. The *pushka* was left open so that he could take money at his discretion. This custom, he told me, originated in Frankfurt.

The custom was that there was only one minyan even if there were a few brothers. The brothers would take turns davening in front of the *amud*. No *sefer Torah* was brought into the house of the *avel*. The people would daven there and then go on to the *beis midrash* to hear *leining*.

Chalitzah in Tsanz

I recall a *chalitzah* which was performed in the large Gribover *beis midrash* in the year 5695 (1935). My father was one of the five *dayanim* required to officiate at the *chalitzah*. Three of the *dayanim* would speak, while two, called "*de shtimer dayanim*," would remain silent. The *chalitzah* was announced in all the town's *batei midrash* the day before.

Long benches were set up, filling half the *beis midrash*. Entering the *beis midrash* was enough to fill one with awe. The three "speaking" *dayanim* were seated with their backs to the northern wall and the other two, with their backs to the eastern wall. The *Rav*, Rabbi Mordechai Zev, did not take off his tallis and tefillin after davening but stood opposite the *beis din* still wearing them during the entire procedure. All the *dayanim* had the *Shulchan Aruch* open before them.

The *taharah* board used by the *chevrah kaddisha* stood at a slant behind the *beis din*. When I asked my father what the black plank was for, he replied that since it is customary for the *beis din* to summon the deceased to *chalitzah*, the place behind the *taharah* board was reserved for the deceased.

The *yavam* stood at the center. The *yevamah* walked in a little later, her face wrapped in a black shawl, accompanied by another woman. The *yavam* spat before the *yevamah*, as is commanded in the Torah, and the *beis din* walked over to inspect the spit if it was white (because of the *din* "a *yevamah* who spits blood..."). The *chalitzah* was repeated, since there were some doubts as to whether the *yavam* was left-handed, and in that case he is obligated to do it twice. The *beis din* only had a right shoe so they had to order a left shoe to be made especially for the occasion.

CHAPTER 12
CHARITY AND GOOD DEEDS

As an introduction to my description of charity and *chesed* in Tsanz, I would like to relate an anecdote told about the Divrei Chaim.

Galicia is a very large province. In those days, the only way to traverse the country was either by horse and wagon or on foot. The journey could take days or even weeks to complete. During the day one would travel, while the nights would be spent in a *kretshma* (inn). These guest houses, usually situated at a crossroad, were places where one could eat, sleep, and refresh oneself. Adjoining the *kretshma* was a stable for the horses. Bearing in mind the difficulties of traveling, one can appreciate that owning a *kretshma* was a valuable source of income for thousands of people, the vast majority of them Jews.

The right to own a *kretshma* was given by the local squire to the highest bidder. The Jews had a mutual understanding among themselves not to outbid a fellow Jew.

Owning a *kretshma* was not an easy job. A hefty part of the earnings went toward the exorbitant rent demanded by the squire. In addition, the police force and other important town officials were entitled to drink their fill, free of charge. Finally, more often than not, the common peasants would pay their debts in installments, because they were very poor and could not afford to pay all at once.

CHARITY AND GOOD DEEDS

Most of the *kretshma*s were located outside town or in small villages where the only Jew in the locality was the *kretshma* owner. Many of the Jewish owners adopted their fellow peasant's mannerisms and lost their refined bearing, becoming coarse countrymen.

It once happened that a Tsanzer Chassid offered a higher bid for a certain *kretshma* than the person who owned it at the time. This person happened to be a particularly low and vulgar fellow.

Hearing that it was a Tsanzer Chassid who had outbid him, the enraged gentleman wasted no time and determinedly rushed to the Divrei Chaim to complain that a Chassid of the Rebbe had broken the time-honored tradition not to outbid another Jew for the rights to own a *kretshma*.

The *Rav* summoned the Chassid and demanded an excuse for his unjust behavior. The Chassid protested that the *kretshma* owner was an irreligious lout. It was a mitzvah to wrong such a person — to bury him! Why was the *Rav* sticking up for him?

The Tsanzer Rav rebuked him, "Since when do you know so well whom one is permitted to wrong and who not? The Torah teaches us the contrary. Rashi tells us in *parashas Bo* that when Hashem saw that the Jews had no merit in which to be redeemed from Egypt, he gave them two mitzvos — the blood of Pesach and the blood of milah. This raises a question: we know that the Jews did have many mitzvos to their credit. How? In *parashas BeShalach*, Rashi comments that only one-fifth of the Jews left Egypt, the rest having died during the three days of darkness, as they were wicked people. If so, the remaining Jews must have been occupied doing countless mitzvos during the three days — burying their fellow Jews. Why, then, did they need the merit of two additional mitzvos? It must be that it is not such a great mitzvah to bury a sinner. Therefore I warn you to retract your bid and return the *kretshma* to this man, even if he may not be much of a *tzaddik* in your eyes."

In the second volume of the *she'eilos v'teshuvos* of the Divrei Chaim (*Choshen Mishpat*, question 47) a similar incident is mentioned. The Divrei Chaim wrote a very sharp response to Rabbi Avraham Chaim, the Lisker Rav, who gave permission to his Chassid

The Vanished City of Tsanz

to outbid for a *kretshma* which belonged to an irreligious man. He writes, "I am greatly surprised at your ruling, for if you decree that with a sinner the mutual agreement does not apply, then it will *never* apply. Unfortunately, contempt exists among us, and if you rule thus a person will condemn anyone he sees fit with the title 'sinner.' Even if a person is more tolerant of others, there are no set limits where you can decide to draw the line."

Similarly, when the Divrei Chaim heard someone rebuking another, especially in the field of poor davening or lack of piety, he would summon the rebuker and ask, "Did you ask him if he has eaten yet?"

The answer would obviously be no.

"Know," continued the Divrei Chaim, "that a person should concern himself with his own spirituality and other people's physical needs. You do the opposite: you are concerned about your own physical needs and other people's spirituality!"

Jewish poverty, Zborov 5675 (1915)

This was the general policy in Tsanz. Friends were carefully chosen, yet when it came to giving a meal or helping out another person, it made absolutely no difference what his spiritual caliber was.

The town of Tsanz was famed for its *tzedakah* and *chesed* throughout Western Galicia. It was the Tsanzer Rav, the author of *Divrei Chaim*, who had implanted this trait in his Chassidim.

CHARITY AND GOOD DEEDS

Every Friday, hundreds of impoverished people came to Tsanz to spend Shabbos there. Destitution had forced them to trudge from town to town collecting money to send home to their starving families. Many of them lodged in the *hachnasas orchim* home, founded and run by Reb Avraham David Shiff.

At the davening on Friday night, the *gabbaim* saw to it that every household had a guest to take home over Shabbos. If, as was often the

Jewish poverty

case, there were more guests than hosts, the *gabbai* would allocate the remaining visitors to the *shochetim*. The *hachnasas orchim* of these *shochetim* was outstanding. The *gabbaim* did not leave the *beis midrash* until they had seen to it that every stranded visitor had a home where he could eat his Shabbos meals.

Rabbi Meir Ba'al HaNess Kollel Chibas Yerushalayim

All the rabbinical grandchildren of the Divrei Chaim held the *tzedakah* of Rabbi Meir Ba'al HaNess Kollel Chibas Yerushalayim in the greatest esteem, far and above other charities. Whatever the misfortune or problem, they always advised the sufferer to put a sizable amount of money in the Rabbi Meir Ba'al HaNess *pushka*, with the words *"Elokei d'Meir aneini"* (G-d of Meir, answer me).

Once, on the twenty-fifth of Nissan, the yartzeit of the Divrei Chaim, I was at the home of Reb Avraham David Schiff when he was hosting the Tzieshinover Rav, Rabbi Yechezkel, the son of Rabbi Simchah Yissachar Ber Halberstam, author of *Divrei Simchah*, and his uncle HaRav HaTzaddik Rabbi Itzikel Gewirtzman, the Pshevorsk-Antwerp Rav.

Suddenly a great commotion erupted. The key of Reb Avraham David Schiff's business had vanished. Reb Avraham David, looking strained and worried, was at a loss. Rabbi Itzikel and Rabbi Yechezkel both advised him to give eighteen groschen to the *tzedakah* Rabbi Meir Ba'al HaNess, accompanied by the words "and G-d opened his eyes" (*Bereishis Rabbah* 52). Reb Avraham David heeded their advice, and presto, he found the keys. Happiness and peace of mind were restored.

A Good, Decent People

The Tsanzer Jews took great care only to use a refined vocabulary. Even the simple coach drivers did not use vulgar or coarse words. People were careful not to tread on or abuse a newspaper written in Yiddish or Hebrew, even if it was issued by an irreligious publisher, because they were written with the letters of the *alef-beis*. All irreligious newspapers, even if written in Yiddish, were banned from Orthodox homes.

Here I will take the liberty of elaborating a little on the general attitude of decency and goodwill which reigned in the Jewish community. In truth, an entire chapter should be dedicated to this subject.

A Hungarian *Rav* once visited the Divrei Chaim. The Tsanzer Rav confronted him with the sharp question, "Do you close your Gemara in order to help out another person?"

This question illustrates how important the concept of kindness was in Tsanz. From childhood, the importance of *chesed* was drilled into each person's heart and mind. Great stress was laid on *middos*

CHARITY AND GOOD DEEDS

tovos and *derech eretz*, too. Every child knew well that should he meet an elderly person he must greet him with a polite "good morning" or "good Shabbos." If an elderly person criticized a child, the child would never justify himself, regardless of whether he was indeed right or not.

When I arrived at Auschwitz, I was shocked to hear religious people using a lowly, vulgar vocabulary, which even the porters among us would not use. It was then that I realized how genteel even the simple people among us were. The Chassidic Jews were especially particular about their speech and good deeds. It was only after the war that I encountered people calling themselves Chassidim, dressed in the "full uniform," who acted and spoke like common peasants.

Gemilus Chasadim of Reb Shmelke Schiff

When the Nazis besieged Tsanz, they used cannons to bombard the city. There was hardly a window that was not shattered by the fierce attack. The Jewish quarter, mainly centered on Kazimierza Street (known as the Jewish Street), suffered especially severe damage. Many of the *batei midrash* were greatly harmed, including the Divrei Chaim's house and his *beis midrash*, the Talmud Torah, the Shinover Rav's house and his *beis midrash*, and the Gribover *beis midrash*.

One day, notices were displayed prominently in Yiddish throughout the ghetto announcing that anyone who required new windows should turn to Reb Moshe Fish, the window wholesaler. As the signs promised, he replaced all the broken windows free of charge. This arrangement lasted a long time, with nobody knowing the identity of the anonymous benefactor.

One day the Gestapo seized four Jews, accusing them of thieving. Reb Shmelke Schiff, the son of Reb Avraham David Schiff, was among them. They were all sent to Auschwitz, where they perished.

After this incident, the window wholesaler, Reb Moshe Fish, stopped his distribution of free windowpanes. It was thereafter revealed that the mysterious giver had been Reb Shmelke Schiff. Before the war, he had been considered stingy in comparison to his extremely generous father, Reb Avraham David Schiff. His father had introduced the concept of a *hachnasas orchim* home for the many visitors who traveled through Tsanz. This goodhearted soul used to make his rounds every evening to all the *batei midrash*, looking for prospective "clients." It was only after Reb Shmelke's death that the people realized he'd been a worthwhile heir to his father's great *chesed*.

The Englander Family

The name Englander was well known by all the Tsanzer inhabitants as belonging to a distinguished family of *ba'alei chesed*. The father, Reb Avraham Shabsai Eber HaKohen, was a devout Chassid and very close to the Divrei Chaim. Reb Eber was the owner of a tavern, from which he earned just about enough to make a living. He had two sons, Yaakov and Moshe.

One night, at midnight, a fire broke out in the backyard of Reb Eber's gentile neighbor. Reb Eber's entire property was in danger of being consumed by the leaping flames. He hastily ran up the hill to where the Divrei Chaim was returning from the mikveh and in great panic told him of the serious situation.

The Divrei Chaim hurriedly walked back with Reb Eber. As they approached his home they noticed a tongue of flame already licking the corner of Reb Eber's wooden roof. The Divrei Chaim motioned with his holy hands and said that the fire was not traveling in the direction of Reb Eber's home, but in a different direction, far away. At that moment the wind changed direction; one could actually see the burning piece of wood being dragged off the roof and blown far away. The wood reached the home of a peasant and set fire to it, razing it down to the ground.

Reb Moshe Englander

Reb Moshe Englander, the son of Reb Eber, struggled hard to make a living. One day he went to the Divrei Chaim and lamented that he did not have the money to pay for his sons' tuition. The Divrei

CHARITY AND GOOD DEEDS

Chaim said to him, "Why do you worry so? I will pay your tuition."

"The *Rav* wants to turn me into a common beggar, *chas v'shalom*," replied Reb Moshe.

The *Rav* responded by blessing him with abundant wealth.

A short time later, Reb Moshe went to a small, local beer factory, Okotshim, and offered to be their agent throughout Galicia. The manager immediately agreed to the proposition. Reb Moshe became the sole representative for the factory and became very successful.

The Divrei Chaim once took a stroll. He stopped outside Reb Moshe's tavern, which had belonged to his father, Reb Eber. Reb Moshe offered him a glass of Okotshim beer. The Divrei Chaim then remarked that Okotshim beer was a beer of high quality. Soon word spread around town that Okotshim beer was excellent and could be purchased at Reb Moshe's. Everybody began drinking this brand of beer. Due to Reb Moshe, the small, unassuming firm Okotshim became one of the largest beer factories in Galicia!

After the Divrei Chaim passed away, Reb Moshe Englander became a Chassid of the Shinover Rav, the Divrei Yechezkel. Reb Moshe purchased a coach with horses for his Rebbe. The Divrei Yechezkel then presented Reb Moshe with a gold watch and said to him, "*Es zol dir git gein* — It should go well with you." From that time on, Reb Moshe became more and more prosperous, fulfilling the Divrei Yechezkel's blessing. He soon became one of the wealthiest men in Galicia.

A remarkable story once happened to Reb Moshe on Pesach night. The family was sitting at the seder table, when Reb Moshe's wife, the daughter of Reb David Klausner, descended the cellar steps to get something. Suddenly, to her immense horror, she caught sight of a corpse of a newborn gentile child lying sprawled across the floor. Reb Moshe's wife realized that this must be a blood libel. She quick-wittedly hid the child in the folds of her dress and, without a word, calmly went back to the table.

A few minutes later, a loud banging was heard at the door. The police stormed into the house and made their way directly to the cellar. They made a thorough search, and when they could not find the body, they sent two of their men to search the entire home. Their search proved fruitless.

They began interrogating Reb Moshe. Reb Moshe calmly answered their persistent questioning, unaware of the danger at hand. Disappointed, the police left empty-handed.

It was only the next morning that Reb Moshe's wife told him of her gruesome discovery. She told him that she had put the child in her dress so that the police would assume she was pregnant and would not question her. She did not tell her husband at the time, for she foresaw that the police would interrogate him, and if he knew her awful secret he might break under pressure. Also, because Reb Moshe was a *kohen*, she knew he would leave the house if he was aware that there was a corpse on the premises, which would have greatly aggravated the situation.

Reb Moshe immediately went to the Divrei Chaim and told him the gory story. The Tsanzer Rav summoned his *shamash* and gave him the corpse, telling him to bury it after *yom tov* in the nearby forest.

The Englanders supported the Shinover *rebbishe* court and the Tsanzer-Shinover yeshivah. They employed a special accountant for the sole purpose of taking care of their *tzedakah* accounts. When passing their house, one could see queues of poor people awaiting their turn to request a donation.

Reb Eber Yehoshua Englander

Reb Eber Englander was a benevolent person and was involved in many acts of *chesed*. He ran the secretariat of the Chevrah Linas HaTzedek, an organization that cared for the sick and ailing. Their services included arranging for a doctor to come during an emergency; providing medical equipment such as wheelchairs, thermometers, and crutches; and sending overnight companions to the lonely and sick. The Linas HaTzedek fund also assisted people in paying for their prescriptions, since in those times there was no such thing as medical insurance.

CHARITY AND GOOD DEEDS

In order to be assisted by this organization in time of need, one had to pay a membership fee of ten groschen a month for a single family. Linas HaTzedek was centered in Reb Eber's home, the only building in the Jewish Street to own a telephone. In an emergency, one would go to his home to use it.

If one needed a favor from the police, Reb Eber would arrange it. His tavern was frequently patronized by the police and their officers, so he was on friendly terms with them. If a person was caught doing something illegal, such as dealing in precious stones, cigarette lighters, or saccharin (Poland claiming the sole monopoly on them), Reb Eber would use his connections with the police, and the person would be freed.

Reb Chaim Falik's

Reb Chaim Falik's surname was Kernkraut, but he was known as Reb Chaim Falik's, since in Tsanz people were called by their father's Jewish name rather than their surname, a custom originating with the Divrei Chaim.

Reb Chaim Falik's was ten years older than the *Rav*, Rabbi Aryeh Leibish. For many years, being a widower, he lived alone in the Tsanzer Rav's sukkah (the *Rav* had a brick sukkah, a rarity in those times). He refused to move in with his children for fear that he would be a burden to them. He provided himself with all his needs. On Sukkos he stayed at the home of his son-in-law Reb Yaakov Tzolman, so that the sukkah would be available for the *Rav* and his family (the men only; in Tsanz women did not enter the sukkah during the *yom tov*).

Reb Chaim Falik's had perfect hearing and sight until his death at the age of ninety-four. He did not even need spectacles! I once heard the *Rav*, Rabbi Aryeh Leibish Halberstam, remark that the blessing of longevity which is mentioned in regard to one who observes *kibbud av va'em*, does not only imply old age, but to be as fit in old age like Reb Chaim Falik's. That was the real blessing of long life!

The Vanished City of Tsanz

The *Rav* would elaborate on the concept. The blessing of long life is mentioned five times in the Torah, he said: for the mitzvah of *kibbud av va'em*; for the mitzvah of *shilo'ach hakein*; regarding a king — "so that his days of rulership should be lengthened"; for the mitzvah of *tzitzis* — "so that your days and the days of your children should be increased"; and for the mitzvah of having precise scales in trade. However, there is a fundamental difference between the mitzvah of *kibbud av va'em* and *shilo'ach hakein* and the other three: regarding the former two mitzvos the *pasuk* tells us, "...so that your days should be lengthened *and they should be good for you.*" If one is in the same condition in his old age as Reb Chaim Falik's, said the *Rav*, then he has merited the blessing of "your days should be lengthened, and they should be good for you."

Rabbi Aryeh Leibish went on to relate Reb Chaim Falik's history. "Reb Chaim Falik's was born in Vizhnitza, Galicia, to very poor parents. He was an only child, yet his parents sent him to learn in Tsanz even before he became bar mitzvah.

"In Tsanz he was given *essen teg*. (In Galicia a boy who was sent away to learn was allotted a different home for every day of the week where he could eat his main meal. This was called *essen teg*. If a boy could not find himself a home where he could eat, he would literally have to fast that day. Unfortunately, this was not a rare occurrence.)

"Reb Chaim Falik's parents lived in great poverty, and they did not have the means to send money to their son in Tsanz. Little Chaim assisted them instead. Every Thursday morning after davening he went around to all the *batei midrash* in Tsanz to collect money, which went straight to his parents in Vizhnitza to enable them to buy what they needed for Shabbos.

"Because of this," concluded Rabbi Aryeh Leibish, "Chaim Falik's, their only son, deserved a long, fruitful life. The *pasuk* '...so that your days should be lengthened and they should be good for you' was fulfilled for him in every respect."

CHARITY AND GOOD DEEDS

Chaim Levi Kiegel

In Tsanz there lived a unique person known as Chaim Levi "Kiegel" Stern. Although he himself was an impoverished fellow, he would collect money from others for the sole purpose of doing mitzvos and good deeds. He literally had a mobile *gemach* — stored in his massive boots! In there one could find anything which Reb Chaim Levi thought could be of use to anybody: *tabak* to sniff, cigarettes to smoke, petrol and stones for cigarette lighters, aspirins in case somebody had a headache, even toilet paper! Chaim Levi Kiegel had it all — free of charge.

He could usually be found in the *beis midrash* of the Chevrah Shomrim. Everybody in Tsanz, even strangers, knew about Chaim Levi Kiegel's boots. Chaim Levi was overjoyed when someone found something he'd been looking for in his boots.

Every boy who stepped into Chevrah Shomrim on his way to *cheder* and said, "Good morning, Reb Chaim Levi," was rewarded with a piece of sugar or a pretzel, according to his choice.

Reb Chaim Levi would never speak during davening or Tehillim. It was a pleasure to daven in Chevrah Shomrim, for there was total silence during the prayers. Woe to the person who spoke in the middle of davening or during *leining*. Reb Chaim Levi would throw him a sharp look. If the person ignored him, he would simply walk over to him and tread on his toes with his huge, heavy boots — hard. The soles were made from the rubber of a used tire so that the person who merited a taste of his boots remembered well not to speak during davening for a good many weeks after that.

After finishing the *se'udah* on Shabbos day, Reb Chaim Levi used to go to all the Jewish homes to collect the leftover food (hence his nickname "Kiegel," after the kugel he collected). This he distributed to the poor wanderers who came to Tsanz on foot to spend Shabbos, exhausted and starving from the week's arduous journeys. It was true that these unfortunate individuals had been provided with a place to eat, but they were often still hungry between meals, especially on the long summer Shabbosos.

The Vanished City of Tsanz

Before Pesach, Reb Chaim Levi set aside a large pile of fleecy white feathers near his tallis and tefillin. Upon request every person was presented with a feather for *bedikas chametz*. Before Sukkos he purchased a set of *arba minim* in order to offer the mitzvah to anyone who did not have his own. He would ask the people to recite a *berachah* aloud so that he could answer "amen."

Chaim Levi "Kiegel" Stern

Yosef Franzblau

As various Chassidic *batei midrash* such as Tsanz, Bobov, and Shinova opened up, the number of people who davened at the Talmud Torah began to dwindle. Yosef Franzblau, the *gabbai* of the Talmud Torah, tried to find a solution to this problem.

Sure enough, he hit upon a plan. He figured that if the children davened there, their fathers would very likely follow. So he announced to all the children that anyone who davened in the Talmud Torah from beginning to end would receive a *rogeleh* (roll). If the youngster came in the middle of davening, he would get only half a *rogeleh*.

As he had foreseen, the children were attracted by this tempting offer and began to daven there regularly. At the end of davening, the baker came in with a large basket filled with fresh, warm *rogelech*. Reb Yosef Franzblau himself was in charge of the distribution. He had a marvellous memory and knew exactly which child had come in at

CHARITY AND GOOD DEEDS

From right to left: Yoske Torum, Naftali Epstein, Yossele Rosenblum, Pinye Kinsinger, Mendel Torum, Zalman Shein, Aharon Berliner, Shiyaleh Halberstam (the Glisker Rav's son), Hersh Berliner, Stengel, Yidel Mustbaum

what time. He donated the *rogelech* accordingly: a child who had been there the whole davening received a whole *rogeleh*, a child who had come in middle received half, a child who had come a little later received a quarter, and so on. His plan indeed worked, and before long the children brought their fathers along, and the Talmud Torah minyan thrived once again.

Landlords and Tenants

The last Tsanzer *rosh hakahal*, Reb Shalom Yonah Tenzer, owned a large apartment building on the main street of the town — Jagellonska Street. The apartments at the front were rented to shopowners. One of them was leased by Moshe Shmuel Friedman, a Jewish watchmaker. Moshe Shmuel had not paid rent for quite a few years, and Reb Shalom Yonah wanted to evict him. But Moshe Shmuel refused to move. Only when Reb Shalom Yonah provided him with another apartment near the train station and put down one year's rent in advance for him did Moshe Shmuel agree to vacate the apartment.

The Vanished City of Tsanz

Reb Aryeh Leib Gelb of Tsanz owned a very large apartment building on the Jewish Street, near the Tsanzer Rav's *beis midrash*. The building housed forty families, of which not one paid rent! They were confident that since their landlord was a Jew, and a goodhearted soul, too, he surely wouldn't throw them out. Reb Aryeh Leib also owned a grocery store, a steam press to iron laundry, and a matzah bakery, all located in that same building.

One day Reb Aryeh Leib Gelb noticed that his tenants were displeased with him. "Why are you angry with me?" he defended himself. "You live in my apartments and don't pay any rent. I don't charge you for the groceries you take. I even let you bake matzah without asking for payment, and yet you are still angry with me?"

"We have a complaint to make," they replied. "We were told that it was written in the local newspaper that the landlord is obliged to pay for repairs. You don't pay for our repairs..."

Reb Moshe Shemayah of Tsanz

Reb Moshe Shemayah was a Tsanzer *Yid* who emigrated to Yerushalayim many years before the war. In Yerushalayim he has established generations of Torah-observant families.

I once asked him, "What made such a young person like you leave Tsanz?"

"It is thanks to a Tsanzer gentile, a rabid anti-Semite," he replied, and he told me the following story:

"I lived on the *Yiddisher Gass*. Every morning, at 4 A.M. I would meet my friend and learn with him. The *bachur* lived on the Piekela. We used to alternate our learning places: one week I went to his home on the Piekela, and one week he came to the *Yiddisher Gass* where we learned in the Tsanzer Rav's *beis midrash*.

"I had to go through the main road to get to the Piekela. One day I came across a group of railway workers going to work. Seeing a Jew in the distance, they began to make their sinister approach. I was all too aware of their evil intentions and, trying to salvage the situation, I said 'good morning' in the most friendly voice I could muster. It was a wasted effort. One of the workers struck me a blow on the head, knocking out two teeth. I collapsed on the floor, bloodied and unconscious. As soon as I regained my senses, I vowed then and there not to remain in that cursed country, where a friendly 'good morning' merits a beating and the bashing out of teeth. *I will travel to Eretz Yisrael*, I firmly resolved.

"When I arrived home and told my mother what had happened and what I had therefore decided, I was merely laughed at. My family and friends thought I had simply lost my mind! G-d alone is witness to the difficulties I encountered in carrying out my ambition. In order to procure the necessary funds for my journey, I sold pictures of the Tsanzer cemetery with the Tsanzer Rav's *ohel* in the middle on the way to the port. People were ready to pay a fortune for those pictures.

"It is thanks to that gentile that I managed to realize my dream and to build a family on this holy soil while the rest of my family were all wiped out," concludes Reb Moshe.

Tsanzer Characters

In addition to its great *rabbanim*, philanthropists, and pious Jews, Tsanz could boast of some very unusual, if not eccentric, personalities.

Yossele Sherer (cutter) was the Chassidic barber on the *Yiddisher Gass*. He lived above the mikveh, in a tiny one-room apartment. There was barely enough room for two beds to be placed side by side in his cramped lodging. Until this day, I am at a loss to imagine where he put his five children to sleep! In his living quarters, he also managed to squeeze in an oven and shelf off a tiny room for wood and coal. This room also served as his "parlor." His client sat perched on the wood and coal while Yossele would cut his hair.

Yossele Sherer met no problems with his Chassidic customers; however the job was done, it was good enough for them. If he cut the hair of a more modern, fastidious *bachur* who wanted his neckline to be smartly finished, Yossele would produce an old, rusty razor knife. As soon as the knife scratched the client's neck, blood would spurt a little.

The Vanished City of Tsanz

The customer, feeling blood trickling down his neck, would protest, "Reb Yossele, blood is running down my neck!"

Unperturbed, Yossele would assuringly reply, "If you want to look handsome, you must have patience, for I am not finished yet. I still have the other side to do."

For these sorts of customers, an old musty mirror hung on the wall. However, the mirror only reflected the tip of one's nose, for due to the damp, the quicksilver at the back of the mirror had gradually eroded.

Reuvele the *shadchan* was a story on his own. He was the chief *shadchan* in Tsanz. He encountered no problems with the Chassidic crowd: he suggested a match, and if both sides agreed to it, a meeting would be arranged. The outcome would be either yes or no.

However, even with a Chassidic boy the procedure was not always straightforward. First of all, the boy's hat might be old and worn out. Secondly, his only pair of trousers were more often than not shabby and torn. Finally, his tattered jacket had obviously seen better days and was either too large or too small on him. The boy had to consequently procure a presentable hat and a decent suit for his upcoming meeting.

If the match was made, Reuvele the *shadchan* would advise the new groom to buy a pocketknife before the wedding. "This is necessary," he explained, "for usually a new son-in-law has all due respect for his mother-in-law. He politely refrains from eating when she

Avraham Shiffer

addresses him. The shrewd mother-in-law knows this, so she prepares a lengthy, *rebbishe* story and does not stop talking until it is time to leave. This way, she will get her food back, but you will be left hungry. The only solution for you is to quickly cut off a large piece of bread while she has her back turned to pour you some coffee, and later in the *beis midrash* you can satiate your hunger."

A popular story was frequently told in Tsanz of a father-in-law who had promised his son-in-law a shoe-polish factory for his dowry. After his wedding, the new groom requested to see his shoe-polish factory. His father-in-law obligingly complied. He led him to a bed, and with the handle of his umbrella dragged out a large bowl and a container of black tar.

The astonished son-in-law protested, "This is the shoe-polish factory? A factory must have a building and a chimney."

His father-in-law appeased him. "Do not worry, my son. I will reveal to you the secret of how to produce shoe polish. After that you yourself can build a large factory with a big chimney."

A more modern boy complicated the procedure a little, for he to refused hear of the match before seeing a photograph of the girl suggested. Reuvele did not have a picture; he only possessed a photo of one girl which was produced with a flourish to every boy who demanded one.

Kornhauser the dairyman

When Reuvele's wife passed away, a match was suggested to him. He was warned that she was a *katlanis* — two husbands had passed away in her lifetime. Reuvele replied that such things do not scare him.

The Vanished City of Tsanz

Soon after his wedding, he passed away.

Even the *ganavim* (thieves) in Tsanz were unique characters. The best known of them was Mendele Miller, who came from a very respectable family. His grandfather, Reb Asher Miller, was a distinguished personality, who was very much involved in the *tzedakah* Reb Meir Ba'al HaNess. Mendele Miller did not differentiate between Jews and gentiles; he stole from both alike. He struck up partnerships with fellow *ganavim*, but they did not benefit too much from their thefts, for whatever money they earned went directly to the poor. Mendele Ganav was a true-to-life Robin Hood.

If a Jew felt unjustly wronged by a gentile, he complained to Mendele Ganav. The worthy fellow would then teach the gentile not to start up with Jews anymore.

A gentile merchant and a Jew once haggled about a wagon filled with apples. The gentile wanted five zlotys for the lot, but the Jew was ready to give him only three. The merchant flew into a merry temper and yelled at the Jew, "You swindler! You dirty Jew!"

As soon as Mendel heard of this offense, he indignantly assured the Jew, "You can forget about buying the apples. I will teach that gentile not to insult a Jew." He then went to the gentile and offered to pay him the required amount. He told him, however, that he would first like him to deliver the goods. He led him to the home of a very poor man, Hershel Lustbader, a widower with eleven children, and bade him to deposit the apples in his cellar.

While the gentile was busy pouring the apples through the small opening of the cellar, our friend Mendel Ganav disappeared from sight. His mission had been accomplished: Hershel Lustbader had a cellar full of apples.

The gentile finished his job and went in search of Mendele, but Mendele was nowhere to be seen. An hour later he turned up and said to the furious gentile, "As a penalty for insulting a Jew, you must give me the apples at half price. If you don't like the idea, you can climb into the cellar and take back your apples."

It was not possible for the gentile to retrieve his apples, for the cellar was locked, and the window was too small to climb through.

CHARITY AND GOOD DEEDS

Having no choice, he had to content himself with whatever money he was given.

In 5689–5690 (1929–1930), Poland suffered a bitterly cold winter. People literally died on the streets from the biting frost. At that time, Mendele arranged a large-scale project to provide the poor with wood, coal, and potatoes, essentials unobtainable for a regular price. Mendele imposed the wealthy people with a "tax": they had to donate these three items. If a rich person refused to give, Mendele would offer him an ultimatum: "Either you give or you take. If you do not give, I take it that you are poor, and you will receive goods from me."

There was a wealthy man by the name of Reb Yeshayah. Mendele commanded him to give the poor people one hundred kilos of coal. However, Reb Yeshayah was only ready to give him money, not coal. Mendele threatened him, "You have the option; you give or you take. If you have coal you must give; if not I will give you." Reb Yeshayah stuck to his original offer.

What did Mendele do? Together with two of his colleagues, he dragged two heavy sacks of coal dust and poured it all over Reb Yeshayah's tastefully decorated bedroom. The coals created a thick, black, misty fog. In the end Reb Yeshayah begged Mendele to accept the entire amount of coal which he had demanded, if only he would remove the coal and dirt which had wreaked havoc all over his house!

Mendele Ganav, without asking questions, laid claim to a storage room in our house to deposit his stolen wares. He did not pay rent, of course, but promised my father that as compensation for using the cellar, he would not steal from him. He was true to his word. From that cellar room, he and his assistants (who also helped him steal) distributed the valuable goods to the poor. Mendele was especially busy before Pesach, when he provided the poor with onions and potatoes.

The Tsanzer *rosh hakahal*, Reb Shalom Yonah Tenzer, a wealthy and generous person, once asked Mendele Ganav, "Who put you in charge of providing for the poor people of Tsanz?" to which Mendele replied, "I do not care if a hundred poor people die every day. However, as long as they are alive, it is my duty to see to it that they have food and warm homes."

This is what a Tsanzer thief was all about. He did not benefit at all from his thefts but distributed everything to the poor.

Mendele eventually got married to a girl from Katowitz. He went there to live and repented completely. When he came to Tsanz on a visit, one could not recognize the thief. He had become a better, more refined person, no longer Mendele Ganav but Mendele Miller.

Reb Moshe Mendel Reinhold

Reb Moshe Mendel Reinhold of Tsanz related the following about himself:

"I came from a very poor home and did not have the opportunity to learn much as a boy. The poverty in our home was so great that I was forced to go to work as a young child in order to provide bread. In the meantime, both my parents passed away, and I was left to fend for myself.

"When I turned twenty I went to the Tsanzer Rebbe, Reb Aryeh Leibish, and asked him what would become of me. He told me to find a suitable match and get married. I asked him how I would make a living, and he advised me to open a flour business. He told me that since flour is necessary for bread, I would never be short of income. I was indeed very successful in my business.

"I hired a tutor to teach me what I had missed as a child. He was a respectable person, one of Tsanz's distinguished members, by the name of Reb Shalom Reb Boruchel's. I would arrive at the *beis midrash* every morning at 4 A.M., light the fire, and then learn with my rebbe for four hours, until 8 A.M. First we would learn the *chok* of that day, then Gemara with *Tosafos*. This arrangement lasted for forty years!"

It was interesting to hear Reb Moshe Mendel reason with Hashem in the middle of Shemoneh Esreh. "*Ribbono shel olam*," he would say, "a dowry, a bread, a bread, a dowry," and he would beseech Hashem for all his needs. He was fortunate to earn a decent income and establish generations of G-d-fearing children and grandchildren.

CHARITY AND GOOD DEEDS

His character traits were exemplary. In the year 5688 (1928) there was a severe crisis in the flour industry. The price of flour fell lower and lower, until it became half of its original value. Reb Moshe Mendel ordered an announcement to be made in all the *batei midrash* that flour for Shabbos would be distributed free to all the poor people. When he was asked about this sudden generous offer he answered, "Seeing how Hashem can decrease the value of flour from one day to the next, I want to take the opportunity while there is still time and give as much *tzedakah* as possible as long as the flour still has some value."

He and his entire family were shot in their beds by the Nazi beasts in the Tsanzer ghetto on April 29, 1942, during the pre-May *aktion*.

The Pious Women of Tsanz

Under this title, Nechumele, the second youngest daughter of the Divrei Chaim, deserves first mention. She was famous for her great piety and keen wit.

Nechumele was also known to have helped many people through her prayers. Women came to her with *kvittelach*, and her blessings were often fulfilled. We lived directly opposite the Divrei Chaim's home, where Nechumele lived in her father's apartment. She accepted people in the room where her saintly father used to hold his *tischen*. People came to Nechumele to take counsel for their pressing problems, for she was known to be a very clever woman.

I will add a few brief outlines of other righteous women in Tsanz whom I clearly remember. There was Feigele Saphir, Tzerele, Chatshe Gut, and Esther the *shamashte*. These women bore the responsibility of giving *tzedakah* in secret to those who were too proud to accept. In addition, they were always ready to help another person or do a *chesed* when necessary. Feigele Saphir and Chatshe Gut were women of means, so they gave *tzedakah* from their own money. Tzerele and Esther the *shamashte* did not have the necessary funds, so they would go around collecting in order to accomplish their acts of *chesed*.

They provided for all the poor families, especially those who were sick. Every day they brought the sick a pot of hot chicken soup with

The Vanished City of Tsanz

a piece of chicken and some apple compote. They also assisted those who had just given birth, for in those days people had their babies at home, in tiny one- or two-room apartments. These exceptional women saw to it that the mother and the other children at home had something to eat. They baked a large, square butter cake which they placed behind the pillow of the new mother. When she or her children felt hungry, or if the children were whining or being difficult, the mother could break off a piece of the cake and give it to them.

Chapter 13
MINHAGIM OF TSANZ

We were overwhelmed by the great interest aroused in the Yiddish rendition of the *minhagim* (traditions) of my hometown, Tsanz. We have therefore decided to list the *minhagim* in English. These are the Tsanzer *minhagim* as I remember them from the period when Rabbis Aryeh Leibish and Mordechai Zev Halberstam were *rabbanim* in Tsanz.

Morning Blessings, Tzitzis, and Tefillin

The people of Tsanz learned Gemara or *Chok L'Yisrael* before davening.

Tur with *Shulchan Aruch, Orach Chaim,* was frequently studied in Tsanz.

They were particular to recite the three chapters of Shema after *birkas haTorah*.

The bag containing the tallis and tefillin was carried under the arm and not held by the hand. This was considered more honorable for the tefillin.

The *tallis katan* and *talleisim* were made of Turkish wool, because no flax was grown in Turkey, ensuring that there would be no problems with *sha'atnez* (mixture of flax and wool in a garment). The tallis (*tallis gadol*) had an *atarah* woven of silver. The Rebbes and *rebbishe* grandchildren had two *ataros* — one at the top and one,

The Vanished City of Tsanz

called the *"mittel shtickel,"* in the center of the tallis.

The custom was to kiss the tefillin when taking them out and putting them back in the tallis bag, and when donning them and taking them off.

One did not speak (other than prayers) while the tefillin were worn, not even in Lashon HaKodesh.

A boy who was about to become bar mitzvah did not put on tefillin before his thirteenth birthday. If his birthday was on Shabbos, he began donning tefillin on Sunday.

Shacharis

Birkas hashachar was said while wearing tallis and tefillin, and everyone said it loud enough so that his neighbor could answer "amen."

The *ba'al tefillah* began with אדון עולם. He davened with great *kavanah*, loud and at length, as did the entire congregation.

The *ba'al tefillah* said הנותן לשכוי and not אשר נתן. He recited aloud יהא לעולם אדם and finished aloud ומיחדים שמך בכל יום תמיד. The congregation recited aloud together שמע ישראל. The *ba'al tefillah* began איזהו מקומן aloud.

At Kaddish, after שמה דקדשא בריך הוא, the congregation responded with בריך הוא and not "amen."

When Kaddish D'Rabbanan was said, one added הוא ברחמיו יעשה.

Before הודו one said מזמור לדוד ה' מי יגור (Tehillim, ch. 15).

The *ba'al tefillah* finished aloud with ה' הושיעה, רוממו ה', and יהי חסדך.

In יהי כבוד, one said והוא רחום quietly. Only ה' הושיעה was recited aloud.

The *ba'al tefillah* always said הללוקה הללוקה together.

At לאל ברוך, one said ונזכה כולנו יחד במהרה.

On the weekdays one said אהבת עולם and on Shabbos אהבה רבה. One said ושבור עול הגליות מעל צוארנו.

In the summer, one said מוריד הטל and not מוריד הטל ומוריד הטל משיב הרוח.

MINHAGIM OF TSANZ

One stood during Kedushah only until ימלך וכו׳.

At אב הרחמן שמע קולנו, before כי אתה שומע, one did not say אנא ה׳ חטאתי.

In Tsanz, Tachanun was said on all the *rebbishe* yartzeits, except for 21 Adar, 19 Kislev, and 11 Tamuz. When there was a bris in Tsanz, the whole town did not say Tachanun. Tachanun was also not said on 11–17 Adar and from 23 Adar until after Rosh Chodesh Iyar. Tachanun was also omitted in the week after Pesach Sheini and the week after Shavuos.

אבינו מלכנו was said only during the Aseres Yemei Teshuvah and not on a *ta'anis tzibbur*.

After ובא לציון, one added ה׳ אדונינו. After that, one said תפילה לדוד. On a day in which Tachanun was not said, only בית יעקב was said.

On a day in which אל ארך אפים was not said, one went straight to the שיר של יום. After the שיר של יום, one did not say הושיענו.

Kaddish was said at every interval, even if there was no obligation.

After עלינו of every *tefillah*, the *ba'al tefillah* said אדון עולם.

Minchah and Ma'ariv

In the *Rav's beis midrash*, *minchah* was davened forty to forty-five minutes after *shekiah*. Tachanun was not said, although it was said in shul. The shul was the only place where *nosach Ashkenaz* was used.

Ma'ariv was davened sixty minutes after *shekiah*. However, for *sefiras ha'omer* one waited until Rabbeinu Tam's *zeman*.

Rosh Chodesh

When Rosh Chodesh was on a Sunday, one did not eat a *kezayis* at *se'udah shelishis* (in order to avoid having to say יעלה ויבא and רצה). Even if one happened to have eaten a *kezayis*, one did not say יעלה ויבא.

ברכי נפשי was not said during davening but sung at the *se'udas Rosh Chodesh*.

After putting the *sifrei Torah* in the *aron kodesh* and saying Kaddish, there was a five-minute pause to allow time to remove the Rashi tefillin and put on the Rabbeinu Tam tefillin.

At the *se'udas Rosh Chodesh*, one added one special food in honor of Rosh Chodesh. יהי החדש הזה was sung at the *se'udah*, along with ברכי נפשי.

After *kiddush levanah*, the congregation went back into the *beis midrash* and sang טובים מאורות, but they did not make a *rekidah* (dance).

Once in twenty-eight years, at *kiddush hachamah*, there were two musicians who played טובים מאורות with a marching tune that was specially composed by the Tsanzer composers for the occasion.

Shabbos

A *berachah* was said for taking challah dough from a minimum of 1.25 kilos. The Kiddush cup was 0.86 grams. Others maintained that the required *shiur* is 0.67 grams *(Divrei Yechezkel)*.

In Tsanz, one read each verse of the parashah *shenayim mikra v'echad Targum* (twice the text and once *Targum*). This was contrary to the opinion of the Ba'al Shem Tov, who said that one must read through the parashah twice without pause and only then read *Targum*. If one had to pause in the middle, one paused at a *pey* or *samech*.

Minchah was said a half-hour after candle lighting. One never davened earlier, even on the long summer days. *Motza'ei Shabbos* was according to Rabbeinu Tam's *zeman*.

If a candle was inclined toward one side, one placed a challah on the other side. This was a *segulah* for the candle to move back into place.

A Shabbos clock was used.

Sardine tins were permitted to be opened on Shabbos.

MINHAGIM OF TSANZ

Everybody wore *shtreimlech, bekishes*, and black socks. Only the *Rav*, the *dayanim*, and Chassidim chosen by the *Rav* himself wore white socks.

A *rezhevolka* was worn during called "a *chalat* without buttons."

A Chassidic Jew did not remove his *shtreimel* and *bekishe* the entire Shabbos, except when he slept. Even on weekdays, one did not remove his hat and jacket during the day, especially when outdoors.

Clapping during davening was common; the davening was said with enthusiasm and joy.

Before מזמור לדוד הבו לה׳, one said "בואו ונצא לקראת שבת."

At אהבת עולם, the *ba'al tefillah* began כי הם, and when he reached ואהבתך, the entire congregation joined in.

At שלום עליכם one said מלאכי השלום מלאכי השרת מלאכי עליון. אשת חיל was sung with the famous Ropshitzer *niggun*.

At Kiddush, כי הוא יום and כי בנו בחרת were not said.

The head of the household was *motzi* his family with Kiddush and *lechem mishnah*. Even so each person said the *berachah borei pri hagafen* himself on the wine and *hamotzi* on the challah.

After Kiddush the head of the household put on his *"tisch chalat"* (*tisch bekishe*), but he only tied on the *gartel* for bentching.

The head of the household did not wait until everybody had washed to say *hamotzi*.

At the *Rav's* tisch everyone wore a *bekishe* (not a *tisch chalat*).

The *Rav* recited, rather than sang, אתקינו סעודתא. Afterward, before אזמר בשבחין, they would make a *berachah* on *hadasim* leaves. Then the *Rav* got up from his place and walked till about half the length of the table and back.

One ate a non-plaited challah called a *koilish* at the Friday night *se'udah*. At the Shabbos morning *se'udah* a plaited challah was eaten. My father, *a"h*, told me that this was because of the *din* that "*kavod hayom kodem lichvod halailah*" (the honor of the day takes precedence over the honor of the night).

One did not cut the challah into straight slices but into slanted pieces, large enough to last the whole *se'udah*.

The table stood from north to south (אסדר לדרמא).

After the fish was eaten, one did not wash one's hands, but one drank liquor and said, *"L'chaim!"*

At the *se'udah* the *zemiros* מה ידידות, מנוחה ושמחה, כל מקדש, and תנו שבת ושירה were sung.

Square-shaped noodles, called *"pletzlech"* (to be different from the long ones used during the week), and butter beans were served in the chicken soup. Four types of tzimmes (additional dishes) were served after the chicken: farfel tzimmes (called "the Ba'al Shem's tzimmes"), carrot tzimmes, and plum tzimmes. In the summer, from after Shavuos, pears were eaten instead of plums. The fourth type of tzimmes, liver, was eaten only with the *Rav*.

שיר המעלות was not sung before bentching, only recited. The person who was honored to lead the bentching said הב לן ונברך when taking the cup of wine.

Barley was eaten during the meal only, since there is a question of whether one has to say the *berachah borei minei mezonos* on it.

Before davening on Shabbos morning, one did not eat but only drank coffee with milk. A sugar cube was dipped into the coffee. The *berachah shehakol* was said before the sugar was popped into the mouth.

Shacharis on Shabbos morning commenced between 9:00 and 9:30 A.M.

At יהי כבוד, one ended with ונחלתו לא יעזב, and the *pasuk* והוא רחום was omitted on Shabbos and *yom tov*. The chazzan ended aloud with the *pasuk* ה' הושיעה. On the weekdays, the *pasuk* ה' הושיעה was recited aloud, and והוא רחום was said quietly.

האל הפותח was sung, apart from the verse אין ערוך לדואין זולתך אפס בלתך was sung. אין ערוך לך ה' אלקינו ומי דומה לך which was recited.

MINHAGIM OF TSANZ

- At אהבה רבה, the *ba'al tefillah* recited aloud מהר והבא until קוממיות לארצנו. At the words כי אל פועל ישועות אתה, the whole congregation joined in together.

- צור ישראל was also said together with the *ba'al tefillah*. גאל ישראל was said quietly (only on Shabbos).

- ממקומך was only sung on *Shabbos mevarchim* and *yom tov*. If the *ba'al tefillah* had a good voice, he was allowed to sing it on an ordinary Shabbos.

- After Kedushah, the men put on their *shtreimlach* until *mussaf*, or until Rosh Chodesh bentching.

- Only a *gabbai tzedakah* was honored with removing and replacing the *sefer Torah*.

- An honorable layman was given the title *"chaver"* when he was called to the Torah.

- יחדשהו was sung with the well-known Tsanzer *niggun*.

- אנעים זמירות was said, but the *aron kodesh* was not opened.

- One did not give a *kiddush* in honor of a bar mitzvah; only a *se'udah* on the boy's thirteenth birthday was given.

- On Shabbos *sheva berachos* there was also no *kiddush* in shul, in order not to embarrass those who could not afford it.

- אתקינו סעודתא and חי ה' וברוך צורי were sung before Kiddush on Shabbos morning.

- Kiddush was said standing up and not while wearing a tallis.

- After Kiddush, one ate a piece of cake, said *al hamichyah*, and washed for challah immediately afterwards. The *Rav* would make a break of one and a half hours.

- At the meal, one ate fish, eggs and onions, *galareta* (calf's-foot jelly), cholent (which was of a more liquidy nature, not thick), and *lokshen kugel*. On Shabbos Rosh Chodesh, an extra kugel was served — challah kugel. Potato kugel was only eaten on Pesach.

The Vanished City of Tsanz

The *zemiros* sung at the *se'udah* of Shabbos day were ברוך ה' יום יום until שבת היום לה', and ברוך אל עליון, כי לא יזנח לעולם ה'.

At *minchah* on Shabbos the *ba'al tefillah* donned his tallis only after אשרי and ובא לציון. At *minchah*, one did not announce "יעמד פלוני בן פלוני," but the *gabbai* would personally summon the people who were called up to the Torah.

During *gelilah*, one said אודה and אשרי איש.

After *minchah* on Shabbos, when one went home for *se'udah shelishis*, one did not say "good Shabbos" anymore.

One washed and ate *se'udah shelishis* at home, and then returned to the *beis midrash* with a *kezayis* of challah in order to bentch there.

The *zemiros* sung at the third meal were מזמור לדוד ה' רועי, בני היכלא, and נמליכו וניחדו until בבואו מאדום. One then stood up and said ה' מלך twice and continued with ברוך אל עליון, דרור יקרא, שבת היום, אל מסתתר, אין כאלקינו, and שהשלום שלו.

Se'udah shelishis sheva berachos was celebrated at home and not in the *beis midrash*. One sang דוי הסר with a special tune. The one who was honored with bentching drank from the cup even after the *zeman* of *motza'ei Shabbos*, but the one who said *sheva berachos* did not do so. The *kallah* drank from the cup but not the *chasan*.

The *zeman* for davening *ma'ariv* was according to the opinion of Rabbeinu Tam: seventy-two minutes after *shekiah*. At *ma'ariv* of *motza'ei Shabbos*, one did not say ברוך ה' לעולם.

Yom Tov

On *yom tov* evening the *ba'al tefillah* said ברכו with a special tune.

Ma'aravos (the *yotzros* said at *ma'ariv*) and other *yotzros* were sung at the meal.

The women lit candles after *ma'ariv*, before Kiddush, even on the first night of *yom tov*.

MINHAGIM OF TSANZ

When *yom tov* was on Shabbos, the daytime *se'udah* was divided into two; one bentched after the fish. The people who lived near a *beis midrash* davened *minchah* before the second half of the meal.

Every *yom tov* at *minchah*, at ועל כן נקוה לך, the people made a *rekidah* (dance).

When *yom tov* was on a Friday, one did not go to the mikveh in the afternoon *l'kavod Shabbos*.

On *yom tov* which was on a Shabbos, one did not say the י"ג מדות when removing the *sefer Torah*, and the *kohanim* did not *duchen*.

When one did *duchen*, none of the *kohanim* would daven at the *amud*.

After Kaddish of *mussaf*, the people said, "*Yasher ko'ach kohanim.*"

On Shabbos Chol HaMo'ed, one danced at בואי בשלום. One sang שלום עליכם. Before Kiddush one said רבון העולמים until מלך תמיד דרכו. One then sang אשת חיל. אתקינו סעודתא was said only until בהדה אתין לסעדא.

Every day of Chol HaMo'ed, and of course on Shabbos, one sang the *yom tov* tunes of וכולם מקבלים, Kaddish, אל מלך, ישתבח, and the תתקבל at every Kaddish.

Pesach

In Tsanz, one ate only hand-baked matzos. (It is well known that the Divrei Chaim was very much against using machine-made matzos.) For the seder, only *shemurah matzah* was used; during Pesach the women and children ate *shemurah mishe'as techinah matzos*, called "*prosta matzos.*"

The flour was ground in a water mill, not a steam-driven mill. The *Rav* personally oversaw the *kashering* of the mill. For the *shemurah mishe'as techinah matzos*, the flour was ground with a hand mill.

Mayim shelanu was taken from the lake. The same wooden buckets were used every year, even on *erev Pesach*.

The Vanished City of Tsanz

On *erev Pesach*, the holes in the matzos were not punched with an iron roller, but with a sort of wooden fork called a *"shtipel heltzer."*

The *Rav* himself distributed the *erev Pesach* matzah and *charoses* to his Chassidim.

The *erev Pesach* matzah was carefully laid on a bed as soon as they reached home.

Every *erev Pesach*, a matzah was put into a round wooden box with a few holes punched in. The box was hung on the western wall of the shul, serving as an *eiruv chatzeiros*, since Tsanz had an *eiruv*, as did most Jewish towns in Galicia. The matzah lay there until the following Pesach.

One did not extinguish the electric lights at *bedikas chametz*.

On Pesach, one did not use a single thing which was not made at home, even if it had the best *hechsher*. For example, one did not use oil, only *schmaltz*. Cheese and butter also wasn't used during Pesach. Milk was only used if it had been milked before Pesach; it was recooked every day so that it would not become sour. Only children drank milk which was milked during Pesach.

Most Chassidic Jews did not use coffee during Pesach. Those who did use coffee bought it in its shell and roasted it on the fire and then ground it.

Only homemade wine and matzos were used during Pesach. People did not eat at other people's homes. Even a father and son did not eat at each other's homes.

One did not mention the word "bread" during Pesach; instead one said *"chametz."*

If a woman baked matzah in the middle of the year, she would only bake egg matzos, so that the *Pesachdiger* matzos would be something special, only for Pesach. Machine-made matzos were never eaten, even in the middle of the year.

At *ma'ariv*, the *sheliach tzibbur* sang from העושה לנו נסים until ומלכותו.

MINHAGIM OF TSANZ

On the first night of Pesach, one could not visit the *Rav* at his seder, and on the second night only for *sefiras ha'omer*. This was because the entire family sat together; the table was very long, stretching into the next room, where the women sat.

When the first day of Pesach was on Shabbos, one sang שלום עליכם.

After the son said מה נשתנה, the father and the rest of the household repeated it. My father, *z"l*, said that this was because מה נשתנה is also part of the Haggadah, so all are obliged to say it.

On the first night one made a point of eating the *afikomen* before *chatzos*, but not on the second night.

On the seder plate one placed a head of horseradish as *maror*. Ground horseradish was used for *koreich*. One ate lettuce with ground horseradish as *maror*. The lettuce was not placed on the seder plate. The *zeroa* was a roasted wing. One used radishes for *karpas*. (In Tsanz there were two gentile familes who originated from Yugoslavia who grew radishes and lettuce for the sole purpose of selling them to the Jews on *erev Pesach*. It was still cold at that time of year, so they grew them in greenhouses. These families moved to Tsanz in the time of the Divrei Chaim.)

At *ma'ariv*, one sang from המעביר בניו until ומלכותו.

On the eighth day of Pesach, everybody brought *kneidlach* to the *Rav*, and the *Rav* mixed them all together in one big pot. He then ate from it and gave *sherayim* to all his Chassidim.

When the last day of Pesach was on a Shabbos, the *kneidlach* were made on the seventh day of Pesach, in the afternoon.

For the Shabbos after Pesach, challah was baked with a form of a key on it.

Shavuos

Children would stick pictures of armed soldiers riding on horses on their windowpanes. These hinted that Hashem descended onto Mount Sinai with his hosts of angels.

The Vanished City of Tsanz

One did not cut one's hair from Pesach until Shavuos.

At *ma'ariv*, the *ba'al tefillah* sang אהבת עולם.

One stayed awake the entire night of Shavuos and said תיקון ליל שבועות. When dawn broke, one went to the mikveh and then to sleep. Davening was at nine-thirty, like every Shabbos and *yom tov*.

At *mussaf*, one only said the *piyut* אז שש מאות.

After *mussaf*, one made Kiddush and ate cheesecake and cheese *kreplach*. After a half-hour's break, one washed for the meal and ate fish and meat. One sang ובאו כלם from יום שבתון.

Av and Mourning

During the Three Weeks, the *rabbanim* traveled to various health resorts so as not to be at home. This was considered like going into *galus*.

During the Three Weeks the *batei midrash* were painted, because the painters, being without work, were prepared to work for less money.

On *erev Shabbos Chazon* one washed completely, with soap, in honor of Shabbos. But there was no sauna, and the water of the mikveh was only lukewarm.

שיר המעלות was always said before bentching, even on weekdays. One only said על נהרות בבל before bentching only at the *se'udah hamafsekes*.

If Tishah B'Av was on a Sunday, one ate *milchigs* during *se'udah shelishis*. (During the year, people sometimes ate *milchigs* and sometimes not, but in this case special attention was given to eating milk products.)

On *motza'ei Shabbos*, one took off his Shabbos clothing and put on weekday clothing before *ma'ariv*. The *paroches* was taken off the *aron kodesh*.

At *minchah*, one said קרבנות and אשרי before Shemoneh Esreh, and the אין כאלקינו and שיר של יום after Shemoneh Esreh.

MINHAGIM OF TSANZ

In Tsanzer homes, the *zecher l'churban* was placed opposite the door.

In the case of a mourner, only one minyan was assembled, even when several brothers sat together. Each would be the *ba'al tefillah* at a different *tefillah*.

One did not bring a *sefer Torah* from the *beis midrash* to a mourner's house; those who davened at that minyan went to the *beis midrash* after davening to hear the Torah reading.

The tablecloths were removed from the tables at a mourner's home.

Selichos was not said in the home of a mourner.

A mourner sat at a different place from his own in the *beis midrash*, for a whole year in the case of his father or mother and for thirty days in the case of another relative.

Elul

יום כיפור קטן was said only once a year, on *erev Rosh Chodesh Elul*.

לדוד ה' אורי was not said after davening, but one said eighteen chapters of Tehillim every day until Rosh HaShanah.

On the first day of Selichos, one recited the whole of Tehillim from 3 A.M. until 5 A.M. After that, Selichos was said. All the *batei midrash* began saying Selichos at the same time; there was no later minyan.

Tishrei

Between Rosh HaShanah and Hoshana Rabbah one dipped the challah in salt and honey.

The *ba'al tefillah* kept his watch on the *amud* on Rosh HaShanah and Yom Kippur so that he could keep track of the time.

On Rosh HaShanah, davening commenced at 7:30 A.M. and finished at 5 P.M. There was a break of one and a half hours.

The Vanished City of Tsanz

One did not say the *yotzros* before Shemoneh Esreh, only אור עולם, סלח, and חטאנו.

During the break, the *Rav* and the *ba'alei mussafim* went to the mikveh. The *Rav* then went to the main shul to blow shofar, since he was the *Rav* of the town, and then to his own *beis midrash* to blow shofar and to daven *mussaf*.

The *Rav* did not give a *derashah* before shofar-blowing. He only gave a *derashah* twice a year, on Shabbos HaGadol and Shabbos Shuvah.

One did not eat before hearing the shofar. Some drank coffee with milk.

Before hearing the shofar, one said למנצח לבני קרח seven times.

One said the *piyutim* of Kedushah — וחיות, etc.— standing up, before ימלך at *shacharis* and before אדיר אדירנו at *mussaf*.

On Rosh HaShanah one said אתה קדוש and לדור ודור. On the first day, one said זכר תחלת, אנסיכה מלכי, and אשא דעי; on the second day, one said אנוסה לעזרה, אפחד במעשי, and אהללה אלקי.

When Rosh HaShanah was on a Shabbos, one did not bow down to the floor at ואנחנו כורעים.

After *mussaf*, the *Rav* blew another 100 shofar blasts.

At Shemoneh Esreh, one sang מי כמוך, מלך עליון, אדם יסודו, אתה הוא, חמול על מעשיך, וכל מאמינים, ויאתיו כל, היה עם פיפיות, זכרנו היום, מכלכל חיים, ארשת שפתנו, הללו אל בקדשו, אלקינו היום תאמצנו, ונתנה תוקף, אין קצבה, and הרת עולם.

When the Selichos of the י"ג מדות happened to be on Friday it was changed to Thursday. The reason was that on the day of שלש עשרה מדות there was a great *hisorerus* in Tsanz. The whole of סדר קרבנות was said after *chatzos*. Many people fasted until after the reading of קרבנות. On Friday there was no time for all this because of the preparations for Shabbos.

The Tsanzer Chassidim went to Tashlich on Rosh HaShanah. The Shinover Chassidim went on שלש עשרה מדות.

MINHAGIM OF TSANZ

During the Aseres Yemei Teshuvah, one said the version of שיר למעלות אשא עיני written between ויהי בנסוע and בריך שמה. One did not say the שלש עשרה מדות after ויהי בנסוע, before שיר למעלות.

On *erev Yom Kippur*, the *gabbai* handed everybody a piece of cake, so that if, *chas v'shalom*, it was decreed that somebody must stretch out his hand in need, he should be *yotzei* with this.

In Tsanz, people did not extend hands to each other in greeting, not even to say *"mazel tov."* However, when a visitor came from another town, one did shake hands to say *"shalom aleichem."* On *erev Yom Kippur*, too, before כל נדרי, everybody extended their hands to each other to beg forgiveness and to wish each other a *"gemar chasimah tovah, ir zalt ois betten ales gut."* On *motza'ei Yom Kippur*, one said *"ir zalt haben ales gut oisgebetten."* From the following day until Hoshana Rabbah one said *"a gitten kvittel."*

In Tsanz one did not say:
At *ma'ariv*: אותך אדרוש, אמנם אשמנו, and אתה מבין;
At *shacharis*: אך אתום, איומה בחר, אנא אלקים, אדר יקר, אנוש מה יזכה, ליושב תהלות until נאמירך, אין כמוך, מי כמוך, אפסי ארץ, אשר אומץ, אתה מבין and אדברה, אחד until האדיר בשמי, אין מספר, אילי שחק;
At *mussaf*: אשר אימתך, אמרו לאלקים until אין ערוך from אנוש איך, אילי מרום, and אמיצי שחקים, but at the Avodah one said אתה כוננת and not אמיץ כח and אתה מבין;
At *minchah*: אתה מבין and אל נא.

The *sheliach tzibbur* sang:
At *ma'ariv*: כי הנה כחומר, אמנם כן, סלח נא אשמות, סלח נא, יעלה, אדון עולם, and ואתה מאמירנו until כי אנו עמך;
At *shacharis*: מעשה, אמרו לאלקים, אתה הוא אלקינו, מכלכל, זכרנו, כי אנו עמך and חמול על מעשיך, האדרת והאמונה, על ישראל אמונתו, אלקינו, ואתה מאמירנו until;
At *mussaf*: בראש השנה, ונתנה תוקף, מעשה אלקינו, אמרו לאלקים, ויאתיו כל, וכל מאמינים, חמול על מעשיך, אין קצבה, אדם יסודו מעפר, היום תאמצנו, כי אנו עמך, and היה עם פיפיות.

The Vanished City of Tsanz

The same applied for *minchah* and *ne'ilah*.

Many people stayed in the *beis midrash* from כל נדרי until after *ne'ilah*.

Sukkos

Most Jews in Tsanz bought a *lulav* without *keneplech* (bent at the point).

In Tsanz the women did not sit in the sukkah, in accordance with the *Zohar*.

One was not particular to sleep in the sukkah.

All the *yotzros* were said. The *yotzros* which had been omitted on Yom Kippur were sung on Sukkos at the *se'udah*.

The whole of *sefer Devarim* was read from a *sefer Torah* on Hoshana Rabbah night. After that there was a *se'udas ushpizin* in the *Rav*'s sukkah. At midnight, everyone went to the *beis midrash* where the whole Tehillim was said.

The *hoshanos* were tied with the leaves of a *lulav*. In the outlying villages, the Jews tied the *hoshanos* with stalks from the *hoshanos* since they did not have *lulav* leaves.

On Hoshana Rabbah, the shofar was blown between every *hakafah*.

When Shemini Atzeres was on a Shabbos, the *kohanim* would *duchen* on Hoshana Rabbah.

On Shemini Atzeres day, there were *hakafos*, but people only danced at the seventh.

In shul, the parashah of Yaakov and Eisav was *leined*. They did not *lein* in the *Rav*'s *beis midrash*.

Every *hakafah* had its special tune, which was only sung once a year. For the *leining* of *chasan bereishis*, too, there was a special tune.

אמונים אשר נאספו, from *shacharis* of Shemini Atzeres, was sung at the *se'udah*.

If Simchas Torah was on a Shabbos, one danced at בואי בשלום.

MINHAGIM OF TSANZ

Chanukah

The *Rav*, and many other Tsanzer descendants, would light the Chanukah candles at 8:30 P.M. After lighting, one sang מעוז צור, למנצח בנגינות, מזמור שיר חנוכת הבית, and רננו צדיקים.

Every day, except for Friday, *pesukim* beginning with three different letters of chapter 119 of Tehillim were recited.

One sat by the Chanukah lights for half an hour.

At *shacharis*, one sang מזמור שיר חנוכת הבית.

The *shamash* would light the menorah in the *beis midrash* between *minchah* and *ma'ariv*. There was an old custom to throw towels at him.

Nittel nacht was kept on January 6 from 6 P.M. till 12 P.M., even though the gentile's holiday was on December 25.

Purim

At *minchah* of Ta'anis Esther, the people wore their Shabbos clothing and gave half a shekel.

Purim was a serious affair in Tsanz. At *ma'ariv* and *shacharis* the davening was serious and thoughtful.

In the morning, before the reading of the megillah, the *gabbai* announced that one should have in mind at the *berachah* of *shehecheyanu* the mitzvos of *mishlo'ach manos* and *matanos l'evyonim*. This *minhag* was initiated by the Divrei Chaim.

After reading the verses ליהודים היתה אורה and ויאמר המלך תלוהו, a special tune was sung.

After *shacharis*, the people would visit the *shochetim*, where they were served *noont* (honey and nuts) and drank *"l'chaim."* One did not get drunk. In Tsanz, there were no Jewish drunks, not even on Purim.

The *simchah* only began in the late afternoon, after all the mitzvos had been done.

On Shushan Purim, a calf was slaughtered. There was a play in which actors acted out *akeidas Yitzchak* and *mechiras Yosef*. The rejoicing on Shushan Purim was even greater than on Purim day itself.

When Shushan Purim was on an *erev Shabbos*, one danced during בואי בשלום.

Weddings

At an *aufruf*, the *machatanim* and the *chasan* davened at home Friday night; they did not go to the *beis midrash*. Though the *Shulchan Aruch* says that when one davens at home one should not say מגן אבות, in Tsanz it was said at home, too, in accordance with the Arizal.

On Shabbos morning before davening, many people collected the *chasan* and escorted him to shul with a special tune.

On Shabbos afternoon, *bachurim* went to the *chasan*'s home and sang *zemiros*. No married men were present. This was called *"der forshpiel."*

Most weddings in Tsanz took place on *erev Shabbos*, to keep down the costs. The *chuppah* took place before the door of the town shul, one hour before candle lighting.

At the *kabbalas panim*, before the *chuppah*, the ladies were given *esrog* jam.

Only *bachurim* of sixteen years and older were present at the *kabbalas panim* before the *chuppah*. No married men attended. The *shamash* would go around with a list of the *chasan*'s acquaintances on it. It was an honor for a boy to be listed on that sheet because that meant that he was officially recognized as one of the "older" *bachurim*. When the time came to go to the *chuppah*, the *machatanim* and other guests came to collect the *chasan* and the *bachurim* went home. A *bachur* did not attend a *chuppah* except for his brother's or sister's.

At the *sheva berachos* of Friday night, the friends and relatives of the couple visited the young couple and presented them with kugel, cake, or other delectables. There was singing and rejoicing, and a merry atmosphere prevailed.

At Shabbos *sheva berachos* one also said דוי הסר.

A grand *melaveh malkah* was celebrated on *motza'ei Shabbos* with music. Sunday morning, the *machatanim* journeyed home. The *chasan* wore his *shtreimel* the entire week, but there were no other *sheva berachos* apart from Shabbos. Only the Rebbes and very wealthy people celebrated *sheva berachos* every night of the seven days.

Weddings were not celebrated after the twenty-second of the month.

When a *rekidah* was made, one only danced from right to left.

Children

At a *shalom zachor*, *zachor kichelach* — heart-shaped biscuits — were served. My father, *a"h*, explained that since it is called a "*se'udas shalom zachor*," one serves *mezonos*.

The Tsanzer Rav was honored with being *sandak* at every bris.

After a certain incident, the Divrei Chaim introduced a rule that a *shochet* may not be a *mohel*.

The *mohel*'s knife was not placed under the baby's head.

On the morning of a bris, one sang רוממות אל בגרונם at *shacharis*. וכרות was recited verse by verse.

The baby's father did not say *shehecheyanu*, even it was his first child.

A baby girl was usually given her name on Shabbos. If somebody named his baby daughter on a weekday, she was called "*a vochendiger meidel*," a weekday girl.

When a child turned five, a party was made for him on Shabbos afternoon. Cake, fruit, and drinks were served. This was called a "*chumash se'udah*." Family and friends of the family and the Rebbe and classmates of the child were invited. *Pekelach* were distributed

to the children. One little boy asked the one celebrating:
"*Yingele*, what are you learning?"
"*Chumash.*"
"What does '*Chumash*' mean?"
"Five."
"Five what?"
"There are five *sefarim* in the holy Torah."
"What are they called?"
"The first one is Bereishis, the second Shemos, the third VaYikra, the fourth BeMidbar, and the fifth Devarim."
"And what *Chumash* are you learning, *yingele?*"
"VaYikra."
"What does '*Vayikra*' mean?"
" 'And He called.' "
"Who called?"
"Hashem."
"Whom did He call?"
"Moshe Rabbeinu."
"Why are you learning VaYikra?"
"Because in VaYikra it says the *seder* of *korbanos*, and if we learn the *seder* of *korbanos* it is as if we have actually sacrificed the *korbanos* to Hashem."

After that, the child recited a few verses of VaYikra.

The child was adorned with all sorts of jewelry, just as one did to a baby at a *pidyon haben.*

One did not cut the *payos*, but when they grew longer than the face, one burned off the ends.

Additional Minhagim

One was very particular not to use a newspaper which had Hebrew lettering for mundane purposes, even if it was an irreligious newspaper. One was also careful not to tread on it. An irreligious newspaper was never allowed into the home.

MINHAGIM OF TSANZ

Only Yiddish was spoken in the home.

One was careful to use refined language only; even the porters and deliverymen did not use vulgar words.

The first year after a young man got married, he was not allowed to daven in front of the *amud*. Generally speaking, only elderly men davened in front of the *amud*.

Cooked food was only eaten after one had washed for bread, because of problems with the *berachos*.

To distinguish between *milchigs* and *fleishigs*, three curves were cut into the *milchiger* crockery.

If a knife which was made of two parts became *treif*, it was stuck into the ground ten times in different places.

The Rebbes wore flat velvet hats. Everybody else wore high velvet hats called *"plushener* hats." Nobody would be seen in the street without his hat and jacket. Even at home they were seldom taken off. The reason was that since Hashem is everywhere one needs to dress with respect.

After the *tisch* Friday night the Chassidim used to make a *rekidah* singing רננו צדיקים.

When saying *korbanos* on Rosh Chodesh, ובראשי חדשיכם was not said.

CHAPTER 14

THE BUXBAUM FAMILY

My Grandfather Reb Yerachmiel

My grandfather Reb Yerachmiel Buxbaum was a great *talmid chacham*. He was a member of the *beis din* of the Tzechover Rav, Rabbi Baruch Kanner. He was a son of Reb Moshe Golda's, who was a son of Rabbi Nassan'el Dayan, *dayan* in the *beis din* of the Divrei Chaim. Reb Moshe Golda's was also called Rabbi Moshe Dayan, as he, too, was one of the *dayanim* of the Divrei Chaim's *beis din* a few years after his father.

Since the *dayanus* was not adequate to support his family of eight children, Reb Moshe subsidized his income by traveling to Hungary to buy linen of drab gray. His wife, Chava, would wash them until they were snow-white and then sell them to the peasants of the nearby villages.

One day, Reb Moshe's two youngest sons, Avraham and Nassan, began crying in *cheder* for no apparent reason. The *belfer* (assistant teacher who accompanied the children to school every day) tried to calm them down. The children could not be consoled. The *belfer* asked the teacher what he should do with the two sobbing children. The teacher shrugged his shoulders and told him to take them home. When their mother couldn't calm them down, she became very concerned, because her husband's arrival from Hungary had been unaccountably delayed. She rushed to the Divrei Chaim to ask his advice. The *Rav* pulled his tallis over his head. He remained in this position for a few minutes and then removed the tallis. "Go home," he announced. "Everything will be all right."

Deep in the night, Reb Moshe arrived home exhausted and emotionally drained. "I have to *bentch gomel*," he exclaimed. He then related the harrowing ordeal he had just undergone. "We were on our way home, riding through the forest on our horse-drawn sleigh," he said. "It was snowing heavily, and our driver could not see where he was heading. After a while, we lost our way. Suddenly we were surrounded by fierce robbers armed with axes. They raised their arms as if to hack us to death. An image of the Divrei Chaim flashed through my mind. Then the driver whipped his horses, who galloped away as fast as they could in the darkness of the night. I turned around and saw an incredible sight: the robbers were standing with their hands suspended in the air, as if paralyzed!"

Reb Moshe's wife listened with bated breath to this chilling tale. After a few minutes of discussion, they realized that this story had happened at the precise moment that she had gone to the Divrei Chaim and he was meditating under his tallis!

My grandfather Reb Yerachmiel was a watchmaker by profession and an expert in his field. He did not earn much, for he refused payment from *talmidei chachamim* and *rebbishe* grandchildren. He was therefore very poor. Despite that, he was always in good spirits, and one would have been forgiven for imagining he was one of the wealthiest people in Tsanz. He had a good word and a smile for everyone. On *erev Pesach* he would bake *shemurah matzah* and sell it. He would jokingly remark that thanks to the *shemurah matzah* he had livelihood for half a year: he sold so few matzos that there was enough matzah for him to eat until Rosh HaShanah...

Shlomo Tenzer, the son of the last *rosh hakahal*, Shalom Yonah Tenzer, was a very good businessman even as a *bachur*. He worked together with his father in his large grain business. Because of that he did not have time to learn all day. He had a *seder* three or four times a week with my grandfather Reb Yerachmiel. With time his business grew very big, so much so that there was a time that he was not able to come to my grandfather for his *seder*.

The Vanished City of Tsanz

One day my grandather happened to meet Shlomo in the street. He said, "*Shalom aleichem!* How are you? By the way, with whom do you learn?"

Shlomo answered, "I am learning with you, Rebbe."

My grandfather remarked, "If that's the case, then at least bring me my wages."

Shlomo straightaway paid my grandfather his wages, and he started going again to his *shiur*, in spite of the fact that he was very busy with business appointments.

My grandmother, the *rebbetzin* Rechel, the daughter of Reb Moshe, was one of the most respected ladies in Tsanz. She fasted every Monday and Thursday, but that did not deter her from going on foot to the nearby villages to sell textiles. My father, who was her only son, told me that when he was a little boy she would wake him very early and send him to the *beis midrash*. My father had only one sister, who married Reb Shmuel Bodner. They and their nine children all perished *al kiddush haShem*.

One of my fond childhood memories is helping my grandmother clean for Pesach. In the midst of my cleaning I once came across two packages and curiously asked her what they were for.

"One package contains clothing and tablecloths for Pesach which I do not use during the year, and the other contains candles and clothing for the deceased."

With childhood innocence, I asked my grandmother, "Why do you need to prepare this package in advance? Surely the items can be provided when needed."

"If I happen to pass away on *yom tov*, I do not want anyone to have to desecrate *yom tov* because of me," she replied.

Indeed, so it was. My grandmother passed away on the second day of Rosh HaShanah, with the funeral taking place on that day. She wrote in her will that she did not want any praise to be written on her tombstone, only her name. Her wish was respected, and her tombstone was simply inscribed with her name, age, and the date of her death.

My grandfather Reb Yerachmiel had five brothers and two sisters. The eldest, Rabbi Berish'l Dayan, served as *dayan* in Tsanz for forty years. Reb Yitzchak, the next brother, lived in Cracow. My grandfather was the third son, followed by the fourth brother, Reb Toivye. The fifth brother, who lived in Hungary, Reb Avraham'le, and the youngest, Reb Nosson Mordche, lived in Limanow. My grandfather's sisters were Shifra and Osnas.

The second youngest, Reb Avraham'le, was involved in the blood libel of the Hungarian town Tisa-Esler in 5642 (1882). He was one of four *shochetim* accused of killing a gentile girl in order to use her blood for matzah. Through terrorizing a little Jewish boy, the *shamash*'s son, the gentiles had persuaded him to testify against the *shochetim*. A clever lawyer proved that the little boy could not have seen what he said that he saw. The boy claimed he saw everything through a keyhole while he was standing on the ground. The only trouble was, the lawyer told the court, that the keyhole was much too high for such a little boy to see through.

At the time of the blood libel, Reb Avraham'le's wife, Perel, made an appointment with Emperor Franz Joseph to ask him to order the police to release her husband from prison. When an audience was granted, she was given three weeks to prepare what to say.

When she stood in front of the emperor she became so nervous that she forgot everything. Emperor Franz Joseph, seeing how nervous she was, said to her, "Please be seated and calm down. I am only a human being." When she heard the emperor speaking so kindly to her she remembered what she had to say. She then told the emperor how ridiculous the blood libel was and asked if the emperor could order the police to release her husband. She also begged him to free the others. The emperor promised to do what he could for her husband. The others, though, he couldn't release, lest his people accuse him of freeing murderers. Reb Avraham was released shortly afterwards.

In his old age Reb Avraham came back to live in Tsanz, where he became a *melamed*. The Hershkowitz family of Jerusalem are his grandchildren.

My great-uncle, Reb Berish'l Dayan, was one of the select few ordered to wear white socks on Shabbos by the Tsanzer Rav, Reb Aryeh Leibish, a sign that he was a *talmid chacham* and G-d-fearing

The Vanished City of Tsanz

Jew. Few of the five to six hundred congregants who davened in Tsanzer *beis midrash* wore white socks on Shabbos. Such great men like *dayanim*; the *rosh beis din,* Rabbi Avigdor Teitelbaum, who was a son of the Krenitzer Rav, Rabbi David Teitelbaum, and a son-in-law of the Piekeler Rav, Rabbi Shalom Halberstam; Rabbi Feivish Landman; and our neighbor Rabbi Mordechai Yosef Saphir, who succeeded my great uncle Rabbi Berish also wore white socks, as well as my father, Reb Nosson Mordche. The remaining Chassidim in Tsanz wore black socks on Shabbos.

The *dayanim* used to sit in the *beis midrash* donned in their tallis and tefillin all morning. They did this so that if anybody had a *she'eilah* he knew where to find them. Every Monday and Thursday they would fast. *Din Torah*s were usually held in the *beis din* courtroom in the afternoon. However, if there was an urgent case (a *get* or a *chalitzah*), the *dayanim* would finish davening earlier so that they could start the case in the morning.

Once, on a Friday morning, when Reb Feivish Dayan was sitting and learning, as he usually did in the *Chassidisher beis midrash,* a woman approached him with a chicken in her hands. Reb Feivish noticed that the approaching woman's chicken had a broken wing. As she got nearer Reb Feivish called out, "Why does everybody come to me with their *she'eilos?* Let them go to Reb Berish'l Dayan, who sits in the Gribover *beis midrash*." After saying that he turned away and refused to answer her *she'eilah.*

Having no choice, the woman went and consulted Reb Berish'l Dayan, who measured the distance of the fracture on the wing from the body of the chicken and then told her that her chicken was kosher. The relieved woman thanked Reb Berish'l Dayan. As she turned to go home, she made a disparaging remark about Reb Feivish Dayan, because he couldn't be bothered to answer her *she'eilah.* Reb Berish'l Dayan said, "Be happy that he sent you to me. The halachah is that if the fracture is more than two fingers' width away from the body of the chicken it is kosher." (The measuring has to be done with the *dayan*'s own finger. If he has small fingers the distance of the fracture can be a lot less than with a *dayan* who has large fingers.) "Since Reb

Feivish is a large gentleman with wide fingers, the fracture would have to be a lot further from the body of the chicken to be kosher. Therefore he sent you to me. I am a small man with narrow fingers, and therefore your chicken is kosher."

My Father, Rabbi Nosson Mordche

My father, Rabbi Nosson Mordche Buxbaum, was an extremely diligent learner. As a young boy, he had been a student of the Brezaner Rav, Rabbi Shalom Mordechai HaKohen Shwadron, author of *Mishpat Shalom*, *Das Shalom*, and other *sefarim*. My father was also a student of the Oswitziner Rav, Rabbi Yehoshua Pinchas Bombach. In a letter to my father, the Oswitziner Rav addressed him as "my beloved student, a sharp young man, well versed in all subjects, Nosson Mordche."

My father had learned in Belz, too. He received rabbinical ordination from the Tarnapoler Rav, author of *Chavatzeles HaSharon*. He married the daughter of Reb Yaakov Lehrer of Tzieshinov, and he lived there, supported by his father-in-law. He acted as *dayan* of that town without payment.

The Tzieshinover Rav, Rabbi Simchah Yissachar Ber Halberstam, a son of the Divrei Yechezkel of Shinov, thought very highly of my father, and my father was always welcome in his home. My fa-

My father, Rabbi Nosson Mordche, *h"yd*, in 5702 (1942)

ther would record the *chiddushei Torah* which the Tzieshinover Rav had said at the Shabbos *tisch*. The greater part of the *divrei Torah* written in the *Rav's sefer Divrei Simchah* had been recorded by my father. His contribution was acknowledged in the introduction to the *sefer*.

Eventually, my father returned to his birthplace, Tsanz. At the beginning, he learned privately with students, but this did not offer an adequate income, since he was not interested in teaching rich children who would not bother with their studies, and poor, diligent boys could not afford to pay him.

It once happened that one of his students, embarrassed that he did not have the money with which to pay my father, did not turn up to learn. My father personally went to his home and asked him to come and learn, despite the fact that his father couldn't pay. That student is one of the distinguished *admorim* in New York today.

There were no official yeshivos in Tsanz until 5665 (1905). The *bachurim* studied in the *beis midrash* in pairs. If they came across a difficulty in their learning they would approach the *talmidei chachamim* who sat and learned there as well. These scholars were called *yoshvim*. When a yeshivah was finally established, it only provided *shiurim* but no food and lodging. There were approximately two hundred poor boys who had come from other towns to study in the yeshivos of Tsanz, Bobov, and Shinov. These *bachurim* ate at various households and slept in private apartments in the system known as *essen teg*.

Until 5692 (1932), Rabbi Avraham Hersh Friedman acted as *rosh yeshivah* of the Tsanzer yeshivah. Then my father took over under the guidance of Rabbi Aryeh Leibish Halberstam, the Tsanzer Rav, and later under the guidance of his son Rabbi Mordechai Zev.

About 250 *bachurim* learned in the yeshivah. There were four *roshei yeshivah*. My father was *rosh yeshivah* of the oldest class. The yeshivah had a very good name and achieved a remarkably high academic standard. Many of the *bachurim* later went on to learn in the Lubliner yeshivah.

THE BUXBAUM FAMILY

In the summer, my father would rise at dawn and, taking a folding chair with him, go to the woods on the outskirts of town to inhale the fresh air. This was necessary for his health because he suffered from asthma. He took along *sefarim* and a student to learn with. My father reviewed the whole of the first section of *Yoreh De'ah* with one of his students, Reb Chaim Herbst, a Bobover Chassid who lives in New York today, during these early-morning sessions.

My father never ate meat except at home. He also did not eat bread purchased from the bakery, because the Jewish bakery workers who worked throughout the night did not wash *negel vasser* when dawn broke.

I once asked my father, "Why does one say about a child who does not have good reading skills, '*Er zetst vi a beker* — He reads like a baker'?"

My father answered, "When a baker heats up his oven, he wants to utilize every inch, because the more full an oven is the better it bakes. So he puts a loaf of bread here, a cake there, a challah and a kugel somewhere else, sticking them anywhere even if they do not match."

When my father set out on a journey by train he always took along with him a flask of water and a cup with which to wash his hands. On his travels, he never ate cooked meals at other people's homes, only that which he had brought with him.

My father once attended the bar mitzvah of one of his students — Shimon, the son of Reb Mendel Wasner, a well-to-do Vielipoler Chassid. Shimon was an only son among eight daughters. Reb Mendel owned a large apartment and could celebrate the *simchah* in his own home with great pomp and splendor, as befit a wealthy person such as he. (On Shabbos even a prosperous man such as Reb Mendel never made a *kiddush* for a bar mitzvah so that the poor would not feel awkward or ashamed.)

The most distinguished men of the town graced the *simchah*. Among them was a close friend of Reb Mendel, a well-known *poseik* in Tsanz. The *bar mitzvah bachur* was seated between my father and this *Rav*.

The Vanished City of Tsanz

אדמו״ר מספינקא עם הגבאים עלה לעקידה אויעווינע י״ג סיון תש״ד
The *admor*, Reb Yitzchak Isaac of Spinka, *h"yd*

When the goose meat was served, my father did not eat his portion. The *Rav* noticed this and loudly announced, "Nosson, in such a pious home as Reb Mendel's one may surely eat the meat."

My father replied that he did not abstain from the food because he didn't trust Reb Mendel's kashrus, but because of his policy never to eat meat outside his home.

A little later, while everyone was enjoying his meat, a tumult broke out when somebody discovered a *she'eilah* in the form of a broken bone. The *she'eilah* was brought to this *Rav*. The *Rav* probed the piece of meat and then ruled that the goose was *treif*. Since all the geese had been cooked in one large pot, all the clay pots had to be broken, and the others had to be *kasher*ed.

The *Rav* then stood up and declared for all to hear, "You should know that the occurrence which has just transpired is my just reward for having embarrassed Rabbi Nosson in public. I beg his forgiveness, for when somebody has a rule not to eat in a strange place, one has no right to mock him for it."

This story demonstrates the piety of the *Rav* who, despite his stature, ignored his pride and publicly asked forgiveness.

THE BUXBAUM FAMILY

The Spinker Rebbe, Rabbi Yitzchak Isaac Weiss, once lodged at our home when he came to Tsanz for the Divrei Chaim's yartzeit. A great and pious man, I recall that at night, before he went to sleep, the Spinker Rebbe would place his hand on the mezuzah and with tears coursing down his cheeks stand there and pray for one full hour.

Many people came to the Spinker Rebbe with *kvittelach*. He carefully placed them between the pages of *masseches Shabbos*, which he was studying at the time. Full of childish curiosity, I was eager to discover what was written in these *kvittelach*. I opened the Gemara in order to take a peek, but to my chagrin my father discovered what I was about to do. He strictly forbade me to read the *kvittelach*, telling me that to read somebody else's *kvittelach* came under the *cheirem d'Rabbeinu Gershom*, just as reading another person's letter did.

When the Spinker Rebbe arrived home from the yartzeit he told his son that he had reviewed the entire *Hilchos Mikva'os* with his host, Rabbi Nossele Buxbaum, who knew them all by heart!

Anti-Semitism in Poland

In order to continue with my father's biography, it is necessary to interrupt my narrative and give a brief overview of prewar anti-Semitism in Poland.

The vehement hatred of the Poles against the Jews increased in its intensity with each passing day. It originated from the very top — the government itself — and the church and its priests used to spread vile, malicious rumors, inciting hatred against the Jews. From the year 5693 (1933) till 5696 (1936) anti-semitism was officially forbidden, but the Poles who mistreated Jews were let off lightly or sometimes not even punished at all.

The following story demonstrates to what extent this inexplicable hatred went. It was on the morning of Shemini Atzeres in 5695 (1935). A thief had tried to break into the Laderers' leather shop, which was situated on the ground floor of their apartment. One of the sons, a *bachur*, was on his way to davening when he heard suspicious noises coming from the shop. He went to investigate. The thief heard his

The Vanished City of Tsanz

footsteps and jumped out of the window with the stolen goods. The *bachur* gave chase and pursued him into a narrow alley leading to the church. There the thief took out a knife and murdered the boy.

The *chevrah kaddisha* requested of the priests permission to remove the bloodied earth so that they could bury it, in accordance with Jewish law. The priests flatly refused. As for the murderer, he was senteneced to the outrageously lenient penalty of a one-year imprisonment.

In summer of 5690, Skladkovski, the premier minister of the Polish government, publicly declared that it was legally permitted to wield an economic war against the Jews. When the female minister Priester proposed a bill forbidding Jewish slaughter, it did not take much persuasion for the Polish government to pass the law. A short while later, a new law was introduced, stating that every merchant must write his name on a plaque outside his office. This was to enable the Poles to discriminate between a Jewish business and a gentile business and thereby discourage them from buying from the Jews.

In addition, the Poles used to appoint picketers, teenagers who would stand outside Jewish shops on market days and prevent any Pole from shopping there. The Jewish peddlers who used to travel to the small villages with their bundle of wares were more often than not accosted by violent thugs. The rogues would steal their wares and any money they had and mercilessly beat them. They had no fear of being apprehended, because the police would invariably be on their side, offering them protection. Placards bearing the words "Do not buy from Jews" hung in prominent places. It is easy to see why Hitler chose the majority of his extermination centers to be established in this land. Reeking with anti-Semitism, it paved the way for him to pursue his ideals unhindered.

Still, there were one or two benevolent gentiles. One such was Yuzek the water-carrier, who, with the help of his wife, used to lug buckets of water to the Jewish Street in the years prior to the war .On winter Shabbosos, they would also heat the ovens in the Jewish homes. They were very faithful to us Jews, so much so that when a law was passed forbidding gentiles to enter the ghetto, they literally cried with sorrow.

But even they were affected by anti-Semitism. One of their jobs was to carry sacks of vegetables, potatoes, and other essentials into the cellar. For some mysterious reason, they steadfastly refused to do this job from a month before Pesach. Instead, they deposited the sacks by the door of the cellar. My mother asked them, "Why is it that you do not mind carrying the sacks into the cellars throughout the year, but refuse to do so the whole month before Pesach?" They always managed to evade the question. One day my mother persistently nagged them to give her an answer.

Yuzek reluctantly replied, "The priest of the church warned us not to let the Jews persuade us to enter their cellars before Pesach. He told us that we were risking our lives, for the Jews were liable to kill us in order to use our blood for matzos! I told him that we own the keys and the cellars are empty, but the priest told us that we were nevertheless in danger, for a *tzaddik* sits in the cellar and waits for a gentile to enter so that he can squeeze out his blood."

A Year in Amsterdam

In 5693 (1933), the year Hitler came to power in Germany, we received a letter from a relative in Amsterdam, Elazar May. In it he enclosed visas for our entire family, with permission to come to Holland.

My mother was all for it, living in fear of the terrible anti-Semitism which was rampant in Poland. My father decided to travel there first in order to survey the religious situation in Holland. He stayed there for nine months. On his way to Holland, he traveled through the town Ozshorod (Carpatan Russ) in Hungary. There he was hosted by Binyamin Steinmetz, a very distinguished person and a great *machnis orchim*. Reb Binyamin had an only son who used to prepare the beds for the guests. He once said to his son, "Don't think that you have accomplished the mitzvah of *hachnasas orchim* merely by making the beds. You must lie down on the bed and see if it is comfortable. If you prefer a soft bed, then you must see to it that your guest gets one, too."

When my father told him he was on his way to Holland, Reb Binyamin said to him, "How much will you earn in Holland? I will

The Vanished City of Tsanz

pay you that amount, and you will stay with me." My father stayed there for three months and learned with his son privately. Together they went through the first part of *Yoreh De'ah* with *Pri Megadim*. After that he left for Amsterdam. (The son of Binyamin Steinmetz survived the war and lives in New York.)

In Holland, our relative took my father to a prestigious doctor to treat his asthma. He also provided him with a position as *Rav* in a shul, where my father gave a *shiur* to a group of men.

Though he stayed in the boardinghouse of a very religious woman, my father did not eat any meat or milk products during his entire stay. His diet consisted mainly of bread dipped in coconut milk. My father lost ten kilos that year.

In Galicia, when somebody saw someone else eating, he would say, *"A gitten apetit* — Enjoy your meal," to which the person eating would answer, *"Kimt mit essen* — Please join me." To that, the other person would say, *"Ah dank* — Thank you." This was merely considered good manners and not an invitation.

My father told me that once, when he was having his bread dipped in coconut milk, someone said to him, *"Ah gitten apetit."* He courteously answered, *"Kimt mit essen,"* just as he used to do at home. Much

Der Yiddishe Gass in 5753 (1993), where our house stood

THE BUXBAUM FAMILY

to my father's chagrin, the other gentleman in all innocence accepted the invitation and sat down to join him.

My father was offered a permanent position as *Rav* of a shul. However, he refused the position and returned to Tsanz. I asked my father why he had turned down the offer. He replied that while he was visiting Amsterdam, a friend from the town Reisha, Galicia, had also settled there with his family.

"The children had arrived with long, curled *payos*," continued my father, "but slowly they became shorter and shorter until, by the end of the year, they had disappeared completely. I am afraid that the same thing will happen to you. I am therefore ready to forgo the fortunes Amsterdam may have to offer."

In my father's absence, I went on Shabbos to the *tisch* of the Tsanzer Rebbe, Rabbi Aryeh Leibish. The *Rav* always inquired of me, "What does your father write from Amsterdam?" Feeling very honored, I joyfully reported to my mother that the Rebbe had asked about my father. My mother, too, derived great pleasure from the Rebbe's interest.

The courtyard of my house in Tsanz

The Final Destruction

My father spread Torah in his town until the last minutes of the final destruction of Tsanz. When the S.S. murderers invaded the town, they closed down the shul. The *batei midrash* were packed to capacity with the thousands of refugees who had been driven from their homes from the beginning of 5700 (1940). They came from Lodz, Sheradz, and other towns. Yet my father persisted on giving *shiurim* in the *cheder sheini* of the shul, known as "the *polish*." By the end of 5700, however, the situation had became extremely precarious, with people being constantly grabbed off the streets and shipped off to death camps. As a result, the davening and *shiurim* held in the *cheder sheini* were abandoned. *Minyanim* were held in private homes only, behind locked doors and barricaded shutters. When a knock was heard, everybody fled to the bunkers which existed in almost every building. At the beginning, this was the key to salvation, but soon even this didn't help, for the Nazis discovered all the hiding places.

II
THE WAR YEARS

INTRODUCTION

It is said that the saintly Reb Pinchas'l Koritzer, *zt"l*, once sighed, *"Ribbono shel olam*, do not inflict upon a Jew all that he can bear..."

Centuries of untold suffering have taught us that Jews are capable of undergoing relentless hardships. Nevertheless, when I look back at the bloodstained years of the terrible destruction which befell Europe and I remember, as in a nightmare, the indescribable pain which we were forced to endure, I cannot understand. I simply cannot comprehend how we were able to tolerate the torture, and how we managed to withstand the odds and remain alive.

This question — how we managed to stay alive — must remain unanswered. However, I do believe that it is an obligation for every Jew who survived the destruction beginning in the year 1939 and ending with the liberation from the Nazis' murderous hands in the year 1945 to record his experiences as a remembrance for all time. As the Torah tells us, "Remember what Amalek did to you." Our children and grandchildren must know how we suffered. They must realize that not a single Jew remained alive by a stroke of good luck, but, as the saintly Belzer Rav once said, "Every Jew who survived the war was accompanied by two angels who guarded his every step."

I have pondered many times how it was possible that the intellectual *"Herren Volk"* (master nation) could stoop to such animalistic, brutal deeds. How could it be that level-headed people, middle-aged, with families of their own, were capable of cruelly inflicting upon their victims indescribable torture until finally killing them? Many times the *Herren Volk* would bring along their wives and children to witness the bloody scenes they performed.

The children of this *Herren Volk*, in line with the "educated" upbringing their parents gave them, joined the Hitler Youth Clubs. With brutal enthusiasm, they happily took part in the elimination of the Jewish inhabitants of Tsanz.

Even the very young relished in discovering Jews, beating and bullying them, and then handing them over to the Gestapo.

A Small Example

It was summer, in 1940. A group of Jewish boys were on their way home from the village known as Old Tsanz, where they had obtained a bit of food for their families, to my hometown, New Tsanz. On the way they were accosted by a group of Hitler Youth gangsters and a few Polish hooligans. The mob forced the boys to throw the food on the floor and trample it. Then they murderously beat them. When their sport was over, they handed the boys over to the Gestapo. The eldest of the group, however, a nineteen-year-old, they kept for their own entertainment.

The ruffians dragged the boy to a factory that manufactured lime, a glue substance that is boiled and used for the formation of furniture. There the boy was ordered to undress and wash himself well. They even handed him soap. After he obeyed them, they firmly tied his hands and feet together and poured boiling hot glue on his body, one load after another, several times.

They waited until the previous coat had hardened before pouring another load, until his body appeared to be entirely covered with a suit of steel armor and he could not breath or move a single limb. They stood by and watched with glee as the victim helplessly battled Death, until the odds overcame him.

The murder was carried out under the supervision of a superior

INTRODUCTION

S.S. officer, assisted by a *Volksdeutsche* who belonged to a Hitler Youth Club. (*Volksdeutsche* were people whose ancestors had come from Germany to live in Poland 150 years before the second World War. They had kept their German identity and still spoke German among themselves. Hitler used them as a fifth column.)

The *chevrah kaddisha* reported that a terrible shudder ran through them when they were given the corpse. His eyes were wide open, as if jumping from their sockets. His face was swollen and puffy, a result of trying to catch his breath through his mouth and nose. His entire body was tinged blue, and from his nostrils ran two lines of dried blood.

After this murderous act, when the *chevrah kaddisha* had buried the corpse, the S.S. sprawled themselves on the broken tombstones in the cemetery and boisterously sang the well-known German ballad: "*Tennenbaum* (pine tree), how lovely are your leaves..."

This gruesome tale is only an example to illustrate what life was like under the heel of the Nazi regime. Once again, the question comes to mind: how could this have happened?

It is pointless even to try to answer such a question, because it is beyond human comprehension. Our only duty is to record what transpired, so that it should, G-d forbid, never be forgotten; the heartbreaking question must be persistently asked again and again, for generations to come.

According to my calculations, eighteen thousand Jews were killed in the Tsanzer ghetto. This is in contrast to the official *Judenrat* documents where the number appears to be less. About two thousand people in the ghetto did not register with the *Judenrat*, in the hope that the Jewish O.D. (police) would not become aware of their existence and consequently not search for them in the frequent *aktion*s. Unfortunately, this ploy was of little use to them because the Nazi murderers, headed by the Gestapo chief Heinrich Haman, *y"s*, pursued them till the bitter end. They were dragged out of the most well-concealed hiding places and flung onto oxen wagons. The wagons were dusted with chalk, which soon began to choke them. Those who did not die

The Vanished City of Tsanz

on the journey from thirst or suffocation lived to see the final step in their journey in hell — the gas chambers of Belzec.

The extermination was finalized on 16–17 Elul 5702 (August 29–30 1942). Obviously, one mourns over the destruction of the six million individual Jews, but nevertheless each town bespeaks a Kaddish for its own fathers and mothers, and its precious, innocent Jewish children.

With a heart hardened by suffering and pain, by unbearable hardships and excruciating beatings, I will now recount the final, heartbreaking saga in the splendid history of the Chassidic community of Tsanz. May this serve as a eulogy at the open grave of the martyrs, who are now in Gan Eden after being tortured physically and spiritually, after being choked to death in the gas chambers of Belzec, and after being consumed in the flames of the crematoria.

With the elimination of Tsanzer Jewry came the elimination of a community with traditional, Chassidic values going back many generations — generations boasting refined Torah scholars, gems of youth, and Chassidic men who were girded with Torah and G-dliness. Let this brief, inadequate outline of their suffering and troubles be hallowed by their children and by the entire Jewish nation as a lamentation for the generations to come.

Chapter I

THE OUTBREAK OF WAR

I hereby begin my tale of the harrowing experiences of the thousands of Jews in the Tsanzer ghetto. I divided the main narrative into four chapters:

The first chapter deals with the era lasting until the beginning of 1940. It describes the random killing of Jews, confiscation of Jewish property, forcing the Jews to wear the sign of degradation — *"Jude"* — and subsequently enforcing laws robbing them of their independence.

The second chapter involves the period lasting from the beginning of 1940 till May 1941: the establishment of the ghetto, driving the Jews out of the towns and villages surrounding Tsanz into the ghetto, the constriction of Jewish trade, and occasional deportations to concentration camps.

The third chapter discusses the period from June 1941 until summer 1942: the closing off of the ghetto walls, the complete dissolution of all Jewish trade, hunger's terrible climax, living quarters becoming increasingly cramped due to the closing off of more and more ghetto streets, the outbreak of the typhus epidemic, and increasingly frequent mass-slaughter actions.

The fourth chapter deals with the period of summer 1942: the preparation for mass deportation, the liquidation of the ghettos surrounding Tsanz (Old Tsanz, Limanow, Amsana, Gribow), the final liquidation of the entire Tsanzer population, and their deportation to Belzec.

The Vanished City of Tsanz

The epilogue, the fifth chapter, describes the era from summer 1942 until summer 1943: the deportation of the few remaining forced laborers in Tsanz to concentration camps, Tsanz becoming *Judenrein* (empty of Jews), and the death of the deported forced laborers in the death camps.

The rest of this section describes my own experiences until the end of the war.

German Espionage in Poland

Prior to the outbreak of war there was a popular ice-cream firm by the name of Penguin, with branches spread across the country. In Tsanz, too, the firm had two outlets, one situated opposite the *Starostova* (where official documents such as passports and visas were issued, as well as papers concerning the military services) and the other, just opposite the train station.

A week before war broke out, Poland began mobilizing its army. The situation was such that the Polish army did not possess sufficient uniforms for all the new recruits in Tsanz. As a result, one soldier was given a military jacket, the other a pair of military trousers, and so on. This gave the army a rather pathetic look, far from the regal and heroic picture an army usually displays. Strangely, at the very same time that the uniforms were being distributed, the German radio station in Berlin scoffed at the Polish army's primitive inefficiency, inasmuch as they didn't even possess adequate uniforms for the soldiers in New Tsanz!

This broadcast aroused suspicions of espionage. The secret police in Tsanz began investigating how the information about the uniforms could possibly have reached Berlin. They strengthened their patrols at the *Starostova*.

One night, a group of watchmen heard curious sounds coming from the Penguin ice-cream booth. As they softly approached the booth, the sounds quieted. Their suspicions aroused, they loudly banged at the door. There was no response. Without further ado, they kicked the door open with their massive boots and encountered a pale-faced *Volksdeutsche* clutching a radio with which he had been

THE OUTBREAK OF WAR

corresponding with Germany. It turned out that the entire ice-cream firm was a massive spy network spread across Poland.

Prior to the German conquest of Tsanz, the police officers and prison wardens fled. Before they fled, the wardens opened the prison doors and released all the captives, except for the *Volksdeutsche* spies. The prison wardens took these spies with them when they fled Tsanz and later murdered them in Melitz.

The Germans would not let such a deed go unanswered. Three months later they retrieved the corpses of the spies, brought them back to Tsanz, and buried them with great pomp and ceremony. On the day of the burial, the Germans planned to organize a pogrom against the Jews on the grounds that they were guilty of the murder. However, there lived in Tsanz a *Volksdeutsche* by the name of Yenkner who owned a mill and enjoyed a very friendly relationship with the Jewish bakers — even conversing with them fluently in Yiddish! He intervened on the Jews' behalf and told the Germans that the *Volksdeutsche* spies had been murdered by their prison wardens, and that the Jews had nothing to do with their murder. Mr. Yenkner vouched for the Jews' innocence, on his life and honor. The Germans believed him,

Nazi officers in Tsanz, 1941

since his son was one of the murdered spies, and thus the Jews were spared a bloody pogrom.

The Germans Are Here!

September 1, 1939. On that momentous and fateful day, the first shot was fired in Poland, signifying the beginning of the downfall of Eastern Europe in general and the gruesome end of millions of European Jews in particular. We Jews felt that the coming days spelled death and destruction to Polish Jewry, but nobody, not even the most pessimistic among us, ever dreamed of the horrible mass executions which awaited us in the coming days. However, as time wore on and the sounds of the German war machines came closer and closer, the barbarous aims of the Nazis became more and more clear.

Tsanz was one of the first Jewish settlements to suffer at the hands of the Nazis, to feel the taste of their heinous cruelty as they strove to annihilate Jewish bodies and crush the Jewish spirit.

The Mass Escape

Directly after the outbreak of war, many Tsanzer Jews fled town. The men in particular were desperate to escape, as rumors were circulating that the Nazis were capturing men and sending them to the front to clear minefields. I, too, with my father, fled to Bobov on foot, where we hired a coach together with the Muszyna Rav, who had come to Tsanz as soon as war commenced. We traveled in the direction of Reisha.

(The Muszyner Rav, Rabbi Aryeh Leibish Halberstam, was the son of Reb Moshe, the Bardiaver Rav, who was the son of Reb Baruch, the Gorlitzer Rav, a son of the Divrei Chaim. The Muszyner Rav's father-in-law was Rabbi Shmuel Rokach, a son of the second Belzer Rav. The Muszyner Rav's son-in-law was Rabbi Shmuel Friedman, son of Rabbi Avraham Hersh Friedman, who was *rosh yeshivah* in Tsanz before my father took over that position.)

At every bridge we crossed on the way to Reisha, a sentry was posted to guard against sabotage. In Dembitz the bridges were especially carefully guarded, as there was an ammunition factory in that town which had suffered heavy bombing earlier in the day.

Here we were to experience a typical example of Polish anti-Semi-

The Stichiner Rav sitting in the coach

tism. The Polish officer guarding the bridge flew into a rage as soon as he caught sight of my father and the Muszyner Rav in their true Yiddish garb and began shouting to the driver, "Halt! Stand still! Here are the two rabbinical spies who are guilty of the fire which is burning down the town of Dembitz. I myself saw these very rabbis signaling to the German planes which bombed Dembitz." He then turned to the occupants of the coach and yelled, "You are all under arrest!"

With these words, he leaped onto our coach and ordered the driver to bring us to military headquarters where the rabbis were to be tried as spies. There was no doubt of the verdict: death.

The driver, who was a Jew, had to serve as interpreter, since my father and the Muszyner Rav could not speak Polish. He pleaded on their behalf with the indisputable logic that Dembitz was burning since the morning and these "spies" had only just arrived after nightfall. However, the officer staunchly clung to his accusations; the rabbis were German spies, and it was of no importance exactly how this was possible.

The situation was grave. The driver knew well that in a military court our word would carry no weight against the word of a Polish officer, and he began bargaining with him as a last, desperate attempt to save our lives. The transaction began. Ten zlotys? No! Twenty zlotys? No! Thirty? Forty? At last the officer nodded in agreement. And so it was that for forty zlotys, the rabbis were no longer spies.

After this transaction, the officer grew quite amiable toward us. He even went so far as to give us a piece of friendly advice:

"The Polish army stationed in Reisha have a right to confiscate your horses and coach for the army's use. Here, take this and bandage up the young one." (He was referring to me. I was eighteen years old.)

I was firmly bandaged over the head, and over the eye for good measure, to give the impression that I was heavily wounded. The officer bade me to sit up front, next to the driver, in order to evoke sympathy from the Poles and be permitted to keep our coach and horses. However, all this was to no avail. As soon as we arrived at the outskirts of Reisha, the Polish soldiers on duty mercilessly ordered us off the coach, forcing us to continue our journey on foot.

Our first stop in Reisha was the home of the Koloshitzer Rav, Rabbi Chuna Halberstam. His home was crowded with refugees who had fled from the surrounding towns. Soon after our arrival, the Rebbe himself entered his home, utterly exhausted. He had been grabbed by the Poles and was forced to clear the bombed-out railway tracks of dead corpses, fallen debris, and heavy iron railings. The Poles used to drag passersby to do this backbreaking work for them. That day they considered themselves especially fortunate to have caught a rabbi whom they could scoff at with added relish.

When the Koloshitzer Rav walked in, pale and weak from exhaustion, the first thing he did was to ask if everybody had eaten. Only after being answered in the affirmative by each individual did he allow himself to rest his weary body and have something to eat.

THE OUTBREAK OF WAR

After having refreshed himself somewhat, the Rebbe turned to my father and said, "Nosson! I will go with you in exile," for we intended to escape further to Sokolow. With these words, the Rebbe donned his fur coat, took his tallis and tefillin and a few other possessions, and set out with us. However, the terrible ordeal he had suffered that day took its toll, and after walking steadily for one kilometer his weakened legs gave way. With a heavy sigh he stopped and said, "I feel my strength is beginning to wane. I must go back to Reisha."

My father and he looked at each other in despair as many unspoken words passed between them. The future was so forbidding and unsure; who could know when — if ever — they would see each other again? With a broken heart he wished us success and turned to go back home. My last memory of him, trudging home wearily, will remain engraved in my mind forever.

After the Nazis besieged Reisha, the Rebbe escaped to a hidden bunker where he underwent many hardships. Finally, on the second day of Chol HaMo'ed Sukkos 1942, the sadistic murderers discovered his bunker in Fristik. He was arrested and taken to a prison in Yasla. On that very same day — 18 Tishrei — the Rebbe was unceremoniously shot together with a few other Jews. Thus another of prewar Europe's greatest *gedolim* joined the millions of *kedoshim* who died sanctifying Hashem's name.

One of the survivors of that group, Shimon Blumenstock, who had been together with the Rebbe in prison, relates that the Rebbe had promised him he would emerge from that living hell alive. Indeed, he is alive today, testifying that the holy Rebbe's blessing had come true.

My father and I traveled further to Sokolow, and there we sojourned. My father did not have the strength to go further.

At the Tzion of Reb Elimelech Rudniker

In Sokolow, the Jews informed us that Reb Elimelech Rudniker, *zt"l*, was buried in the Jewish cemetery nearby. We took this one-time opportunity afforded us and went to pray at his graveside.

Reb Elimelech Rudniker was a grandchild of the renowned

The Vanished City of Tsanz

Rebbe, Reb Elimelech of Lizensk. The townspeople of Sokolow related to us a fascinating tale which happened during World War I (1914–1918).

The peasants of all the surrounding towns of Sokolow had gathered together to vent their bitterness and frustration on the usual hapless scapegoat — the Jews. Intending to loot the Jewish shops, the rabble armed themselves with choppers, knives, sticks, and any other weapon they could lay their hands on and marched toward the town in one noisy, disorganized mass. However, as they advanced toward the border, they miraculously made a U-turn and turned back toward the direction they came from — much to the immense relief of the terrified Jews.

Some time later, the baffled Jews inquired of their gentile neighbors what had caused this sudden change of heart and were told this amazing tale: As the mob approached Sokolow, an aging man with a long, gray beard and a stick in his hand appeared seemingly from nowhere and with astounding strength began hitting the people closest to him on the head. Judging by the gentiles' description of the old man's appearance, it seemed that this was Reb Elimelech Rudniker, *zt"l*, who had come to save the lives of his fellow townspeople long after he had passed away!

We prayed at his graveside with added devotion, beseeching Hashem that just as He had saved the Jews of a terrible disaster not so long ago, He should come to our aid in the bitter and desperate plight in which we now found ourselves.

When the Polish army dispersed and fled in terror and confusion, with the cry that the Germans were advancing, we realized that there was no point in escaping further than Sokolow. It is interesting to note that even in fear for their lives, with the Germans hot at their heels, the Poles found the time and presence of mind to break into a Jewish egg warehouse and rob as many eggs as they could manage, stuffing them into their steel helmets!

Together with us, on our first Shabbos in Sokolow, was the learned Kolbosover Rav. Once, when he was sitting with my father, a person entered with a question on one of the laws of Shabbos. After the *Rav* advised him what to do and the person had left, my father respectfully pointed out that the *Rav* had erred in his judgment, the *din* being directly opposed to what the man had been told. The Kolbosover Rav immediately summoned the person and retracted his *pesak*, adding the following words: "I take upon myself not to answer any more *she'eilos* until the war is over. I see that *min haShamayim* (from Heaven) our presence of mind has been taken away." Sadly, this righteous *Rav* was also one of the millions of *korbanos* of the cursed Germans.

(Similarly, before we ran away from Tsanz, we went to the Tsanzer Rav, Rabbi Mordechai Zev Halberstam, and asked him if we should run away or stay put. He gave us the same answer he'd given everyone else who had come to ask his advice: "I don't know! Our presence of mind has been taken away. Do what you think is right.")

On *erev Rosh HaShanah*, the inevitable happened — the Germans invaded Sokolow. The terrified Jews did not dare pray in the shuls but gathered together in private homes. While they were absorbed in prayer, the wild beasts stormed into their homes, claiming they were looking for illegal weapons. Like animals let loose, they raided the houses and seized anything of value — money, jewelry, watches. The unrestrained beasts even pierced the *shtreimel* boxes with their bayonets in their search for "dangerous armor."

Back to Tsanz

We soon came to the sad conclusion that escape was futile: there was nowhere to run, as the entire Poland was in German hands. The situation being such, we could just as well be in Tsanz, with our family. So we stayed in Sokolow until after Yom Kippur and headed back home for Sukkos. My father traveled with a sock on his head, for there was no knowing what would happen to him were he to travel with his beard and *payos* on show.

Thank G-d we arrived home for Sukkos. Not everyone was so fortunate. We heard the chilling tale of the six hundred Tsanzer Jews who were among those killed in Przemyzl when the Nazis entered the town.

The Vanished City of Tsanz

We heard of the horror story in Dinov, where the Nazis herded all the Jews, of which a considerable amount were from Tsanz, into the town shul and set it afire. The heart-shattering screams of agony-stricken humanity pierced the air, until the last *kodesh* returned his holy soul to its Maker. An eerie, deathly silence pervaded, the smell of charred bones the only proof of the inhuman sadism which had just taken place.

We heard, too, of the murder of Tsanzer Jews, killed on the way home from Istrik. We heard and we knew there was nothing we could do. We were helpless in the face of a world gone mad, a world where bloodthirsty monsters were free to kill, plunder, and torture innocent people whose only crime was that they bore the title "Jew."

Despite the nightmarish happenings going on around us, we set up our sukkah in Tsanz, as we did every year. But on the first day of Sukkos the new German mayor, Dr. Hein, rode through town on his horse. Wherever he could gain entry into a Jewish backyard, he galloped in and enticed his horse to kick down and trample the sukkah.

Eleven Jewish Heroes

During the mobilization of the Polish army, when all Polish soldiers had to offer their services, many hundreds of Jewish youths voluntarily enlisted. For reasons unknown, they were turned down. The most likely explanation is that the army was in such total disorganization and disarray that additional soldiers would only have served to increase the confusion which already reigned, demoralizing the troops even further. But as we all know, this attempt to reduce the confusion did not succeed, and the army was almost immediately crushed by the German war machine.

Nevertheless, a handful of Jewish soldiers played an important role in the brief battle of resistance to the German troops, when they marched into Tsanz. After the Polish forces began retreating from the Slovakian border upon which Tsanz was situated, eleven hardy Jewish souls took upon themselves to protect the town by defending the significant strategic pass between the mountains of Tsanz and Gribow.

These brave Jews barricaded themselves behind the mighty walls

THE OUTBREAK OF WAR

of the Evangelical church which overlooked the Jewish quarter, and with heavy missiles bombarded the route through which the Germans marched into Tsanz. Since Tsanz is situated on a hill, this ploy worked wonders. An added advantage was that there were some Tsanzer Evangelical spies among the German troops, and out of respect for them, the German infantry did not dare shoot back.

After two days of defending the city thus, these courageous soldiers still clung to their positions, despite the suicidal situation they

The German army entering Tsanz via the Helena Bridge

faced. Needless to say, a pitiful handful of brave youths were as good as dead in the face of the Nazi war machine, and the Germans eventually overcame the opposition. The heroism of these fallen victims was the talk of the town for a long time afterward among Jews and Poles alike.

On Wednesday, September 6, 1939, at 4 A.M., the first of the German scout patrols was seen in Tsanz. Half an hour later, the first division of the German army marched into the town.

Before war broke out, the total population in Tsanz was thirty-five thousand, of which the Jews numbered close to twelve thousand. Only a minimal number of Jews managed to leave West Galicia in time to escape the Nazi conquest, and thus it was that almost the entire community was delivered into the hands of the monstrous sadists on that fateful Wednesday.

On the very first day, the Jews were made to feel the bitter taste of their captors who were to enforce a "new order." A few Jews were arrested for the sole crime of standing on the street. Some youths were taken as civil prisoners.

The following day, Thursday, the Nazis' affliction of Jews began in earnest. Without any warning, the Nazis barged into Jewish homes and grabbed men for forced labor. The unfortunate men returned home that evening barely recognizable, so bruised and bloodied and utterly worn out were they from the backbreaking work to which they had been subjected.

Two days later, on Shabbos, the Germans organized a "spectacle" to entertain the local townspeople. By demand of their female war correspondents, they dragged a group of Jews with long beards and *payos*, clad in *bekishes*, to pose for a group photograph. To enhance the effect of this would-be caricature, they seized the town *"meshugane"* and planted him right in the center. The photograph was later displayed in Streicher's *Der Sturmer* as an illustration of the "Jewish warmongers" who enticed Poland to fight against the Third Reich.

Their fiendish enjoyment not yet satisfied, they took Rabbi Hersh Halberstam, the last Tsanzer Rav's brother, who had a bushy beard and *payos*, and placed a large flat hat with a wide brim on his head. They then positioned him among a group of Jews — I among them — who were commanded to point at him with accusing fingers. A photo was taken and later displayed in *Der Sturmer* with the comment that the Jews in New Tsanz were rebelling against their rabbi, who was persistently swindling them.

Soon after the German invasion of Tsanz, the *Volksdeutsche* and Polish hooligans began plundering Jewish homes and robbing their possessions. However, the German authorities soon put an abrupt end to this; stealing from Jews was their privilege, and nobody was allowed to challenge this monopoly.

THE OUTBREAK OF WAR

Meanwhile, our situation was worsening with each passing day. About a week after the first German soldier was seen in Tsanz, the dreaded S.S. put in their appearance. We were afraid to go out in the streets, for apart from the danger of being accosted by a German and having our beard and *payos* cut off or singed with burning matches, there was the danger of being dragged off for forced labor. Even our homes did not provide shelter, for the wicked sadists would break into them, searching for possible hiding places, from which they would drag us off to work.

The work was mainly an opportunity for these savages to kill, torture, and humiliate Jews. Old men were forced to go on their knees and clean the sidewalk or were harnessed to wagons and made to pull them along like horses, accompanied by beatings and whipping amidst jeers of scorn and mockery. I myself was forced to clean toilets with my bare hands. The first victims to be humiliated thus were those who lived in the marketplace — the suitable location for local entertainment.

Pulling out an old man's beard

The Vanished City of Tsanz

The Polish citizens delighted in these scenes and stood by, encouraging and cheering their "hated" conquerors.

Jewish trade came to an abrupt halt for fear of being seen outdoors. Panic was greatly magnified when two German soldiers planted a bomb in the shul known as the *Chassidishe beis midrash*. Luckily, the bomb caused relatively minor damage; had a fire broken out, over one hundred refugees who sheltered there would have found themselves in the streets without a roof over their heads.

A few weeks after Tsanz was invaded the Gestapo arrived, with the infamous Heinrich Haman as their leader. They immediately took charge of Tsanz and its surrounding villages, with the Jews, of course, being the worse for it. Their first command was that the Jews provide a *Judenrat*, which would be responsible for carrying out their demands.

The Gestapo were quick to discover that in Tsanz there were many *batei midrash*, apart from the main synagogue. Anticipating a valuable gain, they ordered that all the candlesticks and chandeliers of every synagogue be delivered to their headquarters within eight days. With great effort, we removed from the main synagogue its ten massive chandeliers, each one weighing over a thousand kilos, in which hundreds of candles burned every Friday night, and buried them in a huge hole in the shul's courtyard.

We imagined, as we mistakenly imagined so many other things, that this ploy would be successful. It was not to be.

Making fun of Jews

THE OUTBREAK OF WAR

The Gestapo weren't satisfied with the many other chandeliers they had received and insisted on receiving the main synagogue's ten magnificent chandeliers as well. They threatened the *Judenrat* that if their command wasn't obeyed within eight days, six of its members would be duly shot. The *Judenrat* immediately ordered us to unearth the chandeliers and have them delivered to the Gestapo right away. Interestingly enough, upon my visit to Tsanz on Lag Ba'Omer, in 1993, I could discern the marks of the pit in the shul courtyard where we had buried those chandeliers.

On Shushan Purim 1940, a number of people arrived from Cracow under the illusion that in Tsanz the situation was better. Among them was the famous Bobover *talmid chacham* and *badchan*, Reb Alter Glaser. The following day, my friend Reb Nechemia Shengut, who lives today in Bnei Brak, went to visit Reb Alter and found him learning Mishnah. Reb Alter interrupted his learning and asked, *"Nu*, are we going to get together today in honor of Purim?"

In response to his suggestion, the Bobover Chassidim assembled together. Reb Alter composed ditties and brought happiness to the hearts of those gathered there. With his delightful sense of humor, he mocked the Germans and made light of the miserable situation the Jews found themselves in. For several blissful hours the Chassidim's worry and despair was dispelled. War, Germans, death, and torture were pushed to a far corner of their minds; instead they were lost in a world of laughter, joy, and happiness.

A year later, on the last Purim in the Tsanzer ghetto, the Bobover Chassidim were in a state of gloom and depression when they heard of the death of over twenty distinguished fellow Chassidim in Bobov. Once again, Reb Alter managed to lift their spirits a little by singing the following song over and over:

> Listen, my dear *Yiddelech*,
> It's time to stop your crying.
> Keep strong, holy *Chassidim'lech*.
> Do not fear anyone
> Because it won't be long anymore.

The Vanished City of Tsanz

But soon, soon enough
We will meet with song.
The holy Mashiach,
He will console you
And bless you with everything good.
Nu, it's time to stop your wailing.
Wipe your eyes, my dear Yisraelik.
We have just read the megillah
And said "Al HaNissim."
Let's sing songs in honor of Purim,
in honor of Amalek's obliteration.

Life in the Ghetto

My eldest brother, Moshe, lived in Cracow before the war. He was employed by my mother's brother Leizer Lehrer, who dealt with stocks and shares. My uncle had strong connections with Holzer Bank, a large bank in which many Jews held accounts, and also with the Viennese Union Bank. Through these connections, he learned that immediately after Hitler invaded Austria, Poland enforced the

Street scene in the ghetto of Tsanz

THE OUTBREAK OF WAR

In the ghetto on *der Yiddishe Gass*

Deviezen Sperre law which prohibited the removal of money from the country. This was done to protect the economy from a currency shortage.

When this occurred, my uncle Leizer told my brother Moshe that if he or any of his relatives had money, he should purchase gold dollars, which were worth double as much as paper dollars, the paper dollar being four and a half zlotys against the dollar and the gold dollar nine zlotys against the dollar.

Our family was not very wealthy. I, however, did have some money in the post office — the accumulation of a few years' Chanukah *gelt* and pocket money saved from various opportunities. Being the youngest at home, I used to receive money from the many guests my parents hosted at the Tsanzer yartzeit. Apart from that, my uncle Shmuel Bodner, although not a man of means, never failed to give me a generous tip. All this together amounted to approximately two hundred zlotys. My father also had two hundred zlotys and my brother, one hundred zlotys.

My brother Moshe took the entire amount, plus his own money, to Cracow and exchanged it for gold dollars. The precious gold dollars were sewn into my trouser breeches; I was bought an extra-wide pair just for that purpose. Every few months my breeches were split open and a piece of gold removed, either a 2.5 gold piece or a 5 gold piece.

In this way we were able to support ourselves somewhat in those bleak, dismal times. But not for long. In the summer of 1941 the Gestapo arrested several Jews — the only name I remember is Yitzchak Landau — and threatened to shoot them within forty-eight hours unless they were redeemed by a certain amount of American gold dollars. Hearing this, a few young men undertook to redeem the captives and went around pleading that whoever had gold dollars should hand them over for the great mitzvah of *pidyon shevuyim*. My father relinquished the last few gold dollars we had. The captives were indeed released, but we starved, not having anything else of value left to sell.

When the few wealthy Jews of Poland heard that it had become illegal to transfer funds abroad they understood that a war was imminent and that the last place to keep one's money was a Polish bank. They began illegally smuggling their capital across the Polish border into Vienna and Switzerland. The money was sent with Czechoslovakian citizens, since the Czechoslovakian passport at that time did not require a visa. However, in December 1938 the inevitable happened. One of the messengers was caught by the Polish Secret Police carrying a large amount of dollars as he boarded the plane on his way from Warsaw to Zurich. He was arrested and the entire amount confiscated.

As soon as the news reached my uncle, he feared that the police would soon be after him, since he had been one of the organizers. My brother Moshe devised a plan to smuggle him out of Poland before the police had the chance to arrest him. In accordance with his plan, Moshe came to Tsanz and consulted with Mr. Eber Englander, who had good connections with the police. Reb Eber agreed to help him out, and that very day he carried out the first step: registering Leizer Lehrer with the police as a visitor in Tsanz.

The next step was fabricating a tale that my uncle had become very sick that day. A doctor's letter was procured stating that he must undergo an emergency operation in Vienna right away. Upon production of this letter, the *Starostova* immediately issued a passport and visa to Vienna — invaluable papers to my uncle in his predicament.

All being arranged as planned, my uncle took the international train, which ran from Cracow to Vienna, stopping in Tsanz on the way. As the train drew into the station in Tsanz, my uncle espied Moshe standing on the platform. The doors opened, and Moshe quickly handed him the important documents before the guard blew the whistle and the train left the station. With these papers, my uncle had no further trouble leaving Poland.

As we had suspected, the next morning the police were at our doorstep demanding to search our house, my uncle having been registered as residing with us. Of course, their search was fruitless.

Meanwhile, my uncle traveled to Vienna, where he remained unmolested for a few months. Not long afterwards, as he was on his way to his safe in a Viennese bank, the Nazis arrested him and handed him over to the Polish border police. He was imprisoned until the outbreak of war in 1939, whereupon all prisoners were released. However, he was to share the fate of millions of other Jews, and after living in the Cracow ghetto for some time, he was deported and perished in the gas chambers of Belzec, *hy"d*.

Toward the end of 1941 we received a parcel from Holland sent by Elazar May of Amsterdam. Included in it was a tin bottle of olive oil. My mother was ecstatic — at last, here was something she could cook with. My father, however, thought differently: he insisted that the oil be used for the Chanukah menorah. He explained to my mother that since the parcel happened to arrive before Chanukah, it must be a sign that the oil was to be used for the mitzvah of lighting Chanukah lights. (We received a second parcel of everyday necessities from

The Vanished City of Tsanz

Baruch Glatt of Scheveningen in The Hague. Baruch Glatt has a son and grandchildren living in Antwerp today.)

When the Nazis conquered Poland, one of the bitter decrees issued was that all the Jews living near the border must immediately vacate their homes and abandon their property. This was all part of Hitler's master plan — to first gather all the Jews together in the ghetto, so that the Final Solution would be quick, easy, and as convenient as possible.

The Jews living in the countryside had to leave their possessions and come to the ghetto with only the clothing on their backs to call their own. All their cattle, sheep, and poultry, amassed through years of hard, honest work, were promptly inherited by the Poles while the Jews arrived in the ghetto destitute and penniless.

Among the countrymen driven from their homes close to the Slovakian border was a man with a family of ten children by the name of Bochner, from the town of Krynica. The family lived cramped together in a room not bigger than eight square feet, in abject poverty. Taking pity on them, my friend Wolf and I took upon ourselves to collect bread for this starving family every Thursday. In those difficult circumstances, who had enough bread to eat, let alone to spare? Yet the good-hearted Jews of Tsanz, who were famous for their charity, still managed somehow to eke out some food for those less fortunate than they, and every week we handed Mr. Bochner a bag full of bread.

When we entered the dilapidated room, we were greeted by whoops of joy from the starving children, their faces pale and drawn from hunger. It was impossible for Mr. Bochner to put aside the entire bag for Shabbos — his famished children begged him for a piece of bread — and so he gave each one a tiny piece and hid whatever remained for Shabbos.

With tears in his eyes, Mr. Bochner thanked us for this lifesaving sustenance and blessed us that in the merit of this mitzvah we should survive this unbearably cruel and bitter war. As Chazal say, "Prayer fulfills half of a person's request": his blessing came true only for me, but unfortunately not for my friend Wolf.

THE OUTBREAK OF WAR

The Shinover Rav's Foresight

I would like to interrupt my narrative to repeat a story that Rabbi Elazar Oswiecimer, the sixth son-in-law of the saintly Divrei Chaim, related when he was in the Keshanover ghetto. He told this story to Reb Moshe Blum, who lives today in Brooklyn, in 1942.

The *tzaddik* Rabbi Elazar Rosenfeld, *zt"l*, or Reb Elazar Oswiecimer as he was known (named after the town where he lived,

Rabbi Elazar Rosenfeld, known as Rabbi Elazar Oswiecimer, son-in-law of the Divrei Chaim

later known as Auschwitz), was eighty years old at the time. While some Jews were discussing the terrible atrocities going on around them, he feebly called out, "I remember as if it had happened today. Fifty years ago, a *bachur* who lived in Biala had just returned from Shinova. He told me that a wondrous thing had occurred. He was sitting in the Shinover Rav's *beis midrash*, when suddenly the door opened, and the Shinover Rav, the oldest son of the Divrei Chaim, *zt"l*, walked in. His voice trembling with emotion, he called out to all those assembled, "Dear brothers, daven and say *tehillim*, because at this moment a wicked man was born, who will grow up to be even worse than Haman. We must storm the heavens and plead Hashem to remove him from this world before he grows up and causes untold evil to humanity."

Reb Elazer Oswiecimer continued, "We see now what marvelous foresight my brother-in-law, the Shinover Rav, had. Hashem should help that our troubles come to an end."

Forced Labor

At this point, many people were of the opinion that the best way to cope under the Nazis' reign of terror was by cooperating with them and being as loyal as possible. Acting upon the advice of a German officer, Yankel Marin, who with selfless devotion did all he could to lighten the Jews' plight in the ghetto, sent a delegation of Jews before the commanding general proposing to form an *Arbeits Ausschuss* (work committee) which would bear the responsibility of supplying voluntary workers for labor. However, the general rejected the offer, and forced labor continued as usual, spreading terror and suffering

Forced labor in the Piekela district

THE OUTBREAK OF WAR

among the occupants of the ghetto. Those who were forced to work for the army had to transport confiscated furniture and other objects for their German overseers and clean out their barracks and military headquarters.

Eventually, after a couple of weeks had passed, the commanding general agreed to set up a Jewish work committee, with Moshe Rindler at its head. This was a sort of employment agency. All able-bodied men were registered, and every day contingents of workers were provided according to the Nazis' demand. This system greatly relieved the plight of the Jews.

Not long after this problem was resolved, a new trouble came to the fore. Without any reason or warning, the German gendarmes captured a number of Jews as hostages and demanded a sizable amount of money for their release. After the *Judenrat* negotiated with them, they agreed to free two of the prisoners, Pearlberger and Klausner, in order to assist in raising the required sum. Some time later, after the money was raised, the remaining Jews were sent home, battered and bruised from the many beatings they had suffered.

On the High Holy Days, we did not dare assemble in the *batei midrash*. Instead, small *minyanim* of about ten to twenty people gathered together in homes far from the center of town. A watchman kept constant vigil should the dreaded S.S. put in an appearance. Thus we davened, trembling with fear and apprehension.

Directly after Yom Kippur, the *Judenrat* was established. Despite this and the *Arbeits Ausschuss*, which had been functioning for quite a while, the German soldiers still persisted in snatching Jews off the streets for forced labor. In due course an *Ordenung* (order) was established in the *Arbeits Ausschuss*, and every able-bodied man registered was paid a minimal wage. At last, the Germans were satisfied with the system and molested the Jews no longer for the time being.

At the same time the *Judenrat* (of which the *Arbeits Ausschuss* was a subcommittee) were commanded to carry out their first order: to provide money, necessities, and clothing to the Jews of the ghetto.

The Vanished City of Tsanz

The Polish mayor, the advocate Dr. Sicrava, was arrested, and Dr. Hein became mayor in his place. He actually encouraged the Jews to continue their businesses as usual.

In the weeks that followed there was a lull in the ghetto's troubles, and we began to believe that the situation had stabilized.

New Decrees

This relatively peaceful atmosphere in the ghetto did not last long. When the Gestapo, with Haman and Shultz at its head, took over the leadership of Tsanz, the random arrest of Jews began anew. It was only thanks to the intervention of the *Judenrat* that the captives were released, and that only through payment of astronomical sums of money and valuables.

However, no amount of effort on the part of the *Judenrat* could put a stop to the new Nazi decrees that were being introduced daily. The big, well-established shops were taken from their Jewish owners and given to the Germans and *Volksdeutsche* to manage. The smaller shops, which were still in Jewish hands, had to be open on Shabbos. All Jewish shops, pubs, restaurants, and warehouses had to display a Magen David in their windows by order of the general governor Frank. Even the Jewish stalls were obliged to display a placard with a Magen David.

That autumn the Tsanzer Jews, as well as all the Jews in Poland, were stamped with the sign of degradation: on their right arm they had to wear a white armband with a yellow Magen David sewn on, embroidered with the word *"Jude."* Immediately after this law was enforced, new laws came into being: Jews were not to travel on communal buses or trains and could not leave their city without permission.

Even in their blackest pessimism, nobody could have imagined then that this method of singling out the Jews, forcing them to wear their identity bands and reside together in one area, was all part of a well-thought-out master plan, a plan designed to eliminate any possibility of the Jews escaping the net which had been spread out for them, entrapping

THE OUTBREAK OF WAR

them for the final step of complete annihilation. Yet even without the whole truth being known to them, these new laws left the Jews feeling humiliated and helpless in the face of their Nazi conquerors.

The Chanukah "Shpiel"

It was in the beginning of the first winter under the Nazi regime that the Tsanzer Jews started their first horrifying ordeal. It was then that they were faced with the bitter, undeniable truth: they were in the hands of bloodthirsty vampires who were out to brutally exterminate each and every one of them.

The Gestapo were curious to see how the Poles would react to the unspeakable atrocities committed against the Jews. And so, on the last day of Chanukah, the ghetto was surrounded by the S.S. and S.D. (*Sicherheit Dienst*, "security police") holding machine guns. They announced that they were organizing a search for hidden weapons, ammunition, and radios. In reality, this was only an opportunity to rob the Jews of anything of value they may have still possessed.

The raid was thoroughly carried out, the Nazis going from door

Jews forced to sing and dance in the marketplace.

to door. All the men, young and old, were driven from their homes onto the streets so that the thugs could search the houses uninhibited and undisturbed. They overturned the furniture in order to investigate if anything was hidden in the hollow wood. The raid began at dawn and continued until 10 A.M.

After the S.S. had stuffed their pockets with money, jewelry, and anything else of value, they gathered together most of the men, especially singling out those with beards and *payos*, and drove them into the marketplace. The Jews whom they had caught davening were forced to crawl on all fours through mud and dirt still wearing their tallis and tefillin, or pull themselves along on their stomachs carrying candlesticks and menorahs on their heads, kicked and beaten by their oppressors.

With the Jews assembled in the marketplace, the Germans organized a "spectacle." The square was surrounded by crowds of Poles, who all came running eagerly when they heard of the exciting adventure they were about to witness.

Among those gathered in the market were some elderly, distinguished *rabbanim:* the son of the Gorlitzer *rosh av beis din*, Rabbi Naftali Miller; his son the *tzaddik* Rabbi Yoelish, *hy"d*; Rabbi Chuna Hirsh Rubin, called the Sakmarer Rebbe, one of the greatest doers of *chesed* in Tsanz; Rabbi Moshe Frank, author of *Hashem Ekra*; and the Labover Rav, Rabbi Shmuel Aharon Miller. (Rabbi Shmuel Aharon was a disciple of the Shinover Rav, *zy"a*, and also of the first Bobover Rav, *zy"a*. He was a *Yid* full of burning enthusiasm for *avodas Hashem*, occupying the position of *Rav* first in Yedlitch and later in Labowa. He arrived in Tsanz as a refugee in 1940.)

The Nazis forced them to pray, to sing at the top of their voices, to dance and clap their hands, amidst jeers and shouts of scorn and mockery from the crowd of onlookers. Those who became weary from their ordeal were egged on with fearsome blows. As part of the presentation, one Jew was made to ride on another on all fours. This gruesome spectacle lasted four hours, until 2 P.M.

Apart from the wonderful entertainment, the audience derived other worthy benefits: every Pole was permitted to pick a pair of shoes, a pair of boots, or a coat from the dancing Jews. As soon as he made his selection, the Jew was obliged to remove the article of his choice and hand it to him. When the ordeal was over, many of the exhausted Jews were so battered from the countless blows they had received that they had to be taken to hospital. Yet, despite all, they were thankful that they had at least escaped with their lives (although three of those tortured died later, as a result of the beatings).

The majority of Poles were indifferent to their fellow townspeople's suffering, even reveling in the delightful scene afforded them. Nevertheless, one Pole, a pharmacist named Yarosh, acted decently and reprimanded the Poles who took the clothing from the dancing Jews, saying, "Don't rejoice so much in the Jews' suffering, for as soon as the Germans are finished with them, we'll be next." Not long afterwards, in 1940, Yarosh was indeed murdered at the hands of the Nazis.

The Nazis took special delight in torturing the disabled and maimed. In Tsanz there lived a thirty-year-old cripple named Yoske Torem, the son of Reb Mordechai and Feigele Torem. Yoske was crippled from childhood; he was small, pale, and a hunchback. He was killed in a horrible manner: the beasts tied him to a horse's tail and galloped the horse through town for many hours, long after their victim had died.

The Only Jewish Calendar in Poland

In the year 1940, Chanoch Krisher, the owner of the printing company G. Weinstein, perceived that the printers were out of business and there was little chance of a Jewish calendar being published that year. Seeing this, he turned to the sole remaining Jewish publisher and asked for his assistance.

The calendar was calculated by Rabbi Nuta Shloime Schlussel and his son, who were both known as great *talmidei chachamim* and mathematicians. It later turned out that this was the sole calendar in the entire Poland which was circulated that year. It was also the last one to be published, since all the Jewish print shops were requisitioned by the Germans.

The Vanished City of Tsanz

Some Personal Memories

At the onset of ghetto life, the S.S. snatched Jews to clean cars, sweep the pavements, and wash the toilets — anything to humiliate them. With the establishment of the employment agency, headed by the Czech Svaboda (whom the Germans had appointed), summons were sent to all the men, ordering them to turn up for work. Those who did not appear and did not have a doctor's letter stating that they were sick were punished with twenty to twenty-five blows. A Jew by the name of Alter Bauman was responsible for carrying out this penalty.

I received my first summons to work at the beginning of 1940. The administrator Svaboda ordered Alter Bauman to shave off my *payos*. I arrived home very much ashamed of my appearance, but my father consoled me: "If the world will ever be sane again and you will survive the war, you will once again grow *payos*."

All they left me was my black socks.

I was given a heavy hammer and made to walk nine kilometers to the work site. Fortunately enough, my *kapo*, Meibruch, was not a harsh overseer. I was led to a pile of large stones and told to break them into smaller pieces. (These were later used to plaster the roads.) I sat there, right in the middle of the road, feeling like a gypsy. But my lot was

THE OUTBREAK OF WAR

tolerable, and I did not complain.

However, as time wore on, the situation went from bad to worse. Every day, new trouble befell the ghetto occupants. Jews were shot at random — at first with an excuse but later without. One time, an anonymous person stuck a sign on the wall with propaganda against the Nazis. As a result, the Gestapo arrested four Jews and four Poles. They were first sent to a prison in Tarnow where they were tortured. One of the tortures inflicted on them was being forced to immerse in a barrel of boiling hot water. When their bodies were completely scalded and they were left weakened and bereft of energy they were shipped off to Auschwitz.

The four Poles returned but not the Jews. The families of the victims received a letter that they must send two German marks to the post office. In return they each received a small box with ashes. On each box was inscribed the name of their loved one. This was their last remembrance of the person sent off to Auschwitz.

I can recall only three of the four names. One was Shmelke Schiff (whose grandmother, Tzlova, was a sister of Rabbi Itzikel, *zt"l*, of

The Jewish orphanage in Tsanz

Pshevorsk-Antwerp, *zt"l*). Another was Rabbi Moshe Ungar, the son of Rabbi Benzion Unger (who was called *"der hoiche Benzion,"* the tall Benzion), a descendant of the Dombrover Rav, Rabbi Mordechai David. The third was HaRav Benzion Westreich, a son of the Kaintshiger Rav and a son-in-law of the Tsanzer *dayan* Rabbi Mordechai Yosef Saphir (and a brother-in-law to Rabbi Moshe Kleinman who lived in London after the war).

The nine-kilometer walk to and from work was proving to be a great strain on me. Consequently, my father turned to a former pupil of his, Baruch Berliner, for assistance. Baruch was one of the members of the *Judenrat*, and, being a good-hearted fellow, he arranged for me to receive via the employment agency a job in the Jewish orphanage caring for the children. This orphanage functioned under the name of its founder, Shmuel Mashler. He was a very warmhearted person, who did a lot of good before the war. In prewar times every child was well dressed, fed, and well looked after and was also taught a trade. In this worthy institution, five hundred children from the Tsanzer ghetto were served breakfast and lunch.

Due to the financial situation of the ghetto Jews, only one orphan per family was allowed entry to the orphanage. The Gestapo forbade us to learn with the children either Jewish or secular studies, and so about the only thing we could do with them was sing. And sing we did, from breakfast until lunch. My work was pleasant and rewarding — serving meals to innocent young orphans.

I received a permit, signed by General Governor Frank in Cracow, stating that I may not be snatched for forced labor. this permit was given to all the employees of the J.S.S. — Jewish Social Security — the official help committee. The permits, however, were worthless in the face of the all-powerful Gestapo, who grabbed Jews off the streets for deportation, permit or no permit.

The Anti-Semitic Tirade of the Evangelical Priest

At the end of November 1939 extracts from the infamous neo-Nazi, anti-Semitic newspaper *Der Sturmer* were distributed in the city.

The article consisted of fabricated stories accusing the Jews of having a hand in the murder of ten Tsanzer *Volksdeutsche* (which we have already written about earlier). It also claimed that the Jews always bore a hatred against the Evangelical church, besmirching its members at every opportunity. The article was based on an interview with the local priest. Ironically, this priest had always been on good terms with the Jews, even speaking a fluent Yiddish.

The reporters of this vulgar, slanderous newspaper brought proofs for each of their accusations and even had "authentic" photographs to illustrate their lies. The snapshots were accomplished by force; with the aid of the S.S., Jews of all ages were caught and made to stand in various positions in order that these "caught-just-in-time, true-to-life" photographs would arouse feelings of hatred and revenge among the German population.

Among the pre-plotted photos was a picture of Jews mercilessly mutilating a German soldier and preparing to shoot him. Luckily, the caption wrote, the Gestapo arrived in the nick of time to save this unfortunate soldier. They also wrote that Jews consider it a "mitzvah to kill Aryans." They displayed pictures of Jews sitting together in heated discussion, with the comment that they were predicting the imminent downfall of the German empire. These photographs were seen by millions of German citizens nationwide.

The First Refugees Arrive

In November 1939, the survivors of the first ghettos to be liquidated — from the Lodz and Shirardz areas — began to arrive in Tsanz. At the train station they were welcomed by members of the help committee: Yisrael Friedman, Refael Klein, Dov Hirshtahl, and Miss B. Finder.

At the train station, we were met with an unforgettable and heartbreaking scene. The arriving Jews were beaten and bloodied, physically wounded and totally crushed in spirit. There was a look of utter resignation in their eyes. Overwhelmed with despair, they stood in gray rows, a shocking testimony to the organized method of mass execution the Nazis were to use against us. Drained of energy, weak from hunger, the men, women, and children were driven along by the S.S., trembling from fear of the beatings which constantly accompanied them and the cold, for which they were so inadequately clothed. In this fashion, they were taken to the barracks of the Polish army.

We were occupied until late evening with the new arrivals. The wounded had to be treated and bandaged and later settled for the night together with the other refugees in the large *batei midrash*.

The following day, the families with small children were relocated into private homes or in the deserted homes of the foresighted ones who had fled this holocaust in time. The other refugees remained in the *batei midrash*.

We listened with horror to the spine-chilling tales they told us about the treatment they had undergone at the hands of their heartless killers. Broken and depressed, we returned home after hearing of the unspeakable suffering they had endured.

The refugees, however, were left greatly uplifted. Hope was rekindled in them when they saw the selflessness and good-heartedness which reigned in the Tsanzer ghetto. The committee devoted themselves body and soul to ease the plight of the terrorized victims. They hung up notices that clothing was needed for the refugees. The response was overwhelming. That very day the help committee's office was filled with clothing and other necessities. Greatly strengthened, the refugees felt that maybe the circumstances weren't so terrible after all.

CHAPTER 2

THE GHETTO AND THE FIRST LABOR CAMP

1940—1941

After the nightmarish Chanukah ordeal, peace reigned in the ghetto, but not for long. A few weeks later, a raid took place on all the Jewish shops. Fortunately, the storeowners only suffered a scare and monetary loss but no physical harm.

With the advent of the first winter in the ghetto (1939–1940) the Jews already felt the pinch of shortage of food and other necessities. In the autumn of 1940 a new influx of refugees arrived in the ghetto. On October 29, the residents of the border and those living in Krenitz, Muszyna, Zshegiastov, and Piwnicna were ordered to vacate their homes by November 30, leaving behind all their possessions. They were to move into Tsanz, the biggest town in the vicinity.

As the stream of refugees poured in, housing conditions in the ghetto grew from bad to worse. The possibility of earning a livelihood was also drastically reduced, as more and more shops were being requisitioned by the Germans. Only a handful of Jewish businesses on the other side of the ghetto wall were still in Jewish hands.

Despite the odds, several Jews continued to manage their businesses on a large scale. One of them was the brush wholesaler, Chaim Peterfreund. Reb Chaim was the *mohel* in Tsanz. A deeply pious man, he not only refused payment for his services as *mohel* but always presented a gift to the father of the baby! At one point his German business partner reported his doings to the Gestapo, and it was only with great effort on the part of the *Judenrat* that he emerged alive.

That autumn the new mayor, Schmidt, issued another decree: the Jews must leave the Old Tsanzer street and the marketplace. As a result, the difficulties of cramped living quarters became even worse. On that day Schmidt also issued a second law banning Jews from the streets on market days (Tuesday and Friday) until midday, another blow to Jewish trade.

A short time later a new order was enforced, adding to the daily worsening of poverty. The Polish police were commanded by the Gestapo to inspect all Jewish packages. Two Polish policemen, Soyke and Griss, carried out this order with great enthusiasm — and every bony chicken or hard-earned crust of bread carried by a Jew was confiscated.

The Jews' suffering at this time wasn't limited to hunger, cold, inadequate clothing, and crowded, unsanitary living quarters. They also had to contend with the spontaneous killings, beatings, and other cruel methods the Nazis used to embitter their lives.

In December 1939, the *Untersturmfuhrer* Heinrich Haman, *y"s*, was appointed head of the *Sicherheits Polizei* in Tsanz, consisting of the S.S., Gestapo, and *Kripo* (criminal police). Haman was an unbelievably cruel and heartless man, a blonde beast. His sadistic bloodthirstiness was insatiable, and nothing in the world

Heinrich Haman, the chief murderer of Tsanz

THE GHETTO AND THE FIRST LABOR CAMP

seemed to move him. Haman bragged to the *Judenrat* soon after his henchmen had overtaken Tsanz, "My name is Heinrich Haman. You Jews know well what the name 'Haman' implies, but this time there will be no Esther to come to your rescue." Sadly, he managed to fulfill his threat with resounding success, eliminating Tsanzer Jewry slowly and methodically. He accomplished his goal in the most horrible ways imaginable; those whom he led to the cemetery to be shot were forced to dig their own graves and undress before being killed.

His assistants, too, were bloodthirsty hounds who tried to outdo each other in cruelty. They were Johann Bornholt, the head of the criminal department, a wagon driver by occupation; Reinhard and Hunziger, the Gestapo members; and the *Volksdeutsche* Gurka, who came from the village of Shviniarsk and the official interpreter of the Gestapo. This gang of virulent killers, apart from robbing and blackmailing, would pounce on Jews in the ghetto, arrest them, and take them to Gestapo headquarters. There they were tortured and later sent home, mutilated and more dead than alive. However, this was only an introduction to the inhumane methods of murder which the gang, headed by Haman, were to later use.

Johann Bornholt, Haman's right-hand man

The Jewish Hospital

The Jewish hospital, situated on Kraszewski Street, had been in existence for many years. At the end of 1938 the Jewish committee, headed by Reb Shalom Yonah Tenzer, carried out a major refurbishing

The Vanished City of Tsanz

The Jewish hospital

project. The building was renovated and beds, medical equipment, and machinery were brought in. However, just when all was ready for public use, war broke out, disrupting all plans for its imminent opening.

When the Nazis raided the town they broke into the hospital and robbed it of everything of value, down to the last bandage. Only the walls remained as a silent testimony to what once was.

The severe shortage of housing due to the influx of refugees necessitated the use of the hospital as accommodation. When the need for a hospital became extremely urgent, as the local state hospital would not admit Jewish patients, the help committee was confronted with a tragic situation — the refugees who sheltered there refused to be turned out into the streets. With much persuasion, the help committee succeeded in emptying two or three rooms for the seriously ill.

I vividly recall being summoned to the *Chassidishe beis midrash* "asylum" to assist in removing a very sick person. He was called Mr. Znamirovsky, a short, thin redhead. We found him weak and drained, deteriorating daily due to the poor conditions in the asylum. We transported him by horse and cart to one of the hospital rooms and

THE GHETTO AND THE FIRST LABOR CAMP

bedded him down on a makeshift, wooden bed. Soon after, the second patient appeared. Mr. Schwartz was a short young man, with very dark, expressive eyes, bespeaking pain and suffering. Both were from Lodz. These were the first two patients, and after their arrival the need for further facilities became increasingly more urgent.

We received permission from the Occupation Authority to import beds from the Jewish hotels in Krenitz. Avraham Enker "lent" them to the hospital. The head doctor was Dr. Jacob Segal.

Gradually, the hospital became more and more established. Nurses were put through training courses, and doctors volunteered their services in their spare time. The administration was run by Yisrael Friedman, who showed tireless devotion in his efforts to keep everything running smoothly.

The vast improvement in the hospital's functioning was largely due to the unceasing efforts of Dr. Stockli, the director of the state hospital. He was a Christian, but his wife was of Jewish descent (she was in hiding). Even in a time of harsh ghetto regulations, when entry by Christians was strictly forbidden, Dr. Stockli faithfully tended to his Jewish patients and refused to accept payment for his services. When he operated on my grandmother he gently assured her that she should not be afraid, because he had received a blessing from the Belzer Rebbe, Rabbi Yissachar Dov Rokach.

The hospital was a blessing to those who could not have otherwise afforded the luxury of medical care. Above all, it was a haven to the steadily increasing number of refugees who lived in the asylum in shocking conditions — cramped and neglected, with a horrifying lack of hygiene.

Many Jewish girls devoted themselves wholeheartedly to the worthy task of taking care of the sick. Despite the many hours of work they did, they accepted no payment. In fact, not only was the hospital a place of refuge and healing to the sick, but it was a lifesaver to many Jewish women and girls, and some men, who were thus spared the harsh conditions of forced labor.

In the last few days of the ghetto's liquidation word went round that the ill people would not be moved, since the Germans "would not carry out such a heartless deed." Hearing this, many Jews took their weak and ailing parents to the hospital. The Germans' "mercy" was yet to be proved. A week after the general liquidation the Gestapo, headed by Haman, entered the hospital and shot the invalids in their beds. The doctors and other remaining staff were taken outside to the yard, where they were also shot.

The Public Kitchen

The help committee carried a heavy burden in its responsibility for the welfare of the refugees. Apart from housing them they also had to provide them with food. The first public kitchen was located in the orphanage founded and run by Mr. Shmuel Mashler. Yisrael Friedman and Dov Hirshtahl acted as secretary, while Shlomo Landau was food officer.

The most difficult task was shouldered by Refael Klein. He was responsible for the finances and was forced to tax the already hard-pressed Jews. This tax was in addition to the regular collections carried out by the *Judenrat*.

Even as the financial situation in the ghetto became more and more difficult, due to the confiscation of Jewish businesses and the withholding of payment for forced labor, midday meals and bread rations had to be distributed to the exiles. In addition, money had to be raised for the constantly rising demand for medical supplies.

A second public kitchen was set up in the women's section of the Gribover *beis midrash* in the Jewish Street. This kitchen was headed by Yekel Englander. Later, when the Nazi Frank, governor general of Cracow, ordered the establishment of the J.S.S. (Jewish Social Security) in Cracow, headed by Yechezkel Gutreich, the help committee was dissolved and both public kitchens were given over to the J.S.S.

If the meals served in the kitchen had any taste when the first refugees arrived, soon enough the portions became smaller and tasteless, as the food shortage became more severe and the constant stream of new arrivals steadily increased.

THE GHETTO AND THE FIRST LABOR CAMP

Isser Eisenberg's Gemilus Chesed

Isser Eisenberg manufactured thread in the ghetto years, a precious commodity in wartime. For this reason, Eisenberg was granted a *pasirshein* — a pass which allowed him to leave the ghetto in order to obtain the raw materials for his work. When he visited gentiles in the nearby villages, he exchanged the bit of thread which he had not surrendered to the Germans for flour.

Isser Eisenberg could have amassed a fortune from the flour. Instead, he gave everything away to the public kitchen. Usually it was a fifty-kilo sack once a week. He and the philanthropist Reb Yekel Englander gave sustenance to thousands of people. The flour was made into a soup which was distributed daily to the needy. As a result, the price of bread fell from sixty zlotys a loaf to thirty zlotys.

The Martyrdom of the Benzion'lech

It was in the year 1940. The Gestapo had caught a smuggler and found a letter written in Yiddish on his person. It was addressed to Menashe Yechezkel Flaster, a Shinover Chassid who lived on the *Yiddisher Gass*. The Gestapo demanded his capture.

Menashe Yechezkel Flaster immediately went into hiding. Thereupon, the Gestapo arrested the rabbinical family Eichenstein (known as the *"Benzion'lech"*) and threatened that the prisoners would not be freed until the hunted made his appearance.

The Gestapo commanded the rabbinical sons to issue an appeal, as the spiritual leaders in Tsanz, that the wanted man should be hunted down and delivered into their hands. However, no amount of barbarous tortures and excruciating pain inflicted upon them was of any avail. The Rebbe and his sons stubbornly refused to do what is forbidden in the Torah — to deliver a Jew into gentile hands. Tragically, they paid for this with their lives and were deported to Auschwitz.

CHAPTER 3

THE LAST YEAR IN THE TSANZER GHETTO

June 1941–Summer 1942

With the Nazi invasion of the Soviet Union on June 22, 1941, the realization of the Final Solution in Tsanz, and in the whole of Poland, was brought into effect with alarming speed.

Before the invasion, the inhabitants of the villages surrounding Tsanz were ordered to leave their homes and move into the ghetto. After the invasion, even those who lived in Tsanz but did not reside in the Jewish quarter were forced to move into one of the two ghettos in town — either the ghetto bounded by Kazimierza Street (also known as "the Jewish Street"), the Third of May Place (the Jews called it the "*Tepperplatz*"), and Piarsky Street; or the ghetto which comprised the Piekela and the area of the Kamienica River up to the Pzetukova, which is next to the cemetery. Until the end of 1941 the ghettos were not walled in, but exit was forbidden without a special permit. Those who dared leave the ghetto without permission were shot on the spot.

The entire Jewish population of Tsanz, together with those of the surrounding villages and the hundreds of refugees from other cities, were squeezed together into the two small ghettos made up of several narrow, dingy streets. This resulted in horrifying overcrowding. In general, four to five families, averaging over twenty persons in all,

THE LAST YEAR IN THE TSANZER GHETTO

lived cramped together in a one-room apartment with a kitchen.

In the summer of 1941, the work camps became a nightmare for the ghetto inhabitants. The former chief of the ministry of labor, Westhold, was replaced by a German, Metta. Originally Camp Lypia was the only work camp, but new sites were set up in Rozhnov, Kamionka, and Muszyna for the purpose of building roads for travel.

Formerly, Jews enlisted voluntarily for work in the hope of earning a piece of bread to satisfy their constant, gnawing hunger. However, under the new leadership, people were grabbed off the streets and forcibly taken to work camps. The first victims to suffer thus were the starving, helpless refugees who were packed together in the asylums of the ghetto's *batei midrash*.

The Ordenungs Dienst

The brutal snatching of unfortunate souls for forced labor, the dreaded *aktion*s where groups of Jews were rounded up and sent to Auschwitz, the random shootings — all would not have been able to be carried out so efficiently and effortlessly by the Gestapo if not for the vicious, murderous deeds committed by the Jewish Police (the *Ordenungs Dienst*, or O.D.), who served their masters like a pack of faithful hounds.

In 1940 the Jewish *Ordenungs Dienst* was formed by the *Judenrat*, by order of the Germans. Responsibility for it was handed over to a shoe merchant, Aharon Moses. He continued to set up the organization which so successfully assisted in causing abject misery and the eventual downfall of the Tsanzer Jews.

At the helm of this lowly group stood a vulgar fellow by the name of Y. Folkman from Kozhov (Schlesjin). It was well-known in the ghetto that this Folkman had already been involved in criminal activities back in Schlesjin. His deputy was Blaustein, a Russian-Polish Jew who had formerly lived in Vienna. The group consisted of elements similar to themselves, outcasts of society.

The mere appearance of the Jewish Police with their white armbands was enough to send chills of fear through the hearts of the Jewish population. They immediately understood that another tragedy was in

The Vanished City of Tsanz

Meeting with a collaborator before an *aktion*, 1941

store for them. The hooligans wore proud, brazen expressions, smugly observing their cringing Jewish counterparts, as if they themselves belonged to the "superior race." Although they were only permitted to be armed with rubber truncheons, they wielded their power with the same animalistic sadism displayed by the Gestapo. They were available for their Nazi superiors' every call, even doing more than what was required of them. (In the ghetto's last days, when selections and deportations were taking place daily, they used blackmail just like the Gestapo in order to squeeze out the last remaining money and valuables from those who could afford to redeem themselves.)

There were a few individuals who retained a spark of humanity, warning the people who were on Folkman's next deportation list even if it meant risking their lives. Amongst these praiseworthy men were Yidel Binder and Schlesinger. Another of the more decent members of the O.D. was David Ullman, the son of Leibish Ullman. He was one of my father's students. Whenever he received a list of Jews to be rounded up, he would go to each Jew in turn and warn him to go into hiding, for in an hour's time he and another group of policemen were

THE LAST YEAR IN THE TSANZER GHETTO

coming to get him. Soon enough, though, when he consistently failed to capture the men on his list, he lost his job as policeman.

My mother was actually saved by one of the O.D.'s. It happened as follows:

One day, at 5 A.M., the Jewish Police raided the ghetto in a hunt for one hundred people required by the Gestapo. When this would happen the men quickly escaped to bunkers which had been built in every house for this purpose. However, during this *aktion* I wasn't quick enough, since the O.D. had broken down the door of our house with lightning speed.

I heard the banging at the door and my name, Solomon Lehrer, being called. I was struck with heart-stopping fear. With sickening clarity, I knew it was too late to reach the hiding place situated on the first floor. On the spur of the moment I thought of a plan and hurriedly dived under my bed, desperately pulling the bedspreads over the sides so that I would not be seen.

As soon as the police entered the room, they yelled at my mother to reveal where her son Solomon was hidden. When she feebly claimed that she had no idea where I was, one of the policemen went over to the direction of the bed where I was hidden. He firmly placed his hand on the bedspread and bawled at my mother, "Liar! His bed is still warm. This is a sure sign that he slept here today. Give me the key of the cellar where he is hiding. Immediately!"

I lay there under the bed and listened to the entire proceedings, trembling with fear. My mother kept her head and calmly handed them the keys of the cellar. As soon as their heavy boots resounded on the cellar steps she signaled to me that the coast was clear. I promptly scrambled out from under my bed and raced up the steps to the bunker. After a futile search the police ascended the cellar steps and warned my mother that the list of those they had not succeeded in capturing would be given over to the Gestapo, who would personally come to get the fugitives.

I was not the only one whom the O.D. had failed to round up. Knowing only too well that our capture spelled almost certain death, I, together with the others who had managed to elude the police, went

The Vanished City of Tsanz

into a safer bunker. Taking all precautions not to be recognized on the streets, I disguised myself as a girl. Thus clad, I crossed the street to the first floor of Rebbetzin Nechumele's home, the former home of the Tsanzer *tzaddik*, the holy Divrei Chaim, *zt"l*.

The entrance to the bunker was situated behind a *sefarim* cupboard in the women's section of Nechumele's *beis midrash*. One shelf was emptied of *sefarim* and we crawled through the shelf and into the bunker. After all seventy of us were safely inside we replaced the *sefarim* and closed the trapdoor. We sat and said *tehillim* for the duration of our stay.

The following day we returned to our homes. That day, the Gestapo themselves came to search for those on the list who had not been caught. This time my father also came with me into hiding, for the order was that if the person on the list could not be found, his brother or father should be taken instead.

The S.S., accompanied by a Jewish policeman, entered our apartment and with the aid of dogs began searching our home. An icy fear squeezed my heart as we heard the raucous barking of their hunting dogs. We heard the soldiers pounding with their heavy boots all over our home, but they did not manage to find us. Suddenly we froze with fear as we heard an S.S. soldier take out a revolver, place the nozzle on my mother's head, and threaten to shoot if she did not reveal where her husband and son were hiding.

With bated breath we heard my mother tremblingly reply that her husband was a drunk who did not come home at night, and her son, too, was a lout who rarely came home.

Standing with the revolver still pointing to her head, the S.S. murderer barked, "You are lying! You Jews are not drunkards!"

However, my mother stuck to her story. Still standing in the same position, the S.S. man turned to the Jewish policeman and said, "Tell me, is this woman telling the truth or not?" upon which the Jewish policeman uttered the fateful words, "Yes, she is telling the truth." This Jewish policeman happened to come from a very degenerate home, yet he had always acted decently.

THE LAST YEAR IN THE TSANZER GHETTO

Hearing this, the Nazi returned the revolver to its holster and left our home.

Folkman, the chief of police, faithfully cooperated with the Gestapo, hoping to find favor in the eyes of the murderers. However, it was not to be. When we arrived in Auschwitz from the camp in Shevnia at the end of 1943 and we were standing before a selection, Folkman stepped forward and proudly declared, "I was the chief of the Jewish O.D.'s in New Tsanz and its surrounding areas," confident that this would earn him direct passage to life.

In reply, the officiating S.S. man hit him with the butt of his gun and yelled at him, "Cursed dog! Go immediately to the left," pointing in the direction of all those destined to die in the gas chambers.

Another Jewish policeman from Reisha suffered the same fate. As soon as he announced that he was one of the O.D.'s in the Reisha ghetto, the S.S. bade him go to the left. They intentionally sought to get rid of those who had assisted them, in order that nobody should remain who could later testify as to the scope of their damning deeds.

Apart from the *Ordenungs Dienst*, a Jewish *Block Dienst* was also formed. They were responsible for supplying the *Arbeits Amt* with the required amount of laborers. Stashek Kraus was appointed head of the *Block Dienst*. He, like Folkman and Blaustein, did not originate from Tsanz; apparently they could not find enough wicked, cruel people with low characters in Tsanz. Although the *Block Dienst* was established by Folkman they were generally not as cruel as the O.D. Nevertheless, they did include some exceptionally wicked members, such as Moshe Green and Yitzchak Roper, who had little to do with Judaism even before the war.

It is needless to say that, as always, the role of bloodhound did not serve to save the Jewish police from their Nazi overlords when their services were no longer required. As mentioned above, Folkman met his fate in Auschwitz. Blaustein and his gang suffered their just reward in the death camp in Shevnia.

I must add here that only one who experienced the ghetto and concentration camps has the right to condemn the Jewish Police.

The Vanished City of Tsanz

Today's generation, which has been brought up in luxury with telephones and refrigerators and does not know what it means to be hungry and not have a piece of bread to still one's hunger, cannot judge. The world turned upside down. Upper-class people lost their humanity and turned into brutal animals overnight when confronted with suffering, cooperating with the Nazis in order to get a slice of bread, while simple people showed extraordinary courage in the face of adversity and refused to cooperate with the Nazis in order to save their skins.

The First Aktions

For a time, the chief of the Gestapo in Tsanz, the *Hauptsturmfuhrer* Heinrich Haman, was satisfied with robbing Jews of their money and jewelry. He used to boast to the *Judenrat*, "Everything belongs to me; your money, your lives, all is mine." But in spring 1941, he began to wield his power over Jewish lives. This was to be expected, with his bootlicker, Folkman, bragging, "I have fifteen thousand Jews available to be sold to you."

THE LAST YEAR IN THE TSANZER GHETTO

Toward the end of summer 1941, in the month of Elul, the *rabbanim aktion*, or *caftan Juden aktion*, as it was commonly called, took place. When a tank train exploded at the Tsanzer train station, ten Jews, mainly *"caftan Juden"* (i.e., *rabbanim* and those clad in Chassidic garb) were taken as a punishment and sent to Auschwitz, where they met their death.

Among the unfortunate victims seized in this *aktion* were two sons of the Tsanzer Rav, Rabbi Aryeh Leibish Halberstam: Rabbi Efraim and his younger brother, an emaciated and pale man, Rabbi Hersh. The other captive, also from a rabbinical family, was Rabbi Moshe Eichenstein.

During the Jewish holidays the Nazi tormentors increased their barbarism. In this way they intended to scoff at the Jewish religion and customs and to degrade Jewish pride as much as possible.

Rosh HaShanah 1942, the third Rosh HaShanah under the Nazi regime, spelled darkness and gloom for the Tsanzer Jews. The troubles began in the month of Elul, a week before Selichos, when the O.D. stormed Jewish homes in the darkness of night and dragged away one hundred Jews to their assembly point, situated in the school on Kochanovska Street.

From right to left: a Gerrer Chassid from Lodz, Mendel Bodner, Leibish Chaim Shia's, and Moshe Gewirtz

The Vanished City of Tsanz

In the early hours of the morning, the captives were brought to the Gestapo's headquarters. The Nazis arranged the trembling Jews in two rows and commanded them to run while their captors mercilessly beat them with leather whips. The Germans watched with delight as the Jews desperately tried to avoid the biting leather. When the Nazis became bored of this sport, they handed the Jews some gardening tools and led them to an empty plot where the prisoners were ordered to plant a garden. They were given two weeks to complete their "work," under the following conditions: two-legged and four-legged Gestapo dogs constantly chased the Jews, murderously hitting and biting them, constantly thinking up new evil and vicious ideas to worsen their plight. One of their barbarous games was ordering the Jews to dig pits and pour dirt over each other up to their necks. It was only two days before Rosh HaShanah, with the garden smoothly laid out with gravel, that they were finally permitted to return to their homes.

On the morning of Rosh HaShanah the Jews gathered in small groups to pray. (They had long stopped using the *batei midrash* for that purpose.) Suddenly the Gestapo burst into their homes and dragged out approximately two hundred Jews, hitting them with wooden truncheons and whips. With the aid of dogs they chased the Jews to the garden which had just recently been completed. This time they were ordered to plow the yard, pulling out thorny plants with their bare hands, all the while being hit by the Nazis with fearsome blows. This gruesome sport ended with those Jews being imprisoned. It was only due to a great sum of money raised on their behalf that the prisoners were spared a death sentence.

A short time after the High Holy Days, in the month of Cheshvan, another *aktion* took place which surpassed all previous ones. Some thirty Jews or so had fled the Nazis to Soviet-occupied East Galicia. When the Germans conquered that area, too, the Jews were brought back to Tsanz, where Haman ordered them all shot in a mass execution.

The *aktion*s for similar mass executions were occurring more and more frequently, covering larger areas in the ghetto. In January 1942, the so-called "cigarette *aktion*" took place. There were some hardy people, mainly youngsters, who would risk their lives to earn a piece of bread for themselves and their families by illegally selling cigarettes which they obtained from Polish wholesalers. One fine day, without any warning, Haman ordered a search for all cigarette dealers. They were arrested and taken to the Gestapo building, where he personally shot them for the crime of selling on the black market. The murdered consisted of two groups: one group of forty and one of fifty. The majority of these innocent souls were young children. The Poles who had provided them with cigarettes were deported to Auschwitz, but they returned alive and well not long afterwards.

At the beginning of 1942, not long after the cigarette *aktion*, the housing *aktion* took place. Haman ordered the arrest of a large number of Jews, accusing them of speculating and investing in properties. They were taken straight from the prisons, where they were held, to the cemetery, where they were all shot under Haman's smug observation.

These particular *aktion*s are engraved in the memories of the few who survived, because of the names which Haman identified them with. However, there were countless more *aktion*s which weren't privileged with individual names. Each was done under a different pretext but all with the same intention: to terrorize the Jewish population, robbing them of their sanity. The reasons given varied: sometimes to punish, sometimes to eliminate those who weren't fit for work anymore. Frequently, a list for an *aktion* of wealthy people was compiled to enable the Nazis to demand a sizable ransom. Apart from the preplanned *aktion*s for which the Jewish Police provided lists of names, many *razia*s took place, in which any Jew who happened to be found on the streets was grabbed and taken away.

A considerable number of those caught in the *aktion*s were shot in Tsanz. Others were deported to concentration camps. From 1940, people had been sporadically sent to Auschwitz, but it was only from the beginning of 1942 that transports were sent to camps in Rabka and Pustkow, near Dembitz. The camp in Pustkow was originally built for the purpose of building roads, but the camp in Rabka was built with

The Vanished City of Tsanz

the sole intention of torturing and starving its prisoners to death.

On Pesach 1942, the massive Pustkow *aktion* took place, in which numerous Jews were deported to the camp in Pustkow. Yet even on relatively "ordinary" days, when no *aktion*s took place, the Jews were at the mercy of the animalistic whims and murderous bloodlust of their Gestapo masters.

Haman's henchmen, Johann Bornholt, Reinhard, and Hunziger (with Millung occasionally acting as his substitute), would roam the streets of the ghetto at night, seeking to satiate their hunger for blood. A Jew whom they accosted on the streets was considered fortunate if he merely suffered burn wounds from having his beard and *payos* set on fire.

The Nazi beasts would storm into Jewish homes, thrusting women off balconies, shooting children before the eyes of their mothers, or men in the presence of their wives and children, or the entire family in one shooting spree (as happened to the Gluck family). This was considered entertainment, their leisurely pastime.

The commander of this barbarous Gestapo gang, Heinrich Haman, did not let himself be outdone in cruelty by his colleagues. He had already proved himself at the beginning of 1942 with the following episode:

Haman was taking a stroll with his wife and several sixteen-year-old youths on the Helena Bridge, when they came across four Jews. He stopped and ordered his sixteen-year-old companions to shoot the Jews. The youngsters, who weren't very proficient at aiming, only man-

A Nazi killing a defenseless woman, her child in her hands

THE LAST YEAR IN THE TSANZER GHETTO

aged to wound their unlucky victims. Haman himself then took the gun and finished the job in order to teach the young German generation the art of shooting Jews dead.

The following ghoulish tale illustrates to some degree to what unimaginable levels of cruelty the handsome, blonde, tall, blue-eyed epitome of the "superior race" could stoop. Haman often came to Old Tsanz to spend his spare time in Finder's Restaurant, gorging himself on fish and liquor. The restaurant had long been requisitioned by a *Volksdeutsche*, but its original proprietors, the Finder family, worked there as his employees.

It happened once that Haman came into the restaurant and demanded liquor. Finder's son-in-law, Fried (from Cracow), told him that at the moment there was no liquor available. Haman flew into a rage and, as a punishment, led Fried into the yard. He tied him to a fence, gouged out his eyes, cut off his tongue, and finally shot him.

In addition to the Jews' suffering from the frequent *aktions*, interlaced with murderous deeds such as the one mentioned above, a terrible hunger reigned in the ghetto. Seven hundred grams of bread, thirty grams of meat, and twenty grams of sugar was the miserly weekly ration for one person. Later, the bread

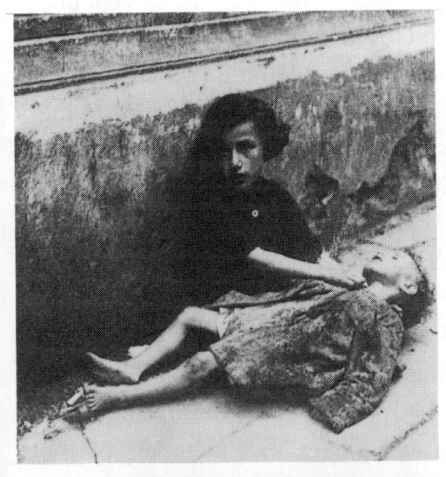

Children starving to death

quota was cut even further, to no more than 250 grams a week. In desperation, the Jews sold all their household goods, down to their last bit of clothing, in order to obtain a piece of bread or a small potato, extra bits of food smuggled across the ghetto wall.

The Winter Clothing Aktion

With the advent of winter in 1942, the Jews had to endure the bitter cold in addition to their gnawing hunger pains. The cost of coal and wood for heating was sky-high, and the material was very difficult to obtain. People chopped and burned their furniture to warm up their apartments somewhat. There were no electric lights either, since the Nazis had cut off the electricity supply to the ghetto.

In these dark and difficult days, filled with suffering, hunger, and cold, a new trouble befell the miserable ghetto inhabitants, in the form of the winter clothing *aktion*. This *aktion* not only robbed the Jews of every bit of warm clothing they still possessed but took away their only chance of selling their clothes in exchange for a few potatoes.

The winter clothing *aktion* was carried out by way of a decree: within twenty-four hours all Jews had to bring to the Gestapo building their furs, coats, sweaters, hats, and gloves. Six members of the *Judenrat* were arrested as hostages to ensure the exact fulfillment of the order. Yet even after the clothing was delivered and the hostages were set free, the Nazis raided the homes to search for clothing. Needless to say, if even a torn cardigan was found the owner was immediately led out of his house and shot.

The winter clothing *aktion* may have still left the Jews with something to sell for a piece of bread — their furniture and household utensils. But this last resort was only temporary. Pesach time, a furniture *aktion* took place whereby all furniture was confiscated. The bare rooms of the interior of the homes, coupled with the narrow, dark, unlit streets outside, threw a morbid depression over the entire ghetto.

With the onset of winter, at the beginning of 1942, an epidemic of stomach typhus broke out. The Jews lived in shocking sanitary conditions due to overcrowding. Consequently, by spring 1941 the

THE LAST YEAR IN THE TSANZER GHETTO

poorest among them were plagued by lice. In 1942 disease was rampant, spreading illness and death throughout the population.

As was their wont, the Nazis hung up placards all over Tsanz, announcing in big, bold letters a warning against Jews: "JEW LICE BLACK TYPHUS." Even the merest suspicion of the dreaded plague was enough to instill in the gentiles a deadly fear of approaching the ghetto for the next few weeks. This served to greatly increase the Jews' plight, for no food was brought in — either legally or by smuggling. It also provided the vampire Haman with another excuse for dragging people off to Auschwitz for the "crime" — either true or imagined — of suffering from the disease. A few days later the families would receive an official telegram confirming the death of those sent away.

The Pre-May Aktion

The *aktion*s bore the mark of typical German efficiency in finding a Final Solution: the Jews were gradually being wiped out so that the last remaining few would not pose much of a problem. Until April 1942, the almost weekly *aktion*s resulted in the murder of up to one hundred Jews. The climax came in the pre-May *aktion*, when a mass execution and a night of bloodletting took place, with the victims numbering in the hundreds. This was an introduction to the final liquidation of the Tsanzer ghetto, which was accomplished four months later. The pre-May *aktion* turned out to be symbolic of the heroic resistance of the ghetto inhabitants.

The *kiddush haShem* displayed by the Limanover *Judenrat* shortly before the pre-May *aktion* gave the Tsanzer Jews the blueprint for their future actions. Some time before April 1942, Haman commanded the president of Limanow's *Judenrat*, Mr. Sola Shnitzer, to supply him with a certain number of Jews to be shot. Shnitzer firmly refused to obey the command and proudly declared that he would let himself be shot rather than accept the role of selecting Jews to be killed. Enraged at this brazen reply, Haman decided to get even with this audacious president of the *Judenrat* when the opportunity presented itself.

On April 20, Haman once again went down to Limanow and

summoned Shnitzer, ordering him to provide him with 150 elderly Jews to be condemned to death. This time, too, Sola Shnitzer clearly and firmly refused to comply. Haman promptly removed his revolver from its holster and shot Shnitzer on the spot. Soon after he ordered all the other twelve members of the *Judenrat* shot. Their corpses were then propped up against the wall of the *Judenrat* building. (Six of them are known to us by name: Chaim Freilich, Yosef Shtiel, Yidel Shochet, Aharon Shochet, Mordechai Nichfreger, and Wasserman).

Eight days after this *kiddush haShem*, the pre-May *aktion* was carried out. It began on April 28. The massacre ended the next night, on April 29.

On Tuesday, April 28, at 5 A.M., the ghetto was surrounded by the S.S. and Jewish Police. The Jewish Police, following lists they had drawn up, seized three hundred people from their homes and took them to the Gestapo building. They were mercilessly beaten, and dogs were enticed to lunge at them. After that, they were led to a tower and locked up in pitch-black cells. It is known that the entire night an orchestra played in the prison courtyard with the arrested being forced to dance to the music. "This is your death dance," Haman called out with glee, as he watched from the balcony together with the wives and children of the S.S. monsters.

The following day, at twelve noon, the arrested were driven to the prison courtyard. An *appel* (roll call) was carried out to ensure that all those on the list were present. The gruesome play of the day before was repeated, and they were beaten and viciously bitten by the dogs.

Once again they were driven back to their cells. At 3 P.M. they were led out in three groups, each of which comprised one hundred men. They were taken to the cemetery on the other side of the town. Before them paraded forty soldiers. Behind them marched the Gestapo, headed by Haman. A villainous smile played on his lips as he piped a merry tune and played with a ball, throwing it in the air and catching it again. Anyone who did not have the foresight to hide and was spied by Haman on the way was immediately snatched and forced to join the marching victims. The previously six arrested members of

THE LAST YEAR IN THE TSANZER GHETTO

the *Judenrat* were also seized. I vividly recall watching this horrifying scene from a window. The prisoners walked with downcast eyes, knowing full well what was in store for them.

When they arrived at the cemetery, the unfortunates were forced to undress completely and neatly fold their clothes. They then had to lie down in rows facing the earth. They were lying on the ground waiting for death to release them when suddenly a voice broke the deathly silence. It was HaRav Yosef Moshe Zehman. (He was a son of HaRav HaGaon David Tevel Zehman, the Dukler Rav, the author of *Minchas Soles*, commonly known as Reb Tevele Dukler. Rav Yosef Moshe was a great personality in town, who used to give *shiurim* to packed audiences. Though he knew the entire Mishnah by heart he used to keep a Mishnah open before him so that nobody would perceive this. We children, however, often noticed that he had a *Nezikin* lying before him while he was lecturing on *Taharos*.) He stood up in the face of his executioners, with their machine guns drawn, and in a strong voice consoled the condemned. They were suffering for the Jewish nation, he told them, and the salvation must surely be near. He then turned to his murderers and yelled out loud, "Jewish children will yet survive to take revenge upon you!"

Lying on the ground, a woman named Goldberg-Shapira also awoke from her passive stance and began mocking and cursing the

Even the town "fool," Yumin Shabbos, knew he was going to die. Before he was killed he cried, "Leave me alone. I still want to live."

The Vanished City of Tsanz

A group of Nazi officers visiting the town before an *aktion*

Nazis, forecasting their imminent doom. The sound of a revolver interrupted her words: she was the first to fall. A further barrage of bullets followed, killing those around her. (The O.D. and *Sanitar Dienst* stood by placidly, watching this wholesale massacre.)

When the gunfire finally ceased, not all were dead yet. Some were only wounded. The Nazi beasts were sparing with their bullets — they needed them for other victims.

Meanwhile, the dead had to be seen to. Methodically the O.D. arranged the bloodied bodies, of which many still showed signs of life. Three hundred and sixty bodies in all were piled up in a mass grave. The O.D. were commanded to trample the corpses with their boots so that they would occupy the least space possible. When all were packed in, the grave was covered with dirt. For many days after, clots of blood were seen on the surface of the grave, the innocent blood of tortured Jews.

A bleak depression and helpless frustration settled over the ghetto inhabitants. The world was a black place, and there was nowhere to run. Their faces expressed pain and despair; their hearts were filled with unbearable grief.

THE LAST YEAR IN THE TSANZER GHETTO

After this great triumph over a few defenseless Jews, the Gestapo, together with the policemen who had helped them in this mass murder, returned home happy and joyful, singing the popular, anti-Semitic song, "When Jewish blood from the knife does flow..."

The Slaughter Night

The bloody day was followed by a bloody night. In celebration of the successful massacre the Nazis got drunk. Late that night they once again stormed the ghetto and replayed their heinous deeds a second time. They did not even bother to pound at the doors but broke them down and barged into the houses. Entire families were murdered.

Among others, they broke into the home of the Kannengisser family. The father, mother, and two daughters were instantly killed by Nazi bullets. The two sons were asleep at opposite ends of one bed. Moshe lay with his head to the door and Mordechai with his head facing the window. One of the S.S. thugs lifted the bedcover covering little Moshe. Another Nazi had called out that it was a shame to waste a bullet on such a small boy, but the words were barely out of his mouth when several shots ended the short life of young Moshe Yosef.

His brother Mordechai, covered with the bedcover, felt his brother's warm blood trickling down his body. The Nazi beasts thought there was no one left to kill and began smoking cigarettes, entertaining each other with coarse tales of their murderous deeds. They left the kitchen and with raucous laughter wished the dead they had left behind, *"Dobra notz"* (Polish for "good night").

The Nazis hung around the house, killing the occupants of all the other apartments. Finally they left, leaving a deathly silence in their wake.

Only now did little Mordechai dare creep out of his bed. He tiptoed into the kitchen. A river of blood met his eyes. His mother, his father, his sisters, his brother...all were dead. In the duration of not even fifteen minutes his world had collapsed. He had become a deserted orphan, alone in the world. This youngest Kannengisser, a personal witness to these horrifying Nazi atrocities, survived the war in a concentration camp and currently resides in Israel.

It was not until the following day that the full extent of the atrocious deeds committed on that fateful night came to light. Children were discovered dead under the beds where they had been hiding. Corpses of men were found behind the cupboards where they had squeezed themselves. They had remained there in a standing position until the next morning.

The massacre ended with a weird twist of fate. When Haman stormed the home of Aharon Neustadt, he encountered a friend of his from the Gestapo, Kestner. As he aimed his revolver to shoot at the last remaining member of the family, a young girl, Kestner called out, "Haman! Enough blood for today!" In reply, Haman turned his revolver toward Kestner and shot him. The Gestapo members immediately spread a rumor that the Jews had killed a German officer. This episode would have ended with a pogrom and the deaths of thousands of Jews, if not for the fact that Kestner was still alive when his friends brought him by ambulance into the hospital. In the last minutes of his life he feebly whispered that his friend Haman had shot him. This tiny spark of humanity in a Nazi saved the Jews thousands of deaths.

The next day, April 30, the burial of the hundreds of murdered victims took place. The funeral was organized by a member of the *chevrah kaddisha* and a few volunteer assistants. It was arranged under the surveillance of the O.D. I myself scraped the blood of Liebish Gelb off the walls of his apartment with my bare hands.

Haman's Downfall

Soon after the war ended, I and a few other survivors from Tsanz searched for Haman and his assistants. Our quest was fruitless. It was only due to the efforts of the relatives of the murdered German, Kestner, that Haman was discovered fifteen years later. He was located in the German town of Bochum, working in a factory under a false name. After he was found, the other twelve murderers of Tsanz were also hunted down, thanks to their friend Haman, who thought that it would be a shame that only he get punished and they get off scot-free.

THE LAST YEAR IN THE TSANZER GHETTO

About one hundred Tsanzer survivors came to testify at their trial in Bochum. I, too, was there, together with another Tsanzer Jew, Avraham Hollander, who now lives in Antwerp, Belgium.

As I entered the courtroom and caught sight of all those S.S. thugs seated on the accusation bench, darkness swept over me and I fainted. Up until then I had not really believed that these murderers were actually alive. Now there sat Haman, without a tie, since he had tried to commit suicide several times.

There was no doubt at all that the accused would not be punished for the many merciless beatings we had suffered at their hands. The issue was only whether they were guilty of murder or not.

I testified that I personally witnessed Haman shooting two people — Leib Gelb and Feigel Saphir, the *dayan*'s wife. Haman's lawyer, Avel, tried to denounce my testimony, claiming that I had twice declared that I had seen Haman kill two people, while a third time I had said, *"Ich fermute* — I assume." I explained to the judge that I was not very fluent in German since I only knew what I had learned in the concentration camps. I had thought *"Ich fermute"* was "I am sure" in German. The judge accepted my response and my testimony.

The court sentenced Haman and three other Nazis to life imprisonment. The others escaped with light sentences since there wasn't adequate testimony against them.

CHAPTER 4

THE FINAL DAYS

Leaving Tsanz

About a week after Shavuos 1942, I received a note from the work committee ordering me to pack my bags and report to them within three days. I was to be sent to a labor camp in Muszyna, near Krenitz. My father consulted with his student Baruch Berliner to see whether I should comply with their orders or go into hiding. He told my father that I should obey them, since there was a greater chance of staying alive in the labor camps than in the ghetto.

My father parted from me with the following words: "You can be of no further service to me here in the ghetto. Have a safe journey, and may Hashem watch over you."

For my mother there were no words. She could not speak, only cry. Words were unnecessary, for each felt in his heart what the other must be thinking. And so we departed with a silent ocean of tears. That was the last time I ever saw my parents.

All those summoned reported to the agency. We were taken to the train station from where we traveled to Muszyna in a wagon designed for oxen.

The Liquidation of Surrounding Villages

After the pre-May *aktion* and the bloody night of April 29, the Jews in Tsanz instinctively sensed what fate lay in store for them.

THE FINAL DAYS

Their fears were confirmed when news reached their ears of the liquidation of other ghettos.

Since autumn 1941, some Jews had already been building bunkers in their apartments. Now more and more were following suit. The *aktion*s of seizing Jews and deporting them to concentration camps became more and more frequent in the months of May, June, and July. The transportees numbered in the hundreds. At first they were all sent to Rabka, a place of no return. From July, some were sent to Tengabozsha and Lypia.

The Jews gradually perceived that the Piekela was intended for the able-bodied while the *Yiddishe Gass* was for those incapable of work. A desperate scramble ensued to move into the Piekela. The Piekela was crowded with workmen: carpenters, tailors, shoemakers. It housed several fur factories, where large shipments of fur garments were made for the Germans. Those who still had the means paid huge sums of money to the *Arbeits Amt* for the "privilege" of receiving a work permit. Consequently, it turned out that mainly the wealthy, who could afford to bribe and pay for an apartment, succeeded in moving into the Piekela. Eventually, the Nazis, in their unlimited cruelty, reduced the ghetto area of the Piekela by two streets and gave them to the Poles. In spite of the severe overcrowding it caused, the Jews' feverish haste in moving into the Piekela was not diminished. Soon enough, though, the Nazis put a stop to this, too.

Zehman, the Tsanzer deputy to the mayor, Dr. Hiller, set up a committee meeting together with Svaboda, the chief of the *Arbeits Amt*. Every Jew, regardless of age, had to present himself at this meeting. All those who were judged incapable of work — the aged, the invalids, and the weak — were led away in wagons prepared for this purpose. They were taken to ghetto B, the walled-in ghetto on the Jewish Street. Those fortunates considered suitable for work received permission to reside in the open ghetto, the Piekela, which was officially declared the worker's ghetto. The guard around the ghettos was reinforced by Ukrainian Black Police.

For those in ghetto B, the crowded living conditions now became

The Vanished City of Tsanz

The Piekela during wartime

even more intolerable. The Nazis saw to it that those in the Piekela wouldn't be too comfortable either, by closing off even more streets. Thus the ruthless killers accomplished yet another achievement: wearing out the Jews, shattering their nerves, and making their lives miserable by having them constantly move from one place to the next.

Only thus can one understand why even in the latter half of

THE FINAL DAYS

August, a mere few days before the Jewish Police were informed of the total liquidation of the ghetto, the Piekela was reorganized yet again, and the Jews were once more forced to move from their living quarters. Move...move...move...until the final move to the "heaven *Kommando*" (extermination camps).

Needless to say, the unrestrained terrorizing of the downtrodden, starving ghetto inhabitants continued mercilessly. Haman and his gang renewed their besieging of homes, wiping out whole families at a time. At one such *aktion* Haman thought up a new, innovative way of eliminating Jews: he entered the ghetto accompanied by Gestapo members, seized six Jews, tied them up with rope, and thrust them into the Dunajec River. Among them were Messrs. Berger, Shechter, and Neuheit.

August 1942, the month of the mass extermination of the Warsaw ghetto and numerous other ghettos in Poland, was also listed on the Nazi calendar as the month for liquidation of the Tsanzer ghetto and four smaller ghettos surrounding Tsanz.

At the beginning of August, the ominous footsteps of the ghetto's doom echoed in the distance. A tax of half a million zlotys was levied in order to squeeze the ghetto population of its last bit of worthwhile possessions. Barely two weeks later, a new tax of a million zlotys was imposed. Two days later, a tax of half a million zlotys and two thousand pieces of kitchenware, new or almost new, was forced upon the Jews. The Jews of the four towns of Old Tsanz, Limanow, Amsana, and Gribow also had to give their share. Furthermore, the Jews of those four towns had to vacate their homes and move into New Tsanz.

Thus the stage was set for the total extermination of the Jews of Tsanz and its surrounding areas. On August 16, the German order of the evacuation of the four towns was proclaimed. In their typically organized fashion, they arranged the evacuation in the following order: Old Tsanz on August 17, Limanow on August 18, Amsana on August 19, and Gribow on August 20.

The Jews from those towns had to present themselves in Tsanz on the designated day at the designated location in the ghetto. They were only permitted to take along up to twenty kilos of personal belongings. The old and infirm who could not walk the entire way were told to report to the S.S., who would "arrange transportation." The S.S. themselves also made selections, deciding who was fit to walk and who should be taken. Lorries were present on the roadside, ready to spirit away the sick and aged. But those lorries never turned up at their destination of Tsanz. Instead, they were driven to a deserted area behind the town, where the elderly and infirm passengers were all shot down in a mass execution and buried in huge graves.

Those who had undertaken the long walk to Tsanz were escorted by armed soldiers. It was a scorching hot day, and they arrived drained of energy and terribly thirsty. Many had discarded their baggage on the way, not having the strength to continue carrying it.

In Old Tsanz the 100 to 150 sick and disabled, who had voluntarily reported themselves as being unfit for the long walk, were led to the woods near Poprad (on the way to Macjekova), where they were shot. The others walked, closely watched by the Gestapo and O.D., to the walled-in ghetto of Tsanz. Forty strong and able-bodied men were selected and ordered to report to the *Arbeits Amt* in the open ghetto.

In Limanow, the Gestapo appeared on August 18. There, approximately 160 old and weak Jews were gunned down. The execution took place behind Briehaus Marz, in the direction of Stary Viesh. The others were led to Tsanz on foot, a distance of twenty-six kilometers.

Mass Slaughter in Amsana

The worst fate of all four towns was suffered by the Jews of Amsana. These Jews were so destitute that they could not possibly scrape together the exorbitant taxes demanded. Some fifteen to twenty thousand zlotys were missing from their contribution. As a punishment for this unforgivable "crime," the entire town shared the fate of the aged and weak. Approximately eight hundred souls, among them children and babies, were carted onto trucks and taken to a predug mass grave where they were all mowed down. Only 120 able-bodied people were "pardoned" and led to Tsanz.

THE FINAL DAYS

In this wholesale slaughter, the assistance of the Polish Fascist *Yanakas* ("good" boys) was enlisted. Two full trucks designated for their transportation arrived at the scene.

The Liquidation of Gribow

Finally, on August 20, it was Gribow, the largest among the four towns, that suffered its turn.

The liquidation of the Jews in Gribow followed the same procedure as in Tsanz except that they were permitted to purchase food outside the ghetto walls. It was only at the beginning of 1942 that the Jews of Gribow were banned from the gentile streets and forced into a few narrow roads scattered throughout the town. The Jews themselves had to build paths and steps in order to get from one street to the other without encroaching on gentile boundaries.

At that time an incident occurred which made the Poles afraid to sell food to the Jews. A Polish woman, Sukonava, was caught selling milk to a Jewish woman. The Polish police punished her by forcing her to dance with a Jew in the marketplace on Sunday af-

Sukonava, the gentile woman forced to dance with Jews

ternoon when all the Christians were on their way home from church. After that the Poles were afraid to risk dealing with Jews. As a result, a ravaging hunger presided in that ghetto, too.

The *aktion*s in Gribow took place at the same time as the *aktion*s in Tsanz. On April 29, 1942, in connection with the pre-May *aktion*, the Jewish police in Gribow captured thirty people and sent them to the prison in Tsanz. They, too, were part of the group killed in the Tsanzer cemetery. In addition, another ten Jews in Gribow were shot in the presence of the *Judenrat*.

After the pre-May *aktion* many more *aktion*s took place in which men were either deported to labor camps or, more often, sent to the prison in Tsanz. As in Tsanz, the old and weak were shipped off to Rabka as "practice" for the Gestapo training unit whose members were taught how to shoot by experimenting on them.

On August 19, 1942, a day before the liquidation of Gribow, the sick and disabled were ordered to appear in the Stelmuch School building. The next morning, at 4 A.M., they were commanded to assemble outside the *Judenrat* building.

Haman arrived accompanied by the Polish mayor and, with a riding whip in hand, selected those who were to be seen to immediately. The Gestapo, taking special aim at the heads, mercilessly beat those chosen and led them away to be shot. Some were taken to Gradek, five kilometers from Gribow, and some to Piantova. In some cases daughters could not bear to part with their mothers and joined the group, willing to share whatever fate was in store for them.

A detailed report of the mass execution was later heard from the Poles who had sat on their rooftops and watched the gruesome scene. The condemned group would have easily fit into one truck, yet they were led away in several shifts. Back in Gribow they had been told to undress, and they arrived at their place of death in only their undergarments. As they ascended the truck in Gribow, and as they unloaded in Gradek, the Nazis beat them murderously and sometimes caused a few broken bones, trying to squeeze out of them every bit of suffering before finally finishing them off forever.

THE FINAL DAYS

As in the other towns a few able-bodied people were selected among the town's population for work. Fifteen hundred people were driven out, in the burning heat, across a stretch of twenty-one kilometers to Tsanz. They arrived in the walled-in ghetto in the Jewish Street at 7 P.M.

As in the other towns, the Nazis kept behind a few young men in Gribow to keep some semblance of order in the deserted ghetto streets.

The entire area surrounding Tsanz was now free of Jews. The two ghettos in Tsanz were packed with the exiles of Old Tsanz, Limanow, Gribow, the pitifully few of Amsana. At the beginning of 1942 the two ghettos were crowded to choking point with eleven thousand Jews; now, on August 20, fourteen thousand Jews were squeezed in. On that same day the Jews were officially informed that this was no more than a well-thought-out plan to concentrate the entire population in one place so that in three days time they could be evacuated together.

By now, the majority of people had become indifferent to the suffering, starvation, and disease which ran rampant in the ghetto. They realized that there was no choice but to resign themselves to their fate, since those who did succeed in escaping the well-guarded, walled-in ghetto — and they were very few — were killed by the Poles once they got out.

The Ghetto's Last Era

It was Friday, August 21, 1942, 9 A.M. Haman, the Gestapo chief, summoned the members of the O.D., the *Block Dienst*, and the *Sanitar Dienst*. He formally informed them that on Sunday, August 23, the entire ghetto population was to be transferred elsewhere. At 5 A.M. all Jews were to assemble at the Dunajec River, between the Helena Bridge and the train bridge. Everyone should be dressed in their finest clothing and bring along the key to his apartment, with an address label attached. Every person was permitted to bring along ten kilos of food and fifteen kilos of personal belongings.

Barely two days were left until the final deadline — two days filled with dread, confusion, and preparation for the long journey

The Vanished City of Tsanz

ahead. The final journey. Like ostriches in the sand the people brushed aside the rumors which had been circulating in Tsanz the last few months — tales of deportations, of wholesale murder in the death camps, of Belzec and Auschwitz. Only a handful of foresighted Jews tried a last desperate attempt to save their lives by fleeing to the woods or to the homes of Polish acquaintances. The rest let themselves be convinced that they were being sent to the Ukraine to work in the fields.

A frantic rush to sell property ensued. Poles suddenly appeared as if from under the ground, seeking to buy furniture, clothing, and other possessions. This was in spite of the strict Polish and German guard surrounding the ghetto. At first with pretended sympathy, and later with open mockery, they offered ridiculous prices. When the Jews tried to bargain with them they brazenly shot back, "Where you are going, you don't need your money. You're going for soap..."

On Shabbos, August 22, a day before the liquidation, two hundred Jews were seized and taken to the cemetery where they were ordered to destroy all the tombstones. Not even a remembrance was to be left of the city Tsanz.

Motza'ei Shabbos, after midnight, masses of people with bundles on their back were already seen trudging toward the assembly point at the Dunajec. The 120 people who worked in the fur factory were ordered to hold on to their work permits. Also with them were the forced laborers of the labor camps in Lypia and the barracks of Novoyova, the camp where roads were constructed.

The Jews walked in an organized fashion, arranged according to the roads where they lived. At the end of every "liquidated" street an officer stood with a list of all the inhabitants of that street. At 5 A.M., Sunday, August 23, all the residents of both ghettos stood at the designated place.

At 6 A.M. Haman arrived, flanked by the chief of the S.D. (*Sicherhiet Dienst*), the head of the *Arbeits Amt*, Svaboda, all the German officials, all the members of the Gestapo, and a group of Polish police.

THE FINAL DAYS

The place was surrounded by S.S., machine guns drawn, and the unfailing participants at every *aktion* — dogs. Firstly Haman ordered the collection of 250,000 zlotys, claiming that the last tax of a million zlotys which the Jews had to pay "did not cover the cost of the liquidation."

Around 9 A.M. Haman began a selection. Those whom he whipped in the face had to stand on a hill nearby together with the other able-bodied people. The rest were condemned to die.

As in Gribow, moving scenes were enacted as those chosen for work — and life — refused to be parted from their loved ones. With fortitude and pride they walked away from the hill where they were told to stand to join those who were to be deported.

Haman openly scoffed at those selected for death, saying, "Those who aren't designated for work *Kommando* are designated for 'heaven *Kommando*.'" Those destined to die were so terrified of their captors that they stood in silent resignation, not expressing even the slightest emotion of fear. The Nazis had cast a hypnotic spell of terror on them. The only sound to be heard from the miserable group was the occasional sobbing of wives and mothers who had been torn from their husbands or sons.

Among the condemned, some hundred people or so had fainted from standing so many hours in the intense heat. Haman had them all shot; some of them he personally killed. A while later, ten of those selected for work were ordered to dig a mass grave in the cemetery and bury the corpses.

The selection lasted for two hours. When it was over, close to eight hundred people chosen for work stood on the hill. The remaining Jews, amounting to over thirteen thousand men, women, and children, were led under close guard to ghetto B, the Jewish Street. Dejected and despairing, many of them left their suitcases and belongings lying by the river.

Those on the hill were led into several houses on Kraszewski Street in ghetto A, near the Kamienica River. Toward evening the Nazis drank bottle after bottle of wine, celebrating the "heroic *aktion*."

The Vanished City of Tsanz

It is impossible to describe the hellish conditions which now faced the thousands of people crowded together in the ghetto of the Jewish Street. They not only suffered from severe hunger and thirst, but even from lack of air to breathe. In some houses there were so many people squeezed together that there was no place to stand, never mind rest their weary bodies. There was a lack of sanitary provisions in the homes and exit for that purpose was forbidden. The ghetto had long ago been cut off from electricity and fresh water. As a result every room became engulfed in the overwhelming odor of human waste. This was all part of the well-organized plan of the "superior race": to dehumanize the Jews and degrade them so that, with their lives soured to such an intolerable degree, they would look toward death as a blessed release.

The Jews were sent away to the extermination camp Belzec in three transports. The deportations began on Tuesday, August 25, and ended on Friday, August 28. Over one hundred people were crammed into each wagon. The wagons were spread with sawdust and the resulting suffocation proved to be the second stage of their hellish suffering.

Those who did not die from thirst and lack of oxygen on the way to Belzec experienced the third stage of hell — the death camp. There the majority of the Tsanzer Jewish community were silenced forever. They were gone, together with the smoke of the Belzec crematoria.

Belzec

The Belzec death camp was built in the of winter of 1941–1942. It started the full-scale extermination of Jews on March 17, 1942, operating until the middle of December of that year. In this short period of time the Nazis managed to kill a maximum number of Jews. Belzec, which was built for the sole purpose of killing Jews, was located in a clearing in a dense forest, near the train line which runs from Lublin to Lemberg or Cracow, north of the Rava-Ruska junction in East Galicia. Today it lies on the border of Russia and Poland. In this deceptively picturesque place about six hundred thousand people

THE FINAL DAYS

from the Jewish communities of East and Central Galicia gave up their lives *al kiddush haShem*.

The leaders of this death camp laid great importance on fooling the new arrivals into thinking that this was a peaceful place. This was necessary so that they could send the people to their deaths more easily. The view of the camp and the treatment that greeted a transport of Jews was tranquil. No graves, pits, or gas chambers could be seen by the victims, who believed they had arrived in a transit camp. The Nazi S.S. monster Christian Wirth strengthened this belief by announcing that they should undress and make their way to the baths for cleaning and disinfecting. They were told that afterwards they would receive clean clothes and be sent to labor camps. Being surrounded by barbed-wire fences and armed guards also kept the victims submissive and calm. The men were sent to the gas chambers before they could grasp what was happening.

The victims were gassed in six large chambers soon after their arrival. The men were the first to go, followed by the women. When it was all over the corpses were thrown into mass graves which were dug by Jewish laborers who were later gassed themselves. In the middle of November 1942 the bodies were dug up and burned. This labor lasted till the end of March 1943. At the same time, all the buildings in the camp were dismantled and a farm house built on the spot so that the whole place would look as if nothing had ever happened there.

The *kedoshim* of Tsanz and its surrounding areas, who surrendered their lives on 16–17 Elul 1942, were gassed on the day of their arrival.

It is worth noting that there was only one survivor of the six hundred thousand men, women, and children who died in that terrible death camp. (Another man and two women also managed to escape from the camp, but they did not survive the war.) His name is Rudolph Reder. He was born in Dembitz and lived in Lemberg. He was an inmate in Belzec from August 17, 1942 until the end of November 1942.

During the Tsanzer liquidation we were in a camp in Muszyna, and so we only heard of the tragic episode a week later. We were told

The Vanished City of Tsanz

by a gentile maidservant who had been an employee of a Tsanzer Jew and now worked alongside us in the camp. She had been able to follow the death transport until Rava Ruska, one short train line away from Belzec. Up until Rava Ruska an ordinary train driver had driven the train. At Rava Ruska a machinist especially chosen for this purpose took over the wheel. He received a bottle of vodka for every transport

he drove into the extermination camp.

Belzec is not a very well-known camp. This is because, as mentioned above, only one person, Rudolph Reder, attempted escape and succeeded, the only inmate to emerge alive from that camp. The S.S. barbarians who worked there were made to swear that they would not reveal any of the atrocities committed in the camp. Because Belzec is not so well known, I would like to quote a short description which Rudolph Reder wrote about it.

> At the train station in Belzec, an evil-looking, elderly German with a bushy mustache took over the train from the driver who

THE FINAL DAYS

The crematoria

had driven it until Rava Ruska and led it into the camp, a distance of one kilometer. When the train arrived at the camp, that same German also assisted the Nazis in chasing out the bewildered people with whips and bayonets.

The old, the weak, and the babies were taken to a mass grave where the S.S. guard Irman, *y"s*, shot them all. He did not appear to be the ruthless killer that he was, a murderer known to be a specialist in finishing off babies and elderly people.

Two or three times daily, a transport arrived. Every day Irman went out to welcome the transportees. As soon as the people had scrambled out of the wagons they were surrounded by Ukrainian S.S. guards and told to surrender their valuables and undress completely. When this was over Irman addressed the assembled. He said the same words every day and to every transport, "You are now going to

Corpses waiting to be burned

be showered, after which you will be sent to work." The people were greatly relieved when they heard those words. Perhaps they would not be killed after all.

His speech achieved the result that the men walked calmly into a barracks marked "Bathhouse" twenty meters away. The women were led into a barracks thirty meters long by fifteen meters wide, where those who had long hair were shaved. Those who had short hair were sent in the direction of the men — that is, together with the men — into the gas chamber.

The shaving lasted for two hours, precisely the amount of time needed to gas the men and clear them away. The women had to be driven into the gas chamber with whips and clubs, for they had heard the agonizing screams of the dying men and knew what was awaiting them.

Seven hundred and fifty people were squeezed into each gas chamber. Those women who hysterically refused to enter despite the beatings they received were stabbed with bayonets, and blood squirted all over the place. The heart-rending sounds of the crying and screaming of the women and children used to freeze the blood in my veins.

After fifteen to twenty minutes all was quiet. The Ukrainian S.S. opened the doors of the gas chamber, and our work began. Using leather belts, we dragged the bodies out by their feet, two workers for each corpse, to a huge, gaping grave one hundred meters long, twenty meters wide, and twelve meters deep. The grave had been dug by 450 workers in the duration of one week. The most horrible part of this gruesome task was that we had to pile up the corpses one meter high above the ground. The entire time blood was pouring from the bodies. The ground became a river of blood, forcing us to wade in our brothers' blood. We had to trample over their bodies, and this was also terribly painful for us. When we finished, we poured sand over the pit. To add to our miserable plight, we were forced to listen to the soothing music of the camp orchestra which played in the background.

THE FINAL DAYS

The camp orchestra, provided to drown out the screaming of the tortured

The barbarian Shmidt, *y"s*, used to beat and clobber us. Occasionally he picked somebody from our group and whipped him twenty-five times. The victim had to count out loud; if he erred in his counting he was whipped fifty times. Nobody could endure fifty lashes, and the next morning the man was usually found dead.

It happened once that a boy who had just arrived with a transport looked around and saw that the camp was enclosed with barbed wire and that every few meters stood a guard. He said, "Did anybody ever escape from this place?" A few of the S.S. overheard what he had said. They viciously pounced on the boy, tore off his clothes, and hung him upside down for three hours. After that they threw him on the ground. When they saw that he was still alive, they stuffed sand down his throat with sticks until he choked to death.

Every day a doctor drew up a list of thirty or forty weakest workers. They were shot at the midday break. The next morning, another thirty or forty workers were selected from the first transport so that the number of five hundred workers would remain constant. It is known that Jewish laborers built the murder factory Belzec, but not one of them survived.

The Vanished City of Tsanz

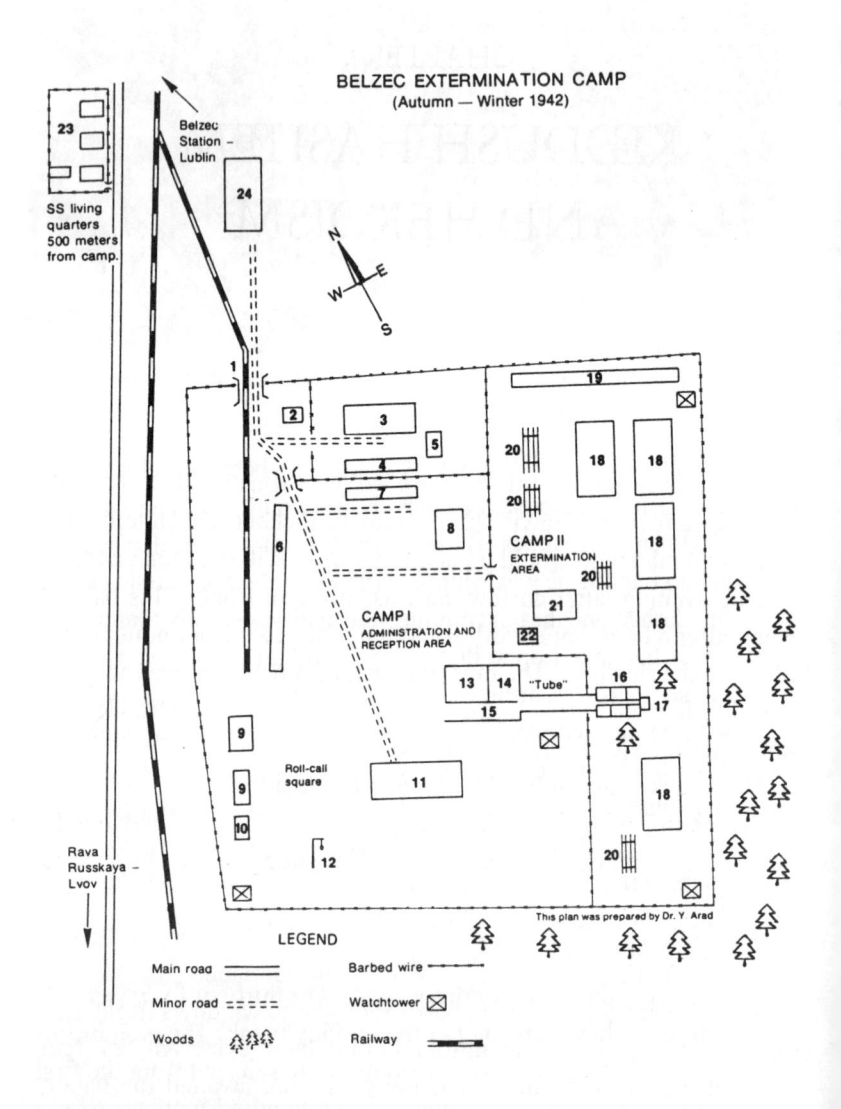

A map of the death camp Belzec

CHAPTER 5

KIDDUSH HASHEM AND HEROISM

Here is a case of true *kiddush haShem* illustrated by Mr. M. Unterberger, a Jewish baker from the Piekela. Mr. Unterberger was a quiet man who would go about his work without much ado.

One evening, after curfew, he was sitting in front of his bakery resting after a hard day's work. He did not notice the ominous figure lurking in the shadows. The man, nicknamed Yochanan, was actually the sadist Johann Bornholt, the chief of the Tsanzer prison. He was famous for his vicious acts of cruelty.

"Where is your armband?" snarled the Nazi.

Trembling with fear, Unterberger rose to his feet and barely managed to stammer the words, "I...I...I'm sitting at the entrance to my home..."

Johann loomed dangerously close to Unterberger, ready to tighten his hand around his arm and drag him off to the Gestapo.

From behind the shuttered, barricaded ghetto windows frightened people watched the scene unfold before their eyes. An icy fear squeezed their hearts, for they knew well what awaited the baker. Johann was sure to shoot him.

However, Unterberger was quick to act. Knowing that there was nothing to lose, he lunged at Johann and threw his whole weight on him. He grabbed him by his neck and, releasing all his pent-up anger and fear, began choking the feared and dreaded Gestapo member.

"You are now as good as dead, for I am about to kill you!" he roared, while in his heart he trembled at his outrageous deed. The S.S. man barely moved; he was at the mercy of a confused and bewildered Jew.

Choking to death, Johann barely managed to raspingly plead, "Let go! Let go! I won't harm you, idiot! Please!"

Sweating profusely, Unterberger relaxed his tight grip for a moment. "Give me your word," he loudly intoned. "Swear by Hitler, by the German pride, that you will not molest my family or me. Go on, plead for your life! It is now in my hands! Only then will I release you. But remember!"

Unterberger had a Jewish brain, and a sudden thought flashed through his mind: Tempted though I am, if I kill this wretched German, who knows how many hundreds of Jewish families will perish as a result? His hands, however, refused to obey his mind. He gave Johann's throat another tight squeeze.

"Go on, swear!" he insisted.

Johann was now in mortal fear for his worthless life, and with incredible humility he conceded, faithfully promising that he would never molest Unterberger or his family, nor any other Jew for that matter.

The next few weeks, Johann did not put in an appearance in that part of the ghetto. He kept his promise not to harm the baker, but as for the other Jews, it did not take long before he once again resumed his cruel tactics in embittering their lives.

It is truly amazing how much willpower was shown by an ordinary baker in that moment, as he restrained himself from killing a Nazi dog in order to prevent the slaughter of hundreds of Jews.

Reb Yossele Frankel

Who in Tsanz had not heard of Yossele Frankel, the son-in-law of Reb Shloimele Burstein, *z"l?* He was an unassuming Jew and despite his humility was known in Tsanz as a learned *talmid chacham* and a pious man.

Reb Shloimele and his son-in-law were two of the most distinguished Chassidic men in Tsanz. Reb Shloimele was a wealthy man, generous with his money and good deeds. He would rise with respect for the *gabbaim* of the charity Rabbi Meir Ba'al HaNess, and indeed to anybody who came to ask for a donation. He would don his *gartel* and then gladly donate the required sum with a friendly smile and a good word. His boundless kindness and humility were reflected in his holy countenance. As he fervently prayed, one couldn't help but imagine that his fiery prayers must ascend directly to the Heavenly throne. He was also president of the Talmud Torah *gabbaim* in Tsanz.

It was a balmy May afternoon in 1941. The Gestapo chief Haman ordered the Jewish Police to arrest the most distinguished and learned scholar in town. The Jewish Police decided on Reb Yossele Frankel. Reb Yossele calmly requested that before he'd be taken to the Gestapo he should be permitted to immerse himself and say *vidui*. With great courage and fortitude he prepared himself for the worst.

"It is G-d's will, and I accept it without complaint. Let us hope that Jewish troubles will finally come to an end," he tried to console his heartbroken family. A hushed silence fell on the streets as passersby dejectedly watched Reb Yossele proudly walking between two white-hatted Jewish Police members. The only sound to be heard was the sobbing of his children.

This was to be one of the rare occasions when an arrested person was seen emerging alive from the Gestapo headquarters. He had merely been kept up the whole night discussing Jewish topics with a learned member of the Gestapo who was familiar with the Talmud.

As remarkable as it may sound, this same Reb Yossele, who went so quietly yet with so much courage, acted completely different on the day before the liquidation, but again with the same valor.

On Shabbos afternoon, 9 Elul 1942, a "pre-liquidation assembly" was organized. It took place on a field on Kochanovska Street, not far from the school where the Jewish Police were stationed. At the assembly the police announced the "rules and regulations" of how one should behave during the liquidation and in which order the events were to proceed so that all should go as planned, with no hitches disrupting the day.

The deputy commander of the Jewish Police, Blaustein, explained to the assembled crowd that the ghetto population was to be transferred by train to the Ukraine, where they would be permitted to live independently. Haman himself had given him this information, he went on, adding that if the Jews would do exactly as they were told no more blood would be shed.

"Any questions?" concluded the deputy commander to the congregated people.

"I want to say something!" called out Reb Yossele Frankel.

Reb Yossele, dressed in his Shabbos finery, complete with *shtreimel* and *bekishe*, stood up on a chair and with a voice trembling with emotion called out to the stunned audience, "Don't believe these murderers! Don't believe a single word they tell you! We are condemned by the Nazis to death! We have nothing to lose! Whoever can should escape! And whoever cannot should say *vidui*. *Shema Yisrael!*..."

Reb Yossele's words were brutally cut off by the police, who forcefully dragged him off the chair.

What admirable *kiddush haShem* and boldness was shown in that wonderful moment!

The Remaining Jews in the Tsanzer Ghetto

A week after the Tsanzer Jewish population was deported to Belzec, the remaining 750 people or so who were selected for work were transferred from their temporary quarters on Kraszewski Street to the deserted houses on the Jewish Street. Approximately two hundred of them were sent to distant labor camps — one hundred to Rozhnov to build a dam at the Dunajec, fifty to the Tartak (wood-chopping) factory in Muszyna, and fifty to the camp in Shendishov.

Five hundred and fifty souls remained in the ghetto. Of these, some were employed in the factory Hobag in Ritra. The majority of those who remained in Tsanz, among them some fifty women and girls, were assigned to the *Raumungs Kommando*. Their job was to clean and sort all the possessions left in the empty, deserted ghetto homes in the Jewish Street. The others, around 120 people, worked in a German fur factory.

Reb Shmuel Gutwein, a specialist in *sefarim*, was assigned the task of sorting all the *sefarim* in the ghetto, which were later shipped to Germany. When his work was completed he was sent to the concentration camp in Shevnia where I worked together with him. He eventually perished there.

The remaining Jews of Tsanz went about their work with bitterness and sorrow. They felt forlorn and alone, their hearts bleeding as they handled the possessions of their dead sisters and brothers. Every room they cleared out, every garment they folded, brought back recent memories of their nearest and dearest who were gone forever, gone with the smoke of the Belzec crematoria. The Germans were quick to assure them that they, too, were, sooner or later, destined to suffer the same fate as their thousands of brethren. When a German woman once stole the blankets which they had salvaged in order to cover themselves at night, she bitingly mocked them, "You don't need them. You're going to die."

The forced laborers worked themselves to exhaustion twelve hours a day, suffering gnawing hunger pains. Every day all they received was 150–180 grams of bread, ersatz coffee, watery soup, a miserly portion of cabbage, and a dab of marmalade. At the beginning their physical and moral well-being was kept strong, thanks to the solidarity and courage of a group of Jews who worked outside the ghetto (in the Tudt factory). Every morning these Jews smuggled items of value out of the ghetto walls, exchanging them with the Poles and returning in the evening with bread, butter, and other food to share with their starving colleagues. Eventually somebody reported their "crime," and on Shemini Atzeres 1943 every one of the thirty-eight people of this *Arbeits Kommando* was taken by Haman to the cemetery and shot, *hy"d*.

The Vanished City of Tsanz

The Jews of the *Raumungs Kommando* endured great psychological suffering apart from their physical plight. They were forced to witness the Gestapo and S.S. members dispose of the articles they had no use for by arranging auctions. These auctions took place in the large Tsanzer shul every Tuesday and Friday, the market days. A *Volksdeutsche* would price the items, and the Poles swarmed in by the dozens in their quest for worthwhile bargains. The money went directly into the already overstuffed pockets of the Nazi bandits.

The bargain hunting became so popular that the Jewish workers of the *Raumungs Kommando* had to stand by the doors, allowing entry in an orderly queue only. Occasionally a Pole would bribe the doorkeeper with a bit of food to be permitted to go in before the others.

The pain involved in seeing this was nothing in comparison to the mental torture they suffered as silent observers to the ongoing searches for the Jews who had gone into hiding. The Gestapo had lists with the names of those who had not appeared at the assembly point by the Helena Bridge on that fateful day, August 23, and they regularly organized raids to dig out the hidden Jews.

Among these were the Saphir family, famous in Tsanz for their warm hospitality and generous deeds. Feigele Saphir was particularly known for her kindness. She lived in a tiny apartment, yet she was never short of space for guests whom she clothed, fed, and offered lodging.

Feigele's son Shimon Saphir built himself a bunker behind his large warehouse, where he hid with his family. Four weeks after the liquidation they were discovered by the S.S. They were led to the cemetery and shot into a grave which other Jews had dug before they, too, were murdered.

Yidel Weinberg suffered a similar fate. He had hired a gentile to lead him to safety from the ghetto. However, the gentile was noticed by the S.S. barbarians and was followed to Yidel's hideout. Yidel was taken to the cemetery on Shemini Atzeres, the same day as the thirty-eight members of the *Arbeits Kommando* mentioned above. On the way to the cemetery Yidel begged the S.S. man escorting him to shoot him then and there, as he was so ill he simply did not have the strength to continue. The S.S. guard mercifully complied.

The S.S. were so thorough with their investigations, sometimes even following up a lead to Cracow, that sooner or later all those who had gone into hiding were caught. The arrested who were immediately taken to the cemetery and shot — such was the fate of about fifty people — were considered fortunate. Sadly, most were not so "lucky" and suffered unbearable tortures before finally being put to death. The Jewish laborers whose work included cleaning the offices of the Gestapo came across instruments which sent shudders of fear through them: whips entwined with iron rods, tweezers to compress fingers and mouths, and steel cupboards where the victim would be locked in together with a vicious dog.

The maniacal hounds disguised as humans thought up a further malicious plan, which surpassed all other methods of torture in its sheer cruelty: Some weeks after the Tsanzer deportation, the Gestapo, by means of special watch guards, captured a group of Jews from Bochnia and other places who had tried to flee to Hungary. After subjecting them to unspeakable tortures in the Tsanzer prison, Haman and his assistant Rudolph satiated their appetite for cruelty by packing the unfortunates into boxes and sending them to the cemetery to be buried alive. Hersh Hertzberg, a tailor from Tsanz who was forced to take the boxes to the cemetery together with three other Jews, heard the chilling groans of the Jews locked in the boxes as they were being transported to the cemetery.

With the ghetto steadily being cleared out, the Germans began gradually deporting more and more Jews when their services were no longer required. Some of them were simply shot as soon as they showed the slightest sign of ailment or weakness.

On Rosh HaShanah 1942 the first group of around forty Jews were sent to a concentration camp in Melitz. At the end of September 1942 about 150 people were sent to Tarnow. The end of October showed another transport being shipped to Tarnow, to a tailoring factory. With the conclusion of spring 1943 over a hundred Jews remained in Tsanz, working in the *Aufraumungs Kommando* (cleaning brigade). Of those, seventy were sent in June 1943 to the labor camp in Shevnia, which is located in the district of Yasla. Only thirty-seven forlorn souls were left behind in Tsanz to clear away the fallen stones and debris of the destroyed ghetto and to clean away the dirt of the Jewish Street. Four weeks later, in July 1943, the German field marshal surrounded the ghetto, and the last remaining thirty-seven Jews were deported to Shevnia.

The Nazis had accomplished their mission. Tsanz was at last *Judenrein*.

The Suffering in the Concentration Camps

The last few hundred remaining Jews in the Tsanzer ghetto were separated and sent to various camps, where they endured unimaginable suffering.

In Muszyna, where I was an inmate, there were one hundred Jewish laborers from Tsanz and its surrounding villages. After the final liquidation of the ghetto on August 23 another forty-nine Jews joined us there.

The Jewish commander in our camp was David Shlussel of Tsanz. He was an extremely refined man who treated the inmates as decently as circumstances allowed him. He was the son of Reb Shalom Shlussel, a distinguished and wealthy person in Tsanz.

The situation in Muszyna changed drastically for the worse after the destruction of the Tsanzer ghetto. The inmates who came from Tsanz and its surrounding areas used to receive packages of food and clothing from the help committee in the ghetto. However, now that there was no one left in Tsanz, many members of that very help committee found themselves in the Muszyna camp, in the same dire situation as those they had formerly assisted. They sent word to Cracow, begging for aid in the form of food, medicine, clothing, and shoes, but nothing was heard in reply.

The most sinister camp of all, where many people were deported before the final liquidation, was Rabka. Situated in West Galicia,

KIDDUSH HASHEM AND HEROISM

Rabka was officially a training unit for the *Sippa* (*Siecherheits Police*) and S.D. (*Siecherheits Dienst*). In reality it was a school for the training of fresh recruits in the most horrible methods of torture and cruel ways of killing. A "course" in the school lasted six months.

When the new recruits arrived, each was given a dog. This dog was to be his pet during the course of his training. He had to look after him, feed him, and wash him. The idea was that the dog was to be his companion and that he should become attached to it.

After six months, when the course was finished, each recruit had to stand in front of his friends and strangle the dog with his bare hands to prove that he had pity on nobody and nothing — not even his companion of the last six months. With that he successfully completed his training.

The camp was located in the Villa Tereska. The transports that arrived at Rabka were promptly put to death by shooting or hanging. This was the fate of two transports of 170 and 150 old and weak Jews, sent by the chief of the work commission in May and June 1942. The Nazis permitted some of the strongest transportees, not more than a tenth of each group, to stay alive in order to wear them out with backbreaking labor and to practice unspeakable tortures on them.

A group of sixty Jews from Tsanz were sent to Rabka in June or July 1942. The *rabbanim* among them were shot immediately by the S.S. commander Rosenbaum, *y"s*. The remaining Jews were forced to drink *gnaiovka* (human waste) and to tear *siddurim* and other *sefarim* which they had with them. Then they were led to a grave and shot. They died with the words "*Shema Yisrael...*" on their lips.

Proch was another murderer who carried out mass slaughter in Rabka.

The few Jews who weren't shot upon their arrival were forced to drag heavy wheelbarrows up a mountain, subsisting on one hundred grams of bread a day. The camp commander Rosenbaum used to follow them from behind, lashing at them with a whip with a lead ball attached.

The head of the military department, Banet, tried to excuse

The Vanished City of Tsanz

himself to a Polish engineer for the atrocities committed. "We want to make as much use as possible of Jewish strength before they are sent on to Madagascar," he lied.

Occasionally, several Poles would be shot together with the Jews. When a group of laborers were hung after a selection, all the other laborers had to assemble to watch the scene. Often, the Jewish laborers were made to bury those who had been killed as well as those who had been shot but still showed signs of being alive. The murderer Rosenbaum once wiped out an entire family for the sole reason that they dared to own the same name as he.

In Shevnia the camp commander was an S.S. member named Grozimek. He used to stroll among the workers, accompanied by a dog and an automatic revolver which was always ready for immediate use.

He once spotted one of the workers, Meir Yechiel Tzimmetbaum, who was wheeling a heavy wheelbarrow laden with sand, stopping to catch his breath for a few seconds. Meir Yechiel (born in 1905) was a relative of mine who lived in Bochnia during the war. After the Nazis murdered his only child during the liquidation, he became so broken and depressed that he could not pull himself together and work with the same energy as the rest of the laborers in Shevnia.

When Grozimek noticed that Meir Yechiel's work was slacking, he aimed his revolver at him and pressed the trigger. The bullet missed its mark and wounded him in the leg. Meir Yechiel started to run, but three Jewish Police caught him and, following Grozimek's orders, tied him up. Bound tightly in rope, Meir Yechiel recklessly called out to Grozimek, "You will all end up suffering the same fate as me; indeed, you murdered us Jews, but you will yet lose this war!"

Lying on the floor, guarded by Ukrainians, Tzimmetbaum was trampled by an S.S. man. Tzimmetbaum then lashed at him, "You have won the war against the Jews but not against the world!"

The S.S. man promptly shot him in the mouth to put a stop to his speeches. Ten O.D. members then dragged him to the *appel* assembly place, where they hung him with his hands behind his back. Every time his

KIDDUSH HASHEM AND HEROISM

hands gave way and his feet dropped a little lower to the ground a Jewish O.D. member who was specially assigned for this task shoveled away the earth from under his feet. Thus he hung, suffering excruciating pain, for seven hours.

In the evening, after *appel*, the camp commander Kellerman arrived together with Grozimek and other Gestapo members. They removed Tzimmetbaum from his gallows and shot him three times. His name will be remembered and glorified as one of the martyred *kedoshim* of the town Tsanz.

Hung by the feet, like Meir Yechiel Tzimmetbaum

In November 1943 the camp in Shevnia was liquidated and its inmates sent to Auschwitz. In 1944 the remaining inmates in the camp in Pustkow were deported to Auschwitz, too. Some Tsanzer Jews were also scattered in the camps in Plashow, near Cracow, and Skarzshiska. At the end of the war, only a handful of the last few remaining Tsanzer Jews survived the infamous death march to live to see the liberation.

CHAPTER 6

MY OWN EXPERIENCES

In the camp in Muszyna we worked for the Hobag company, constructing wooden huts to be sent to Germany to replace the homes bombed by the Allies. Our chief and S.S. commandant was called Treidlar. He was an intelligent linguist who could even converse in Hebrew.

It happened once on *erev Yom Kippur* 1942 that I was unable to go to work as I had suffered a severe blow on my left hand from a sharp, rusty piece of metal. The wound had become infected, and I was ill from blood poisoning. I stayed behind in the barracks and lay on the wooden slats.

Suddenly I heard somebody enter the block. It was Treidlar. He walked over to where I was lying and said, "You Jew! You know well that tomorrow is Yom Kippur, and tomorrow you will die. Get yourself somebody to say Kaddish for you before you perish!"

A shudder ran through my body as his words penetrated my mind. Yet his curse did not materialize, and in spite of the impossible circumstances (apart from placing a damp cloth on my wound, I received absolutely no treatment for the blood poisoning), I outlived him. It must have been the angel Refael himself who healed my hand.

Once, a parcel arrived for me at the camp. It contained a letter written in Yiddish by a Jewish girl who had worked together with my

MY OWN EXPERIENCES

sister Chava in a factory in the Cracow ghetto. Treidlar commanded me to read it aloud. The letter read as follows:

> To my dear brother,
>
> I have never met you, yet I have heard much about you from your sister Chava, with whom I used to work. Your sister is unfortunately no longer here (i.e., she is not among the living), and I therefore took upon myself to stand in her stead, helping you in every way possible even though I do not know you personally. Naturally, I do not know how long I will remain here.
>
> Keep well, and may G-d protect you from all evil...

The S.S. man flew into a rage and barked at me, "Who is this girl who wrote you this letter and sent you the parcel?" I answered him that I did not know who she was, having never met her before.

Treidlar gritted his teeth and muttered, "How is it possible that this girl sends you packages if she does not know you at all? Tell me how you got to know her so well that she sent you this parcel?"

I insisted that I had never set eyes on this girl and had absolutely no idea who she was. He began shouting, "You Jews are one ring of international criminals!"

I never received a second parcel from her and never heard of her again. I assume that she shared the same tragic fate as my sister.

It is impossible to describe the High Holy Days in the Muszyna concentration camp in 1942. The Selichos which we said every morning before praying, the bitter tears which were shed, the crying and wailing, must have pierced the very heavens, as we thought of the fate which had befallen our fathers, our mothers, our brothers and sisters, so brutally killed in all sorts of horrible ways. We prayed before dawn, in the darkness of the night, so that the S.S. barbarians would not notice us. It was difficult to control the broken-hearted assembly, to pray a little quieter.

Once, the S.S. commandant Treidlar marched into our barracks and announced that he wanted to practice "Russian equality." This meant that all must be equal — there would be no rich or poor. We understood what this implied: he would confiscate the bit of clothing and food we had brought from home and divide them among all the inmates. Unfortunately the first half of our predictions came true — he indeed stole our belongings — but as for the second half, none of us ever saw anything back again.

Back to Tsanz

One fine day in November 1942, the Gestapo chief murderer of Tsanz, Haman, arrived unexpectedly. He consulted with the S.S. commandant Treidlar of Muszyna and ordered him to return all the inmates from Tsanz. He feared they were too free in the camp in Muszyna, because the barbed wire running round the camp was not electrified.

A dark fear overcame us when we became aware of the decree. We knew well what awaited us back in Tsanz, which had long ago been declared *Judenrein*. Our dread was doubly increased when we heard what had befallen the thirty-eight Jews who had remained behind working in the Todt company after the liquidation. On Shemini Atzeres, Haman had led them to the cemetery, forced them to dig their own graves, and then shot them.

Haman's plan was not to Treidlar's taste at all, since he knew that as soon as the concentration camp was dissolved, his glorious career would be over and he would be sent to the eastern front. The "east-front" meant his death sentence. This dreaded thought gave him the courage to travel to Haman in Tsanz and request that he let us stay in the camp, "since this is vital for the good of the German nation who are being bombed by the enemies." Chazal tell us, "Prayer accomplishes half." Indeed the S.S. murderer Haman agreed to repeal half his command: 50 percent of the strongest workers would be permitted to stay in the camp while the remaining 50 percent (seventy-five workers) must be sent to him to Tsanz.

The selection for the seventy-five weakest workers to be sent to Tsanz now began. Among the first to be picked was my friend Hillel Landau (who lives today in Brazil) and I, since we were short and skinny — obvious signs of weakness. The S.S. had quite a tough time

MY OWN EXPERIENCES

trying to sort us out, since as soon as somebody was chosen to be among the seventy-five, he promptly went back to mingle among those who were yet to be selected. When the S.S. men saw that they were getting nowhere with us they aimed their revolvers at those chosen and warned us that the next person who tried to back out would be shot on the spot. Having no choice, we stood in our places, resigning ourselves to our fate.

Soon enough, our group was ready to go. Those who remained in Muszyna parted from us with tears in their eyes, for they knew well what awaited us at the hands of the sadist Haman. We were led to the train station, where the police herded us onto oxen wagons and escorted us to Tsanz.

Upon arrival at our destination, the familiar figure of one of the notorious S.S. barbarians, Johann Bornholt, awaited us at the station. As we descended from the wagons, he gave each of us a kick with the sharp-edged heel of his boot, accompanied by the words, "Cursed dog! Out of this wagon quick!" To this day I have a scar on my left leg from the clout I received from him then.

From the station we were led to the infamous Tsanzer prison. The prison door was only wide enough to allow one person at a time to pass, but we trampled over each other in our haste to escape Johann. We were packed into two prison cells, thirty-seven in one cell and thirty-eight in the other. No sanitary facilities were provided and, of course, no food. In any case, we could not have possibly eaten in the face of the ominous death sentence which loomed over our heads. When sanitary facilities were needed, we banged on the prison wall until somebody brought in a bucket.

Finally the long night came to an end. As soon as dawn broke, the S.S. led us into the prison courtyard and asked us if we were cold. A unanimous "yes" was the reply. They ordered us to sing "synagogue songs" and dance in order to warm up a little. They chose Berel Kahana, a man who had absolutely no voice and could not sing at all, to be our conductor. The Nazis stood at the side, scoffing and laughing at the entertainment we provided.

The Vanished City of Tsanz

They then asked us if we were hungry. Again the reply was affirmative, upon which they called out, "Here you will receive no food, but as soon as you reach your uncles in the Jew-ghetto of Tarnow, they will provide you with some grub."

Oddly enough, a good inclination possessed them, and they did not beat us. Opposite us in the prison courtyard we caught sight of a group of Poles being beaten by the S.S.

From Tsanz to Tarnow

The Gestapo then led us to the Tsanzer train station to send us to Tarnow. We were hardly convinced that we were to escape unharmed from the clutches of the S.S. beasts. Yet so it was; we were herded onto oxen wagon and under the careful watch of the S.S. driven to Tarnow.

Upon arrival in Tarnow we were taken to the *Judenrat*, where one of our escorts told them, "This gang has not eaten for two days. You must provide them with food."

So it was. The Jewish Police guided us to the ghetto's kosher kitchen, where we satiated our ravaging hunger with some warm potato soup.

Now there arose a new problem. Where were we to live? Ninety percent of the ghetto's former inhabitants had been slaughtered or perished. The remaining 10 percent were remnants of other liquidated towns and settlements, and they lived in extremely cramped conditions. Looking for a solution, the Jewish Police decreed that every family in the ghetto must take one of us into his home.

I was placed in the home of the Pfennig family. Herr Pfennig worked as a painter for the Tarnover Gestapo. He was none too happy when he arrived home and encountered his uninvited guest. To be fair, perhaps he was justified. The only suit I owned was that which I was wearing, and the jacket was patched up all over with white cloth which I had torn from my shirt and crudely sewn on. I had figured that, as the saying goes, "better an unsightly patch than an attractive hole." Herr Pfennig and his wife politely explained to me that since he was

MY OWN EXPERIENCES

employed at Gestapo headquarters and he must appear neat and presentable, he could not afford to take in unclean guests. I protested, saying, "Where shall I go? The *Judenrat* has stationed me here. I will sit in a corner, and I promise not to be a hindrance." Having no choice, they shrugged their shoulders and agreed.

A few days passed, and I came into contact with some kind-hearted people who provided me with decent clothing. After my appearance underwent a transformation the Pfennigs warmed to me and treated me royally. Herr Pfennig even risked his life for me, in the following episode.

By order of the Gestapo the Jewish Police organized raids from time to time to seize Jews to be sent to concentration camps. It happened once that I was standing on the street with two other boys from Tsanz when a sudden, unexpected raid took place. Seeing the police a short distance away we panicked and desperately looked for a place to hide. Thankfully we heard the voice of a woman who sold potato *pletzlach* calling to us from above. "Children, come up quickly, and I will hide you." Hearts racing, we flew up the stairs to her home. The oven where she baked the potatoes was crowned with two large chimneys. One of them was deceptive and actually led to her attic. She hurriedly directed us up the chimney and whispered loudly, "Quickly, crawl upstairs!"

We had barely reached the attic when we heard the bellowing voices of the Jewish Police who had followed us into her home demanding, "Where are the children you hid?" The woman firmly insisted that she did not know what they were talking about. They began their search, banging on all the walls and doors, but they could not find their prey. However, they were not about to give up. Just as we began breathing a sigh of relief, we heard them climb onto the roof and remove a few tiles, determined to discover the attic hideout. In desperation we tore open a feather duvet and tried to conceal ourselves under the feathers, but to no avail; soon we were discovered. With a whoop of delight they pounced on us and dragged us off to the cellar of the *Judenrat*, where all those captured were thrown.

The Vanished City of Tsanz

On the way to the *Judenrat* I tried to plead with one of the police, Shammai Adler. "Please let us go," I begged. "Of what benefit will it be to you if they shoot us or send us away?" However, my words fell on deaf ears, and we were handed over to the Gestapo.

When we descended into the cellar we almost tripped over the dead body of a Jewish policeman sprawled across the floor. He had been shot by the killer Grunov because he wasn't efficient enough in capturing Jews. Among the other prisoners in the cellar we encountered two brothers who were also from Tsanz, Moshe Mendel and Avraham Gross.

When Mr. Pfennig returned home at night he asked his wife, "Where is the young boy, Zalman Lehrer, who lives with us?" It was 9 P.M. and there was a strict curfew from 8 P.M.

His wife replied, "Who knows if he wasn't seized by the Jewish Police in the ghetto *aktion* today?"

Without hesitation Mr. Pfennig said to his wife, "I will go to the cellar of the *Judenrat* to see if he is there and if I can do anything to get him out."

There was a lot of danger involved in this daring venture. Firstly, it was after curfew. Secondly, the chief of the Gestapo, Grunov, renowned for his murderous deeds, used to guard the cellar himself. However Mr. Pfennig was undaunted, and, grabbing his coat, he made his way to the *Judenrat*.

As soon as he walked through the door he was accosted by the Gestapo murderer Grunov. "Cursed dog!" he yelled. "What are you doing here now? Didn't you finish the painting job at my house?"

"*Jawhol*," answered Pfennig.

"Then what are you looking for here?"

"I would like to learn if the youth who resides at my house is among the captured ones in the cellar. If so, please let me take him back home with me."

"Fine. Go down to the cellar and see if he is there."

Mr. Pfennig descended the cellar steps. As soon as he espied me there, he took hold of me by the arm and led me to the killer Grunov, saying, "This is the youth who lives with us in the ghetto."

"Get out of my sight together with him," Grunov raspingly ordered from between clenched teeth.

To sidetrack for a moment, in the ghetto I came across a daughter of Rabbi Mordechai Yosef Saphir, a *dayan* in Tsanz who had lived in our apartment building and was a close friend of my father. We were frequent visitors in his home and he in ours.

Reb Mordechai Yosef's daughter had the appearance of a gentile. She had changed her name from Saphir to Saraphin, a Polish name, and managed to procure Aryan papers for herself. Thus she was able to smuggle herself out to the Aryan side of the ghetto. I was therefore very surprised to see her back in the ghetto.

"Tzipporah, what are you doing here?" I asked.

"I would rather die here in the ghetto with the Jews than live with gentiles," she replied. "I have therefore smuggled myself back within the ghetto walls." She then went on to relate to me what had happened to another Jewish girl who had also obtained Aryan papers and lived outside the ghetto. She had been drinking a glass of tea, when she broke a sugar cube in half with her hands. The gentiles sitting in her presence immediately turned to her and said, "You are a Jewess, because only the Jews break sugar cubes with their hands." They handed her over to the Gestapo.

There were other ways the Jews unwittingly gave themselves away. If somebody gathered crumbs from the table and did not throw them on the floor, he, too, revealed his identity. I heard that in Brussels, where there were a lot of Jews disguised as non-Jews, the S.S. used to find out who was a Jew by investigating who slept with goosedown and who slept with a blanket. Even the Jews themselves were not aware that they were the only ones who slept with goosedown.

In the ghetto I once came across a ramshackle barn owned by a Jewish wagon driver who possessed an old, bony horse and a wagon. This Jew had to stand at the service of the S.S., carting away the many corpses of those whom they had shot.

The Vanished City of Tsanz

Suddenly, to my great consternation, I caught sight of a boy I knew well from Tsanz, Mendel Turem, the son of Fishel Turem. He lay sprawled in a corner of the dirty barn, feverish and deathly ill with typhus. The pitiful figure was barely recognizable as the boy I once knew.

I was shocked and dismayed, but there was little I could do for him. Seeing him suffer so I was reminded of the *gemara* in *masseches Gittin* which describes the time of the *churban Beis HaMikdash*. The *gemara* tells the story of Marsa bas Beisus, who had been one of the wealthiest women in Jerusalem. The famished woman scrounged among the rubbish in the streets for something to stave off her hunger, when she came across a squeezed-out fig of Rabbi Tzadok. (Rabbi Tzadok fasted for forty years in the hope that the Beis HaMikdash would not be destroyed, breaking his fast every night on the juice of a fig.) In desperation she ate the fig, but the coarse food proved to be more than her refined body could bear, and she died as a result.

This young boy, Mendel Turem, was accustomed to a life of luxury, coming from a very refined and respectable home. Sadly, he could not tolerate the harsh conditions in the ghetto, and he died in that barn, *hy"d*.

One Shabbos morning, while we were praying at the home of the Leizer family, the door was thrown open, and the Gestapo, headed by Grunov, marched in. Filled with terror, many people jumped from the first-story window in a frantic attempt to escape, some even breaking a hand or a foot. One of the people was shot by Grunov as he tried to flee through the door. Fortunately I escaped notice in my hiding place behind a dustbin.

There were two ghettos in Tarnow, ghetto A and ghetto B. In ghetto A all who were able to work were kept together so they would be ready whenever they were needed. Ghetto B consisted of those who did not have a work permit and included all those who were not considered fit for labor. Of course, nobody got any food in ghetto B, because somebody who did not work was not considered worthy of even a slice of bread. It was there that all the *aktion*s took place.

I lived in ghetto B and therefore did not receive any sustenance to keep body and soul together. In order to earn a bit of food I and a friend from Tsanz, Tzvi Friedman (who lives today in Bnei Brak), used to smuggle ourselves at night into ghetto A. We got ourselves a saw and an axe and chopped wood for the ghetto's inhabitants. We knocked down dilapidated ghetto houses for this purpose, since the S.S. did not allow any outside wood to be brought into the ghetto. In payment, we received a bowl of potato soup and bread from the kosher kitchen, which every worker was entitled to each evening when he returned home from work. Needless to say, the work was fraught with danger and risk to our lives, the penalty being death.

There was a certain woman from Cracow by the name of Steinhauer who employed our services as woodchoppers. One day she said to us, "You don't appear to be professional woodchoppers. You will receive food from me even without chopping wood." Indeed, she provided us with food for free. She also gave me twenty dollars which, she said, would be useful in an emergency should I be sent away to a concentration camp.

Before Pesach 1943, I fell ill with typhus. Adjoining the apartment of Mr. Pfennig was the home of Dr. Wachtahl, a doctor in the Tarnow ghetto's hospital (who lived after the war in Bat Yam, Israel). He and

The main shul of Tarnow before the war

The Vanished City of Tsanz

his wife devotedly tended to my every need when I was sick, bringing me cooked meals, since they knew I did not eat at the Pfennig family because of kashrus. Dr. Wachtahl's wife, whose maiden name was Wind, kept a strictly kosher kitchen. Her father was one of the distinguished Belzer Chassidim in Tarnow.

The doctor sent me to the Jewish hospital outside the ghetto, a place for those whose illness was contagious. I stayed there for a few weeks, until after Pesach, and led the seder for all the invalids in the hospital. With this he did me a great favor: I was thereby saved from two *aktions* which took place in the Tarnow ghetto during Pesach.

My strength was greatly revitalized in hospital. As I slowly regained my energy my fever went down. I would have soon been sent back to the ghetto if not for the good-heartedness of the nurses. Before they would take my temperature, the nurse on duty would hand me a glass of tea and the thermometer and say, "You know what you must do now." I understood. I knew that I must have fever in order to be allowed to stay on in hospital, and so I placed the thermometer near the hot glass of tea instead of where I should have. The thermometer instantly showed a reading of above forty degrees. When the nurse came to get the thermometer she seemed pleased that I had understood

Remains of the shul in Tarnow after the war

MY OWN EXPERIENCES

her message and conscientiously wrote down the reading on the board near my bed. Doing this, she risked her own life.

Two weeks after Pesach I was sent back to the ghetto. A short time later I was once again caught by the Jewish Police. This time, however, there was nothing to be done, and I was sent away. Later on, I discovered that this was for the best, since all those who had stayed behind in the Tarnow ghetto were murdered.

In the Rimanov Concentration Camp

I was sent together with a group of 150 people to the camp in Rimanov where we were delivered into the bloodstained hands of the monstrous *Hauptsturmbandfuhrer* Sheid, *y"s*.

The suffering and troubles we were put through in Rimanov were even worse than in Auschwitz. The Ukrainian S.S. outdid the Germans in their unlimited cruelty. There were no fixed working hours; as soon as dawn broke the Ukrainians would beat the Jewish slave laborers on the heads with the butt of their rifles and drive us to work. Our work consisted of dismantling barracks and loading the parts onto wagons, which were then sent to the ghetto in Plashow, near Cracow.

The Visit of Amman Ghet

The commandant of the camp in Plashow was the S.S. *Sturmfuhrer* Amman Ghet, *y"s* (who was put to death in Cracow after the war). One day Ghet came to Rimanov to visit the S.S. commandant Sheid. I heard him boast to Sheid, "Here in this camp I personally silenced twenty-five thousand prisoners forever — Russians, Poles, and Jews." Indeed, we saw Jewish names like Yitzchak ben Yisrael from Vitepsk engraved on the barracks walls.

The plot of ground on which we were stationed belonged to a *Volksdeutsche* landlord. The Germans were eager to vacate the property and return it to its owner. During Ghet's visit he gave our commandant Sheid a "lecture" on how to handle Jews. "You do not know how to treat them," he reprimanded him. "I will give you some lessons."

The Vanished City of Tsanz

Ghet set out three rows, two Jews to every row. Every pair had to carry a board loaded with bricks. "Run!" he barked. The pairs of hapless Jews began running, one behind the other. He then had his dog, Lorry, jump at the first pair of Jews, shouting, "Lorry, bite them!" The dog promptly lunged and sank his fangs into them, tearing away at their flesh until they collapsed and could not rise anymore. When the S.S. beast Ghet saw that the bitten and bloodied victims were close to death he yelled at his dog, "Lorry, *phoy!*" upon which the dog finally ceased his vicious attack. The unfortunate victims were then left to die in agony.

While we tremblingly loaded the bricks on our board, I observed that as soon as the dog heard the word "*phoy*" he stopped his attack. I carefully memorized that word, and when mine and my friend Hillel Landau's turn arrived, and the commandant called the dog on us, I yelled desperately, "Lorry, *phoy!* Lorry, *phoy!*" Indeed, the dog did

Nazi training his dog to kill

not touch us, and we did not suffer even a single scratch. I cannot take credit for my quick thinking; the Creator, Who granted me extra years, also granted me the intelligence to escape the hands of those who sought to destroy me.

We were once going about our work, under the watchful surveillance of the S.S. murderer Sheid, who was standing at a distance, when, with the use of his binoculars, he noticed that I had paused in my work for a split second. Instantly, he raised his revolver and aimed it at me, ready to shoot. To my good fortune, the Jewish policeman on duty had witnessed this interchange, and he swiftly ran over to me, beating me mercilessly. He beat me so severely that for the next seven days I could not see with my right eye. When Sheid approached me and saw how I had collapsed in a heap from the intensity of the blows, he was appeased and replaced his revolver in its holder. I had been saved by the brutal blows of a Jewish policeman. Shaul Tzimmer, another Jew from Tsanz, was not so fortunate, and when he once stopped his work for a moment he was shot and killed by Sheid.

In Rimanov the S.S. constantly drilled into our ears, "As soon as your work is finished, you will all join your *rabbiner* in his cave." They meant the grave of the *tzaddik*, Reb Mendele Rimanover, who was buried to the north of our work site. Indeed, many inmates of Rimanov were sent to join him in his final resting place.

Shevnia

When our work in Rimanov was completed, we were sent to Shevnia, a small village close to Yasla. The remaining survivors of many ghettos — Briggel, Bochnia, Reisha, Tarnow, Cracow, and Tsanz — were also brought to that camp. Their task was to collect and sort out the belongings of our slaughtered brethren. The items of minuscule value were sold to the local Poles, while those of greater value were shipped to Germany. Shmuel Gutwein, the man chosen by the Germans to sort out the *sefarim*, was also sent to Shevnia, where he perished, as I mentioned above.

Our task in Shevnia was to erect barracks. At the beginning, the

The Vanished City of Tsanz

situation was tolerable, but when the survivors of the above-mentioned ghettos were brought in, our circumstances worsened considerably.

In September 1943, a transport of the survivors of the Tarnow ghetto arrived. The S.S. commandant Kellerman decreed that since he did not have sufficient place in his barracks to accommodate the transport, the eighteen hundred Jews should be taken to a nearby field and shot. The unfortunate victims were taken to a large field where they were ordered to dig their own graves. They were then made to completely undress and every single one of them was shot and swallowed by the huge, gaping hole they had dug. Their bodies were burned on the spot. Later, all those who had assisted in the killing were likewise murdered in order to completely wipe away all remembrances of this unspeakable atrocity.

Two weeks later another tragic episode occurred. A Jewish stable manager of the *Hauptsturmfuhrer* commandant, Kellerman, managed to escape the camp in Shevnia. He had been sent on a mission by Kellerman, under the close guard of two Ukrainian S.S. guards. On the way, the Jew invited his escorts to join him in a pub where they could satiate themselves with drink at his expense. The guards were unable to resist the temptation and agreed. While they were drinking, the Jew excused himself and fled via a different exit.

The infuriated Kellerman had his revenge by ordering the killing of ten Jews. When we returned from work that day and were standing on the *appel* assembly ground, we were surrounded by Ukrainian S.S. on the outside and by German S.S. from within. The S.S. picked ten Jews at random, kicked them into the middle of the *appel* assembly grounds, and ordered them to lie face down on the ground. They were destined to be shot. Their tenth victim was a man from the Bochnia ghetto. His son, standing at his side, begged the killers to shoot him instead, but his father adamantly protested. Without further ado the Nazis resolved the argument by shooting them both. Thus, eleven victims were shot instead of ten.

The Jewish *lagerelteste* (leader) of the camp was called Elzner.

MY OWN EXPERIENCES

He proved to be decent and upright, extremely rare for a *lagerelteste*, who always tried to assist his unfortunate underlings. It was highly unusual for the Nazis to allow such a person to keep his position since they needed hard-hearted bullies for their job of eliminating as many Jews as possible. Yet, strangely enough, Elzner stayed on.

Every day when we went to work we would take the bowls in which we had received our meager portion of soup and give it to the Poles in exchange for broken or damaged bowls filled with bread. Upon our return, we were obligated to show that we had brought back our emptied bowl. We showed the broken bowl, and the next day when we received our ration we took a new bowl. So it went, day after day. Elzner was well aware of these goings-on, yet out of the goodness of his heart he turned a blind eye. If somebody had a pressing problem, he would turn to Elzner, who would offer his kindly advice. Indeed, he was dubbed "the father of the camp."

Yisrael Paserina was a young Belzer Chassid who had owned a dairy restaurant in Cracow. In the camp in Shevnia he worked with the delousing *Kommando*. When we arrived at Shevnia and were deloused he summoned me from the gray column of Jews and asked me my name. I was wary of telling him, being ever-suspicious of potential danger. My fears were allayed when he asked if I had two brothers, named Moshe and Hersh. When I answered in the affirmative he said that they often used to frequent his restaurant, and I resembled them strongly. "From now on," he said, "you will receive an extra piece of bread from me every day."

Indeed, he kept his word and provided not only me, but my friend Mates Friezel from Tsanz (who is the mayor of New Square in the U.S.A.), with this life-giving sustenance. Before we left Shevnia for Auschwitz, Yisrael Paserina was among a group of Jews shot.

CHAPTER 7

AUSCHWITZ

On November 3, 1943, 5 Marcheshvan 5704, we were sent from Shevnia to Auschwitz. Before being sent away, the S.S. commander Gzhimek gave us a lecture. "You Jews must learn to work well, because when the *Fuhrer* conquers Palestine you will all be sent there to work."

We were led from Shevnia under the light of the sleek S.S. cars, which illuminated the darkened streets to the train station in Yasla. There we were herded onto a train to Auschwitz. The transfer was carried out by a high-ranking S.S. officer, the *Hauptsturmfuhrer* Von Haze, who was specially brought in to organize the liquidation of the camp's remaining Jews. Before being loaded onto the cattle trucks we were commanded to remove our jackets and shoes, in order to prevent any possibility of escape.

Upon arrival in Auschwitz-Birkenau in the darkness of the night, a few people, assuming they were on an ordinary station platform and unaware of the electrified barbed wire running around the camp, attempted escape. As soon as they reached the wire they were electrocuted or shot by the S.S. guards in the watchtowers.

The first selection now began: "Right, left, left, right." Terror and confusion reigned supreme, and nobody knew in which direction it was more advisable to push himself. The murderers then misled us with their well-known lies: "Those who are weak should board the trucks, and they will be taken by transport." The fate of those who fell into the trap was soon revealed; they were driven directly to the crematoria. Those who chose to go on foot were led to Birkenau.

Rabbi Naftali Ehrenberg, *z"l*, daringly jumped off the truck and mingled among us. The S.S. noticed and promptly issued a new order; we were all to bend down on our knees so that should somebody try the same trick he would be noticed instantly. As for Reb Naftali, the S.S. did not recognize him, and he indeed got away with it. He survived the war and died in America twenty years ago. There were other Jews who also tried to jump off the trucks and lose themselves among those kneeling down, but they were immediately chased back onto the trucks.

Next to us stood a group of fifty people, barely recognizable as human beings, who had been brought from the concentration camp in Magdenburg. These *Musselmen* (the name given to living skeletons or wasted human beings) had let themselves be convinced that they were being taken to Auschwitz in order to recuperate. They were given a piece of bread and led straight to the gas chambers. We, on the other hand, were not given any food.

(During a later selection in Auschwitz-Birkenau, in which we were all selected when we were completely naked, so that they could see at a glance who was fit for work, my friend Hillel Landau and I were sent to the left. I took a quick glance at those standing with us — disabled, hunchbacked, lame and limping — and quickly appraised the situation: we were destined to die. Having nothing to lose, I turned to my friend and said, "Hillel, our situation is critical. We must find a way to get out of here — quick."

Hearts beating with trepidation, we succeeded in returning to those not yet selected. We stood in the row, trembling with fear. Finally, our turn arrived. Standing on tiptoe, for I had observed that the short ones were sent to the left, we were indeed sent to the right this time — to life.)

As I stood there, I noticed one of the S.S. finishing a cigarette and

The Vanished City of Tsanz

throwing the butt to the floor. A Jew standing at my side grabbed the tiny stub and took a puff.

The S.S. turned to me and roared, "Who picked up the stub which I threw down a minute ago?"

I remained silent and thereupon received three clouts on my head with a long pole used to transport barrels of coffee from one place to the other. I collapsed on the floor, unconscious, from the impact of the severe beating. After that incident I realized how fortunate were the ones who did not have an urge for smoking. Those who were addicted to tobacco would throw themselves on the ground and risk receiving severe blows in order to extract one solitary puff from a discarded stub of a cigarette. They would also give away their portion of bread for a puff of smoke. This very often cost them their lives.

At the tattooing procedure we were registered in a massive book and all our details carefully noted down: our father's occupation, our occupation... My number, 161421, was tattooed on my hand, and I was taken to Birkenau, block 14.

The blocks were originally built to be used as horse stables. In every block, designed to house fifty-two horses, nine hundred to a thousand people were squeezed in. There were two columns of bunks facing each other, with a long, thin passage between them. The bunks were three-tiered; every tier was two meters long and had seven people sleeping on it. They resembled shelves in a grocery shop. Between the bunks there was a narrow space of thirty centimeters where we were permitted to stand. It was strictly forbidden to stand in the passage, and anybody caught doing so was smitten with twenty-five lashes. At both ends of the passage there were two large ovens which only served to crowd our intolerably cramped sleeping quarters to an even greater degree.

When the thousand people went to sleep at night or rose in the morning, they all had to move as one, in the same position and at the same time. There were no windows, only small holes near the ceiling, which in winter dispelled the bit of warmth emanating from the ovens and in summer allowed the sun to beat down mercilessly on the wooden block, almost suffocating us with its intense heat.

AUSCHWITZ

Our block was looked upon as a more favorable one since the *blockelteste*, Yidel P., and the *Shtuben Dienst* were considered to be less brutal than their counterparts in other blocks. Nevertheless, their welcoming words were "Galicianer bastards, here you should stay put!"

At night we were given an eighth of a small-sized bread. Officially we were entitled to receive a spoonful of marmalade along with it, but Enoch, the one who distributed the food, gave the seven of us who slept on one bunk one spoonful to share among us.

One person declared, "I didn't get any marmalade!"

When Enoch heard this daring announcement, he barked, "Whoever had too little marmalade should report to me at once."

His order was met by silence. Nobody wanted to reveal who had complained, since we knew well what penalty awaited him. Enoch then commanded all seven of us to dismount from our bunk and to kneel and drag ourselves on the floor on our stomachs. When this ordeal was over, he said, "I believe that no one will dare complain anymore that he received too little marmalade." He was right, of course.

One day I resolved that I would not be able to continue hiding the twenty dollars which I had zealously guarded since my days in the Tarnover ghetto. I walked over to a relatively decent-looking *kapo* and asked if I could change my precious twenty dollars for a plate of soup. His answer was short and to the point. "You see the smoke curling up from that crematorium? You can take the money there with you." I was grateful that he didn't finish me off on the spot. This was the reaction of a decent-looking *kapo*.

Although we saw the smoke emanating from the red-brick chimneys, our hearts refused to believe what our minds told us: that those whom we had seen in the selection only a day before were now no longer. Thus, human nature, in its willingness not to believe the worst, blinded us to the atrocities which our Nazi tormentors were committing right before our eyes.

After the war a man by the name of Blauner, from Gribow, told me the following tale: He had worked in the *Canada Kommando*, the name given to those who assisted in dealing with the newly arrived transports which were selected for the gas chambers. Usually, every few weeks, the members of the *Canada Kommando* were killed and new prisoners made to take their place, since the Nazis wanted to ensure that not a single living witness would remain. Blauner, however, was permitted to stay alive, since he was an expert in the handling of horses, and the Nazis needed him to manage their stables.

This is the story he told me:

Once, a transport arrived from Hungary, and a selection took

Auschwitz

place. Mothers who were carrying children were invariably sent to the left. Blauner noticed a robust-looking woman standing at the side with two children. He tore the children from her arms and, pushing her to the right, called out to the S.S. guard, "She is strong and suitable for work." The S.S. guard agreed. The woman, not realizing that this step was to save her life, showered Blauner with curses and wildly scratched at his hands. After the liberation she sought him out and thanked him for saving her life. She apologized for the scratches and

AUSCHWITZ

Arrival at Auschwitz-Birkenau

curses she had inflicted upon him. At the time she did not know that within an hour no remnant would remain of those mothers who had been carrying children.

Officially our stay in Birkenau was only temporary, in transit to

The first selection upon arrival

The Vanished City of Tsanz

a labor camp. Yet every day we were put to work, dragging heavy boulders from Auschwitz to Birkenau, escorted by S.S. beasts with vicious dogs. Every member in our group was forced to carry a stone over his shoulder, and thus we marched to Birkenau, several times a day, backwards and forwards, in the morning and in the afternoon. Woe was to the one who selected a small stone to take; the S.S. would drag him out of the column and load him with a massive boulder. Needless to say, the boulder would prove to be too heavy for the victim to carry, and he would lag behind. The Nazis would set their dogs on him, who would tear pieces of flesh from his body. The physical exertion of carrying stones was in itself the cause of death for many people.

Those Who Survived

When I was in Birkenau in Kislev 5704, at the end of 1943, the *blockelteste* of my block was a French Jew of Polish descent by the name of Umglick. He was moderately decent — unfortunately there were many who were much worse than he.

A long wait for a turn in the gas chambers due to overcrowding

AUSCHWITZ

Umglick had accused two inmates, Yonah Linker and Yehoshua Hollander from Tarnow, of possessing diamonds. He demanded that the two prisoners surrender the valuables. Of no avail was the insistence of the two that they did not own any diamonds. Umglick bent them over and pushed their heads inside a cold oven so as to prevent them from moving during the murderous beating he gave them.

Umglick was later shot by the S.S. and his body displayed at the entrance of the camp. Rumor had it that he had approached an S.S. guard with five hundred dollars and asked him to smuggle him out of the camp. The S.S. man reported him, and he was shot, his body put on show for all to see and take a lesson.

The two inmates, Yonah Linker and Yehoshua Hollander, survived the war and set up families, while their tormentor was killed. This pattern repeated itself time and time again; those who beat their fellow Jews in an attempt to find favor in the eyes of the Nazis did not accomplish their goal, and sometimes even achieved the opposite effect.

As I have written before, it was seen with startling clarity that those who were destined from Heaven to survive the war were given an instinctive intuition to outwit their captors. But who can understand the ways of the Almighty? There were righteous, innocent people who died a horrible death and unworthy people who died a horrible death. Conversely, there were righteous people who survived the war and, likewise, unworthy people who survived.

I would like to point out that those people who give reasons why this one stayed alive and that one didn't, or claim this person was punished for this reason and that person was not punished for that reason, are obviously people who did not endure the bitter suffering in the concentration camps. I have heard it said that a particular shul was untouched because its members did not talk during prayers. I myself am witness, though, that some shuls where unfortunately people spoke during prayers remained whole, while others, where people were careful not to speak during prayers, were burned down. One can only quote the Belzer Rav, *z"l*: this tragic page in history was

The Vanished City of Tsanz

Outside block 14 with my son-in-law Eliezer Strassman, my son Hershel, and my grandson Leibel Strassman

a Heavenly decree, and those who were destined to live had two angels guarding them at every step of the difficult way.

One afternoon I resolved to skip work. A friend of mine had confided in me that he had dodged the backbreaking labor a couple of times by hiding in the lavatories situated behind the camp gates. When the troop returned from work he would mingle among them, joining them for *appel*.

I followed his advice. While our group went on their way to exert themselves to the point of exhaustion by transporting stones, I hid behind the door of the latrines. Unfortunately, it just happened that that particular afternoon they did not go to work; instead, they were assembled on the *appelplatz* where a selection of people to be sent to a different camp took place. Of course, the count revealed that one number was missing — me.

Inside block 14

After half an

AUSCHWITZ

hour of waiting in breathless suspense, I stuck out my head from behind the door to hear what was going on. I was greeted with a commotion. "One man is missing!" I realized in what a precarious situation I had placed myself and began to scheme feverishly how I could rejoin the prisoners without being noticed. As I stood there, my mind working overtime, I was spotted by one of the S.S. guards. He yelled at me, "Cursed dog! You have held up the entire camp because one man was missing!"

In ordinary circumstances I would have been shot on the spot. However, I was in luck. The *lagerelteste*, known as a particularly brutal man, approached me and said, "Where were you?" Terrified to the core, I answered that I had suffered from severe stomach cramps. To my intense relief, he bellowed at me, "Disappear into the columns now!" without even so much as harming a hair on my head!

At that selection the Germans chose seventy people — I among them — to be sent to the

A block 14 in Birkenau, the holes in the roof providing meager ventilation in the summer and letting in the cold in the winter

A block in Birkenau right after the war

The Vanished City of Tsanz

concentration camp Szwientochlovitz, near Katowitz, a branch of Auschwitz.

We were led from Birkenau to our embarkation point, Auschwitz. There we were told to completely undress and put through another

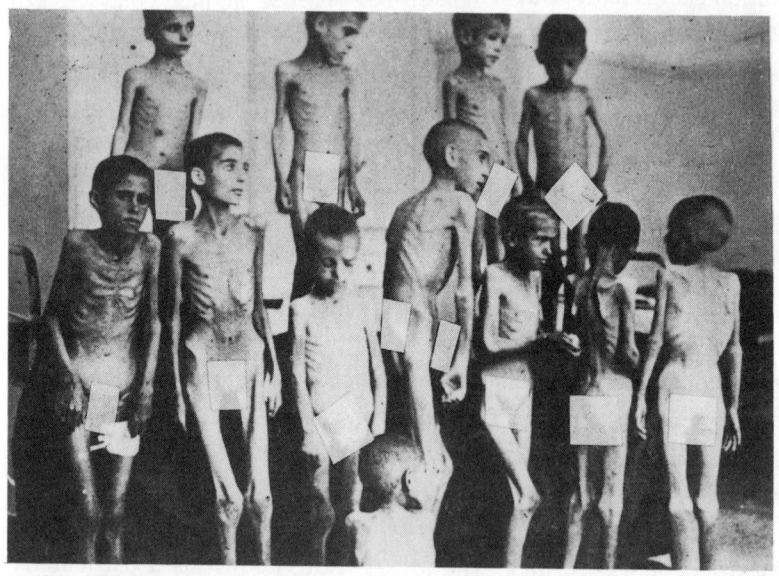

Jewish children ready to be gassed after Dr. Joseph Mengele had finished with them

selection by Dr. Joseph Mengele. Dr. Mengele, who was infamous for his thoroughness, selected the people who had the slightest bruise or cut. Even a bandage, a sign of having been beaten, was enough to make one worthy of the gas chambers.

(Among those condemned to die in that selection was an acquaintance of mine, Reb Alter Boguchval, a Radomsker Chassid. His body was scarred with welts and sores from the fifty lashes he had received after being accused of stealing a piece of margarine. He was a son-in-law of Reb Yossele Roth, one of the Chassidim of Reb Chuna Hersh, *zt"l*, whom I have mentioned previously as one of the most pious men in Tsanz.)

AUSCHWITZ

Tefillin in the Concentration Camp

It was toward the end of 1944 when trains carrying tens of thousands of Hungarian prisoners rolled into the gates of the concentration camps daily. Due to the drastic increase of new inmates, it was virtually impossible to ensure that nothing foreign was brought into the camp, as was the case with the Polish Jews. Consequently, one of the Hungarian inmates succeeded in smuggling in a pair of tefillin.

Since our block consisted of Jews only, the tefillin was concealed in our block. Each day after work, for half an hour, a queue would form of everybody who sought the privilege of donning tefillin. The procedure of hastily placing them on the arm, saying Shema, and tearing them off went by quick as a flash. At first, the Hungarians were wary of us Polish and Galician Jews for fear that we would betray them. However, when they learned with time that we could be trusted, we, too, were permitted to share in the sacred task. We only merited to fulfill this mitzvah for a few short weeks, because Auschwitz was liquidated soon afterwards.

Chapter 8
SZWIENTOCHLOVITZ

Upon our arrival at Szwientochlovitz we were welcomed by the notorious *kapo* Martin Shmitz, a bestial killer who hated Jews with a fiery passion. In no uncertain terms he brusquely warned us that we were too weak for his *Arbeits Kommando*, and we would not be able to tolerate its conditions for more than two weeks. Unfortunately his words proved to be only too correct. He was a cruel taskmaster, and apart from the backbreaking labor we were subject to, he would frequently beat us with deathly blows.

As we descended the truck in which we had come from Auschwitz, a group of seventy *Musselmen* were ordered to climb on. They were sent to Auschwitz to "recuperate" — to get their final rest in the gas chambers.

I felt my strength beginning to ebb as I plodded through the laborious task of loading and unloading lorries with earth. However, I girded myself with the faith that He who granted me the stamina to endure my troubles up till now would grant me further strength to bear what still awaited me.

Block 3 was assigned to me as my sleeping quarters. It was there that I met a Czech who had been sent to Auschwitz for being of Jewish descent, despite having no inkling of what Judaism entailed. He would watch in fascination as I davened *ma'ariv* each evening after work.

SZWIENTOCHLOVITZ

One day he hesitantly approached me. "My name is Dr. Bachner," he introduced himself. "I am an engineer for the construction of bridges, buildings, and cannons. I was sent here for being a Jew, but I have no idea what this means, since my great-grandparents had already become assimilated in Czechoslovakia. I would be greatly interested, however, in knowing a little of the Bible and Talmud. Perhaps you can learn with me?"

I answered him regretfully that by the time I came back from work under the command of Shmitz, with no food to sustain me, I was too drained to even contemplate studying Bible or Talmud.

That evening, after the lights were out and all was quiet in our barracks, I heard a soft thud on my bed. Upon investigation I discovered a piece of bread. I immediately guessed who my benefactor must be. Under the cover of night my friend Hillel Landau and I stilled our gnawing hunger with the unexpected gift. In the morning, I thanked Dr. Bachner heartily, but he only shrugged his shoulders and pretended total ignorance.

That night I told him that if I was not too fatigued after returning from work I would oblige him and teach him a little of the Torah and Talmud. So it came to be that each evening I would satiate his burning curiosity with stories of Moshe Rabbeinu, the Ten Commandments which were given on Sinai, the miracles which occurred at the Exodus from Egypt, and a collection of stories from Gemara. He listened in wide-eyed wonder. Occasionally I would find a piece of bread tossed into my bed.

Dr. Bachner had acquaintances in the camp who used to come and converse with him every evening. They were doctors who worked in the camp hospital — Dr. Shperber, a stomach specialist, and Dr. Ettinger. They noticed that Dr. Bachner had been spending some time with me lately, and they asked him, "Who is this youth?"

"A Polish Jew," he answered. "He is a decent fellow."

Dr. Bachner asked them to assist him in providing me with food. The doctors were in a position to obtain food since their patients were all allotted a plate of soup which was not always eaten; a patient may have died or occasionally was not able to eat. It soon turned out that the two distinguished doctors also became my willing disciples, they, too, being interested in knowing about Judaism despite being totally assimilated.

Apart from my difficult work under the taskmaster Martin Shmitz, I now had three eager students to contend with. I had to have a supply of stories from the Gemara and tales of Chassidic Rebbes ever ready. The doctors had an unquenchable thirst for knowledge, and they

Szwientochlovitz

enjoyed my *shiurim* so much that in return they provided me with a plate of soup every day without fail. They had never heard of the concept of Chassidus, and my tales of the *chesed* and miracles carried out by Chassidic Rebbes fascinated them immensely.

Even worse than the ravaging hunger were the severe beatings and lack of adequate protection from the bitter, relentless cold. In the biting frost of winter 1944, when we were forced to dig pits for a sewer system and I dug with my spade on the frozen ground, flashes of fire sprang up from the impact. I was reminded of the curse "Your ground will become hard as copper."

SZWIENTOCHLOVITZ

By this time I was emaciated from working under the intolerable conditions of insufficient food and lack of winter clothing. The soup which I received from the doctors each evening, hurriedly consumed in one of the hospital latrines so that nobody would discover this treasured secret, proved to be my salvation in those dark and dismal days. The hard labor and murderous beatings which Martin Shmitz so generously showered on me became that much more bearable. Once again, I was shown from Heaven that I would not be deserted.

Infused with new courage and optimism, I began to scheme how I could rid myself of this *Kommando* once and for all. I longed to work in the cannon factory, because the workers there fared much better, for a number of reasons. Firstly, they were sheltered and did not suffer from exposure to the elements. Secondly, their *kapo* was a relatively decent Pole, whereas mine was a ruthless beast who had developed an extra hatred toward me and always sought me out for the most difficult work and toughest beatings. He spitefully called me the *"Talmud Jude,"* and I began to have the uneasy premonition that he was seeking an opportunity to finish me off. I decided to take advantage of my ever-growing friendship with the doctors and asked them to try and get me out of the *kapo* Martin's *Kommando*. Unfortunately, the doctors were unable to assist me in my plight; they themselves were in mortal fear of the notorious *kapo*.

The Visit of the Red Cross

The Nazis were eager to deceive the world into believing that their prisoners were being treated decently, and they agreed to allow a delegation of International Red Cross representatives in to inspect the concentration camps.

The S.S. commander of Szwientochlovitz prepared well for the upcoming visit. His first step in this direction was to ensure that only the prisoners who still had some semblance of well-being would queue up for food at the camp kitchen. The remaining emaciated prisoners would have to starve in their respective barracks until the delegation left. Needless to say, the horrible sights of walking skeletons, the decaying bones of the murdered inmates, and the battered bodies of prisoners were put well out of the way.

However, we did benefit from the visit to some degree. That day we were given a concentrated potato soup from which the members of the delegation themselves tasted a plateful. They licked their lips, nodded their heads in approval, and went away fully satisfied that the inmates were well treated. Thus the Nazis managed to hide their barbarous atrocities, deceiving the entire world into believing their unforgivable lies.

Sunday Afternoon

Every Sunday afternoon we were given free time to do our washing, alterations, or other necessary work. The Russian inmates utilized this time to dig an underground tunnel leading to the other side of the camp's zealously guarded, electrified barbed-wire fence. Their work quarters were stationed in a barracks where construction materials such as spades, forks, and axes were kept. Every Sunday afternoon they gathered in that barracks, and while part of them worked on the tunnel, the others would sit around and sing to drown out the noise of the digging and to obliterate any suspicion. It was an amazing feat: they managed to conceal the earth they had dug up and succeeded in keeping their plan from being discovered until its conclusion.

In the winter of 1944 the Russian inmates triumphantly broke through the tunnel and escaped to the outside world. In the middle of a Sunday night, nine prisoners made their escape — seven Russians, one Pole, and one Jew. The S.S. guard who was on duty at the watchtower noticed suspicious movements in the darkness and immediately began shooting at the objects. However, not one of his bullets reached their target. None of the Russians were recaptured, but the Pole and the Jew were discovered and brought back to the camp. On my way to the camp in Buno I came across the unfortunate Jew. He was pale and trembling with terror, for he knew well what penalty awaited him.

SZWIENTOCHLOVITZ

One of the seven Russians who escaped was a man named Loka, a decent fellow. He worked in the camp as a cook and thereby managed to steal a hefty chunk of bread from the kitchen for the escapees to take with them. It was truly a marvel that he had succeeded in squeezing his heavy bulk through the narrow tunnel.

Starvation

The following incident happened in August 1944. In Szwientochlovitz there worked a German *kapo* from Berlin by the name of Waldemir Heinz, a political prisoner deported for being a member of the Communist party. He was an exceptionally decent chap, which was an extremely rare occurrence. He supervised the inmates who worked in the kitchen cellar. One day I was sent to the kitchen cellar to peel potatoes. My fellow workers whispered to me that I could smuggle out a few raw potatoes and the *kapo* would turn a blind eye. I immediately found myself a partner in crime, and, tying our pants together at the bottom, we dropped potatoes down our shirts where they landed in our trousers. Together we managed to accumulate some forty potatoes in this way.

However, we were not in luck. On our way out of the cellar we were accosted by one of the S.S., who inspected us and discovered our carefully concealed treasures. He counted forty potatoes and conscientiously noted down the number in his notebook. He then accorded us a thorough beating and sent us on our way with the parting words, "Tonight the commander himself will come to confiscate your loot." The German *kapo* was in even greater trouble than we were, for he was accused of the robbery being done with his consent.

It occurred to me that I could minimize the severity of our crime. I let it be known amongst my fellow peelers that I was exchanging big potatoes for small ones. I was immediately bombarded by prospective customers who were even prepared to throw in a piece of bread for the exchange. My forty large potatoes were quickly transformed into forty tiny ones. When the commander came that night he saw that our robbery consisted of minute little potatoes. "These are mere food for pigs!" he said in disgust, but thankfully he did not beat us. Our penalty

The Vanished City of Tsanz

was to wash the latrines — an ordeal preferable to a beating any time.

Once, when we were being apportioned our measly bit of watery soup at dinnertime, a sudden cramp overcame me. Unable to eat, I asked a doctor whom I figured to be a better sort to watch my soup. I excused myself, but when I came back I realized that my guard had eaten my portion. What could I do? If I would report this, the doctor would shot, and I would still remain soupless. So I held my peace and did not say a word. However, my stomach protested. I desperately craved that soup to still my starving hunger. In the afternoon, famished to the core, my suffering brought me to tears. When the *kapo* Waldemir Heinz asked me what was the matter, I tearfully poured out my tale of woe. In reply he promised to give me his portion after work, assuring me that he was not in such great need of it.

Waldemir kept his word. As he handed me his soup he added philosophically, "Remember, my child, what I will tell you now. You are still young and in all likelihood will survive this war. You will see that it is always the victim who weeps and not the attacker. In theory it should be the rogue that ate your soup who should be crying, for he committed a grave misdeed. Yet in practice it is you, the innocent one, who weeps."

The *kapo* Waldemir suffered many beatings at the hands of the Nazis for his kindheartedness to his underlings, yet he laughed at his tormentors in their faces.

One day, as we stood at *appel*, three S.S. men ambled toward us. One of them, Frenzel, the chief of the cannon factory of Szwientochlovitz, was dressed in ordinary civilian clothing. He called out in a voice for all to hear that anyone who was a *machinen dreier* or *berufs shlosser* should report to him at once.

An inexplicable urge told me to enlist myself as *machinen dreier* even though I had not the foggiest notion what this meant. I figured that genuine workers would also volunteer, and I would somehow manage to work together with them. At least this way I would finally rid myself of the despised *kapo* Martin. Boldly, I walked up to the three S.S. men and reported myself as a *machinen dreier*.

SZWIENTOCHLOVITZ

Beating a Jew to death

To my terrible misfortune, not a single other person volunteered his services. The S.S. group doubtfully sized me up from head to toe, assessing my abilities. One of them asked me with narrowed eyes, "Are you a *machinen dreier?*"

"*Jawhol*," I replied confidently, while inside I quaked with fear.

"How many years did you work in this field?" I was asked.

"Three years," I fabricated on the spot.

"Which sort of machines did you work with?" my interrogator persisted. "Large *drei bank* or small *drei bank?*"

I had not the slightest inkling what he meant. Being a small and skinny lad I took a chance and said, "Small *drei bank.*" One of the S.S. men waved with his hand and said, "You are assuredly only a *dreier* and swindler like all the Jews."

I did not respond to his accusation and shrugged my shoulders, straight-faced. In truth he was correct, for I had never in my life even set eyes on a *drei bank*; the only *"bank"* I knew of was my bench in the yeshivah.

Being the only one to have reported for this work, I was sent to the cannon factory and delivered into the hands of the chief of the *drei machinen* department, Klein, a middle-aged fellow. He led me into the work hall to a machine so enormous that I could not even take it all in with one glance. He began to explain to me exactly what my task was. "The handle above is 5,000 k.v.; the handle below is 2,500 k.v." and other technical jargon which sounded like Chinese to me.

The Vanished City of Tsanz

After ten minutes of seeing my stony, expressionless face and getting no reaction, he began to perceive the extent of my knowledge in this field. He flew into a mighty rage and yelled, "Cursed dog! You will immediately be sent back to the camp and sentenced to death! You are no professional but a liar and swindler like all the Jews."

I waited in silence until Klein had finished his tirade. I saw that my life was hanging on a thread and like a drowning man clutching on a straw began to plead, "Herr Meister Klein, please let me say a few words. You are right. I indeed said a lie, but only because of my desperate situation. My father, mother, brothers, and sisters all perished in the gas chambers of Auschwitz and Birkenau. I am the sole survivor of my family. I so much desired to stay alive that I really didn't have a choice but to report as a professional in order to escape the hands of the ruthless killer Martin Shmitz."

Seeing that he was beginning to mellow, I continued to beg, "What benefit will you have if I will be shot? Please, I so much want to live." By this time, I was crying.

Finally, I managed to soften his heart with my pleas. This was only because in Heaven I was ordained to outlive the war.

"Fine, lad! You are in luck. I will not send you back to the camp," he replied magnanimously.

Filled with gratitude, I promised to do the most difficult work for him, and I would never forget his generous favor if he would not send me back.

Meister Klein assigned me a transport task. I was given a trolley and told to transport cannon parts from one machine to the next and from one working unit to the next. That day I *bentched gomel* twice, once for finally escaping the *Kommando* of the *kapo* Martin, *y"s*, and the second time for not being killed for being caught in a lie.

(After the war Martin Shmitz was sentenced in a German court to a mere eight-year imprisonment despite being a mass murderer, since unfortunately not enough people remained alive to give testimony to his murderous deeds.)

The Page of Gemara

The factory in Szwientochlovitz manufactured cannons for the purpose of shooting down aircraft. The various parts of the cannons were wrapped in assorted packaging, among them pages of the *Vilna Shas*. A youth from Bochnia, a Bobover Chassid, also worked in the cannon factory, and one day he came across a page from *masseches Yoma, daf* 38. He carefully concealed the page in his pocket and later handed it to me, knowing that I would derive untold joy from once more fingering a page of Gemara. I hid the precious page, and when I had a moment when I happened not to have any parts to transport, I stood at a side with my trolley and under cover of a large *drei bank* began perusing the page. I did not know, however, that I was being observed.

After a while, a sixth sense told me to turn around. To my horror, I came face to face with the leering countenance of the S.S. man *Obershafuhrer* Leitmeyer. Paralyzed with fear, I stared back at him for I knew very well that "Talmud" was a dirty word to the Germans. *Der Sturmer*, the Hitlerite newspaper, always wrote poisonous slander against the Jews, quoting references from the Talmud against the gentiles.

I hastily threw the paper on the ground, hoping he would not pursue the issue. However, he yelled at me, "Pick up what you have just thrown down immediately!" I hurriedly obeyed.

"Read what it says there," he ordered. I answered him that I did not understand the language; I had just found the paper and was trying to figure out what was written on it.

The S.S. man summoned the intellectuals of our work force, French, Dutch, Greeks, but they all looked puzzled, trying to make head or tail out of the squiggles they saw, some of them even studiously reading the page upside down. Among those whom he consulted was a Pole who told him that he could not read it, but he was certain that it was a page of the Jewish Talmud.

As soon as the S.S. man heard the word "Talmud" his ears perked up. Infuriated, he slapped me hard twice and shrieked, "You swine! Dog! You are studying Talmud during work?"

At that moment he was approached by a French Jew who told him that he knew somebody who could read Talmud. He pointed to the Bochnian youth who had given me the fateful page. The youth was promptly summoned and asked if he could read the language. As soon as he caught sight of me standing near the S.S. guard he trembled in fear for he thought I had reported him. I quietly assured the poor youth that the S.S. fellow was not a terribly brutal man, since he had not killed me on the spot but was satisfied with two slaps. He was only fiercely determined to know what was written in the "dangerous Talmud."

The Bochnian youth could not speak German, only Yiddish, so the S.S. ordered me to tell him to read and translate the page into Yiddish. He then called a Belgian Jew who knew German and Yiddish to interpret the lad's words.

The Bochnian boy began expounding on the *gemara*. That particular page told the story of Nikanor, who went to Egypt in order to purchase gates for the Beis HaMikdash. The Gemara relates the following:

SZWIENTOCHLOVITZ

Nikanor went to Alexandria in Egypt to bring the gates for the Temple. On his return journey to Akko, a strong wind threatened to overturn the ship. The captain ordered all the heavy objects to be thrown overboard in order to prevent the ship from sinking. One of the gates was also thrown into the sea. Seeing that the storm was still going strong, the passengers wanted to throw the second door overboard, too. But Nikanor put his arms round the gate and said, "If you throw the second door into the sea, I go, too." As soon as he said these noble words the waves died down. Upon their arrival to the port in Akko, the first door floated up from under the ship. When the gate was installed in the Temple it was named *"Sha'ar Nikanor,"* in memory of the wondrous miracle which happened to him.

The S.S. man was somewhat appeased, seeing that the Talmud consisted of other material apart from instructions on how to swindle gentiles. He ordered the number on my hand, 161421, to be noted down, and later I was given twenty-five lashes for pausing and reading during work.

Suspected of Sabotage

At the end of summer 1944, when we had more or less adjusted to our suffering and misery, a new trouble befell us. There was a constant underlying sense of friction and jealousy among the inmates, who were always afraid that their fellow prisoners had it that bit more comfortable than themselves. An especially venomous jealousy was felt toward the Jewish doctors, Dr. Shperber and Dr. Ettinger, and other people in a similar position who were able, via their connections, to procure for themselves an extra bit of food.

One of the inmates in our camp, the *lagerelteste*, was the first prisoner to be sent to Auschwitz. He had the number one tattooed on his arm. He had been convicted of murder in a German court and sentenced to life imprisonment. These sort of prisoners were usually appointed *lagerelteste* or *blockelteste* since they were well versed in the ways and means of murder. Another murderer, fifty-year-old Bruno Bradnievitch, had been removed from prison and sent to our concentration camp in order to fully utilize his talents as a killer.

These two murderers, Bruno and Martin, put their evil minds together to hatch a plot which would ensure the killing of the people they loathed, people who had too much intelligence for their liking. Their blacklist included a father and son from Berlin by the name of Schwartz, men of Polish descent who worked as electricians. They also had their eye on a German inmate by the name of Heinz, the *blockelteste* of block 2, a good friend of the doctors Ettinger and Shperber.

The two scheming rogues fabricated an accusation against the *blockelteste* Heinz and against the doctors. I was summoned after curfew and ordered to sign my name to the written accusation. It read as follows:

"On the tenth of August 1994, Dr. Ettinger, Dr. Shperber, and other partners in crime schemed to blow up the S.S. barracks which is situated at the entrance of the camp Szwientochlovitz. They planned to use four boxes of explosives which they prepared. The deed was to be carried out by the father and son Schwartz, the camp electricians, whose tasks included checking the double rows of electrified wire running around the camp every evening. They were to attach the explosives to the wire which would later explode and blow up the S.S. barracks. Until the deed was accomplished, the explosives were to be concealed in a death cellar." (Every body which had been shot or hung was stored in a death cellar until it was delivered to Auschwitz to be burnt or made into soap.)

The *kapo* Martin told me in no roundabout way that they explicitly needed my signature since I had connections with the doctors.

For one moment I stood immobile, stunned by the sheer audacity of the slanderous libel. I gathered my wits together and said, "How can you expect me to give my signature to something I know nothing about?"

The *kapo* Martin turned to his friend and mockingly said, "This is a criminal *Talmud Jude* who knows well what we are referring to but likes to play the fool." When he realized that I had not the slightest intention of signing an accusation against innocent people, he yelled at me, "Disappear to your block immediately! Your end will come together with the accused!"

I returned to my barracks and lay down. But sleep eluded me. My hands and feet literally trembled with fear, and my heart was heavy. I was afraid of what fate had in store for me.

I did not have to wait long. At midnight the *kapo* Martin entered the barracks accompanied by the S.S. commandant of the camp. I was ordered to dress and go with them. I was taken to the doctors' sleeping quarters and ordered to take all their belongings to the S.S. block which was situated at the entrance of the camp. As I entered the block I encountered the doctors and the other accused assembled there.

We were steeped in a plot of sabotage, they informed us. They took us outside and stationed us between the two sets of electrified barbed wire which ran around the camp. We were positioned three meters apart and strictly warned not to speak to each other.

I was the youngest of all the condemned, and, overcome by fatigue, my head dropped toward the electrified wire a couple of times. The S.S. guard on duty warned me, "Watch out! You will die if your head touches the wire!" Once again, I was shown from above that I was destined to live, and live I would, despite the many incidents which should have spelled my death. We were made to stand in this manner the entire long, seemingly endless night, until finally morning broke.

The following day, at noon, two judges arrived from Auschwitz, and we were led indoors, one by one. I watched as each one of the accused emerged from that interrogation with eyes heavy from lack of sleep, their bodies beaten. Soon my turn arrived. I was convicted, they read off a paper, of preparing a case packed with four dozen explosives in the cellar, for the purpose of blowing up the S.S. barracks. The accusation was signed by two witnesses, Manfried and Roth. I tried to plead my innocence, but it was to no avail. One of the judges screamed at me, "Hold your tongue! Your place is on the gallows."

The Vanished City of Tsanz

After each of the accused was interrogated we were led to the same spot where we had spent the night — between the two rows of barbed wire.

At this point, a most wondrous miracle occurred. Before the last interrogation had been carried out, an S.S. man arrived, the commander of all the camp hospitals in Auschwitz, who was on very good terms with the doctors. That day he had planned to visit a different camp, and his arrival at Szwientochlovitz was totally unprecedented.

When the S.S. commander approached the camp entrance, he was astonished to see the doctors standing three meters apart between two rows of barbed wire. He walked up to the doctors and asked them what on earth they were doing there. The S.S. guard advised him not to speak to the doctors for they were guilty of sabotage. The commander snapped at him, "What? Impossible. It is impossible that the doctors would do sabotage. This is only the result of jealousy of the other inmates." He marched into the judges' room and in a rage protested the innocence of the doctors. "They have no need to harm their masters. They lead a good life here; even better than at home. I know four of these worthy people well. They have no reason to risk their lives. I myself guarantee the innocence of the doctors," he lashed out in fury.

The judges took his words into consideration and nullified their verdict of hanging. However, our penalty was not completely lifted, and we were made to wear an IL sign with a red circle on the front and rear of our jackets, an indication that we were suspected of sabotage. This was a great blow to the morale of the doctors, for it meant they could not treat the S.S. outside the camp,

Bruno Bradnievitch

SZWIENTOCHLOVITZ

since the letters IL meant "remain in *Lager*."

With gratitude and overwhelming joy, I thanked Hashem for saving me from certain death. However, the story did not end there. Soon a command was issued in the camp that all those bearing an IL sign with a red point were to be transferred to a different camp as a further penalty. In ordinary circumstances this meant being sent to the coal mines in Yavishovitz or Yavorzhna. Few people emerged alive from there. But we were destined to live. We were sent to Buno-Monovitz.

The two false witnesses, Manfried and Roth, were hung after their deception was revealed. The S.S. added these words: "We need these tattletales, but we do not like them. As long as we need them, that's how long we let them stay alive."

CHAPTER 9

FROM BUNO
TO LIBERATION

Буно

As soon as we arrived at the Buno concentration camp, the doctors volunteered their professional services. The S.S. man who greeted us was *Hauptsturmfuhrer* Dr. Konig. He recognized Dr. Shperber and Dr. Ettinger as his fellow students in a Czechoslovakian university. As soon as he saw them he demanded, "What is this insignia that you are wearing — the IL and the red mark on your clothing?" They related their experience to him. Dr. Konig immediately ordered the removal of our mark of shame, and the doctors were given distinguished positions in the camp hospital.

I was assigned to *Kommando* 62 — the electrical *Kommando*. Experience had taught me that it was always more advisable to enlist as a professional.

My sleeping quarters was block 3. It was a dreaded barracks, the *blockeletste* being Alfred Vedel, a bloodthirsty half-Jew from Berlin.

As I walked into the block I heard somebody announce that if anybody present was a professional barber, he should present himself to him. Knowing that a barber would receive a plate of soup prior to beginning work, I volunteered my services. I received my soup and quickly ate it. I was then given a pair of clippers and set to work.

378

Naturally, the machine was faulty, with a few teeth missing, and I was no professional. As soon as I began my work, my clients protested, "Ow! It hurts. You are no barber!"

I knew well that they were right, but I begged them not to complain since I had already eaten the soup, and the barbarous *blockelteste* was liable to kill me. I promised my customers that if they would tolerate my amateur efforts as barber just this one time I would never again volunteer. The result was that I gained a plate of warm soup, which was worth everything involved in getting it!

Clean Feet

The *blockelteste* used to organize a "feet inspection" every second day. Woe to the one whose feet weren't meticulously clean. He was mercilessly beaten to a pulp. Washing ourselves in Buno was no mean feat, since the wash barracks was situated in the center of the camp, quite a distance from our barracks. When we came home from work in the evening, totally exhausted after standing on our feet for twelve long hours, we did not have the strength to tackle that long walk.

Knowing this well, the feet inspection only served to give the *blockelteste* Alfred Vedel an excuse to beat those who simply could not muster the energy required to wash themselves.

It happened once that I was in no physical shape to undertake the long walk to the wash barracks after a particularly strenuous day. After curfew, at 8 P.M., Alfred Vedel announced the dreaded words "Feet inspection!"

I became hot and cold all over from sheer terror. I knew that my feet were hopelessly black since that day I had worked in the cable *Kommando*. Luck was with me, and this time he began his inspection at the other end of the block. I made use of the time this allowed me to wash and scrub my feet with my saliva and dry them with the underside of my cover. I watched in trepidation as he went from one inmate to the next, until he arrived at my bunk.

"Stick out your feet," he barked. I obliged and with the help of a pocket flashlight he carefully examined my extended feet, starting from the toes and continuing upwards.

"Well, you are the cleanest man of the entire block," he declared. As a reward, he handed me a pair of whole shoes to replace my torn ones.

Davening Ma'ariv

On Sukkos 1944, I got nine men to assemble at my bed in order to make a minyan for *ma'ariv* after the lights were out. The prayers were said quietly and without any undue noise. However, Alfred Vedel heard something going on, so he began beating a few suspects. None of his beatings reached the true culprits, and we members of the minyan escaped unscathed.

I was later told that at the death march of Buchenwald before the liberation the inmates turned upon Alfred Vedel and killed him.

My Prayer for a German

As mentioned above, my policy was always to enlist as a professional. They had greater chances of staying alive as they did not have to do harsh labor while standing outdoors suffering from hunger and cold with inadequate clothing. In line with this policy I worked as an electrician in Buno.

In the electrical *Kommando* 62, my taskmaster was Florian, a German from Obershlesian, Katowitz. He was not a particularly brutal man, but he had one weak point: he was in constant terror of being sent to the eastfront.

One afternoon, Florian caught me davening *minchah* and snapped at me, "Don't you know that you may not pause during work?" I answered that I had been praying to G-d for the health of all His subjects, and for the health of Master Florian.

"If so," mused Florian, "perhaps you can ask your G-d not to send me to the army, since I am afraid to go to the eastfront. If you succeed in persuading your beloved G-d not to send me to the army," he promised me, "I will be good to all of you in this *Kommando*, and none of you will be overworked."

FROM BUNO TO LIBERATION

I spoke in all sincerity with a Jewish companion with whom I worked. "We must pray hard for the well-being of Master Florian, for this will prove very beneficial for us." (This Jewish companion was from Sakmar; unfortunately, I do not recall his name. He was a refined and gentle person, a great scholar. He told me that he had been a *dayan* in Sakmar. He later died at my feet when Buno and Auschwitz were liquidated and we were transported in open wagons to Buchenwald in January 1945.)

Together we recited a few chapters of Tehillim by heart. When we had finished, I walked over to Master Florian and told him that we had arranged with our G-d that he would remain with us in Buno until the termination of the war. He was not satisfied with my promise and demanded a guarantee. Only then would he see to it that we would not be overworked. I immediately agreed, telling him I was even willing to give him a written statement.

My partner, the Sakmarer *dayan*, wondered at my daring deed. "How can you guarantee him 100 percent?" he asked. He was especially concerned after hearing Master Florian threaten that if this arrangement with G-d proved to be untrue and he would be sent to the eastfront, he would beat me to death. I answered him that the risk I had taken was minimal. Firstly, the merit of benefiting so many Jews with lighter work would surely stand in my stead. Secondly, if he were to be sent to the eastfront, the chances that he would live to come back and take revenge were very slim indeed.

Once Master Florian went home to Katowitz for the weekend. He came back raging with anger, waving a red note before my eyes. The note was an order for him to appear at army headquarters in Katowitz. Fuming at me for having fooled him, he yelled at me thunderously, "Well, what do you say now?"

I quickly responded that the red note was meaningless. "My beloved G-d promised me that you will stay here; therefore you need not despair. However, you must make an effort on your own behalf, because we Jews believe that G-d says, 'Do something and I will help you.' You told me that your father is eighty-six years old, your mother is dead, and your two brothers are in the army. You must send a request for exemption to the military chief, saying that you cannot desert your father."

My idea appealed to him, and he followed my advice. He sent his request by express delivery to Katowitz. When he traveled home for the holidays, my heart beat rapidly with fear that my "miracle" would not work and my life would be at stake. But, thank G-d, the "miracle" succeeded. Master Florian came back from his holiday vacation in high spirits, bringing me a small bread as a token of appreciation for his exemption from the army. He indeed kept his word, and we did not have to work very hard under his jurisdiction for the duration of our stay in Buno.

Our work consisted of dragging electrical wire backwards and forwards through the length of a tunnel in a massive factory named Buno Works. He warned us that if we heard the sound of heavy army boots, we should prepare for an inspection by the S.S. and make ourselves look busier than usual until they would pass and we could once again resume our casual speed.

The light work and the fact that it was done in a warm, protected tunnel lessened our constant hunger pangs to some degree and prepared us for the future troubles which lay in store for us — the torturous death march we were made to suffer on the way to Buchenwald when the concentration camp Buno was liquidated.

The Liquidation of Buno

On Thursday, January 18, 1945, Auschwitz and Buno were liquidated due to the advance of the Russian army. We were hastily gathered together and led on foot to Glievitz in a journey lasting the entire night. In Glievitz we lay under the open sky, deprived of food until the following night. We were then packed like sardines into roofless oxen wagons, one hundred people to each wagon, exposed to the bitter cold and falling snow.

The S.S. sat in the watchtowers built at the end of the wagon, observing us keenly lest we dare try to escape. We did not receive any food or drink, apart from the two or three breads which the S.S. tossed into each wagon. A fierce battle ensued in which the stronger ones managed to snatch a precious chunk of bread while the weaker ones were trampled. The Sakmarer *dayan* who had worked with me in Buno was trampled right near my feet as he tried to get himself a bit of food. He was thrown off the wagon, together with all the other corpses who had died of hunger or cold on that dreadful journey.

We stilled our thirst with the falling snow. The sensation of the cold fluid going down our parched throats was heavenly. However, the snow which fell on our heads proved to be too little to quench the thirst of all the people, so we thought of a strategy. We removed pieces of string from the dead bodies which lay around us in abundance and tied them together, attaching a small bucket at the end. We dropped the bucket on the ground, and as the train sped along, snow was gathered in the bucket. The S.S. begrudged us even this bit of snow and tried to shoot at the string, thereby severing the bucket. Thankfully, they failed in their efforts.

As we traveled through Czechoslovakia, on our way to Buchenwald, the train entered a tunnel, slowing down as it did so. It was dawn, and a few Czech gentiles were on their way to work. When they espied the tragic scene of thousands of prisoners being sent off to labor camps in roofless wagons, they took pity on us and threw us their bread. The S.S., however, confiscated the food they had given us and shot in the air a couple of times to scare off our benefactors.

Finally, after two whole days of this nightmarish journey, the train arrived at Buchenwald. Here our troubles began anew. Weak from hunger and exhaustion, I barely managed to stumble to my barracks, block 59. We were given new numbers which were not tattooed on our bodies but on our clothing. I now bore the number 122377 in addition to the number I had received in Auschwitz, 161421. I cannot recall if we received food that day or not, I only remember that the *kapo*s and the delousing service checked us from head to toe to see if we carried any valuables on us. Apart from an abundance of lice, they found nothing.

The following morning, when I was woken up, I realized that the bodies on either side of me were frigid — deathly cold. I tried to wake them, but there was no response. Sadly, by now I was used to coming in contact with dead bodies, and I did not recoil in fear. The other inmates soon discovered that one of the corpses had two gold teeth and they promptly set to work removing them. I was fortunate that I did not have a part in this extraction, for the *blockelteste* beat the two inmates to a bloody pulp. They were not beaten for having desecrated the bodies, but for having stolen what rightfully belonged to the *blockelteste* and *kapo*s.

That January, Buchenwald was packed with thousands of inmates who had been gathered together from all the camps in the vicinity of Auschwitz. There was no room to accommodate them all, and they died like flies, suffering from hunger and exposure to the outdoors in the bitter cold. In reality, Hitler, *y"s*, had issued a command that all the remaining inmates must be exterminated, but the S.S. knew well that when there were no camps left to run, they would be sent to the eastfront, which spelled certain death. They

At work in Buchenwald

wanted the concentration camps to remain at all costs, and it was for this reason that we were not all eliminated.

After we had been in Buchenwald a few days, they began selecting professionals — barbers and *machinen drier*. In tune with my longstanding principle, I signed up as a professional in order to be able to work indoors. I was one of fifty other workers. We were sent to Zonnenberg, where there was a factory for airplane parts (originally a toy factory).

During the first week, my work consisted of cleaning up a lot adjacent to a hospital for wounded Hungarian soldiers. Once, I was scrounging through a heap of rubbish in search of some food, when an S.S. guard caught me. When we returned to camp I received a penalty of twenty-five lashes. One S.S. firmly gripped my head while two others hit me alternately on my backside with leather whips which were entwined with steel wires. When the excruciating ordeal was over, they yelled at me, "Get out of sight!"

I was so beaten that there was no way I could move. They continued beating me until I collapsed in a dead faint. They poured cold water over me and ordered two inmates to carry me to my barracks. The next day my body was swollen and bruised with welts, yet I was forced to go to work as usual. The swelling did not go down for two weeks after the in-

A beating on the backside

The Vanished City of Tsanz

cident, but Hashem gave me the stamina to endure this, too.

My next assignment was in the factory, one weekday shift and one weeknight shift. During the night shift we received a bit of watery soup at midnight. One of the nights happened to be Pesach, in April 1945. Just before midnight the German *Ubermiester* of the factory announced that "despite it being *Sonnenabend* (Passover) we would receive no soup, as penalty for the fact that the bread which he had brought to work that day had been stolen." Whether this was true or not, nobody knew.

We sat at our machines and quietly murmured extracts of the Haggadah in the tune of Eichah. "*Avadim anachnu l'Hitler, y"s, b'Germany ub'ezras Hashem...* — We are slaves to Hitler, *y"s*, in Germany, but with the help of Hashem we will outlive them and live to see our salvation."

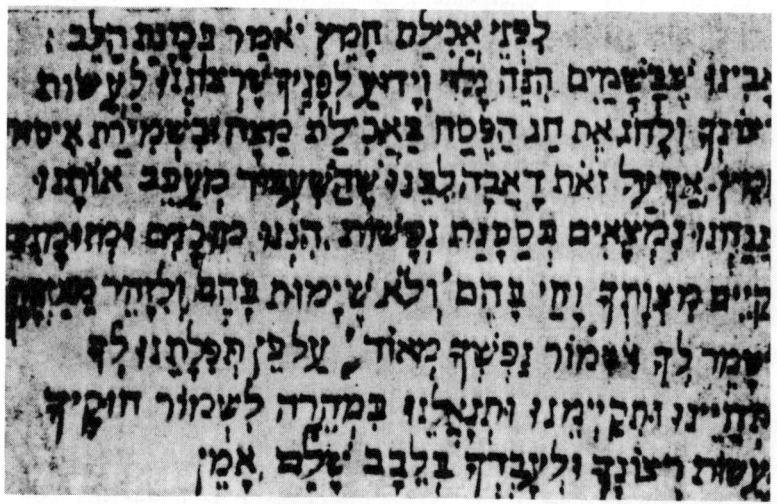

A Pesach prayer said in the camps

The Death March

The death march began the last day of Pesach. With the steady advance of the American and Russian armies, the S.S. began leading us through mountains and valleys to avoid confrontation with them. This was in violation of Hitler's order that every last remaining Jew should be shot so that they would not live to gloat over his downfall. As already mentioned, the S.S. were willing to keep us so that they would not have to fight the enemy.

Approximately 500 of us walked out of the gates of Zonnenberg, yet merely 240 people were liberated. The remaining prisoners were shot when they did not have the physical strength to continue walking. One S.S. guard watched out for people who were dragging their feet or leaning on someone else. He would kick the weakened victim so that he stumbled and fell, whereupon he would shoot him.

The last two weeks before the liberation a lot of people who had managed to endure the intense suffering in the concentration camps collapsed. We were forced to march on foot with no food. In desperation we ate the grass which we saw on the way, and an earnest conversation ensued about which sort of grass was tastier. In addition, the persistent lice almost consumed us alive, and we had no facilities to wash ourselves.

The S.S. killers knew how to fend for themselves. On the way they killed a horse and roasted its flesh. The tantalizing smell was pure torture. We were permitted to drink water from a nearby lake, and, cupping the water in our hands, we drank thirstily. We continued walking on foot through Carlesbad and Marinbad. In Marinbad we slept under a roof for one night.

Our S.S. escort was an Austrian from Vienna. When he noticed that the village we had just entered was surrounded by American soldiers he attempted to play at being a decent guard. Suddenly, he began to talk to us gently, assuring us that we should not be afraid; he was planning to surrender to the American troops, and he would ensure that no harm would befall us. Soon, however, an S.S. man rode up to him on a horse and informed him that one part of the village was unguarded and we could march out through there. Like a puff of smoke, the geniality of the commandant vanished, and, resuming his original bestiality, he gruffly snapped at us to march further.

Meanwhile, three inmates had hidden themselves in a canal pipe. The S.S. commandant ordered his soldiers to shoot them through both ends of the pipe. The corpses of the three inmates remained wedged inside.

The next day we were surrounded by two small American tanks. The soldiers shot in the air to scare the Nazis into surrendering. The S.S. immediately displayed a white flag. They preferred to give themselves into the hands of the Americans, who would treat them as war prisoners, rather than the Russians, who would promptly settle with them on the spot.

The Liberation

Tuesday, 25 Iyar, May 8, 1945. With Hashem's help, the yoke of our Nazi oppressors was finally removed by the American army. We must have appeared to our American liberators as insane. We were wild for food; the first morsel of food which I received from an American soldier was a sugar cube. I swallowed it whole, paper and all. We were so oppressed by our years of enslavement that it took a while for us to adjust to a life of freedom.

My first free step was to go into a German farmer's house and ask him to wash and scrub my lice-infested body. Later, I fell ill and was taken to a temporary hospital. My body had become completely swollen as it had been deprived of food and water for so long that it could not withstand the large amount of fluid I swallowed after the liberation.

As I lay in the hospital bed, I was approached by a tall Russian official who asked us how he could be of service. I told him that we were not permitted to eat but only to drink milk. "If that is the case," he said, "follow me and I will provide you with milk."

My swollen feet could barely withstand my weight, but I nevertheless hobbled after him in the hope that he would give me some milk. Instead, he led me to a barn and, untying one of the cows who were kept there, gave me the rope, and said simply, "You need milk. Here is a cow."

I tried to explain to the officer that I was an invalid and I could barely drag my feet: how could I milk a cow? But the officer was adamant; I must take the cow to give me milk. I wearily pulled the cow along to oblige him, but as soon as the officer was out of sight, I breathed a sigh of relief and deserted the cow. The Russian officer meant well, but I could not use his favor. There was barely enough room for me in the hospital, never mind a cow.

"Born in Amsterdam"

After eighteen days in the hospital I gradually regained my strength and began planning for the future. I decided to pair up, for both practical and moral support, with another Jewish patient who was in the same position as I — lying in the hospital with no friends or relatives. His name was Jerry Weiss (today he lives in New Jersey). We traveled together to Pilsna, in Czechoslovakia, a displacement camp for concentration-camp survivors established under the auspices of the U.N.R.A. and the Red Cross. From there the survivors of the concentration camps were sent back to their country of origin.

I was determined not to set foot on the cursed Polish soil, where our parents, brothers, sisters, and millions of other *kedoshim* had perished. I therefore conspired with Jerry to report at the registration office that we were born in Holland. I had a vague recollection of an address in Holland, from a parcel which we had once received. There would be no documents to contradict our statement since the concentration camps had left us bereft of everything. My friend agreed that the story would be that we came from Keisergracht 186, Amsterdam.

The next morning we entered the office of the U.N.R.A. and queued in the line for Dutch citizens. We optimistically imagined that our ploy would go through without any hitches. Our turn finally arrived, and we entered the office. The officer asked us in German where we were born. I promptly replied, "Amsterdam, Keisergracht 186."

He then began speaking in Dutch to me. I did not understand a word of his speech. To add to my discomfort, my friend, who is prone to giggling fits, began laughing. When the officer saw our response, he perceived exactly what we were up to and ordered the door of his office to be locked.

When we were alone with him in his office, he turned to me and asked in Yiddish, "Are you Jewish?"

The Vanished City of Tsanz

"Yes," I replied.

"Why did you lie to me that you are Dutch?" he demanded.

"It is true that we were born in Poland and not in Holland," I admitted, "but we lost everything there — our parents, our family, our friends. We do not want to return to that cursed land for all the money in the world. We had no choice other than to lie about our birthplace."

The officer was moved to tears by my words. After a short silence he wondered aloud, "But how did you know the address in Amsterdam? The address actually exists?"

I replied that when we were in the Tsanzer ghetto, at the end of 1941, we had received a parcel of sustenance from Amsterdam. I went on to relate to him how my mother had wanted to cook with a tin of olive oil from the package, but my father had said that since it arrived just before Chanukah it should be used for beautifying the mitzvah of lighting the menorah. My mother had agreed, in spite of the terrible hunger we suffered then.

The officer listened with increasing admiration to my tale. When I had finished he said, "Right. It remains as you have said. I will hereby issue two documents stating that you were born in Amsterdam, Holland, Keisergracht 186. Tomorrow at 3 P.M. a military aircraft is transporting the Dutch survivors of the concentration camps back to their birthplace, Holland. Do not forget that you are Dutch!"

So it was. The following afternoon, at 3 P.M., a Red Cross automobile came to collect all the Dutch citizens, us among them. However, the airport in Amsterdam was out of action, because the runway had been bombed and as yet had not been repaired, so the aircraft was unable to land there. The airplane made a detour and landed in Brussels, Belgium.

CHAPTER 10

IN BELGIUM

To us it made not the slightest difference where we landed, for we had no relatives either in Holland or in Belgium. Our aim — that we should not be sent back to Poland — had been achieved. We arrived at Brussels on June 8, 1945, one month after the liberation.

At the airport the border police strictly controlled the entry of all the refugees, since many S.S. men had mingled among the freed inmates in an attempt to escape detection. It was easy for them to falsify their identity, because none of us possessed documents. However, the police had other means; every S.S. man had a tatoo engraved under his arm. With the help of this tell-tale sign, six or seven S.S. men who had tried to masquerade as refugees on our flight were arrested on the spot.

Our entire fortune consisted of a small, dried-out piece of bread and a small packet of butter. We were still under the effects of the terrible conditions in the concentration camps and therefore carefully hoarded the bread and butter for a worthier occasion. The food had been held in reserve for over two weeks already. As we entered the control room of the border police, the police chief wrinkled his nose and pinched his nostrils when the smell of the rotten butter wafted through the room. A torn picture of Hitler lay on the floor, and the officer bade us to discard the stale bread and the stinking butter on it.

The Vanished City of Tsanz

However, we were reluctant to surrender our precious possessions and stubbornly clung to them.

The chief realized that he was dealing with two concentration-camp survivors, and he ordered a policeman to bring bread, milk, and chocolate into the room. We ate till we could eat no longer, and then he patiently tried to explain to us that we could safely discard our rotten remains, since in Belgium there was no lack of food. Finally, we agreed to comply.

That night we slept at the gendarmerie, and the next day we were visited by members of Brussels' Jewish help committee who assured us that we were not alone in the world; they would concern themselves with our welfare.

The help committee gave us vouchers which allowed us to sleep in a hotel at their cost. We could not relish the luxury of an ordinary bed, since we were so used to sleeping on hard bunks. That night we slept on the floor. Gradually, however, we became accustomed to sleeping on a bed once more.

Rabbi Levi, *z"l*, presented us with brand-new tefillin, and the help committee arranged for a *tallis katan* to be sewn for each of us, according to a design which I had sketched. A kosher kitchen was established. Food was still being rationed in those days, but the Belgian government allowed concentration-camp survivors to receive a double ration.

During the day we had nowhere to go as we had no relatives in Brussels. If it happened to be a rainy day and we needed shelter, I and my companion, the Sosnovtzer Rav's son Reb Yaakov England, would board tram line 15 until the rain would subside. We chose line 15 because it circled the whole of Brussels, so we could travel round and round without being noticed.

One day, there was a particularly heavy downpour. After having covered the scope of Brussels twice, the conductor, puzzled at our peculiar behavior, approached us and tactfully asked us our destination, kindly offering to tell us where to disembark. We answered that we had no idea where our journey would lead us; we were simply seeking protection from the rain. He seemed amused and told us we could sit on

IN BELGIUM

the tram as long as we pleased, without having to pay the fare.

In Brussels I was treated by a Jewish doctor, Dr. P. Goldstein, who refused to receive payment for his services.

My fellow countryman from Tsanz, Mr. Yitzchak Gelb, offered to accommodate me in his home. His parents had been neighbors of mine in Tsanz. His father, Mr. Aryeh Leib Gelb, was shot in his home by the Gestapo chief Haman on April 29, 1942, and his mother was thrown out of the window of her second-floor apartment by Johann. She perished on the spot.

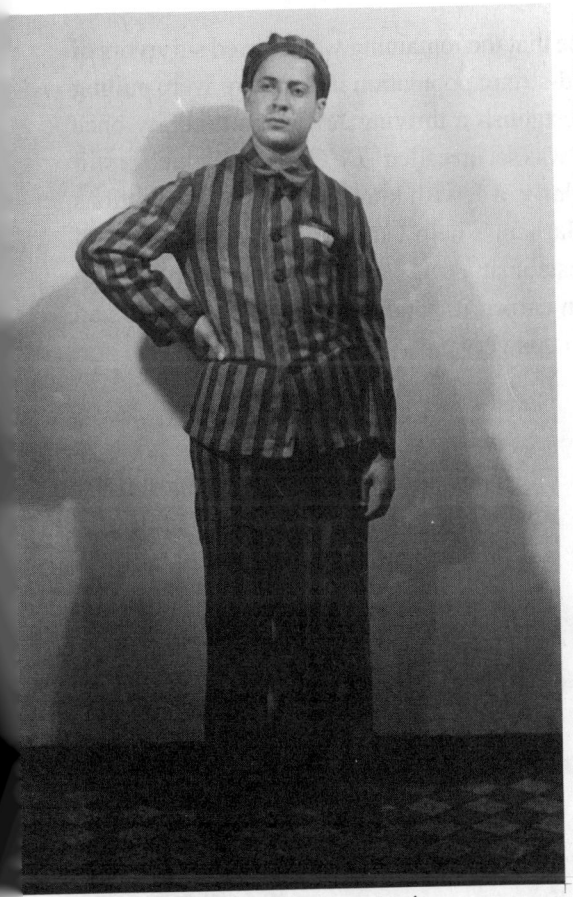

After a few months in Brussels I regained my strength to some degree and resolved to visit Antwerp, where I heard religious life was slowly being rebuilt. In Antwerp I met a few of my countrymen from Tsanz, and I came into contact with other Chassidic Jews. I decided then and there that this would be my permanent residence.

My very first earnings came thanks to the mitzvah of *kibbud av*. When I was a young boy in Tsanz, my father urged me to observe him knotting a *lulav* to learn the technique. I was totally uninterested then, but my father kept on

In Brussels in August 1945 after recuperation

The Vanished City of Tsanz

prodding me, saying that the extra knowledge couldn't harm me. Reluctantly I obliged. In Antwerp, as I passed a *sefarim* shop, the owner, Mr. Kahan, beckoned to me and said, "You are a Galicianer. Perhaps you can tie a *lulav?*" Mr. Avraham Drenger happened to be standing there, and he advised me to demand good payment for my services since Mr. Kahan would be unable to sell his merchandise without it. I asked for one thousand Belgian francs (a sizable amount in those days) and a *sefer*. He immediately agreed. And so it was that my first business deal was struck in the merit of the mitzvah of *kibbud av*.

I was delighted to see that the remaining war-scarred survivors of the former fifty-thousand-strong population in Antwerp were pulling themselves together to establish a thriving Jewish community once again. A help committee was set up called *"De Centrale"* which is still in existence today. Similarly, a Jewish kitchen and other institutions were organized. With Hashem's help I met my partner in life, and together we merited to establish a true Jewish home. Slowly, gradually, Antwerp once again earned its reputation for its generosity and kindness, which exists to this very day.

The *gabbaim* of the charity Rabbi Meir Ba'al HaNess Kollel Chibas Yerushalayim

IN BELGIUM

Let us hope that, in the merit of the generosity which exists in the Antwerp Jewish community, the present difficult financial situation will improve, and we will live to see revenge upon all our enemies who took part in the extermination of European Jewry. Above all, may we live to see the Final Redemption.

A Visit to Tsanz

About fifty years after the war I visited Tsanz. The trip had a tremendous effect on me, and it is superfluous even to try to describe my feelings at seeing my birthplace after so many years. At first glance it was difficult to recognize the place as the town I knew and loved so well. Of the splendid beauty and charm which the town once boasted, only the exterior of the main synagogue is still standing in its former glory.

My son-in-law Reb Eliezer Strassman, my son Reb Hershel, my grandchild Reb Leibel Strassman, our guide, Professor Jonathan Webber, and myself, spent the day there. We hoped to see at least some remnant of the city which once was.

Together with the president of the Cracow Jewish community in 1993

The Vanished City of Tsanz

Inside the shul in Lanset on the trip we made with Professor Jonathan Webber

IN BELGIUM

We arrived in Tsanz late at night and stopped at the first hotel we saw. When we stepped out of the hotel in the morning I noticed that we were standing opposite the home of Reb Chuna Hersh Rubin, *zt"l*. The house still stands intact. The headquarters of the community center and a small *beis midrash*, Beis Nassan, are also two of the few buildings to remain erect.

We also visited the grave of the saintly Divrei Chaim, *zt"l*, where thousands of Jews used to flock to pray.

One other thing has remained in its intensity: the passionate hatred of the gentiles. Some of them concealed it, and some of them showed it openly, but it was clear that anti-Semitism is still strong, despite the fact that they had not set eyes on a Jew for fifty years!

I owe a debt of gratitude to Professor Jonathan Webber of Oxford, who gave of his valuable time and guided us through the length and breadth of Galicia.

Discovering My Sister

There is a concept in Judaism of ending on a good note. Therefore, upon completion of my sad and tragic tale of the destruction of European Jewry, I would like to relate an incredible occurrence which happened to me more than thirty years after the war was over. The miraculous background events which led to my meeting with my sister Golda, who had survived the concentration camp Auschwitz, is an amazing story on its own.

I had not seen Golda for forty-two years. She had moved to Czechoslovakia in 1935 and married there, and since travel in those days was not common, she never came back to Tsanz for a visit. I did not dream that she was alive. I had a faint hope that one of my brothers or sisters was alive, but I was sure my sister Golda was dead. The reason why lies in the story that follows.

In Birkenau, I once became aware that a transport of the last remaining women in Teresienstadt had arrived at Auschwitz. Knowing that my sister Golda was an inmate in Teresienstadt, I tried to gather as much information as I could about that transport. I risked my life by approaching an elderly S.S. man who did not appear to be as brutal as his colleagues and asked him, "Does the women's camp adjoining us consist of the transport from Teresienstadt?"

"Yes," he replied.

"If so, why is it that we were shaved from head to toe while they don't even have their heads shaved?" I persisted.

"Be happy that you are here," he growled. "In this camp for men you have a greater chance of staying alive. The women are being sent directly to the *Himmel Kommando*." I understood that this meant that they would all be gassed.

Tragically, my fears proved to be correct. At the end of the week not a living soul remained in the women's camp. Since I had assumed that my sister was in that transport, I was certain that she, too, had perished.

I had always hoped that I would yet live to see a surviving member of my family, but as for Golda, I was certain she was no longer alive. After many years had elapsed I confronted the bitter realization that I was the only living member of my family.

I became aware only many years later how it came about that my sister survived. Just before the women's camp was about to be gassed, the Nazis called out, "Who among you is a nurse?" My sister and another woman stepped forward. With this gesture they were saved at the last minute.

The two women were given work as nurses and managed to stay alive. This in another clear indication that those who were destined to survive the war were given the intuition from Heaven of what to say and how to talk. They were the only two out of more than ten thousand women who were not sent to the gas chambers.

After the war, my sister, too, made every effort to find a surviving member of her family. She registered my name and perused the lists of the Red Cross and HIAS, but could find no trace of my existence. The reason for this is as follows: In Tsanz, as in all of Poland, one had to get married officially in a courtroom. My father was determined not to get married there, since one was forbidden to wear a hat there, and

IN BELGIUM

a large cross was displayed in the place where he was to declare his marriage vows. Therefore, when we were born, we were registered under my mother's maiden name, Lehrer, and not under my father's name, Buxbaum.

Together with the Pshevorsker Rebbe

Therefore, I gave my name as being "Lehrer" for the camp records. My sister Golda did not know this since she left Tsanz when she was still quite young, and she got married in Czechoslovakia where this problem did not exist. Thus, she searched for surviving members of her family under the name Buxbaum; there were no survivors by that name.

When my seventh child was born, a girl, I informed the Pshevorsker Rebbe of Antwerp, the *tzaddik* Reb Itzikel Gewirtzman, *zt"l*, that I would like to name my newly born daughter Golda, in memory of my sister Golda, who had died in Auschwitz. The Rebbe advised me to add another name, Golda Bas-sheva. He remarked that one cannot be certain that our relatives had indeed all perished, and a child should be named after a deceased and not after somebody who is still alive.

Every year, the former citizens of Tsanz (headed by Mr. Shmuel Gutwein), in Antwerp would organize a remembrance gathering for the eighteen thousand martyrs of Tsanz and its surrounding areas who were murdered by the Nazis, headed by the Gestapo chief Heinrich Haman.

In Israel, too, the former Tsanzer citizens commemorate the death of their countrymen. It takes place annually in Tel Aviv on the yartzeit of the majority of the Tsanzer ghetto's inhabitants, on 16–17 Elul.

After the liberation, my sister remarried a Czech by the name of

The Vanished City of Tsanz

Yosef Strulowitz. She moved to Israel and settled in Be'er Sheva, where she still lives today. For many years she was not aware of the annual Tsanzer gathering in Tel Aviv. As the years went by, the attendance at the gathering grew larger and larger. Consequently, the organizers widely publicized the date and venue of the commemoration a good two weeks before it was to take place.

My friend Moshe Lauer was one of the main organizers of the event. I was in very close contact with him; he often came to Belgium to visit me, and whenever I happened to be in Israel I always stopped at his home in Ramat Gan. In the summer of 1977 he came to Antwerp for the occasion of the bar mitzvah of my youngest son, Tzvi Yaakov (Hershele). A short time after he returned to Israel, the Tsanzer gathering in Tel Aviv took place. My sister Golda heard of the upcoming event on the radio and decided to attend for the first time ever, curious to know who of her former townspeople had survived the war.

At the commemoration, the organizers see to it that the name of every participant is noted down. When Golda entered she gave her married name, Golda Sahar. Further inquiries revealed that her maiden name was Buxbaum and that she was the daughter of the Tsanzer *rosh yeshivah*, Reb Nosson Buxbaum. Hearing this, my friend Moshe Lauer and my former neighbor in Tsanz, Toivia Katz (who has also visited me a number of times in Belgium), asked her if she had any connection with her brother, Zalman Lehrer from Belgium. "My broth-er Zalman?" she exclaimed in astonishment. "My youngest brother was called

A memorial gathering for the martyrs of Tsanz

400

IN BELGIUM

Zalman, but I know he died in the Tsanzer ghetto. I have made thorough investigations as to the possibility of his still being alive, but I always came to the same response: no Buxbaum is registered in the lists of concentration-camp survivors."

They tried to calm my distraught sister and told her to take a seat. Delicately they told her, "Your brother Shlomo Zalman Lehrer is alive and resides in Belgium. We will immediately connect you with him by telephone." Needless to say, the astounding discovery made a lasting impression on the participants in that year's gathering. Thanks to this event, a brother and sister met each other after almost half a century.

Immediately after the gathering was over, my friends Moshe Lauer and Toivia Katz phoned me in Belgium. They told me to take a seat and then asked me if by any chance I had a sister Golda. I answered in the affirmative. They went on to tell me the unbelievable news that she was still alive and would contact me the next day. I will never forgot that phone call. My heart refused to believe what my ears told me: my sister Golda had actually emerged alive from the burning inferno of Auschwitz!

Our boundless joy at that telephone conversation is indescribable. Both of us had long given up all hope that there was still a surviving member of the family.

The wondrous piece of news was soon reported in newspapers and radio stations in Israel, Belgium, and Holland. It infused new hope in war victims who had despaired of ever discovering any surviving family members. I was even surprised by two phone calls from gentile families in Holland, congratulating me on the amazing turn of events.

It is interesting to note that my sister's first visit to Belgium was on the occasion of the wedding of my seventh child, the daughter whom I had named Golda.

"The wonders of Hashem speak for themselves" (Bereishis 18:14). Can we comprehend the way Hashem runs the world?

מזכרת נצח לעילוי נשמת

אבי מורי הרה"ג
רבי נתן מרדכי הלוי בוקסבוים הי"ד
רומ"ץ ציעשנוב ור"מ דישיבת 'בני תורה' בצאנז

ואמי מורתי
מרת יוטא הי"ד

נהרגו על קידוש השם במחנה השמדה בעלז'יץ
ע"י הנאצים ועוזריהם ימ"ש

ט"ז - י"ז אלול תש"ב

אחותי איידעל הי"ד
בעלה הר"ר ברוך פיש הי"ד

אחי צבי (הערש) הי"ד

נהרגו על קידוש השם בלמברג בחודש אלול תש"ב

אחי משה הי"ד
אשתו ובנו הילד יוסף הי"ד
נהרגו על קידוש השם בדאמבראווע בחודש אלול תש"ב

אחותי חוה הי"ד
נהרגה על קידוש השם בקראקא בחודש אלול תש"ב

זקני הרה"ג ר' ירחמיאל
בן הרה"ג ר' משה בוקסבוים זצ"ל המכונה ר' משה גאלדע'ס
רומ"ץ בצאנז
נפטר חודש סיון תרצ"ו

זוגתו זקנתי הצדקנית מרת רעכיל ע"ה
נפטרה ב' דראש השנה תרצ"ה

חתנם ר' שמואל באדנער הי"ד
זוגתו-כתם שבע ותשעה ילדיהם הי"ד

מזכרת נצח לעילוי נשמת

זקני הרה"ח ר' **יעקב** ב"ר יחזקאל יונה לעהרער ז"ל מציעשנוב
מו"ל "קונטרס רבי צבי חריף"
נפטר חודש סיון תרפ"ב בקראקא

זוגתו-זקנתי מרת **מאליא** הי"ד
נהרגה עקה"ש בשנת הפ"ו לחייה בקראקא בחודש אלול תש"ב

בנם הרה"ג ר' **יחזקאל יונה** הי"ד
ראב"ד סטרי
נהרג עקה"ש יחד עם אשתו ובניהם בעיר סטרי

בנם **לייזער** הי"ד
בתם **רחל** הי"ד
נהרגו עקה"ש במחנה השמדה בעלז'יץ אלול תש"ב

בתם **מארגאלי** ע"ה
נפטרה ו' אייר תרצ"ט בצירך (שווייץ)

חמי ר' **גרשון** ב"ר יצחק לעהרער ז"ל
נפטר כ"ג שבט תשל"ה באנטווערפען

חמותי מרת **ליבא** בת ר' יצחק אייזיק הכהן **דארף** ע"ה
נפטרה כ"ה אייר תשל"ז באנטווערפען

הונצח ע"י בניהם
ר' **יששכר דוב** ור' **ישראל** הי"ו
ובתם חי' **מלכה** תחי'

חתני היקר באנשים האברך החשוב
הר"ר **יחיאל אפרים** ב"ר פסח **טיפנברונר** ז"ל
נלב"ע בדמי ימיו ט"ו סיון תש"נ

הוקדש ע"י חותנו המחבר

L. Strassman, Iyar 5757

STAIRS TO
LADIES GALLERY

GRIBOVER
BEIS MIDRASH

ROAD

ENTRANCE

RABBI ARYEH LEIBISH'S
SEAT

EAST ↓

CHASSIDISHE
BEIS MIDRASH